RESTORATION HISTORIANS
AND THE ENGLISH CIVIL WAR

ARCHIVES INTERNATIONALES D'HISTOIRE DES IDEES

INTERNATIONAL ARCHIVES OF THE HISTORY OF IDEAS

74

ROYCE MACGILLIVRAY

RESTORATION HISTORIANS
AND THE ENGLISH CIVIL WAR

RESTORATION HISTORIANS
AND THE ENGLISH CIVIL WAR

by

ROYCE MACGILLIVRAY

MARTINUS NIJHOFF / THE HAGUE / 1974

To
My Mother
And to the Memory of
My Father

DA413
M32

PRINTED IN THE NETHERLANDS

CONTENTS

ABBREVIATIONS

Aubrey, *BL* John Aubrey, *"Brief Lives," chiefly of Contemporaries, set down by John Aubrey, between the Years 1669 & 1696,* ed. Andrew Clark. 2 vols. Oxford, 1898.

Baxter, *RB* Richard Baxter, *Reliquiae Baxterianae: or, Mr. Richard Baxter's Narrative of The most Memorable Passages of His Life and Times,* ed. Matthew Sylvester. London, 1696.

BM British Museum.

Burnet, *OTA* Gilbert Burnet, *Burnet's History of My Own Time: . . . Part I: the Reign of Charles the Second,* ed. Osmund Airy. 2 vols. Oxford, 1897-1900.

Burnet, *OTR* Gilbert Burnet, *Bishop Burnet's History of His Own Time,* ed. M. J. R[outh], 2nd ed. 6 vols. Oxford, 1833.

Airy's edition of the *Own Time* extends only to the death of Charles II; for later events, Routh's edition must be used.

Clarendon, *HR* Edward Hyde, Earl of Clarendon, *The History of the Rebellion and Civil Wars in England Begun in the Year 1641,* ed. W. Dunn Macray. 6 vols. Oxford, 1888.

Clarendon, *L* Edward Hyde, Earl of Clarendon, *The Life of Edward Earl of Clarendon, . . . in Which Is Included, a Continuation of His History of the Grand Rebellion. Written by Himself.* 2 vols. Oxford, 1857.

Clar. S. P. *State Papers Collected by Edward, Earl of Clarendon,* ed. Richard Scrope and Thomas Monkhouse. 3 vols. Oxford, 1767-1786.

DNB *Dictionary of National Biography*

Dugdale, *SV* [Sir William Dugdale], *A Short View of the Late Troubles in England.* Oxford, 1681.

EHR	*The English Historical Review*
Gardiner, *HE*	S. R. Gardiner, *History of England from the Accession of James I. to the Outbreak of the Civil War 1603-1642.* 10 vols. London, 1883-1884.
Hacket, *SR*	John Hacket, *Scrinia Reserata: a Memorial Offer'd to the Great Deservings of John Williams, D.D. . . . Containing a Series of the Most Remarkable Occurrences and Transactions of his Life, in Relation both to Church and State.* [London], in the Savoy, 1693.
HLQ	*The Huntington Library Quarterly*
HMC	Historical Manuscripts Commission
Nalson, *IC*	John Nalson, *An Impartial Collection of the Great Affairs of State.* 2 vols. London, 1682-1683.
N & Q	*Notes and Queries*
OPH	*The Parliamentary or Constitutional History of England; From the earliest Times, to the Restoration of King Charles II,* 2nd ed. 24 vols. London, 1761-1763. Commonly known as *Old Parliamentary History.*
Rushworth, *HC*	John Rushworth, *Historical Collections.* 7 vols. London, 1659-1701. All references are to the set shelfmarked 2072 f. in the Reading Room of the British Museum.
Warwick, *M*	Sir Philip Warwick, *Memoires Of the reigne of King Charles I. With a Continuation to the Happy Restauration of King Charles II.* London, 1701.
Wood, *AO*	Wood, *Athenae Oxonienses,* in Anthony à Wood, *Athenae Oxonienses. An Exact History of All the Writers and Bishops Who Have Had Their Education in the University of Oxford. To Which Are Added the Fasti, or Annals of the Said University,* ed. Philip Bliss. 4 vols. London, 1813-1820.
Wood, *F*	Wood, *Fasti,* in the same.

PREFACE

This is a study of the histories of the English Civil War or some aspects of it written in England or by Englishmen and Englishwomen or published in England up to 1702, the year of the publication of the first volume of Clarendon's *History of the Rebellion*. By the terms of this definition, Clarendon is himself, of course, one of the historians studied. Clarendon's *History* is so formidable an achievement that all historians writing about the war before its publication have an air of prematureness. Nevertheless, as I hope the following pages will show, they produced a body of writing which may still be read with interest and profit and which anticipated many of the ideas and attitudes of Clarendon's *History*. I will even go so far as to say that many readers who have only a limited interest or no interest in the Civil War are likely to find many of these historians interesting, should their works come to their attention, for their treatment of the problems of man in society, for their psychological acuteness, and for their style. But while I intend to show their merits, my main concern will be to show how the Civil War appeared to historians, including Clarendon, who wrote within one or two generations after it, that is to say, at a time when it remained part of the experience of people still alive.

A word is necessary on terminology. Whenever no misunderstanding seemed likely to result from my doing so, I have used the words "English Civil War," "Civil War," and "war" to refer not only to the actual fighting in England but to the whole connected series of political upheavals and revolutionary developments in the British Isles from 1637 to 1660, that is, from the breaking out of the Scottish revolt to the Restoration of Charles II. This usage has obvious defects, but there seems to be none better. "Puritan Revolution" and "Rebellion" are politically loaded in a way that makes them difficult to use in a context where some neutral term is necessary, and the former, in the sense in which it is usually understood, is so anachronistic with respect to seventeenth-century thought that I do not see how it could be used at all in interpreting the thought of most of these early historians. "Revolution" is less troublesome than "Puritan Revolution" and "Rebellion," but I do not think that this term either could be used repeatedly, as a convenient term for this purpose must be, without incurring objections similar in kind if not in degree. I hope that my use of "Civil War" and so forth in this sense produces no difficulty for readers. Wherever there was danger of misunderstanding occurring, wherever my meaning in using these words was not sufficiently clear from the context, I have, I hope, discovered the difficulty in manuscript and rephrased my thoughts in words less open to ambiguity.

While I have included a general survey of the Civil War historiography of the period, with discussion of trends and patterns and notice of even some of the very minor historians, I have concentrated upon the more important historians whose names appear in the headings and subheadings of the chapters.

A word is necessary on the problem of what is a "history" of the Civil War. Besides histories in the more ordinary and unquestioned sense of the term, I include as "histories" biographies and autobiographies, memoirs, historical essays, printed collections of documents, the relevant sections of histories of England, Europe, or the world, narratives or "relations," and replies made to other writers' histories. I do, however, exclude verse, religious treatises including sermons, political treatises, merely polemical pamphlets, and works of a belletristic nature. In dealing with writings so extremely varied I have not found it possible to follow a mathematically exact rule of what is a history and what is not, but it was usually evident enough for practical purposes in any particular case whether the work was a "history" or not. By "historian" I mean anyone who wrote a "history" in the sense indicated above without trying to limit the term to those who most deserve it – to professionals such as Dugdale or amateurs of undoubted achievement such as Baxter.

In the following study I exclude as part of my defined subject matter Scottish, Irish, continental, and other non-English historians unless, like Burnet, they wrote Civil War histories in England or had them published there within the period indicated. I do, however, occasionally refer to continental historians when they cast light on the works of their English brethren or are relevant to some strain in English thought.

In my research and writing I have incurred many debts of gratitude. My obligations to Professor W. K. Jordan of Harvard, under whom this study was begun, go back many years. His unfailing kindness, courtesy, and helpfulness in dealing with his students set a high standard for all

university teachers. I am grateful to the staff of the Widener and Hough-
ton Libraries at Harvard, the British Museum, the Institute of Historical
Research at the University of London, the Bodleian, the City of Nottingham Museum and Art Gallery, the City of Nottingham Public Libraries,
and the University of Waterloo Library, Waterloo, Ontario. The Marquess of Bath, the Marquess of Bute, and the Corporation of Nottingham
have very kindly allowed me to read manuscripts they own. For financial
assistance I am grateful to the Canada Council, to the University of Waterloo, and to the American Philosophical Society, which gave me a grant
from the Penrose fund.

Material that has already appeared in the *Journal of the History of
Ideas, The Lakehead University Review, Notes and Queries,* the *Dalhousie Review,* and the *Humanities Association Bulletin,* is reprinted
here with permission.

I am grateful to the British Museum, the Bodleian, the Marquess of
Bath, and the Marquess of Bute for permission to print material from
their manuscripts.

CHAPTER I

INTRODUCTION

Most of the histories of the English Civil War written or published in England before 1702 can be clearly labelled as either Royalist, Parliamentarian, or Whig. The attitude that the writer takes to the political issues of the war and to any later events in English history that he has opportunity to notice is generally sufficient to indicate which of these labels should be applied to his history, but occasionally it is also useful to refer to what is known about his life to help identify his political views. Of course one can also develop other systems of arranging the histories in groups, but no other system, it seems to me, is likely to be found that will correspond so well to the natural divisions separating the histories or that will present the classifier with so few doubtful cases when put into practice. I do not think that one can make a uniformly clear-cut distinction between Royalist and Tory histories, or between Parliamentarian and republican histories, and so I have regarded Tory histories as part of the Royalist group and republican histories as part of the Parliamentarian group. Only a few histories reveal no political associations or leanings or reveal them so imperfectly that one cannot be confident in identifying the histories with the name of any political faction.

In terms of their political identification the histories of the Civil War published in England up to 1702 can also be seen as the products of three distinct and successive periods in English publishing.

In the first period, lasting from the First Civil War to the end of the Commonwealth in 1660, both Parliamentarian and Royalist histories were published. Under the rule of the victorious Puritans, Royalist historians such as Peter Heylyn, Hamon L'Estrange, and William Sanderson were unable to speak for their cause as vigorously as their Parliamentarian counterparts, but they do reveal in their histories a modest, but firm, attachment to the lost cause.

The second period, lasting from the Restoration in 1660 to the Revolution of 1688, provides an especial problem. In dealing with it one must take into account the possibility of Parliamentarian works of the pre-Restoration period being reprinted with the old dates unchanged. Thus the first volume of Rushworth's *Historical Collections* seems to have been surreptitiously reissued at least once in this period with the original date of 1659.[1] It appears likely, however, that such disguised historical reprints were negligible in number. There were relatively few good pre-Restoration Parliamentarian histories anyway, so publishers must have felt little attraction to this particular form of forbidden fruit, and had surreptitious reprinting been much used presumably contemporaries would have remarked upon it more often.

If we overlook, then, any other disguised reprints that may have existed, we can say that the histories published between the Restoration and the Revolution of 1688 are nearly all Royalist with only a few histories of wanly Parliamentarian tendency appearing, all (apart from a very few exceptions) in a cluster about 1680. No single theory will explain the publication of every one of these volumes in the cluster, but it is significant that political circumstances facilitated the reemergence of Parliamentarian histories at this time. The lapse of the Licensing Act in 1679 and the crisis of the Popish Plot and the succession struggle made the government unable to supervise the press as effectively as before, while the political and religious crisis produced an enlarged interest in historical issues.[2] To this time of unrest belong the second and third volumes of Rushworth's

[1] Wood, *AO*, IV, 282, says it is "There again by stealth, bearing the same date, an. 1675," and a writer of Jan. 30, 1681/2, *OPH*, XXIII, Appendix p. 219, says it was republished "Not many Years ago" with the 1659 date.
[2] The liberty of the English press at this time of crisis has been noticed rather than extensively studied by modern writers. See, for example, J. Walker, "The Censorship of the Press during the Reign of Charles II," *History*, n.s., 35 (1950), 238, and James Sutherland, *English Literature of the Late Seventeenth Century* (Oxford, Clarendon Press, 1969), p. 354. For similar contemporary notices, see Aurelian Cook, *Titus Britannicus: an Essay of History Royal: in the Life & Reign of His Late Sacred Majesty, Charles II* (London, 1685), pp. 424-425; [William Howell], *Medulla Historiae Anglicanae. Being a Comprehensive History of the Lives and Reigns of the Monarchs of England*, 3rd ed. (London, 1687), pp. 445-446; Anthony à Wood, *The Life and Times*, ed. Andrew Clark, 5 vols. (Oxford, 1891-1900), II, 457-458; and, unless the passage is an eighteenth-century interpolation, Sir Richard Bulstrode, *Memoirs and Reflections* (London, 1721), p. 299; cf. p. 393; for an enquiry into the authenticity of these memoirs, see C. H. Firth, "The 'Memoirs' of Sir Richard Bulstrode," *EHR*, 10 (1895), 266-275. Sir Robert Southwell wrote to the Duke of Ormonde, July 5, 1679, "I am told that now the press is at liberty one Dr. Burlace, . . . is actually printing that Narrative of the Irish Rebellion, which I sent your Grace, . . ." HMC, Ormonde n.s. IV (London, 1906), p. 529; cf. pp. 378-379. This narrative presumably is Clarendon's manuscript work on the Irish rebellion, which Borlase uses in his *History Of the Execrable Irish Rebellion;* see the discussion of Borlase in chapter VII below. Baxter, *RB*, III, 187, says that "The act restraining the Press being expired, I published a Book that lay by me to open the case of Nonconformity . . ."

Historical Collections (1680) and his volume on the *Tryal* of the Earl of Strafford (1680). We cannot ascribe the appearance of the two volumes of the *Historical Collections* to the aforementioned press liberty and crisis, for it seems that Rushworth would have published them about this time in any case, but he does seem, as we shall see in a later chapter, to have taken advantage of the press liberty to make some Parliamentarian additions to his text that the censor would not otherwise have allowed. This time also saw reprints of the first volume of his *Historical Collections* (1659; reprinted 1682), of Sir John Temple's history of the *Irish Rebellion* (1646; reprinted in two editions, 1679),[3] of Thomas May's *Breviary of the History Of the Parliament Of England* (1650, 1655; reprinted 1680), and of the very fairminded life of Cromwell called *The Perfect Politician* (first published 1660, just before the Restoration; reprinted 1680, 1681). Then too appeared Edmund Borlase's *History Of the Execrable Irish Rebellion* (1680), which is Parliamentarian in its implications though not in its open professions. While the first edition of Whitelocke's *Memorials* (1682) contained little to offend Royalists its author had been a prominent Parliamentarian and its tendency must have been to lead readers towards a more intelligent view of the Parliamentarian mentality. Earlier than this cluster of works centering about 1680, the nearest thing to a serious challenge to the Royalist monopoly of politically conscious histories was a reprint (1673) of Francis Osborne's *Works* containing his "Historical Memoires" of James I. The "Historical Memoires" should not be considered a history of the Civil War, as they touch upon it only marginally, but Osborne's unfavorable reflections on James I were certainly ammunition for the Parliamentarian side. The *Works* reappeared as part of the "cluster" with the date 1682.

In the third period, lasting from the Revolution of 1688 to 1702, Parliamentarian, Royalist, and Whig histories were published. The dynastic revolution is reflected in the appearance of a few histories attacking the Stuart family.

These three periods conform more or less to what one would expect in view of contemporary political conditions, but the second period deserves

---

[3] The Earl of Essex in a letter to Secretary of State Coventry, Jan. 5, 1674/5, exculpates Temple from having consented to the recent publication of an account, of which Temple was the author, "concerning the cruelties committed in Ireland at the beginning of the late war." Arthur Capel, Earl of Essex, *Letters Written by ... Earl of Essex, Lord Lieutenant of Ireland, in the Year 1675,* 2nd ed. (Dublin, 1773), p. 2. The *DNB* (s.v. Temple), relying perhaps only on this letter, says that a new edition of the *Irish Rebellion* appeared in 1674, but if so, it is not recorded under Temple's name in Wing's *Short-Title Catalogue* and I have found no reference to an extant copy elsewhere.

additional comment. No doubt the censorship is a sufficient explanation for the long dominance of Royalism in the politically conscious histories published between the Restoration and the Revolution. During the one interval in which the censorship was weakened, Parliamentarian histories did appear. But it is hard to escape the conviction that at the same time the humiliating failure of the Parliamentarian cause both before and at the Restoration had left most of its former defenders in such moral disarray that they found little further defense possible, that censorship and demoralization weighed upon them together.

The contrast between Royalist and Parliamentarian historians as far as confidence is concerned can be most clearly seen if we extend our enquiry into this period, which so far has dealt with histories published then, to include also histories *written in the period but not published till after it.* The Royalist histories written or published in this period are morally and politically aggressive. The Parliamentarian histories written or published in the same period are commonly weak or silent in the defense of the Parliamentarian side; this was to be expected in histories intended for publication under the restored Stuarts, but one may suppose that if there had been many prospective historians about of strongly Parliamentarian convictions more histories from their pens would have survived in manuscript from this period to be published at a later date, as did the histories of Ludlow, Mrs. Hutchinson, Clarendon, and other historians both Parliamentarian and Royalist. If by some miracle of premature liberalism there had been no censorship in this period, presumably a wider variety of Parliamentarian histories would have been published, if only for the sake of exploiting to the full the legal possibilities of profit in the book trade, but it is hard to believe that as a whole they would have matched the assurance and plausibility of the Royalist histories.

Edmund Ludlow and Mrs. Lucy Hutchinson, who wrote their histories in this period (though they did not publish them at that time) and confidently defended their cause were spared the usual embarrassment because of the minority to which they belonged. As republicans they had a far more coherent and tenable cause to defend than most of their fellow Parliamentarians. The consistency and unyielding principles which made Edmund Ludlow and John Hutchinson impractical in the world of politics from the execution of the King to the Restoration paradoxically made their careers easy to defend in following years.

When the Whig historians began to write they faced an easier task than their Parliamentarian predecessors because as Whigs they had morally disentangled themselves from the wreckage of the Parliamentarian cause and were free to pick and choose in their praise and condemnation. Disappointingly, as far as histories published up to 1702 are concerned the Whig historians' greater freedom of maneuver merely resulted in their defense of the Parliamentarian cause being limited and selective and their historical treatments of the war are few in number and unremarkable in quality.

As we turn now to the problem of the sources from which the historians covered in this study wrote, it should be mentioned that the following examination is based on the historians who *wrote* during the years covered by the study, whether their histories were published then or later. Apart from a very few minor sources which may have occasionally been used, their sources may be classified as follows: (1) personal experience, (2) books, (3) newspapers, newssheets, and newsbooks, (4) unprinted manuscript material, and (5) enquiry among persons who had experienced the war.

Personal experience. It usually turns out, when enough information is available about a historian's life to make a judgment possible, that he had some kind of personal involvement in the war or its aftermath – an involvement which often included some form of deprivation or suffering. This involvement will be illustrated in the short biographies which will be given of the major historians covered in this study.

Seventeenth-century historians of the Civil War form a group which is, by reason of its personal experience of and nearness to the war, unique among the successive generations of historians of the war. Every great historical upheaval, unless it proceeds so very quietly as to be almost unnoticeable (like the Industrial Revolution in its early days), produces a similarly privileged generation. In this period, when unprinted documents of the war were seldom opened to historians or, at least, as will be seen, were seldom used by them, it is nonetheless rare, even among the simplest of the general histories, to find a history whose contents were totally derived from other printed sources. Even if a historian had no factual material drawn from his own experience to offer concerning national events, he could at least reveal his personal reactions to the war. The *feeling* of what it was like to live in the times of the war, a feeling that later historians have had to recapture by laborious study, by legitimate efforts of the imagination, and by uncertain conjecture, was a part of the experience of these historians. For this reason, even the dreariest Civil War history of the period is an original authority, revealing indirectly as well as directly the ideas and feelings of Englishmen as they faced the actuality and the memory of the Civil War.

Personal experience sometimes passed through the form of memoranda which were later incorporated in or used in writing histories. Sir William Dugdale's *Short View* is based partly on a record of events kept by Dugdale at Oxford during the war. Richard Baxter took "Minutes of Proceedings and Events, as they occurred," which provided the foundation for the *Reliquiae Baxterianae*. Sir Philip Warwick professed to be writing his *Memoires* "from a fraile memory and some old ill-digested notes." [4] The exact process by which Bulstrode Whitelocke formed his annals, the original narrative from which his *Memorials* were extracted, is not clear, and Whitelocke is known to have destroyed some of his papers through caution or fear, yet there can be little doubt that he used memoranda of some sort. He sometimes gives conversations in dialogue form, yet it is unlikely that he remembered them so well that he was justified in reproducing them, in this form, merely from memory, some years after they had taken place. He may have relied upon invention to expand his unwritten recollections, but given Whitelocke's character, this is an unlikely explanation. The literary device of wholly or partly invented speeches was, in any case, rarely used by English historians of this period. They recognized its use in the classical historians, but even the classical precedent seems to have been insufficient to render it respectable in their eyes. [5]

Nearness to the war brought disadvantages as well as advantages to the historians. For one thing, they suffered the disadvantage of lacking much knowledge that only time would bring to light. It is, moreover, worth investigating the difficulty they faced in their relationship to political authority, an authority which often was at variance with their past or present political allegiances; the difficulty they faced in being impartial in the modern sense of impartial; and the danger – not quite as slight as it may seem at first sight – that some of their material would be distorted because they used it conversationally in the form of anecdotes before they used it in their histories.

The difficulties the historians faced in their relationship to political authority were more indirect and harder to establish than one might at

---

[4] Dugdale, *SV*, preface, sig. [A3]ᵛ; Baxter, *RB*, preface by Matthew Sylvester, sig. [b4]; Warwick, *M*, p. 207.

[5] There may be an invented speech in Hacket, *SR*, Part II, 215, constructed on the basis of some reports of what was actually said. Something of the same end as that aimed at in invented speeches was attained, with less violation of historical truth, by the device of citing the opinions of different groups of people rather as if the writer had taken a public opinion survey; see, for example, Thomas Fuller, *The Church History of Britain*, ed. J. S. Brewer, 6 vols. (Oxford, 1845), VI, 91-93, 175-177, 312-315, and Richard Perrinchief, "The Life of Charles I," in *Works* of Charles I, 2nd ed. (London, 1687), p. 13.

first expect. Despite occasional complaints about the dangers of writing contemporary history, often supported by the familiar maxim that he who follows truth too close to the heels will have his teeth struck out by it, there seems to be no example of a historian who suffered at the hands of the authorities for his historical views on the war except Clement Walker,[6] who was imprisoned because of the publication of the second part of his *Compleat History of Independency*. Historians collided more commonly with authority or with great men on issues unconnected with their historical opinions about the war. We find that David Lloyd went to prison as a result of publishing a foolish work about the Countess of Bridgewater, John Nalson was punished by the House of Commons for indiscreet pamphleteering, Richard Baxter stood trial before Judge Jeffreys on a charge of seditious writings, and Anthony à Wood was made to smart for libelling the late Earl of Clarendon, whose probity as Lord Chancellor he had impugned. But while historians avoided punishment for their historical views on the war, the realization that they could be punished if they spoke too carelessly must have often prevented statements they would otherwise have made.

Under such conditions, impartiality in the modern sense could flourish only with difficulty, yet the principal impediment to this kind of impartiality seems to have been moral rather than political. There were professions of impartiality in abundance, of course, and probably only the very rare historian applied himself to the writing of a deliberately dishonest history. Professions of impartiality did not mean necessarily, however, or even usually, that the historian would make no decision with respect to the rightness and wrongness of the two contending sides. When John Nalson named his furiously Royalist reply to Rushworth the *Impartial Collection* he was not misusing words. What he meant was that although he recognized as indisputably true the rightness of the Royalists and the wrongness of their enemies, he would not heighten or reduce this existing contrast by misrepresenting events. If someone believed as Nalson did that one side in the war was morally right and the other morally wrong, he was clearly bound to favor the morally right side. To expect that contemporary historians should apply present-day standards of "impartiality" to the study of the Civil War is simply to expect them to violate their own moral principles. An early eighteenth-century work on historical method expressly names "the Rising of a People against their lawful Prince" as an

---

[6] If posthumous injuries are to be included it should be added that Thomas May's body was removed from Westminster Abbey after the Restoration, no doubt partly because of his Parliamentarian histories of the war.

example of a case in which the historian is obliged not to be impartial: "we cannot say, that the most sacred, most inviolable Authority, God has placed upon Earth should be treated of with Indifference." [7] With this seventeenth-century English historians of the Civil War would have agreed, except that they would have preferred to think of themselves as combining their political sentiments with their impartiality instead of, as this work proposes, making a temporary breach in the impartiality. It was in their sober and reasonable spirit and not in a spirit of self-delusion or nonsense that John Watson's frenziedly pro-Stuart *Memoires of the Family of the Stuarts* (1683; continued only to death of Mary, Queen of Scots) is described by the anonymous writer of its preface as being "full of Loyalty and Impartiality." [8]

Without much reliable evidence, and on the basis principally of speculation and suspicion, one may suggest that a further disadvantage derived from nearness to the war was distortion as a result of anecdote-telling. It is likely that much of the material that appeared in the more personal accounts had previously been told and retold by the historian-participants themselves in conversation. This process, which polishes anecdotes, also distorts facts. The process is all the more dangerous because as someone tells and retells a story he tends not to see that its facts have been repeatedly changed slightly in the interest of improved literary form and even if he does notice that this has happened he is tempted to prefer the improved form to the simple, uninspired truth. Without, again, much reliable evidence, and on the basis principally of speculation and suspicion, one may suggest that Warwick's *Memoires* and, even more likely, John Price's *The Mystery and Method Of His Majesty's Happy Restauration* went through the shaping experience of anecdote-telling. Distortion resulting from anecdote-telling was also, of course, a problem to historians who were not dealing with their own experiences and observations but picked up misleading anecdotes from others, but in this form the problem is not peculiar to historians who have shared in the events they are describing. It has simply become the problem faced by all subsequent historians of the war, who have had to work with other people's testimony and to separate, as much as possible, the poetry from the truth in it.

Books. It is difficult to tell what books an English historian of this time has consulted. Books are sometimes mentioned in marginal references or

---

[7] P. N. Lenglet du Fresnoy, *A New Method of Studying History,* trans. and improved by Richard Rawlinson, 2 vols. (London, 1728), I, 282.
[8] [John Watson], *Memoires of the Family of the Stuarts* (London, 1683), preface, sig. (b) 2ᵛ.

in the text, but contemporary documentation practices did not require that all books used or even all books from which quotations were taken be named. If a work is specifically named, the reason may be only that the writer wished to correct or commend some opinion expressed in it. In view of the lack of a rigid system of documentation, it is often difficult to say how much a book that is named has been used. Has it been greatly used, briefly consulted during the process of writing, or perhaps only glanced into many years before? Comparison of content in two works is not of much use in establishing the debt of one to the other; unless there is echoing of phraseology or some other clear indication of debt, the investigator is always impeded by the difficulty that similar material may come about in a number of ways. On the other hand, examination of the works mentioned in histories does at least give an idea of what contemporary works were thought important and it does give some clues – unfortunately, we can seldom consider them much more – as to the individual historian's printed sources.

Some works, such as Baxter's *Reliquiae Baxterianae,* have little documentation and few clues as to printed sources, but if Baxter named books very sparingly in his history, many others were less sparing in theirs. The references to printed historical works relating to the war or to the first two Stuarts of two historians who documented more heavily than most can be outlined as follows.

John Hacket's *Scrinia Reserata* (1693), despite its date of publication, was written, except for probably minor additions, before the Restoration. In it Hacket refers to the *Eikon Basilike,* Hamon L'Estrange's *Reign of King Charles,* Sanderson's *Raigne of King Charles* and his corresponding work on the reigns of Mary Queen of Scots and James VI and I, Sir Anthony Weldon's *Court and Character of King James,* Sir Edward Peyton's *Divine Catastrophe of The Kingly Family Of the House of Stuarts,* Arthur Wilson's life of James I, the collection of documents called the *Cabala,* Thomas Fuller's *Church History,* two or more of Heylyn's works, Laud's diary as edited by Prynne, and Archbishop Spottiswoode's *History of the Church of Scotland.* In view of the period to which *Scrinia Reserata* belongs, this list of works may be regarded as more than satisfactory. The only serious omission is the first volume of Rushworth's *Historical Collections* and Hacket must have virtually completed his task before that was available to him.

Sir William Dugdale's *Short View of the Late Troubles* (1681) is mainly a product of the reign of Charles II, but Dugdale used materials he had written as early as the First Civil War. In this work, which despite its title is a good-sized folio, Dugdale refers to Rushworth's *Historical Collections,* Edward Husbands' *Exact Collection* of documents, Henry Scobell's *Collection of Acts and Ordinances,* Heylyn's *Cyprianus Anglicus, Aerius Redivivus,* and *A Short View of the Life and Reign of King Charles,* Richard Perrinchief's life of King Charles I, Gilbert Burnet's *Memoires* of the Hamiltons, James Heath's *Brief Chronicle Of the Late Intestine VVarr,* the *Eikon Basilike,* Walker's *Compleat History of Independency,* Sanderson's *Raigne of King Charles,* the French version of Robert Mentet de Salmonet's *History* of the war, and Anthony à Wood's history of Oxford University. Dugdale was a hardworking professional scholar, and this list shows that he had acquainted himself with the best books then available to a historian of the war. When he was preparing the text for a second edition of the *Short View* [9] (an edition which never appeared in print) he drew his additional material "especially," [10] he says, from Whitelocke's *Memorials,* which had been published since the preceding edition.

Historians gained less from the historical writings of their contemporaries than they might have done because of the frequent delays, at least in the major works, between writing and publication. Heylyn's *Cyprianus Anglicus* and Hacket's *Scrinia Reserata* were not uncommon in that one waited most of a decade and perhaps longer and the other waited more than thirty years for publication. When Clarendon's *History* was published knowledge of the war was greatly advanced by it, but if Clarendon or his literary executors had chosen, the *History,* though probably not in an unexpurgated form, could have been published at least a quarter of a century before. On his death in 1674 Clarendon had left a will in which he permitted his literary executors to publish his writings as they thought fit.[11] The brilliant and perceptive *Memoirs* of Colonel Hutchinson by his wife Lucy remained in manuscript right up till the nineteenth century. From the point of view of the present, one may especially regret the delay in publication of this work. The world has missed the opportunity of seeing what the seventeenth and eighteenth centuries would have made of

[9] Dugdale's text for the second edition survives as Bodleian MS Gough Gen. Top. 120, with a licensing note dated March 3, 1686/7. For more information on this proposed second edition, see R. MacGillivray, "Sir William Dugdale As Historian of the English Civil War," *The Lakehead University Review* (Lakehead University, Canada), 2 (1969), 123-124.

[10] Bodleian MS Gough Gen. Top. 120, p. 1, "An Advertisement to the Reader"; Dugdale to second Earl of Clarendon, Jan. 24, 1684/5, Bodleian MS Eng. lett. c. 130 f. 25. Notes from another source by Dugdale on Whitelocke's *Memorials* are printed by W. D. Macray, *N & Q,* 7th ser., 7 (1889), 303-304.

[11] His will is printed in T. H. Lister, *Life and Administration of Edward, First Earl of Clarendon,* 3 vols. (London, 1837-1838), II, 489-490.

so excellent a woman writer and so vivid a portrait of a Puritan and republican husband and wife. The commonest reasons for delay in publication seem to have been the conventional feeling that autobiographical
writings should not be published till after one's death, if at all, family dislike of exposing any kind of intimate writings to the public gaze, the desire of some writers to write for their families only, desire not to offend
the living, and hostile political circumstances. As far as political circumstances are concerned, it is noteworthy that we find the publication of
Royalist histories being delayed under the restored Stuarts even when on
ideological grounds the publication could not have been thought undesir-
able.

Newspapers, newssheets, and newsbooks. For purposes of an examination of the sources employed by the historians, it is unnecessary to distinguish between newspapers and the various kinds of newssheets and newsbooks which originally gave birth to newspapers and continued to exist
along with them. Though the newspapers were distinguished from the
others by continuing more or less periodically in separate issues, their high
mortality lessened the force of the distinction, and separate issues of
newspapers were like newssheets and newsbooks transient publications
concerned with passing events. Earlier English and continental newspapers existed and single, non-repeating publications dealing with news-
worthy events were an institution nearly as old as western printing, but the
great torrent of English newspapers begins with the early Long Parliament and the years 1641 and 1642.[12]

Writers say even less about their use of these various publications than
about their use of books. However, Dugdale in his heavily documented
Short View reveals to the reader his extensive use of newspapers – the *Perfect Diurnal*, the *Weekly Accompt,* and probably others he does not specifically name. *"What falleth within my own cognisance,"* he says, *"I de-
liver with mine own words: what is beyond my knowledge, in the words
of my Authors; most of which I have quoted: the rest being taken from
the common* Mercuries, *and other public-licensed Narratives of the chief-
est occurrences in those times."* [13] When Clarendon was writing part of
his *History* during the last years of Charles I, he was cut off, as a political
fugitive on the Scilly Isles and in Jersey, from many sources of information. He apologetically describes himself as writing "without any other

---

[12] I have found Joseph Frank, *The Beginnings of the English Newspaper 1620-1660*
(Cambridge, Mass., Harvard University Press, 1961) a most useful guide to the Civil
War press.
[13] Dugdale, *SV,* preface, sig. [A3], and his marginal references to his sources, *passim.*

help than a few diurnals" and "upon the stock of an ill memory, refresh-
ed only with some few pamphlets and diurnals." Whitelocke in his annals
reveals his own reliance on "Diurnals." [14] Perhaps it is no very daring
conjecture that most historians would use newspaper-type publications
in their research if copies happened to be easily accessible. For writers of
the more personal accounts, such as autobiographies and memoirs, their
value would often be marginal, but for a writer of general histories they
provided information difficult to obtain elsewhere. The poor reputation
of these publications for honesty and accuracy may have confirmed writers in their reluctance in naming them as sources. Wood indicates what
judgments might be built on this reputation when he says that Sanderson's histories "are not much valued, because they are mostly taken from
printed authors and lying pamphlets" and that Heath's *Brief Chronicle
Of the Late Intestine VVarr* "being mostly compiled from lying pamphlets, and all sorts of news-books," contains "innumerable errors . . . especially as to name and time." [15]

Unprinted manuscript material. Vast quantities of manuscript material
relating to the Civil War existed, but this material was not readily available to historians. While some was in government repositories of documents, much that has since come into public repositories was then in private hands, and private owners of manuscripts relating to matters so
controversial and touching so closely upon the reputation of families might
justly hesitate to expose them to investigation. No matter where the material was to be found, the historian would usually have to contend with
masses of uncatalogued or ill-catalogued papers. If he were looking for a
certain document, or documents on a certain topic, he would have none
of the present-day bibliographical aids to assist him. While the value of
manuscripts was realized, manuscript research of the modern extensive
sort was little used by the seventeenth-century historians of the war. The
historians did rely on their own personal papers, if they had any that were
relevant, and if other promising manuscripts were by chance readily at
hand they consulted them, but one gets the impression that manuscript
research was not a line of enquiry they found it very pressing to pursue. In
any case, the weight and immediacy of personal experience in many of the

---

[14] Sir Edward Hyde to Mr. Secretary Nicholas, Nov. 15, 1646, and to Charles I,
Dec. 12, 1647, *Clar. S. P.,* II, 288, 385; Whitelocke's "Annals," BM Add. MS 37345
ff. 20ᵛ, 126ᵛ, 239. These passages in Whitelocke are omitted in Bulstrode Whitelocke,
*Memorials of the English Affairs: . . . King Charles the First, to King Charles the
Second* (London, 1732). For use of newspapers, see also [Josiah Ricraft], *The Civill
VVarres of England Briefly Related* (London, 1649), "To the Impartial Reader," and
C. H. Firth's life of John Rushworth in *DNB*.
[15] Wood, *AO,* III, 565, 664.

histories probably made the kind of data obtainable from manuscripts seem relatively unimportant. In the general histories, in which the role of personal experience was usually relatively light, the elementary narrative of events which was generally all that the writers felt obliged to provide could be formed easily enough without manuscript research.

The extent of manuscript use by individual historians is difficult to gauge because of the practice of imperfectly identifying sources. However, a certain amount of evidence on manuscript use is available both in and out of the histories. Rushworth and Nalson, in compiling material for inclusion in their great printed collections of documents, were manuscript users by the very nature of their task. Rushworth had access before the Restoration to the public records of England [16] and to the public records of Scotland which had been brought to England as a result of the Cromwellian conquest of Scotland.[17] Nalson in the reign of Charles II had access to the office of the Clerk of the Parliament, "from which he was apparently allowed to take almost anything he pleased," and to the Paper Office, "though there he was apparently allowed only to take copies." [18] Various persons contributed to his efforts. He was allowed to copy papers belonging to the Duke of Ormonde, he obtained a document or transcript of a document from Archbishop Sancroft, and Lord Keeper North furnished him with a transcript of the Earl of Manchester's unpublished memoirs.[19] Burnet had the good fortune to have the family papers of the Hamiltons opened to him. The difficulties faced by a historian in dealing with controversial events of such recent date are shown by his action in concealing some material discreditable to Charles I in the resulting *Memoires* of the Hamiltons. Dugdale used Warwick's unpublished *Memoires* in preparing the intended second edition of his *Short View.* Hacket used papers of Archbishop Williams for his *Scrinia Reserata.* Clarendon used various manuscripts in writing his *History.* When Edmund Borlase wrote his *History Of the Execrable Irish Rebellion* he had the good fortune to have at hand a manuscript of Clarendon's unpublished history of the Irish rebellion from which he borrowed unabashedly.

---

[16] At Longleat House in the Coventry Papers, XII, f. 45, is a catalogue of "Councill Bookes" surrendered by Rushworth, dated June 6, 1660. This catalogue is mentioned in HMC, 4th Report, Part I (London, 1874), p. 231.

[17] Rushworth, *HC,* II, preface, sig. B2.

[18] "Introduction to Volume I. of the Calendar," by F. H. Blackburne Daniell, HMC, 13th Report, Appendix, Part I, i.e., Portland I (London, 1891), p. iii. For Nalson's recourse to these repositories, see Nalson, *IC,* II, 790, and I, introd., p. lvi, II 713, respectively.

[19] Daniell, "Introduction," p. iii; Nalson, *IC,* II, introd., p. ix; I, introd., pp. vi-vii; II, 206. He says, I, introd., p. lxxviii, that "I have not had the happiness to procure many private Papers" and hints that he would like contributions of these.

Enquiry. The historian seeking information could consult persons whose experience made them seem likely sources of information. Thus Clarendon and Nalson appealed to prominent Royalists for information.[20] It was an easy matter to question an old friend, an old soldier, or anyone else who appeared likely to possess information; and, indeed, such appeals cannot always be distinctly separated from the ordinary processes of conversation. Often an informant is alluded to in a history, with or without his name, but with no indication of what effort was made by the historian to obtain the information imparted.

This discussion of the sources employed by the historians points to a contrast. In theory at least, a common body of information about the Civil War is open today to all scholars of the Civil War. Seventeenth-century historians of the Civil War did not enjoy the same common fund of information. While books and newspaper-type publications were open to all, subject only to the difficulty of finding copies, manuscripts were not open to all, whatever opportunities may have been given to the occasional fortunate enquirer, and personal experience and opportunities for gaining information about the war through conversation and enquiry varied, sometimes very sharply, from person to person. In addition, the information gained through personal experience and through conversation and enquiry was liable to be distorted by political prejudices. One may see in this set of circumstances part of the reason for the variation in interpretations among the seventeenth-century historians of the war.

---

[20] Sir Edward Hyde to Lord Widdrington, Aug. 5, 1646, *Clar. S. P.,* II, 246; John Nalson to Duke of Ormonde, Aug. 7, 1682, HMC, Ormonde n.s. VI (London, 1911), pp. 415-416. In an undated and unaddressed letter, *OPH,* XXIII, Appendix, p. 232, Nalson seeks a meeting with the Earl of Macclesfield, from whom he hopes to obtain information.

CHAPTER II

ROYALIST AND PARLIAMENTARIAN
HISTORIANS BEFORE THE RESTORATION

1. Survey of the Historians

The principal genres of historical writing used by the people who wrote histories of the Civil War in the years before the Restoration will be evident from the following, but a few general observations about these genres may be included to serve as an introduction and to fill the gaps. Autobiographical patches often appear in the histories, but no full length autobiographies or memoirs dealing sufficiently with the war to be considered as histories of the Civil War for our purposes appeared in print so early. Biographies of prominent Civil War figures published in this period tend to be political histories rather than studies of a human being; with one or two exceptions, the best biographies, judged as biographies, were written later or, if written in this period, were retained for publication later. The lack of autobiographies and memoirs and the literary deficiencies of biographies give the printed histories of this period taken as a whole an air of drabness that is not characteristic of their successors after the Restoration; one must, however, except from this general charge of drabness the works of Heylyn and Fuller, who have been selected for detailed treatment later in this chapter. Several printed collections of documents appeared, most notably the first volume of Rushworth's *Historical Collections*; further notice of these will be reserved for the chapter on Rushworth and Nalson. Finally, it may be said that neither now nor at any later time did the war give rise to any new genre of historical writing in England, though it gave a great impetus to certain genres already existing, especially autobiography and biography.

Throughout this period one has to distinguish between printed reports of current events, such as a recent battle, and histories in a more developed sense. Gradually, as the hostilities between Charles I and his Parliament continued, writers begin to produce narratives of events which, in one sense, were little more than a string of news reports, and, in another sense, were elementary or embryonic histories. An example of such works is George Wharton's *Englands Iliads in a Nut-Shell* (1645), published anonymously at Oxford, which relates events in annalistic manner under dates from December 1641 to March 24, 1644/5, and prints Laud's scaffold speech and some verses on the death of Sir Henry Gage. Wharton mentions Marston Moor, but he hardly seems to regard it as a Parliamentarian victory.

A number of more fully formed histories appeared in print before the King's execution, but most – though not all – of these early histories were poor and colored by a desire to publish propaganda for the author's party. Such primitive histories continued to be published throughout the century on the Civil War and on other subjects; and their significance as Civil War histories in the pre-execution period is simply that at that time they held the field with few rivals, not yet being offset by a sizeable body of good histories dealing with the war. For the sake of completeness in giving a picture of the historiography of the war, we ought briefly to examine these primitive histories as well as the better ones as they appeared before the King's execution. In compensation, the reader will be spared a recital of the similar histories for the period from the execution to the Restoration, though it should be mentioned that among such histories in this latter period two assaults on the royal cause, the astrologer William Lilly's life of Charles I in *Monarchy or No Monarchy in England* (1651) and Sir Edward Peyton's *The Divine Catastrophe of The Kingly Family Of the House of Stuarts* (1652) are lively, scandalous, and still highly readable. Among the pre-execution histories we may first notice John Vicars' *Englands Worthies* (1647), a simple collection of pictures and brief military biographies of the Parliament's commanders. His *True Information of the Beginning and Cause of all our troubles* (1648) is a scrappy history or chronology probably meant for a popular audience and is distinguished only by an attractive set of pictures of war events. His *Magnalia Dei Anglicana* (1646), a much longer and much more ambitious work than either of these, combines sober narrative with rhapsodic celebrations of the Parliament's righteousness and success. Josiah Ricraft's *A Survey of Englands Champions* (1647), reissued later in slightly extended form as *The Civill VVarres of England* (1649), contains pictures of Parliamentarian commanders, brief eulogistic descriptions of their deeds and characters, and an interesting, slapdash attempt to calculate the number of soldiers killed on both sides. Sir John Temple's history of *The Irish Rebellion* (1646), issued at a time when the Irish rebels were still unquelled, is better than these works of Vicars and Ricraft but shares the same flavor of pamphleteering.

Joshua Sprigge's *Anglia Rediviva; Englands Recovery: Being the History Of the Motions, Actions, and Successes of the Army under the Immediate Conduct of His Excellency Sr. Thomas Fairfax* (1647) contains little of intellectual interest but is a craftsmanlike journalistic account of the military operations of the war. In its time it must have been a useful companion for any Parliamentarian who wanted to be informed about the progress of his cause. Cromwell is still a minor figure in the book and Sprigge hardly seems to see in him anything more extraordinary than a good commander. The King is little more than a mere name moving in and out of the story. Sprigge does not probe into the causes of the war, except in an unsatisfactory and vague way in the first chapter, and he is even more vague about the war aims of the Parliamentarians.

From these works it is rewarding to turn to John Corbet's *A true and impartiall History Of the Military Government Of the Citie of Gloucester* (2nd ed., 1647). In this predominantly military history with its geographically limited interests, Corbet does not attempt to give a comprehensive account of the war. He deserves, however, to be singled out for attention because of his views, briefly stated but perceptive, on the role of social divisions and religion in the contest. Gloucestershire or at least the countryside about Gloucester was, Corbet says, inclined to the Parliamentarian cause because it had "no excessive number of powerfull Gentry," who are willing to submit to princes so long as they are allowed to tyrannize over their fellow man. Instead, the inhabitants were chiefly a more liberty loving people, "Yeomen, Farmers, petty Free-holders, and such as use Manufactures that enrich the Country, and passe through the hands of a multitude." There, too

the Country-man had of his owne, and did not live by the breath of his great Land-lord; neither were the poore and needy at the will of the Gentry, but observed those men by whom those Manufactures were maintained that kept them alive. By which meanes it came to passe that neither they of the middle ranke, nor the needy were devoted to the examples of the Gentlemen who turned back, betrayed their trust (and are alwaies more apt to be corrupted, or mistaken in judging of the common interest) but had learned to reverence their Liberties, and to acknowledge their native happinesse.[1]

From these remarks one may suppose that the needy were lucky enough to find that "observing" their economic masters and valuing their liberty

---

[1] John Corbet, *A true and impartiall History Of the Military Government Of the Citie of Gloucester,* 2nd ed. (London, 1647), p. 9.

and happiness were practically the same thing. Corbet in any case has little sympathy for the lowest elements in the populace. He remarks that in Bristol "the Kings Cause and Party were favoured by two extreames . . . the one the wealthy and powerfull men, the other of the basest and lowest sort, but disgusted by the middle rank, the true and best Citizens." [2] Corbet also pays tribute to the importance of religion in awakening the intellect and political consciousness of the people of Gloucestershire. "Thus have we found," he says, extending his remarks to a wider theatre, "that the common people addicted to the Kings service have come out of blinde *Wales,* and other dark corners of the Land; but the more knowing are apt to contradict and question, and will not easily be brought to the bent." With evident allusion to Laud and his adherents, he states that "the ambition of the times hath endeavoured the undermining of true Religion, to promote a blind and irrationall worship" in order to produce political servility.[3]

Corbet, who was Richard Baxter's "most faithful and familiar friend," has also been connected with John Rushworth, who is said to have drawn on his services in the compiling of the first volume of the *Historical Collections.*[4] Whatever precisely were the services Corbet afforded, Rushworth does not mention them in the *Historical Collections.* He had, of course, no obligation to acknowledge the help of a paid assistant used mainly in the assembling and transcribing of documents, which was perhaps all that Corbet was.

The poet and dramatist Thomas May published more comprehensive and ambitious Civil War histories than Corbet or any of their pre-execution predecessors in his *The History of the Parliament Of England: Which began November the third, M.DC.XL. With a short and necessary view of some precedent yeares* (1647) and his Latin *Historiae Parliamenti Angliae Breviarium Tribus partibus explicitum* (1650), later issued in English as *A Breviary of the History Of the Parliament Of England* (2nd ed., 1655). May was one of the intellectuals and literary men whose society Edward Hyde, the future Clarendon, cultivated before the war. Later, after May had become the historian and defender of the Parlia-

---

[2] *Ibid.,* p. 14. Cf. also p. 8.
[3] *Ibid.,* pp. 9-10.
[4] Richard Baxter, *A Sermon Preached at the Funeral Of that Faithful Minister of Christ Mr. John Corbet* (London, n.d. [1680?]), pp. 27, [37]; Wood, *AO,* III, 1267. Baxter, *RB,* Part III, 96, says more largely that *"Rushworth's* Collections, . . . were much of his Composure," but only Rushworth's first volume had been published when Baxter wrote the section of his autobiography in which these words appear. It is of course quite plausible that Corbet also worked on the material for Rushworth's later volumes.

ment and, in particular, of the victorious Independents and Army, few grounds for sympathy remained between the two men. In his autobiography Clarendon declared that May commemorated the acts of the rebels so badly "that he seemed to all men to have lost his wits when he left his honesty" and that he deserved to be forgotten.[5] A less politically and emotionally charged and more accurate verdict, it may be suggested, is that May's histories are competent if in no way very remarkable accounts of events. They are of some interest as rarities because after the Restoration few cared or dared to defend the specific part of the Parliamentarian cause that May defended and because May was more a literary intellectual than any other of the seventeenth-century English historians of the war. His pose of detachment seems a mask for the irony and discomfiture of a man who thought himself more a citizen of the airy republic of letters than a participant in the unedifying tumults of his own time and country.

The author of a short, smoothly written, anonymous work called, somewhat misleadingly, *Britania Triumphalis; a Brief History of the Warres* (1654), announces that he is beginning his narrative where May left off. He accordingly covers events from the King's execution to Cromwell's assumption of the Protectorate or, as he epigrammatically says, "from the end of one Monarchy to the beginning of another." [6] Extended to reach to a slightly later period, the book reappeared as *Britains Triumphs* (1656). In his attempt to sum up the causes of the war, the author asserts that

> The first and generall Cause was the Sinnes of the People, who (taking a surfet of ease, plenty and pleasure) and growing wanton thereby, gaz'd after novelty (that magneticall attraction of the Plebeian rout) and as discontented with their present condition, sought felicity in things they wanted, and were still unsatisfied even in the accomplishment thereof: whence is occasioned the hatred of tranquillity, the desire of motion, the loathing of present things, and seeking after future.[7]

This passage, which bears some resemblance to one at the beginning of Clarendon's *History,* is based on the familiar contemporary idea of the evils arising out of a surfeit of peace and plenty. In an appendix to this present study, the idea of the surfeit of peace and plenty is more fully discussed. Among his causes of the war, the author adds the corruptions of the court and "the Pride, Avarice, Ambition and slothfulnesse of the

---

[5] Clarendon, *L,* I, 33.
[6] *Britania Triumphalis; a Brief History of the Warres* (London, 1654), pp. 5, 207.
[7] *Ibid.,* pp. 1-2.

Clergy"; [8] as this and other remarks suggest, he inclines to anticlericalism. Critical of Levellers, the Solemn League and Covenant, and Presbyterians, he seems to approve of religious freedom while disliking the religious anarchy of the time. In some interesting remarks, he notes that even after the fall of the monarchy the people were prone to adore the idea of monarchy, "the Garlick and Onyons of *Egypt* they much hankerd after." [9] He remarks wittily of Charles II's adventures in Scotland, that "he found the greatest difficulty in ascending the Throne, and least enjoy'd it of any Prince that was ever heard or read of." [10] While he submits to Cromwell's assumption of power as Protector and perhaps even attempts a little mild denigration of the preceding government of the republican Parliament, he is neither servile nor strongly Cromwellian and seems to be in no sense a disseminator of official propaganda.

While the House of Cromwell ruled, Royalist views of the dead King and the circumstances of his downfall were unobtrusively expressed by Hamon L'Estrange and William Sanderson. Despite its title, L'Estrange's *The Reign of King Charles* (1655) only goes as far as the execution of Strafford and therefore is shorter in scope than Sanderson's corresponding life of Charles. It is, besides, written with a Royalism of a more moderate and considered sort. L'Estrange admits that, while he has gained information from good eyewitnesses, he himself has "constantly conversed in the vale of rurall recesse, farre from the Court (the prospect and vantage ground of observation)." [11] Sanderson, on the other hand, was an observer at court. This difference of experience is little reflected in the quality of the histories. Fuller praises L'Estrange too warmly when he says that "he hath presented the Publick with an hansome History, likely to prove as acceptable to Posterity, as it hath done to the present Age," [12] but he was certainly a better historian than Sanderson.

It is possible to detect something of L'Estrange's views on the genesis of the war, though he makes no attempt to give a deliberate and complete account of this part of his subject. He praises James I for his learning, for properly making "other Sciences (their most proper imployment) but Drudges, and Serviteurs to Divinity," and for his opposition to the Roman See, the Arminians, and the Presbyterians, but he nevertheless acknowledges that James alienated the affections of the people by pressing them

---

[8] *Ibid.,* pp. 2-5.
[9] *Ibid.,* pp. 85, 5.
[10] *Ibid.,* p. 25.
[11] H[amon] L['Estrange], *The Reign of King Charles. An History, Disposed into Annalls,* 2nd ed. (London, 1656), preface, sig. A3ᵛ, [A4]ᵛ.
[12] Thomas Fuller, *The Appeal of Iniured Innocence* (London, 1659), Part III, 9.

for money and censures him for his extravagance and his supine foreign policy. "And though those dismal Calamities which befell his Son," he says,

were doubtless ampliated by a superfetation of causes; yet was their first and main existency derivative from those recited grounds: Let Court-pens extol the calmnesse of his Halcyonian Reign, . . . Yet can they never truly deny, but that admired *Serenity* had its set in a Cloud, and that he left to his Successor a Crown of Thorns, as being engaged to contend with two puissant Enemies; First, the mighty Monarch of the West, the King of *Spain:* Secondly, the more invincible of the two, an Empty Purse . . .[13]

He is less helpful in explaining how the war developed in the years after James's death, though it is evident from his severe remarks about Laud and the Laudians that he does not consider them blameless, and he goes so far on one occasion as to blame the Presbyterians for "their so principally occasioning our late sad distractions." The Presbyterians concealed their real nature before the war, but they later turned out to have "clawes and asperities . . . far more sharp and terrible then the Prelates." [14] He mentions ship-money and the compositions for knighthood without clear disapproval but certainly without approval. He annoyed Heylyn with his mild criticism of William Noy. When he mentions the Triennial Bill, he remarks that "The distempers of our state, both Ecclesiastical and Political, were eminently derived from the long dis-use of Parliaments, which are in truth the strongest ligaments of the relation Paramount betwixt King and People: . . ." [15] He remarks on the propensity of corporate towns to rebel and he terms the Londoners "the considerable Artificers of" Charles's ruin. When he mentions the death of Portland, he notes the wide divergency of mind existing then between Charles and his subjects.[16]

Further reflections on the origins of the war may be gathered from his remarks about the Short Parliament.[17] He is uncertain, he says, whether it was more unfortunate in beginning so late or in ending so soon. This Parliament, he thinks, "had Power, and probably Will enough to impede the torrent of the late civill War." However, the King would have had to yield to retrenching "some luxuriances of his Prerogative," to the reduction of "Episcopacy to its primitive institution, that is, to the frame by Divine Right (a root which had not sap enough to maintain so spreading

[13] L'Estrange, *King Charles,* pp. 5-6.
[14] *Ibid.,* preface, sig. A3ᵛ; p. 144.
[15] *Ibid.,* pp. 209, 114, 134-135.
[16] *Ibid.,* pp. 128-129, 141.
[17] *Ibid.,* pp. 188-189.

and flourishing a top as was contended for)," and to "more frequent and sociable communication of Counsels with the grand Representative." All these concessions the King did ultimately make when it was too late, but L'Estrange thinks that Charles could have been persuaded to make them even at the time of the Short Parliament. He notes that many have blamed Laud for its dissolution, and without definitely accepting or rejecting the charge against Laud he reflects that the bishops were at that time too active in civil affairs and cites, as a precedent that ought to have been followed, the admirable reticence of Whitgift.

Apart from a few polemical pamphlets on historical topics, L'Estrange's fellow Royalist Sanderson wrote two histories, his *A Compleat History of The Lives and Reigns of Mary Queen of Scotland, And of Her Son and Successor, James The Sixth . . . And . . . First* (1656) and its continuation, *A Compleat History of the Life and Raigne of King Charles from His Cradle to his Grave* (1658). These are mainly political histories, with little information on the personal lives of their subjects. The dullness tinged with grouchiness which is indicated in Sanderson's picture as affixed to his *King Charles* is reflected in his works. His performance as a historian was derided or denounced by Heylyn, Baxter, Evelyn, Burnet, and Wood,[18] but his histories seem to have achieved considerable circulation; he was able to boast in 1658 that "this with modesty I may averr . . . that these Histories sell well, holding up their first good price, and thereby are valued in the commodious and profitable vent, with the general acceptation of those that pay for them." [19] They contained, indeed, much useful material, ill digested though it was, from which the reader could form his own opinions at a time when numerous better histories were lacking. Sanderson has no particular interpretation of the rebellion to expound. His opinion of James I and of Charles I is favorable, and he declares that Charles's apparent failings arose largely from ill advisers. He praises the good times before the war, when the court, gentry, citizens, commerce, navy, universities, and church all flourished. The church was "among all the *Reformed*, . . . esteemed (as in truth she was justly stiled) the *Church Triumphant*." [20] He approves of Laud's action in more fully restoring

---

[18] Heylyn fought a literary battle with Sanderson. For the attacks of the others named, see Richard Baxter, *A Holy Commonwealth, or Political Aphorisms* (London, 1659), pp. 488-489; John Evelyn, *The Diary of John Evelyn*, ed. E. S. de Beer, 6 vols. (Oxford, Clarendon Press, 1955), IV, 94 (entry for July 19, 1676); Gilbert Burnet, *The Memoires of the Lives and Actions of James and William Dukes of Hamilton and Castleherald* (London, 1677), pp. 166, 179-180, 412; and Wood, *AO,* III, 565.

[19] William Sanderson, *Peter pursued; or Dr. Heylin Overtaken, Arrested, and Arraigned upon his three Appendixes* (London, 1658), p. 55.

[20] William Sanderson, *A Compleat History of the Life and Raigne of King Charles from His Cradle to his Grave* (London, 1658), p. 311.

"the ancient usefull *Ceremonies* of the *Primitive Church*" as a means of balancing the Puritans and commends its effectiveness in undermining the Papists, but he censures "the busie Arch-bishop, who must in this time of high discontent, press a full conformity of their Kirk in *Scotland,* with the *English* Discipline." [21] The Londoners were, he finds, unreasonably restive and ungrateful despite the felicity they enjoyed under Charles.

For all his Royalism and his sorrow in describing the King's death, there is evidence that he became reconciled in some degree to the idea of Puritan rule. At the end of his history of Mary and James he says that Charles was *"taken away in the strength of his years and perfections, and none of his (in possibility of Reason) to succeed to any part or portion of his Inheritance."* He also intends, he adds, to write later about how, after the end of the Barebones Parliament, *"it pleased the Almighty to raise a Power which resumed the Peoples protection in monstrous danger of utter destruction,"* and about how at last *"The prosperous effects and issue"* were *"settled into an assurance of the Nations future subsistance."* [22] His various references to Cromwell are never abusive and a few, surprisingly, are mildly commendatory.[23] But no doubt he would have attacked Cromwell with satisfactory malevolence if he had written after the Restoration.

A few lives of Cromwell appeared before the Restoration, and among these was *The Perfect Politician* (1660),[24] sometimes attributed to Henry Fletcher, which stands head and shoulders above any other of the century. A passage describing the appearance of the Cromwellian Army during its encampments in Scotland in 1651 [25] suggests that the author, whoever he was, may have belonged to the Army. A cantankerous allusion in the prefatorial address to the sufferings of the people for Cromwell's sake is so out of keeping with the tone of the rest of the book as to suggest that the author overtaken by prudent afterthoughts or someone else connected with the book felt a need to throw a sop to Cromwell's enemies. Cromwell is treated in the body of the book with intelligent sympathy; the view taken of him is practically modern, except that the author alludes to his

[21] *Ibid.,* p. 299; introd., sig. [A4].

[22] William Sanderson, *A Compleat History of The Lives and Reigns of Mary Queen of Scotland, And of Her Son and Successor, James The Sixth, ... And ... First* (London, 1656), "The Conclusion," sig. Kkkk – Kkkkv.

[23] *Ibid.,* "The Conclusion," sig. Kkkk – Kkkkv; Sanderson, *King Charles,* pp. 321, 698 [correctly 699], 770.

[24] Thomason's annotation on his copy, which is now in the Thomason Tracts in the British Museum, shows that it was in print by Feb. 1659/60.

[25] [Henry Fletcher?], *The Perfect Politician: Or, a Full View of the Life and Actions (Military and Civil) of O. Cromwel,* 3rd ed. (London, 1681), p. 137; cf. also 132 for the horrors of a Scottish spring.

craft and subtlety. *The Perfect Politician* is neutral with respect to the contending factions, being neither Parliamentarian, Royalist, Cromwellian, nor anti-Cromwellian. In cataloguing its merits, it should not be forgotten that the style is often graceful and expressive. "No sooner had the Parliaments Army broken down this bank," the author remarks of the Battle of Naseby, "but like a Torrent they soon overflowed the whole Kingdom." [26]

The author begins his life of Cromwell by noting his honorable extraction. After his early wildness, which the author does not much emphasize, Cromwell became remarkable for sobriety and religion. The troubles in the early Long Parliament which culminated in the outbreak of fighting are explained as the result of God's anger with the English for their "abuse of a long continued Peace, and the blessings thereof." [27] Charles's behavior "in the last scene of his Life," the author thinks, "made many pity him, who before had undervaluing thoughts of his Abilities, looking upon him as too weak to bear the burden of three Kingdoms on his Shoulders." [28] He praises the achievements of the Long Parliament of the early republic. He seems to mean that Cromwell was bribed by the Dutch to make peace with them, and he seems to reprove Cromwell for not producing a settlement and conformity in religion. He notes that Cromwell "became the main stickler for Liberty of Conscience without any limitation," but ungenerously explains toleration as Cromwell's "master-piece in Politicks," which "procured him a party that stuck close in all Cases of necessity." [29] Yet he seems to regard Cromwell as being sincere, at least in part, in his religion. He holds that Cromwell was "better fitted to make a *Prince* of, than the *People* was to *receive him*," but cannot find any other explanation for the swift fall of his house after his death than the finger of God.[30] Perhaps inevitably, the book is more about politics than personal matters, but the author does try, at least a little, to deal with the problem of Cromwell as a man.

S. Carrington's *The History of the Life and Death Of His most Serene Highness, Oliver, Late Lord Protector* (1659) is, by contrast, mainly a eulogy. It does not appear from the book that Carrington had any personal knowledge of Cromwell. He claims to have "continually conversed with the most principal Instruments in these admirable Transactions, persons Unbiased, that had certain and full Intelligence of the highest emergences,

[26] *Ibid.,* pp. 13-14.
[27] *Ibid.,* p. 3.
[28] *Ibid., p. 39.*
[29] *Ibid., p. 269.*
[30] *Ibid., p. 272.*

whether Forreign or Domestick." [31] As Bulstrode Whitelocke is warmly praised,[32] it is interesting to speculate whether he was one of the persons Carrington comprehends in these words. Carrington's weak, disorganized, and half-hearted book is mainly a bare narrative of political and military events, with little information about Cromwell's character and personal life. He includes only a brief and confused account of the origins of the war and his reference to the Parliament "summoned in the year 1641" suggests that his knowledge for such an account was not very reliable. He is at no loss for praise: Cromwell's elegant speech at the beginning of the Barebones Parliament showed that he had "the qualities both of a *Caesar* and of a *Moses*" and his mind "had something of supernatural in it, and partaked of the Divinity." This diligent researcher finds that "Ambition, ... is the onely passion whereof envy it self seems to accuse" Cromwell, but he defends him even on this point.[33] The book is enlivened by bizarre metaphors and flights of fancy, pretentious and unsuccessful ("the quiet Serpent which hatched its poison under the green grass, unawares let slip a Hiss" [34]) and by the first publication of Waller's lines on Cromwell's Spanish War beginning *"Now for some Ages had the pride of Spain."* Carrington's almost worthless book makes practically no contribution to knowledge of Cromwell and makes no real attempt to justify Cromwell's actions or to refute the charges against him. It is such a book as would be produced if a hack writer who shared the standard Royalist hatred of Cromwell were hired to violate his own principles and write Cromwell's life for money. The Stuarts are little mentioned and the King's death is alluded to only in passing.

When the House of Cromwell had fallen and the Restoration was at hand, the anonymous *Metamorphosis Anglorum* (1660) was published,[35] professing to be a letter written by an informant in England to Don Luis de Haro, the King of Spain's principal minister. The real author was Sa-

---

[31] S. Carrington, *The History of the Life and Death Of His most Serene Highness, Oliver, Late Lord Protector* (London, 1659), preface. Perhaps my own negligence or ill luck is at fault, but after considerable enquiry I have been unable to obtain any scrap of information about Carrington other than the few facts he includes in his book. Can his name have been a pseudonym? W. C. Abbott expands his initial "S" to Samuel, but of course any seventeenth-century Englishman whose first name began with "S" was probably called Samuel. W. C. Abbott, *A Bibliography of Oliver Cromwell* (Cambridge, Mass., Harvard University Press, 1929), pp. xvi, 126.

[32] Carrington, *History*, pp. 188-189.

[33] *Ibid.*, pp. 150, 165, 247-248.

[34] *Ibid.*, p. 209.

[35] Thomason dates his copy in April. The passage in [Samuel Dancer], *Metamorphosis Anglorum, or, Reflections Historical and Political, upon the late Changes of Government in England* (London, 1660), p. 106. suggests that the author is a Roman Catholic but this supposition is inconsistent with the passage pp. 110-111.

muel Dancer; the letter form is only a literary device. Covering events
from the death of Cromwell to the Army's redissolution of the Rump in
1659, he mentions the fear of Cromwell felt in Europe and the joy of
most princes, and especially of the Dutch, at the news of his death. His
talent for the expression of intelligent incredulity and his device of casting
his work in the form of a letter to a foreigner enable him to express his
sense of the strangeness of the events which have taken place in England.
"My Lord," he says,

I have often wondred at the English Commonalty; who made their lawful
Soveraigns raising of Ship money, without authority of Parliament, one of
their chief pleas for their raising Warr against him, and yet have since sat
still, and as 'twere willingly yielded to the payment of unheard of duties, and
have been content with what ever burthens and oppressions have been imposed on them, by those whom they stick not publiquely to call extorting
unjust and lawlesse Tyrants.[36]

Similarly, he finds the fall of Richard like "a very *Romance*," and thinks
it will "very hardly find belief in future ages" and that the commotions
in government since Richard's accession are unparalleled since the creation. As a result of these distractions England has been made, in the eyes
of foreigners, "the most ridiculous Nation of the whole world." [37] He
is deeply impressed by the character and abilities of Lambert, but puts
his own hopes on the restoring of Charles II. Indeed, "at least two thirds
of the people of *England*," he determines, are still "faithful and loyal" to
the royal interest.[38] Perhaps the author is a Royalist in the full sense and
has a Royalist past as well as immediate monarchist convictions, but he
maintains his pretense of detachment from English ties and problems
successfully enough to conceal the road which led him to his present opinions.

In addition to these published works, certain other histories of the war
or aspects of it were written wholly or in part before the Restoration but
were published only after that event. Elsewhere we shall consider such
works by Hacket and others in an order corresponding, so far as the principles of orderly arrangement permit, to that in which they were published. Two of these works, however, ought to be discussed here, for the date
of their publication is later than that of Clarendon's *History* and they
find no other convenient place in our chronological sequence.

Sir Edward Walker's *Historical Discourses* (1705) were all or mainly

[36] *Metamorphosis*, pp. 57-58.
[37] *Ibid.*, pp. 24-25, 88-89, 101.
[38] *Ibid.*, pp. 62, 99-100, 111, 92.

written before the Restoration. Walker was Charles I and Charles II's Garter king-of-arms and one of the Royalists who shared the exile of Charles II; not surprisingly, the work is intensely Royalist. In addition, Walker was intellectually and emotionally devoted to a degree even beyond that of most of his contemporaries to the idea of a society of clearly graded ranks in which men observe exactly the right relationship of deference and aloofness to each other. The *Discourses* include, in their several essays, military narratives, a life of Walker's ferociously aristocratic patron, the great Earl of Arundel, a reply to Lilly's assault on Charles I in *Monarchy or No Monarchy in England,* a comment on L'Estrange's history, a treatise on Charles I, and another on the ill consequences of the Stuarts' policies in bestowing honors. The work is interesting chiefly for Walker's awareness, which went beyond that of most of his fellow historians, so far as one can judge from what they wrote, that historical events can be elucidated by the study of the classifications of men in society and of property relationships. He seems to believe that if the ranks of society were only a little more closely regulated, disasters like the Civil War would be less likely to happen.[39] Like Harrington and Mrs. Hutchinson, he sees the connection between the fall of the monasteries and the Civil War.[40] When he sets himself to list "the Causes that seemingly gave Life to the horrid Usurpation of the Commons in our times," he limits himself to a shorter historical period, noting (1) the "Perverseness of many in matters of Religion," (2) the excessive liberality of James I, (3) James's debasement of the nobility by too many creations, (4) the wealth and populousness of London, and (5) the imprudent policy of buying off troublemakers in Parliament by advancing them.[41] The many discerning comments scattered throughout his folio volume seem somewhat inconsistent with the evidence one finds elsewhere in the same volume of inflexibility and pettiness of mind in the author, but they do render it one of the better contributions to the debate on why the late catastrophe happened.

His fellow Royalist M. Wren's "Of the Origin and Progress of the Revolutions in England" (1781),[42] which is a highly compressed historical essay rather than a history in the ordinary sense, is shown by internal evidence to have been written before the Restoration. In its richness of ideas and even in its author's confidence in the importance of a highly

---

[39] Sir Edward Walker, *Historical Discourses, upon Several Occasions* (London, 1705), pp. 50, 311, 334, and chapter 6 *passim.*

[40] *Ibid.,* p. 298.

[41] *Ibid.,* pp. 326-328.

[42] Published in *Collectanea Curiosa; or Miscellaneous Tracts,* ed. John Gutch, 2 vols. (Oxford, 1781), I, 228-253.

intellectual approach to history, it reminds one of *Behemoth*. As it includes some enquiry into the errors of the royal government which helped to effect the downfall of the monarchy, it similarly bears comparison to the book of advice the Marquis of Newcastle wrote for Charles II. Filling only twenty-six pages as published in the eighteenth century, its structure of ideas could easily supply the intellectual framework for a factual narrative of many times this length. The author's insights are difficult to summarize, for they arise from no single fixed theory, but it may be mentioned that he traces the rebellion back to the period of the Reformation, pins some or much of the blame for it on "the Puritan Faction," and does not conceal the errors and worse of King James and the irresolution of King Charles.

We should not leave the survey of these pre-Restoration historians without noticing the appearance, during the period when the Stuart power to control the press was in abeyance, of a number of histories devoted to unsympathetic treatments of James I. Strictly speaking they were not Civil War histories, but the connection between James's unfortunate or unwise government and the war was so obvious to contemporaries at mid-century as to give them a distinct relevance to the war. Sir Anthony Weldon wrote his scandalous *The Court and Character of King James* (1650, new edition 1651 with a section on Charles I) and was answered by the loyal Sanderson's *Aulicus Coquinariae* (1650) and life of James, and by Bishop Godfrey Goodman's *The Court of King James the First,* which was not published till the nineteenth century. Weldon continued his attack on the monarchy at a lower intellectual level (if the work is really his) in *A Cat May look upon a King* (1652), a derisive survey of the English monarchs since William the Conqueror with special attention to James. *The Narrative History of King James, for the first fourteen Years* (1651), is a volume of narrative and documents usually attributed to the bookseller Michael Sparke; by its emphasis on the scandalous events of his reign, it criticizes James by implication. Arthur Wilson's life of James from his accession to the English throne to his death, called *The History of Great Britain* (1653; replied to in Sanderson's life of James) is critical of James in an aloof way that reveals little about the author's own ideological position. Certain passages suggest that Wilson draws on the idea of the surfeit of peace to connect the good times of James's reign with the war that grew out of them. His literary flourishes inform us that he saw himself as a literary man as well as a mere historian. Francis Osborne, writing in a more labored and difficult style, is just as consciously a literary man as he chronicles the failings of James, his court, and his age in his

Historical Memoires on the Reigns of Queen Elizabeth and King James
(1658). Osborne views the world with an astringent irony that finds few
parallels among his fellow historians. Well developed though the intellectual assumptions behind the irony seem to be, it gives the impression of
being the defense of a man who has badly burnt his fingers in the business
of life.

2. Peter Heylyn

As a member of the Arminian party the clergyman Peter Heylyn (1599-
1662)[43] played an energetic, reckless, and at times vindictive part in the
struggles between the Arminians and their opponents that disturbed England in the 1630's. In July 1630 he preached against the feoffees for im-
propriations, his voice being, according to Gardiner, the first to be raised
publicly against them.[44] In 1633 he collected evidence from *Histriomastix*
to be used in the prosecution of Prynne. Bulstrode Whitelocke, commenting on this prosecution, cleverly remarks that Heylyn and Prynne actually
resembled each other, "though so much different in diuinity, or show of
it." [45] In order to undermine the strict sabbatarianism of the Puritans, he
wrote, acting on the King's orders, *The History of the Sabbath* (1636).
He played a large part in the persecution of Laud's rival Bishop Williams,
leading an attack of some of the prebendaries of Westminster Abbey
against him, writing against Williams' views on the communion table,

---

[43] The chief account of Heylyn's life is one of the neglected gems of seventeenth-
century biography, John Barnard's *Theologo-Historicus, Or the True Life of the Most
Reverend Divine, and Excellent Historian Peter Heylyn* (London, 1683), reprinted
with many notes and additions at the beginning of Peter Heylyn, *Ecclesia Restaurata;
or, the History of the Reformation of the Church of England,* ed. J. C. Robertson, 2
vols. (Cambridge, 1849). Additional material supplied by Barnard's rival biographer,
George Vernon, is incorporated in this edition. The life of Heylyn by Mandell Creighton in the *DNB* is excellent, but Heylyn's date of birth must be corrected from his
autobiographical memoranda printed at the beginning of his *Memorial of Bishop
Waynflete,* ed. J. R. Bloxam (London, Caxton Society, 1851). All biographical data
on Heylyn in this chapter, unless otherwise identified, come from Barnard, Creighton,
or the autobiographical memoranda. The Harvard College Library has an unpublished Radcliffe Ph. D. thesis by A. M. Kendall, "A Royalist Scholar: Peter Heylyn as
Historian and Controversialist" (1946). There are many contemporary and near contemporary references to Heylyn, illustrating various aspects of his reputation, such as
the curious references to him as a famous man in James Yonge, *The Journal of James
Yonge [1647-1721]: Plymouth Surgeon,* ed. F. N. L. Poynter (Hamden, Conn., Ar-
chon Books, 1963), pp. 23, 157.
[44] Gardiner, *HE,* VII, 258.
[45] Bulstrode Whitelocke's "Annals", BM Add. MS 53726, f. 80, or Bulstrode Whitelocke, *Memorials of the English Affairs: ... King Charles the First, to King Charles
the Second* (London, 1732), p. 18; see also Samuel Taylor Coleridge, *Coleridge on
the Seventeenth Century,* ed. R. F. Brinkley (Durham, N.C., Duke University Press,
1955), p. 224, for a severe censure of Heylyn.

and suggesting the existence of a confederacy of Williams with Burton, Prynne, and Bastwick.[46] Meanwhile, he was handsomely rewarded in church preferments for his zeal. He played a prominent part in the convocation which met with the Short Parliament, but the assembling of the Long Parliament brought a sudden end to his prosperity.

Heylyn suffered much from the war. He helped to edit *Mercurius Aulicus* at Oxford but subsequently was reduced to the life of a fugitive. Still later he made his peace with the victors and settled down to a life of study and writing. Then, in the second half of the 1650's, he reappeared before the public as a controversialist, directing his attacks chiefly, though not quite wholly, against his fellow Royalists. This choice of target is not surprising: on the ticklish subjects of politics and religion it was safer for him to dispute with his fellow Royalists than with Parliamentarians, while the narrow and cliquish nature of his churchmanship provided him with grounds for finding fault with them. Perhaps he also believed, like other ideological firebrands, that deviation from the truth by however little in a fellow believer is worse than its outright rejection by an enemy. While it is clear that he clung to his old Laudian views about the church, it is hard to be confident of his views at this time about the state. On the one hand, he never publicly showed any lack of firm Royalist opinions against which to nail all waverers and it is difficult to believe that he ever rejected any tenet that was essential to his definition of a Royalist. Yet on the other hand one may wonder, on the basis of a few passages in his writings, whether he had not developed more tolerance for the Cromwellian regime than one is entitled to expect in view of his previous career. It even appears, if the manuscript dedication page inserted in one of his volumes in the British Museum is authentic, that he presented the volume as a gift to the Protector Richard! [47] But whatever precisely his attitude

---

[46] This slander about a confederacy is in Heylyn's *Antidotvm Lincolniense. Or an Answer to a Book Entitvled, The Holy Table, Name, & Thing, &c.* (London, 1637), preface *passim*. The dates involved suggest that it was intended to hurt Williams at a time when, because of his approaching first sentence in the Star Chamber, he was particularly vulnerable in person and reputation. According to Vernon in Heylyn, *Ecclesia Restaurata,* I, cix, the book was in print by May 20, 1637; cf. Hacket, *SR*, Part II, 109. Williams was sentenced in the Star Chamber on July 11. Laud attempts the same incrimination of Williams in his speech of June 16, as reported in Rushworth, *HC,* III, Appendix p. 129.

[47] Copy of Heylyn, *Examen Historicum: or a Discovery and Examination of the Mistakes, Falsities, and Defects In some Modern Histories* (London, 1659), shelfmarked G4681. The dedication reads: "To his Highnesse Richard Lord-Protector of the Commonwealth of England, Scotland, and Ireland; &c. The Author doth Humbly Present this ensueing-Examen Intended For rectifying the Mistakes & Partialities in some Moderne Histories." Heylyn's curious reference to Oliver Cromwell in his *Extraneus Vapulans: or the Observator Rescued* (London, 1656), pp. 272-273, will sup-

to the two Cromwells may have been, and however it may have conflicted with his past career, one can at least easily see that the power of Oliver's protectorate must have had an emotional attraction for someone predisposed, as he was, in favor of a strong despotic government unmarked by the weaknesses of the late King Charles. This nimble and iconoclastic thinker, whose exceptional degree of emancipation from conventional ideas recalls that of Hobbes, was also of all men one of the least likely to resist the spell of a new government merely through unthinking attachment to old ways.

Heylyn survived the Restoration by a few years, but after all his efforts he was not made a bishop. Wood comments that his failure to rise higher than subdean of Westminster "was a wonder to many, and a great discontent to him and his," but that the reason for this failure was "manifest to those that well knew the temper of the person."[48] Presumably Wood is alluding to his rash and violent character, but the near-blindness of his last years must have been a further obstacle to his elevation and one may also wonder how far his flourishing controversies, which were close to being the literary equivalent to street brawling, were consistent with the dignity expected in a bishop.

Though his career as polemicist was marked by his vigorous defense of Laud's principles, there is little indication in Heylyn's life or writings that his acquaintance with Laud and enjoyment of his favor ever extended to anything that could reasonably be called personal intimacy. This point has some importance, for the value of his treatment of Laud and the Laudian period in his histories depends, in part, on whether he was an intimate of Laud or, as seems to have been the case, only an acquaintance and partisan. No doubt he knew Laud well, in the sense that he observed Laud closely and made the most of every piece of information about him that came his way, but he seems to have known him from a distance. Gardiner seems simply to have been mistaken in describing Heylyn as Laud's chaplain.[49] I have not seen this claim made in any seventeenth-century source, and it is particularly significant that it is not

port no firm conjecture but hints at a half-unconscious belief that the Cromwellian power in England was likely to be permanent. See also his *Ecclesia Vindicata: or, the Church of England Justified* (London, 1657), ep. ded., sig. [A3], and general preface to the reader, sig. e2, where he presents arguments to the existing powers, and his *Observations on the Historie Of the Reign of King Charles: Published by H. L. Esq.* (London, 1656), p. 94.

[48] Wood, *AO*, III, 557; Barnard, "Theologo-Historicus," *Ecclesia Restaurata*, I, clxxxii.

[49] Gardiner, *HE*, VII, 258, 329; VIII, 253, 267. So too H. R. Trevor-Roper, *Archbishop Laud*, 2nd ed. (London, Macmillan and Co. Limited, 1962), pp. 82, 108.

made by Heylyn himself or his son-in-law and biographer Barnard, though it is in the highest degree unlikely that they would have passed over in silence a fact so much to Heylyn's honor were it true.

Since Heylyn played the role of controversialist with such éclat, it may not be amiss to discuss the qualifications he had for it. There is much that is mean, narrow, and morally insensitive in Heylyn's view of the world and his times, but it would be wrong to dismiss him as merely a myopic and poisonous insect in comparison with men of well developed sympathies and generous views like Fuller and Clarendon. Heylyn's books provide abundant evidence of his intelligence, learning, diligence, and formidable talent for proving a set historical thesis. To all appearances he was an honest scholar who highly prized truth and accuracy. I am unable to discover any justification for Carlyle's reference to him by the nickname of "Lying Peter." [50] Even his style deserves praise, though it is not a style for all tastes. To be fully a connoisseur of seventeenth-century English prose styles, one needs a certain tolerance for sharp and bitter writing. Doubtless it is a general lack of this tolerance that has prevented the masterly stylistic achievement of Anthony à Wood from being widely recognized. Even Mrs. Hutchinson can only be fully appreciated by someone with a tolerance for acrimonious prose. Heylyn's cruel cutting prose, with its severely disciplined irony, outlined his ideas with precision and clarity and was especially well suited for exposing his enemies' errors.

Conveniently for the reader or student, Heylyn's interpretation of the political and religious issues of the war as expressed in his historical writings does not differ significantly from one work to another and may be expounded by selecting the evidence indifferently from among them.

The most important of his works is the life of Laud, *Cyprianus Anglicus* (1668), which takes its title from the decapitated third-century martyr St. Cyprian, to whom Laud referred in his speech on the scaffold.[51] If it was Heylyn who chose this title, he probably valued the implied parallel because Cyprian had, as Laud interpreted him, "no great opinion of the Roman infallibility." [52] Warmly sympathetic as Heylyn was to some

[50] Thomas Carlyle, ed., *The Letters and Speeches of Oliver Cromwell,* re-edited S. C. Lomas, 3 vols. (London, Methuen & Co., 1904), I, 63, 166; Carlyle, "Laud's Life by Heylin," in his *Historical Sketches of Notable Persons and Events in the Reigns of James I. and Charles I.,* ed. A. Carlyle (London, 1898), p. 274. I have not discovered the contemporary sources from which Carlyle claims to have drawn this epithet. Sanderson, *Peter pursued,* p. 53, claims to have caught Heylyn in a lie, but the incident he describes is trivial and there is probably some simple explanation in Heylyn's favor.

[51] Peter Heylyn, *Cyprianus Anglicus: or, the History of the Life and Death, of . . . William . . . Archbishop of Canterbury* (London, 1668), p. 532.

[52] William Laud, *A Relation of the Conference between William Laud, Late Lord Archbishop of Canterbury, and Mr. Fisher the Jesuit,* ed. Edward Cardwell (Oxford, 1839), pp. 6, 3, 307-314.

aspects of Roman Catholicism, he always stressed the firm Protestantism of himself, Laud, and the Laudian school. *Cyprianus Anglicus* contains little of the personal detail customary in a biography, but gives Heylyn's views on the ecclesiastical history of England from the Reformation to the debacle of the church under the Long Parliament. While it can easily be overvalued as a firsthand account of Laud, it is a fascinating account of the background and development of the Laudian policies, being, in fact, nothing less than the history of an abortive revolution or counter-revolution. Doubtless the word "fascinating" needs to be justified. In the last third of the twentieth century one is not likely to find most readers quick to accept the claim that a biography of a seventeenth-century archbishop, covering some 550 folio pages and argumentative rather than gossipy and personal, is a pleasurable work. Yet if the personal experience of the present writer may be alleged, it can be read with a good deal more pleasure than the tedious and sanctimonious depersonalized lives by Walton.

Heylyn's other works relating to the war may be described more briefly. His *Aerius Redivivus: or, the History of the Presbyterians* (1670) traces the seditious behavior of the Presbyterians in the various countries in which they have existed. Despite the intelligence and the great knowledge of its author, one gets the impression, as he singlemindedly and ferociously pursues his thesis of Presbyterian guilt from one end of the folio to the other, that he has allowed his thesis to get the better of his judgment and of the complexity of his facts. Like *Cyprianus Anglicus,* it appears from internal evidence to have been completed before the Restoration. The brief and anonymous *A Short View of the Life and Reign of King Charles* (1658), one of the best written of Heylyn's works, supplements *Cyprianus Anglicus* with a more thoroughly political interpretation. The works he published in controversies with Hamon L'Estrange, William Sanderson, Fuller and others [53] demonstrated his wide knowledge of contemporary English history and his inability to connive at errors in his fellow writers and forced him to express his views with special explicitness. His *Ecclesia Restaurata* (1661), a history of the English Reformation from the accession of Edward VI, does not touch directly on the Civil War but is useful as an addition to the account of the ecclesiastical background of the Civil War which he gives in *Cyprianus Anglicus* and for the evidence it provides of Heylyn's dislike for many aspects of the English Reformation.

[53] The controversy with Fuller is described later in this chapter, but it has not been thought necessary to describe the others. They are well described by Creighton in his life of Heylyn in the *DNB,* except that the work by William Sanderson which he calls "Post-haste" is correctly called *Peter pursued.*

Heylyn's interpretation of the war in his histories is limited in scope and in sympathy. He deals very thoroughly with the ecclesiastical history of the reign of the Stuarts up to 1640, but his account of political history for the same period is less complete. He makes only occasional and disconnected attempts to account for the origins of the war. In his treatment of events after the outbreak of fighting he generally restricts himself to correcting the errors of others; his references to Cromwell are few and minor. In his views on ecclesiastical history, Heylyn is strictly a partisan of Laud. In his views on political history, he is a Royalist extremist, devoted to the idea of a powerful monarchy and resentful of the contrast between the lethargy of the monarchy and his own energetic principles. No suspicion ever seems to cross his mind that Charles erred in giving so much importance in church and state to the Laudian clergy in those days "when the power of churchmen grew most transcendent," [54] or that Laud's rigor in opposing the Puritans and advancing church policies distasteful to them was unwise. From the completeness with which Laud's policies and achievements were dashed to nothing he appears to draw no conclusion save that of the transience of all human government.[55]

The ecclesiastical history of England from the Reformation to the Civil War, as it appears in Heylyn's histories, is a story of the beneficial principles of the original Reformation, the deviation of the church under Calvinism or at least Puritanism from those principles, then the restoration of the church to a superb height of power and glory as a result of the leadership of Laud favored by a pious king. At the beginning of *Cyprianus Anglicus,* as an explanatory background for his account of the struggles of his hero, Heylyn includes a long essay in which he investigates "upon what *Principles* and *Positions,* the *Reformation* of this Church did first proceed; that so we may the better Judge of those *Innovations* which afterwards were thrust upon her, and those Endeavours which were used in the latter times to bring her back again to her first Condition." [56] As a young man Laud was in intimate contact with the unhappy results of these innovations, for at the end of the sixteenth century, when he was studying divinity at Oxford, "the face of that University was so much altered, that there was little to be seen in it of the Church of *England,* according to the Principles and Positions upon which it was at first Reformed." Calvin's very books had been "made the Rule" in the university "by which all men

---

[54] Clarendon, *HR,* II, 417.
[55] See the moving passages in his *Cosmographie In Four Bookes. Containing the Chorographie and Historie Of the whole VVorld, And all the principall Kingdomes, Provinces, Seas, and Isles thereof* (London, 1652), to the reader, sig. [A5]ᵛ – [A6]ᵛ.
[56] Heylyn, *Cyprianus Anglicus,* p. 1.

were to square their Writings." [57] But Laud by his studies readily discerned

how much the Church had deviated from her self, or most men rather from the Church, in those latter times; how palpably the Articles had been wrested from the *Literal* and *Gramatical* sence, to fit them to the sence of particular persons; how a different construction had been put upon them, from that which was the true and *genuine* meaning of the men that framed them, and the Authority which confirmed them; and finally, that it would be a work of much glory, but of much more merit, to bring her back again to her native Principles.[58]

Difficulties would no doubt have to be met in carrying out such a plan, "But these last considerations being weighed in the Scale of the *Sanctuary*, appeared so light, that he was resolved to try his fortune in the work, and to leave the issue thereof unto God." [59] Proving a fearless and dogged proponent of his views, Laud was branded as a Papist or Papist sympathizer for his pains. Heylyn describes the affronts this zealot had to endure. He remained inflexible, notwithstanding, till at last, without having complied with the times, he carried with him into Canterbury the views he had held in the university.

In his writings on the political history of the reigns of James and Charles, Heylyn does not shrink from criticism of the persons of the monarchs, but he is an unflinching devotee of the institution of monarchy. Whether he shared the belief of Hobbes in an absolute monarchy is an open question, but there is much in his work to arouse a suspicion that he did. His views on the Spanish match, the characters of James and Charles, and the survival of Parliaments in England are the result of his drawing logical conclusions from his belief in the necessity of a powerful, perhaps an absolute monarchy.

Heylyn's reflections on the Spanish marriage are especially striking because they suggest, ominously though not conclusively, that he was callously indifferent to the manner in which the monarchy was to be upheld. James, he says, perceived a great popular faction growing up against him, and "Way he found none to extricate himself out of these troubles, but to proceed vigorously in the Treaty for the Match with *Spain*." [60] Puritans may have been alarmed at the proposed Spanish marriage, Heylyn says, "fearing (and perhaps justly fearing) that the Kings alliance with that Crown might arm him both with power and counsel to suppress those

[57] *Ibid.*, pp. 51-52.
[58] *Ibid.*, pp. 52-53.
[59] *Ibid.*, p. 53.
[60] *Ibid.*, p. 90.

practices which have since prov'd the Funeral of the Church of *England*." [61] Other English Protestants, however, looked at the other side of the picture:

other English hearts there are, of no lesse *Loyalty*, and of as great affection to the Royal Family, and as great *Zealots* of the true *Protestant* Religion here by Law established, who think otherwise of it, and that the ruine of *Prince Charles* might by this match have been prevented. The *Spaniard* being for the most part a more steady friend, than the wavering *French*.[62]

In exactly what way the Spaniards were to act to preserve the monarchy and the Protestant Church of England Heylyn does not explain; his remarks at least allow the possibility that he viewed without fear the notion of Spanish troops being employed in England. Since he also says that the alliance would have armed James "with power to suppresse that Faction, which began then to be dreadfull to him, and have since been the ruine of *Charles*, and his whole Posterity," [63] it is likely that he envisages the assistance of Spain being exerted *before* actual warfare broke out in England. Perhaps the most charitable explanation of these reflections is to suppose that Heylyn imagines James and Charles resorting to Spanish money in the manner in which Charles II was later to resort to French money. It must be said in Heylyn's favor that even the amiable Hacket inclines, though with much caution, to Heylyn's views about the Spanish match being the preservation of Charles. It could be argued that Hacket was reluctantly drawn to this view by his compelling desire to salvage as much as possible of the reputation of Bishop Williams, whose life he was writing, but he adds that what Heylyn has said, "many have Whisper'd." [64] Heylyn seems to have lacked the deep-seated anti-Spanish prejudice of some of his fellow Englishmen. He defends the justice of the Spanish war against Queen Elizabeth, asserting that it was not undertaken for religious purposes and that it was justified by Elizabeth's meddling in the Netherlands.[65]

Despite his enthusiasm for the Spanish marriage, Heylyn is unsympathetic to James. Generally his remarks on James are neutral and even sympathetic, but from time to time, as in his criticisms of James's ecclesiastical policies (with Bancroft in 1610 "died the *Uniformity* of the Church of *England*" [66]) the real acrimony of his feelings escapes him.

[61] Heylyn, *Examen Historicum,* Part I, 193.
[62] Heylyn, *Observations,* p. 9.
[63] *Ibid.,* pp. 8-9.
[64] Hacket, *SR,* Part I ,164-165.
[65] Heylyn, *Observations,* p. 10; Heylyn, *Extraneus Vapulans,* pp. 86-87.
[66] Heylyn, *Cyprianus Anglicus,* p. 62.

Once he speaks of the British Solomon in such sharp terms that the passage, though long, deserves to be quoted at length. This treatment of James seems to have shocked Fuller.[67] It must be remembered that at this time, despite the efforts of Weldon and others, James was still often regarded with considerable admiration. "It cannot be denied," Heylyn declares,

but that he was an Universall Scholar, . . . but that he was Great *Britains Solomon,* that is to say, either the wisest Man, or the wisest King of the *British* Nations, I am not Courtier enough to defend or say. It is true indeed, that he much pleased himselfe with boasting of his *Kings craft,* as he used to call it, but . . . I have heard many wise men say, that they could never finde what that King-craft was: It being no hard matter to prove, that in all publick Treaties and Negotiations, and many private Conferences and debates of Councell, he was out-witted, and made use of unto other mens ends, by almost all that undertook him. And one might say, (I feare too truly) that by putting off the Majesty belonging to a King of *England,* that so he might more liberally enjoy himselfe; neglecting the affaires of State, and cares of Government, to hunt after pleasures; deserting the imperiall City, to sport himselfe at *Roiston, Newmarket,* and such obscure places (which were to him as the Isle of *Capre* was to *Tiberius Caesar*) and finally by letting loose the Golden reines of Discipline, held by his Predecessors with so strict a hand; he opened the first gap unto those confusions, of which we have since found the miserable and wofull consequences. But I know not what temptation hath drawn this note from me, I goe on againe.[68]

He seems surprised at his own audacity, but it must be remembered that in the printed word it is impossible to blurt out the embarrassing truth; what Heylyn says in print, he necessarily says in cold blood. Two personal reasons can be suggested for Heylyn's dislike of James – James's anger with Heylyn over a blunder in the youthful author's first publication, his geography, and James's opposition to Arminianism [69] – but it is not necessary to depend on these alone to see why Heylyn held that James had disastrous consequences.

In view of this severity to the father, it is interesting to enquire what Heylyn thought about the policies of the son, and all the more because one suspects that Heylyn had little natural respect for weak, unsuccessful men. Heylyn was to all appearances deeply devoted to Charles I, he owed much to him personally, and he revered him for his high church po-

---

[67] Thomas Fuller, *The Appeal of Iniured Innocence* (London, 1659), Part I, (56).
[68] Heylyn, *Observations,* pp. 13-14.
[69] The incident of the geography is described in Barnard, "Theologo-Historicus," *Ecclesia Restaurata,* I, xlvi-li. Heylyn, *Observations,* pp. 24-25, tries to take the edge off James's embarrassing opposition to Arminianism by claiming that towards the end of his life his opposition softened considerably.

licies – "there never being a greater Patron of the Episcopal order than he lived and died" [70] – but one may detect in his references to Charles a certain criticism which, unlike his discontent with James, never quite comes to the surface. In a work against Hamon L'Estrange he notes that L'Estrange has said that Charles "vailed" his crown to his first Parliament, and this word leads him to reflect on the various weak concessions made by Charles.[71] Later in the same book he returns from time to time to this theme of Charles's weakness. If London had been properly punished for Dr. Lamb's murder, he says, that example might have prevented the murder of Buckingham and the tumults against the Prayer Book at Edinburgh. The Edinburghers "knew very well (none better) by the unpunishing of the *Londoners* for the Tumult in the death of *Lamb,* that the King had rather *patience* enough to bear such indignities, than *resolution* to revenge them." [72] Had Charles stood firm to his servants, Heylyn reflects elsewhere, "he had never fallen." [73] Similarly he observes that though the Scots could easily have been suppressed in the first Scottish War, Charles failed to quell them.[74] Some of Heylyn's leanings or apparent leanings towards despotism have already been noted; it is not surprising to find him approving the maxim, *"That the Resistancies of the Subject being once suppressed, add strength to that Authority which they sought to crush."* [75] Besides reacting weakly to the aggressions of his subjects, Charles also failed in the legitimate arts of popularity, neglecting, like his father, to uphold the pomp so wisely and successfully employed by Queen Elizabeth.[76]

It is not remarkable, in view of his extremist opinions, that Heylyn completely sides with Charles in his discussion of Charles's disputes with his Parliaments. It is more surprising to find him toying with the notion that the institution of Parliament ought to disappear. This notion hardly appears at all in other contemporary Royalist thought. He refers to the belief at the end of the Parliament of 1628-1629 that this might be the last of all Parliaments in England and says:

And certainly there was very good reason why it might be thought so, the King never having good successe in any of his Parliaments, since his first coming to the Crown; and withall, having an example before his eyes, of the like discontinuance of assembling the *three Estates* in the Realme of *France,*

---

[70] Heylyn, *Cyprianus Anglicus,* p. 243.
[71] Heylyn, *Observations,* pp. 28-32.
[72] *Ibid.,* pp. 66, 146.
[73] Heylyn, *Cyprianus Anglicus,* p. 180.
[74] *Ibid.,* pp. 384, 391; Heylyn, *Observations,* pp. 31, 169; Heylyn, *Aerius Redivivus: or, the History of the Presbyterians* (Oxford, 1670), p. 437.
[75] Heylyn, *Cyprianus Anglicus,* p. 290; Heylyn, *Aerius Redivivus,* p. 357.
[76] Heylyn, *Cyprianus Anglicus,* pp. 241-242.

by the King then Reigning, and that upon farre lesse provocations then were given King *Charles*.[77]

Heylyn disapproves of the calling of the Short Parliament and says:

the calling a Parliament at that time, and with so long warning beforehand, was conceived [by some persons] unsafe: And if it was unsafe, it was more *unseasonable*. Parliaments had now long been discontinued, the People lived happily without them, and few took thought who should see the next: And which is more, the Neighbouring Kings and States beheld the King with greater Veneration, than they had done formerly, as one that could stand on his own Legs, and had raised up himself to so great Power both by Sea and Land, without such discontents and brabbles as his Parliaments gave him.[78]

It is tempting to think that in holding such views Heylyn was being more realistic than many contemporary Royalist historians and thinkers. If monarchy and church were to flourish in that excellence in which Heylyn thought they ought to flourish, did not Parliament have to suffer a total or at least a very considerable eclipse? Other Royalists reflected that although certain Parliaments had ended badly, well regulated Parliaments working hand in hand with a sympathetic monarch could be very good,[79] but was this attachment to an ideal so woefully difficult to achieve in reality anything more than a bit of wishful thinking, an attempt to resolve a mighty constitutional conflict by blandly insisting that it need not exist?

In Heylyn's description of the King's enemies there is a certain lack of connection and clarity. He appears (though it is difficult to be certain) to regard what he calls Puritans and what he calls Presbyterians as identical in pre-war England. At any rate, he sees Charles as the victim of a deliberate campaign of destruction waged by Protestant extremists. He observes the parallel between the Puritans or Presbyterians of England, who were preparing a rebellion against their prince, and the Presbyterians of the Netherlands, who had already thriven by rebellion. If the potential rebels of England wished to enjoy the same "Felicities" as their counterparts in the Netherlands,

they were to entertain those Counsels, and pursue those courses, by which the others had attained them; that is to say, They were by secret practises to

---

[77] Heylyn, *Observations*, pp. 92-93.
[78] Heylyn, *Cyprianus Anglicus*, pp. 393-394.
[79] See for example the Marquess of Newcastle's views on Parliament expressed in his book of advice to Charles II, pp. 214-219. This book is printed without a title in *A Catalogue of Letters and Other Historical Documents Exhibited in the Library at Welbeck*, ed. S. Arthur Strong (London, John Murray, 1903).

diminish the King's Power and Greatness, to draw the people to depend upon their Directions, to dissolve all the Ligaments of the former Government; and either call in Forreign Forces, or form an Army of their own to maintain their doings. And this had been the business of the *Puritan* Faction, since the death of *Bancroft*; when by the retirements of K. *JAMES* from all cares of Government, and the connivance or remisness of Archbishop *Abbot*, the Reins were put into their hands. Which gave them time and opportunity to grow strong in Parliaments . . .[80]

Heylyn also speaks of

those great *Achitophels* of the popular Party, who laboured in the raising of a new Common-wealth, out of the Ruins of a Glorious and Ancient Monarchy. To which end they employed the *Presbyterians,* as the fittest Instruments for drawing the people to their side, and preaching up the piety of their Intentions. Which Plot they had been carrying on from the first coming of this King to the Crown of *England,* till they had got His Sacred Person into their possession.[81]

In *Aerius Redivivus* he shows that the English Puritans or Presbyterians were only continuing the rebellious tradition of their continental colleagues when they "embroiled the Kingdom first in Tumults, and afterwards in a calamitous and destructive Warr." [82] He elsewhere – how seriously one may only guess – professes belief in much, though not all, of the Papist plot reported by Sir William Boswell from the Hague in 1640. Finding the Archbishop and King obdurate in the face of all attempts to spread Popery in England, Heylyn says, the Papist plotters decided to exploit the rebellion which had begun in Scotland and so bring about the death of Charles and Laud.[83] Heylyn's motives for noticing this plot are easily explained. Even if the allegations of the plot were unproven, they were at least a body of evidence, a set of clues, that should not be entirely ignored by a historian, and they gave Heylyn an opportunity to confront the pope-hating Puritans with the idea that the Archbishop and the King were the real enemies of Popery while the Puritans had been tricked into serving its ends.

[80] Heylyn, *Aerius Redivivus,* pp. 433-434.
[81] *Ibid.,* p. 481.
[82] *Ibid.,* p. 480 and *passim.*
[83] Heylyn, *Cyprianus Anglicus,* pp. 451-452. Valerie Pearl, *London and the Outbreak of the Puritan Revolution* (London, Oxford University Press, 1961), p. 7, includes Heylyn among the contemporaries who "attributed all responsibility for the Civil War to the factious Puritan citizens of London." Heylyn is on record as having expressed on one occasion the views of which Mrs. Pearl speaks, if he was the author, as he seems to have been, of the anonymous pamphlet, *Lord have mercie upon us: or, a Plain Discovrse Declaring That the Plagve of Warre, which now wasts this Nation, tooke its beginning in and from the Citie of London* ([Oxford], 1643). However, in his historical works proper Heylyn does not attempt to limit the Puritans or Presbyterians on whom he blames the rebellion to London.

Heylyn had an alert eye for the worldly motives behind the religious professions of the King's enemies, as his remarks cited above on the Netherlanders suggest. Greed for the material possessions of the bishops and desire to transfer the business of the ecclesiastical courts into the common law courts he observes to be much or all of the reason for the destruction of episcopacy in England.[84] Speaking of the Scottish rebellion and the first Scottish war, he says "that though *Liturgy* and *Episcopacy* were made the *occasions*, yet they were not the causes of this Warre; Religion being but the vizard to disguise that businesse, which Covetousnesse, Sacriledge, and Rapine had the greatest hand in." [85] The Scottish rebellion originated, according to Heylyn, not in true religious grievances, but in the determination of the Scottish landlords to resist the attempts of the King to loosen their grip on ecclesiastical property and to weaken their tyranny over their vassals.[86]

3. Thomas Fuller

The historical views of Thomas Fuller (1608-1661) on the English Civil War are found chiefly in two of his many works, in his *Church History of Britain* (1655) and in his *Appeal of Iniured Innocence* (1659). A word is necessary about how the second of these came to be written. When Heylyn attacked the *Church History* in his *Examen Historicum,* he began a controversy which had the fortunate result of forcing Fuller to express with greater explicitness views he had already indicated in the *Church History.* Fuller replied in the eloquent and witty *Appeal of Iniured Innocence,* and when Heylyn had replied in his *Certamen Epistolare, or, the Letter-Combate* (1659), a pugnacious work in which he attacks in all five opponents, the quarrel of Heylyn and Fuller ended in a reconciliation and even, if we can accept the claim of their contemporary biographers, in friendship.[87]

Fuller was a moderate Anglican and Royalist whose life shows what seems today an admirable freedom from party ferocities. This moderation

---

[84] Heylyn, *Cyprianus Anglicus,* p. 495.
[85] Heylyn, *Observations,* p. 151.
[86] *Ibid.,* pp. 151-156; Heylyn, *Examen Historicum,* Part I, 223-224.
[87] Anon., "The Life and Death of That Reverend Divine and Excellent Historian, Dr. Thomas Fuller" (1662), reprinted in Thomas Fuller, *The Church History of Britain; from the Birth of Jesus Christ until the Year M.DC.XLVIII,* ed. J. S. Brewer, 6 vols. (Oxford, 1845), I, xxv; Barnard, "Theologo-Historicus," *Ecclesia Restaurata,* I, clx. Cf. John Eglington Bailey, *The Life of Thomas Fuller, D. D. With Notices of His Books, His Kinsmen, and His Friends* (London, 1874), pp. 652-653. Heylyn describes the reconciliation in his letter to Anne Sadlier, April 23, 1660, BM Add. MS 23206 f. 27.

seemed little more than a vice to Heylyn, who complained of "a continual vein of *Puritanism*" [88] in the *Church History*. It would be wrong to claim that Fuller was, except in the most recklessly enlarged sense of the term, a Puritan, but his theological position, or broad nature, or both together, made him sympathetic to some aspects of traditional Puritanism, such as sabbatarianism. In his *Church History* he sometimes speaks well of people who were Puritans even by moderate men's definitions.[89]

Beyond noticing the great biographical fact of Fuller's moderation, we need say little about his life [90] for our present purposes of understanding his historical writings on the war. He fled from London to Oxford in 1643 rather than take in its original terms a Parliamentarian oath which he had already taken with some reservations. For a time he served as chaplain to the Royalist commander Lord Hopton. After the military defeat of the monarchy he lived on more comfortable terms than most of the Royalist clergy with the victorious rebels, for he managed to hold a church living from 1648 or 1649 onwards, preached in London during the Interregnum, and was even, strange to say, a friend of the regicide Sir John Danvers. Like Heylyn, he did not long survive the Restoration, and Heylyn was spared the indignity of seeing his low church adversary assume the bishopric which is alleged [91] to have been in prospect for him.

In a work published under the date of 1642 Fuller announced his hope of writing "the Ecclesiastical History from Christs time to our dayes," [92] but if he meant that he intended to write a general history of Christianity he later reduced the scope of his plans. What he produced was the ecclesiastical history of Britain or, more exactly, despite the words of the title, the ecclesiastical history of England. Echoing a famous remark by Thucydides or merely joining in the claim of so many of his seventeenth-century contemporaries to be writing for "posterity," Fuller calls the *Church History* "a book to Eternity." [93] Without bothering very much about the precise ideas he had in mind in using this startling and unexpected phra-

---

[88] Heylyn, *Examen Historicum*, introd. to Part I, sec. 8.

[89] He clearly feels some attraction to the idea that profanation of the sabbath was a cause of the war. Fuller, *Church History*, VI, 102-103; cf. V, 62. For his commendation of individual Puritans, see VI, 83-85, 285, 305-308.

[90] The principal lives of Fuller are the anonymous life and life by Bailey mentioned in note 87 above. Unless otherwise identified, all my biographical data on Fuller come from these. Other lives include W. B. Patterson's Harvard dissertation, "Thomas Fuller (1608-1661) and the Puritan Revolution" (1966).

[91] Bailey, *Life*, pp. 684-685; cf. Anon., "Life," *Church History*, I, xxix.

[92] *Thomas Fuller's The Holy State and The Profane State*, ed. M. G. Walten, 2 vols. (New York, Columbia University Press, 1938), II, to the reader, sig. A2 - A3.

[93] Fuller, *Appeal*, Part I, 28; *Thucydides*, trans. Charles Forster Smith, 4 vols. (Cambridge, Mass., Harvard University Press, The Loeb Classical Library, 1962-1966), I, 41.

se, we can apply it very justly in our sense to the *Church History* as a literary masterpiece. The *Church History* stands a good chance of being read for its superb prose when the works of Heylyn, Gardiner, and Namier are forgotten. Fuller carries his narrative only as far as the death of Charles I, tends to avoid political issues and foreign events, and deals cautiously with the revolutionary and immediately pre-revolutionary period by making it his practice, to a very considerable extent, to relate facts and to catalog the views of others rather than to state his own interpretations. It is therefore impossible to learn as much from Fuller about the causes of the war and about the significance of events relating to it as from such a relatively minor historian as Mrs. Hutchinson. It is as the cautious analyst of one process, the progressive concentration of the English church about the opposing poles of Laudianism and anti-Laudianism, that he makes his principal contribution to the interpretation of the war.

Exasperated by Fuller's indifference to many of the cherished ideas of the Laudians and by his sympathy for their opponents, Heylyn drew attention to a peculiar passage in the *Church History*. Fuller had written there that the first three books of his history "were for the main written in the reign of the late king, as appeareth by the passages then proper for the government. The other nine books we made since monarchy was turned into a state." [94] Heylyn hereupon claimed to detect an intention in Fuller of tempering his history to whatever happened to be the existing government, an intention which, he remarks justly enough, "I am sure agrees not with the Laws of History." He also observed that the first three books contained evidence to suggest that even when the monarchy still existed, Fuller's loyalty had been lost.[95] There is no need to accept Heylyn's views about Fuller's disloyalty, but the question of what he did to adjust his history to the prevailing political conditions needs to be investigated. Fuller made a distinction between the good and the bad time-server and found that one could be a good time-server by being *"pliant to the times in matters of mere indifferency."* [96] These words seem to indicate the rule that he tried to follow in writing the *Church History*, for he says that:

I did not attemper my History to the Palat of the Government; so as to sweeten it with any *Falshood*; but I made it *Palatable* thus far forth as not to give a wilful disgust to those in present Power, and procure danger to my

[94] Fuller, *Church History*, I, lix-lx.
[95] Heylyn, *Examen Historicum,* introd. to Part I, sec. 12.
[96] Fuller, *Holy State*, II, 202; Fuller, *Appeal*, Part I, 12.

self, by using any *over-salt tart* or *bitter* Expression, better forborn than inserted, without any prejudice to the Truth.[97]

It is doubtful what amount of distortion Fuller's observance of this principle caused in the *Church History;* probably the tone of the work would have been somewhat different had he written it after the Restoration. In particular, he would probably have developed into more pronounced declarations those little hints and remarks of distaste for sequestrators, plunderers, vandals, sectaries, military rule, and other phenomena of the rebellion scattered throughout his history,[98] a few of them innocently incorporated in passages ostensibly dealing with the events of past centuries.

Turning now to Fuller's treatment of the Laudian regime, we find that he uses the word "Arminian" to describe a group of English clergymen, even though the persons represented under that word usually objected to it. Men promoted by Laud, he says, were generally "men of learning and abilities, though many of them Arminians in their judgments, and I believe they will not be offended with my reporting it, seeing most of them will endeavour to justify and avouch their opinions herein." [99] On the use or refusal of this word stands a difference of opinion, for these so-called Arminians disliked the connotation of innovation and foreign influences which it bore. The name of Arminius was attached to some doctrines, Heylyn complains, yet "the same Doctrines had been here publickly Authorised and Taught before he was born." [100]

In the *Church History* and *Appeal,* Fuller discusses the controversies that arose during the despotism of Charles and Laud out of the Arminians' ceremonialism. Perhaps the most important of these was the altar controversy, in which Heylyn played a prominent part. Fuller's opposition is directed not against a single side in these controversies but against the very existence of them. While he believed that at least part of the ceremonialism in question was unwise and historically unjustifiable, he also believed that the cure for the ill feeling over ceremonialism was moderation. Speaking of these controversies or perhaps specifically of the altar controversy, he says:

Indeed if moderate men had had the managing of these matters, the accommodation had been easy, with a little condescension on both sides ... men's minds, distempered in this age with what I may call a mutinous tendency,

---

[97] *Ibid.,* Part I, 52 (sig. [M2]ᵛ).
[98] See principally *Church History,* I, 66, 384, III, 52, 443, 447, 474, 513, 520, 524, 527, 547, IV, 57, 204, 360, 427, V, 115, 319, 340, VI, 67, 103-104, 108.
[99] *Ibid.,* VI, 302.
[100] Heylyn, *Cyprianus Anglicus,* p. 127.

were exasperated with such small occasions which otherwise might have been passed over, and no notice taken thereof.[101]

Accordingly, he censures Heylyn's notion that doctrinal differences could be patched up with Rome, but that merely ceremonial differences could not be accomodated between English Protestants.[102] He does not explain what relation he believes these controversies bore to the ensuing war; however, it is probably fair to assume from a passage in the *Appeal* that he thought the altar controversy contributed to the origins of the war, for he says that the just anger of God prevented a moderate man from standing up at this time to reconcile the dispute and so permitted "a *Pustle* to *fester* into an *Ulcer*." [103]

Besides being a critic of the Arminians' position on ceremonialism, Fuller rejected the doctrines reprehended under the name of Arminianism as private opinions rather than part of the legitimate belief of the Church of England.[104] He explains in a valuable definition how these doctrines were used to split the Church of England:

We must not forget that Spalato (I am confident I am not mistaken therein) was the first, who, professing himself a Protestant, used the word Puritan, to signify the defenders of matters doctrinal in the English church. Formerly the word was only taken to denote such as dissented from the hierarchy in discipline and church government, which now was extended to brand such as were anti-Arminians in their judgments. As Spalato first abused the word in this sense, so we could wish he had carried it away with him in his return to Rome; whereas now leaving the word behind him in this extensive signification thereof, it hath since by others been improved to asperse the most orthodox in doctrine and religious in conversation.[105]

He does not explain the connection between these two extensions of the term "Puritan" and the Civil War; whatever may have been Fuller's own opinion, the connection seems obvious to the modern reader. It is worth noting that Fuller himself was one of the clergymen whose opinions made them liable to be abused as Puritans in the new sense of the term created by the Archbishop of Spalatro and his imitators.

While Fuller commends Laud's private virtues he also shows, as the foregoing suggests, that he disapproves of some aspects of his character

---

[101] Fuller, *Church History,* VI, 112, 40; Fuller, *Appeal,* Part III, 8-6 (correctly 8-10), 17-18.

[102] *Ibid.,* Part III, 18, 64.

[103] *Ibid.,* Part III, 18.

[104] *Ibid.,* Part III, 8-9; a passage in his *Church History,* VI, 298, is less forthright but seems to have the same meaning.

[105] *Ibid.,* V, 529; cf. IV, 327-328. Heylyn refers to the quoted passage without revealing comment in his *Cyprianus Anglicus,* p. 124.

and cannot commend all his actions.[106] In what is perhaps his sharpest reference to Laud, he takes the liberty in the *Appeal* to demolish Heylyn's story about Laud's intention to throw himself at the King's feet to obtain mercy for Lambert Osbaldeston, sentenced in the Court of Star Chamber for libelling Laud and the Lord Treasurer Portland. He says:

I cannot forget, that when the Sentence in the Star-Chamber, passed on Bishop *Williams,* (where he concurred with the highest in his Fine) He publickly professed, that He had fallen *five times down on his knees* before the King in the Bishop's behalf, but to no purpose. It might be therefore suspected that his intention to do it *once* for Mr. *Osbolston* might not have taken effect. And therefore, had the Arch-Bishop's good resolution been known unto him, Mr. *Osbolston* might most advisedly conceale himselfe.[107]

Under similar provocation from Heylyn he brings forward in the *Appeal* a discreditable fact about Laud's intemperate zeal in displacing his predecessor Abbot which he had thought best to suppress when writing the *Church History.*[108]

Fuller unfortunately does not say enough in his *Church History* about the origins of the rebellion in England to enable us to form a connected picture of his views. He is more comprehensive in dealing with England's neighbour, for he includes an impressive sketch of the origins of the Scottish rebellion of 1637. But from another of his historical writings, his preface to a collection of documents called *Ephemeris Parliamentaria* (1654), it is possible to obtain his opinion on the date of the origins of the rebellion in England:

And now give me leave to say, that the *History* of the *Parliament* represented in this *Book* [i.e., the Parliament of 1628-1629] is *fundamentall* to the *History* of our *Times,* and what valiant penne soever dare undertake the writing thereof, it must lay its *ground-work,* and take its *rise* from this *Parliament.* Herein were vertually contained the seeds of all those *troubles* which since the heat of *anger* hath ripened to the full *height* and *breadth* thereof. For what is said of *Rebeckah,* that *Twinnes were in her bowels,* which made their *Mothers wombe* the *field of their fight,* wherein their *unborn Infancy* gave an *Essay* of that *Antipathy* which would be continued betwixt them when arrived at riper yeares: the same was true here, where the opposition betwixt two parties was begun with much violence and impetuousnesse.[109]

[106] Fuller, *Church History,* II, 480-481, III, 555-556; VI, 40, 44, 107, 127, 298-301, 303; cf. IV, 322-323; V, 141-142, 385; VI, 131-132.

[107] Fuller, *Appeal,* Part III, 25-26; cf. his *Church History,* VI, 132-133.

[108] Fuller, *Appeal,* Part III, 6 (correctly 10).

[109] *Ephemeris Parliamentaria; or a Faithfull Register Of the Transactions in Parliament, in the third and fourth years of the reign of our late Sovereign Lord King Charles* (London, 1654), preface, sig. qq2-qq2ᵛ. The preface is signed "T. F." and is in Fuller's characteristic style.

And he adds that "the abrupt end" of this Parliament "was the beginning of all our miseries." This late dating of the origins of the rebellion, in which, however, he differs from Clarendon by only a few years, is nowhere referred to in the *Church History*. In that work he does refer the issues of the war back to the troubles at Frankfort,[110] but of course to do so is quite consistent with a belief that these issues remained innocuous up till a relatively late date. Similarly, when he speaks of the breaking of the Short Parliament, he says that "from this very time did God begin to gather the twigs of that rod, (a civil war,) wherewith soon after he intended to whip a wanton nation," [111] but in this passage he presumably only means that at this time events entered a new and more desperate stage, one immediately antecedent to the outbreak of fighting.

Assuming, then, the validity for Fuller of the idea of a turning point at the Parliament of 1628-1629, what conclusions may be drawn from this idea? It may throw light on why he at one time proposed to end his *Church History* with the death of James and why he speaks of the reign and character of James in such favorable terms, [112] and it gives the context within which he must have placed the ecclesiastical conflicts of the regime of Charles and Laud. Presumably a historian of the war who believes that its causes are largely to be found in the reign of Charles I, and who therefore studies a contracted ground on which every detail assumes a magnified importance, will see in such conflicts as these greater dissolvents of the public peace than will a historian who believes that the causes of the war must be traced back through many generations.

---

[110] Fuller, *Church History*, IV, 208-209.
[111] *Ibid.*, VI, 163.
[112] *Ibid.*, V, 497 note q, 352, 386, 572; VI, 10.

CHAPTER III

ROYALIST HISTORIANS FROM THE
RESTORATION TO 1702

1. Survey of the Historians

There is no sharply visible rise of information year by year and decade by
decade on the war among the Royalist histories of the war written or
published in the period from the Restoration to 1702, nor is there anything among them that deserves to be called a Royalist progression of
ideas about the war or a significant change in Royalist interpretations of
the war. In this period which, as we have defined it, ends with the appearance of Clarendon's *History,* most Royalist historians of the war give
the impression that their histories would have been virtually the same as
they were if any given predecessor had not existed. Presumably these
statements would not have been true if more of the histories had been
of high quality; most of them were the ancestors of modern textbooks
and modern popular histories, not of Gardiner's scholarly and authoritative volumes.

About the time of the Restoration, five moderate Royalist histories of
this modest sort but of somewhat more than usual merit appeared. *The
History of His Sacred Majesty* (1660), a life of Charles II completed
shortly before the Restoration, and *An Exact History of the several Changes of Government* (1660), completed shortly after the Restoration, have
both been attributed to John Dauncey. These were followed by *The Civil
Warres of Great Britain and Ireland* (1661), perhaps by John Davies,
Francis Eglesfield's life of Charles II, called *Monarchy Revived* (1661),
and W.C.'s *The History of the Commons Warre of England* (1662).
These five histories are well filled with facts and interpretations and still
useful as introductions to contemporary thinking on the war. As their
main views are not peculiar to them and will mostly be expressed elsewhere in this study as we encounter them in more prestigious histories,
there is no need to discuss all five in detail, though for examples' sake we
should pause over the first two, those attributed to Dauncey.

The first of these, *The History of His Sacred Majesty,* covers the life of Charles II from his accession to the crown on the execution of his father, with a few introductory pages on his earlier years. The author says little about the court in exile or about Charles as a person, and one may suppose that he knew little about these matters. He concentrates instead on English political history. He may have been one of the people commonly called "Presbyterians"; this conjecture would be considerably strengthened if we could be certain that he was also the author of the *Exact History.* He has a remarkable passage on the word "Presbyterian":

Yet one thing I shall desire the Reader to take notice of, that when I speak of the presbyterians, *I mean not those moderate people, who are as truly loyal as they are godly; but some amongst them like wolves in sheeps clothing (such as* Straughan *and* Kerry *in* Scotland) *who onely pretend themselves to be* Presbyterians, *but are in their proof found Sectaries . . .*[1]

He describes Charles's adventures in Scotland and admits freely that he took the two Covenants under the tutelage of his Scottish hosts. In discussing Charles's escape after the Battle of Worcester, he comments on "all those miseries & hardships which this poor Prince endured for the sakes of us his Subjects," and he holds that "God was never so merciful to any people, as to us, in delivering his sacred majesty so wonderfully out of the hands of his Enemies." [2] In dealing with the problem of whether the leaders of the republic achieved their great successes because of the rightness of their cause, he turns the argument neatly against them by insisting that they were raised up as a punishment for the national sins but, he is careful to add, as a punishment to the prince "onely for the Peoples sake." [3] In a treatment of Cromwell that resembles, in its much more limited extent, the famous treatment by Clarendon, he recognizes the greatness as well as the wickedness of this "Noble Tyrant." [4] He includes some interesting material on the turning of the nation to its old monarchist attachments with the troubles that followed upon the fall of Richard Cromwell. After Lambert's dissolution of the Rump, the military rulers were in a position in which they could maintain their authority temporarily "by sword-law" but in which "no Government whatsoever, by them establisht," could "be firm or durable, since it must be settled contrary to the *Genius* of the people." [5]

---

[1] I[ohn?] D[auncey?], *The History of His Sacred Majesty* (London, 1660), "To the Readers in general."

[2] *Ibid.,* pp. 75-76, 83, 127, 128.

[3] *Ibid.,* p. 132.

[4] *Ibid.,* pp. 149, 193, 196 (misprinted 169).

[5] *Ibid.,* p. 201.

At the conclusion of his writing, Monck has just readmitted the se-cluded members. The author hopes that the other two estates may also be restored "that these Nations . . . may no longer continue to be the scorn and derision of forreign Countries." [6] If he means that the bishops are one of the missing estates, it is difficult to accept the assumption that he is a Presbyterian; however, the passage suggests that like some of his con-temporaries he thinks of the King as one of the three estates and that the missing estates are the peers and the King. When he eulogizes Charles he does not forget to include his royal brothers:

Nor hath God alone been merciful to us in endowing his sacred Majesty with such Heroick Virtues, but he hath given us a stock of Noble Princes, who seem to Emulate Virtue in one another, and grow like Royal Oaks to main-tain the Honour and Glory of this Nation, but are yet and have a long time been the disgrace of it, all the Nations in *Europe* laughing at the *English* folly, who slight that happinesse which they might enjoy.[7]

He ends the history with a wish or a prayer to God for the calling home of the King.

The opinions of the companion work (if we may for convenience' sake call it that), *An Exact History,* are similar enough to strengthen the possi-bility that one author wrote both, but not strong enough to turn the possi-bility into a certainty. The *Exact History* begins with the execution of Charles I and ends with the calling home of the King and so covers just a trifle more than the same period as its companion. The author stresses, in Clarendonian manner, the wickedness and the greatness of Cromwell, and says that he raised "the Nation to that glory, that forreign Princes both feared and envied it." His passage on Cromwell's death is, in terms of ideas, only a restatement and slight elaboration of one in the preceding work and, again, recalls Clarendon. Cromwell's "great soul," he says,

expired, and went to give an account of his actions in this life, to the great High Court of Justice, who had so often called men to account before his High Courts of Justice here: yet there he might have this surety, which could not be given here, that there are neither *Trepanners* nor *false Witnesses.*[8]

In view of the turn that the religious history of England was about to take, it is curious to notice that this loyal author commends the Long Parlia-

---

[6] *Ibid.,* p. 216; for opposition to the idea that the King was one of the three es-tates, see Warwick, *M,* pp. 183-184, and Clarendon, *L,* I, 131-132.

[7] Dauncey, *Sacred Majesty,* p. 233.

[8] J[ohn?] D[auncey?], *An Exact History of the several Changes of Government* (London, 1660), pp. 275, 273, and *passim*; Dauncey, *Sacred Majesty,* p. 193.

ment as altered by Monck's admission of the secluded members for reaffirming the Solemn League and Covenant.[9]

Though the work in itself is unimportant, we may mention in connection with our reference to Dauncey that he appears as the author of a short life of Henrietta Maria, *The History of the Thrice Illustrious Princess* (1660). The tone of this work is eulogistic; the information commonplace and readily available from printed sources. Henrietta Maria's attempt to pervert the Duke of Gloucester to her own religion is omitted, though it is included in the two preceding works. Inappropriately enough, the dedication is to that "Paragon of Vertue and Beauty," Monck's wife, the Duchess of Albemarle, further described by Clarendon as "a woman of the lowest extraction, the least wit, and less beauty," that Monck "was cursed, after a long familiarity, to marry." [10]

At the peril of once or twice plunging needlessly far into the undergrowth of historical literature, we may note some other histories appearing in the years immediately after the Restoration. William Younger's *A Brief View of The late troubles and confusions in England* (1660) covers events from 1640 to 1660 and is interesting mainly as an intimate document of the revolutionary period: one gets a sense of personal happiness suffusing the book as a result of the Restoration, an event that the author, like many others, regards as an example of God's intervention in human affairs. The *Brief View* is intelligent, well written, and informative, but its material is commonplace. Younger began it, he says, with the intention "to leave it in the Register book of his Parish (in which he first began it) for the use of his successors; but it" grew "too big." [11] With the assistance of materials compiled by William Fulman,[12] the Royalist clergyman Richard Perrinchief wrote a devotedly loyal life of Charles I which appeared prefixed to an edition of Charles's *Workes* (1662) and was later reissued as a separate volume (1676). James Heath, the son of Charles's cutler, was expelled from his studentship at Oxford by the Parliamentarian visitors and joined the Royalist exiles on the continent, but his loyalty must have brought him little or no material reward for in the England of Charles II he was forced to rely on his pen for a living.[13] The result included a bare factual narrative of the Civil War called *A Brief Chronicle of All the chief Actions so fatally falling out in these three King-*

[9] Dauncey, *Exact History*, pp. 371-372; cf. p. 377.
[10] Clarendon, *HR*, VI, 154; for the Duchess, see *DNB* s.v. George Monck.
[11] William Younger, *A Brief View of The late troubles and confusions in England* (London, 1660), to the reader, sig. A2v.
[12] Wood, *AO*, IV, 242; cf. 625.
[13] *Ibid.*, III, 663-664; *DNB* s.v. Heath.

doms (1662), its much larger and much more fully developed successor, called *A Brief Chronicle Of the Late Intestine VVarr in the Three Kingdoms of England, Scotland & Ireland* (1663), and a biography *Flagellum: or The Life and Death, Birth and Burial of Oliver Cromwel The late Usurper* (1663). The abusive *Flagellum* is the best known of the early lives of Cromwell; its lively scandal and invective have been well described by W. C. Abbott.[14] William Yonge's *Englands Shame: or the Unmasking of a Politick Atheist* (1663) is an abusive Royalist life of the unfortunate Hugh Peter.[15] The author knew Peter, for that divine lived at his house for a time under the Commonwealth and he urged on Peter's prosecution at the Restoration and was a witness against him at his trial. Reading between the lines, one can detect a slightly uneasy conscience in the author. Had he acted wrongly? Surely not, for does he not demonstrate the wickedness of Peter to the full satisfaction of the reader – and of himself? He claims that Cromwell's eldest son was hanged at Tyburn for murder.

The histories, well known in their time, of Sir Richard Baker and the physician George Bate were first published before the Restoration but had continuations added to them afterwards. Baker's *A Chronicle of the Kings of England* extended in its first edition (1643) to the beginning of the reign of Charles I. Subsequently enlarged in successive stages by other hands to include the full reign of Charles I, the Civil War, and even later events, it continued to be reissued in new editions into the eighteenth century. Its account of the Restoration is especially important. Bate's Latin *Elenchus Motuum nuperorum in Anglia* (1649) dealt with the events of the war to 1649; it was subsequently continued in Latin by Bate himself and by Thomas Skinner and was also issued in an English translation.[16] Bate and Skinner, who show intelligence, though of an unpleasant kind, are unmeasured and rancorous in their Royalism and write with the

---

[14] W. C. Abbott, *A Bibliography of Oliver Cromwell* (Cambridge, Mass., Harvard University Press, 1929), pp. xvi-xviii.

[15] This book is discussed on pp. 46-48 of Raymond Phineas Stearns, "Hugh Peter and His Biographers," *Proceedings of the Bostonian Society at the Annual Meeting, January 15, 1935* (Boston, Published by Order of the Society, 1935). See also the references to Yonge in Stearns's *The Strenuous Puritan: Hugh Peter 1598-1660* (Urbana, University of Illinois, 1954).

[16] Wood, *AO*, III, 828, says that Clarendon assisted Bate with the loan of papers and George Vernon, quoted in Barnard, "Theologo-Historicus," *Ecclesia Restaurata,* I, cxv, says that Heylyn revised Bate's *Elenchus* before publication, but (unless Heylyn is merely being coy) this latter statement conflicts with Heylyn's words in his *Extraneus Vapulans*, p. 199. For fervent Royalist tribute to Bate's plausibility as a historian, see Henry Foulis, *The History Of the Wicked Plots and Conspiracies of Our Pretended Saints* (London, 1662), preface, sig. (b2).

rough assurance of people who know their own minds and will not readily connive at error in their readers.

Several works of narrower scope take Monck and the Restoration as
their topics. Thomas Gumble wrote *The Life of General Monck* (1671)
from personal experience of the general, for he was Monck's chaplain
and Monck used him in the public business that led up to the Restoration.
Gumble shows a certain moral obtuseness in his defense of the disingen-
uous aspects of Monck's career. He defends Monck's service under the
Long Parliament and Cromwell as necessary if he was to carry out his
hopes of one day doing the King service. Of Cromwell he takes a severe view, only admitting that "There was something generous in him." [17]
John Price, who was another of Monck's chaplains, was able, like Gumble,
to remember graphic details from the general's famous march into England. "The Frost was great, and the Snow greater," he writes in one passage, "and I do not remember that ever we trod upon *plain Earth* from
Edenburg to *London*." [18] His *The Mystery and Method Of His Majesty's
Happy Restauration, Laid Open to Publick View* (1680) is naive and
egocentric and sometimes inadvertently conveys the impression that the
author, who seems to have been a man of unusual guilelessness, was one
of the guiding spirits behind the pliable general. Perhaps the work reflects
the distortions of years of anecdote-telling. Thomas Skinner, the continuator of Bate's *Elenchus,* wrote *The Life of General Monk* (1723; 2nd
ed. 1724), marked by warm admiration and lifeless and dull rhetoric.
John Collins' "Mysteria Revelata," [19] dated 1674 but first published at
the end of the nineteenth century, contains a peevish attempt to claim for
its author part of the credit of having brought about the Restoration. It
is more an argumentative personal narrative than a history in the ordinary sense and Mrs. S. C. Lomas, who edited it for the Historical Manuscripts Commission, justly calls Collins "a foolish man," but it deserves
notice here for Collins' attacks on the account of the Restoration in the
continuation of Baker's *Chronicle* and for his belief, contrary to that of
Gumble, Price, Skinner, and other defenders of Monck's deliberate ra-

---

[17] Thomas Gumble, *The Life of General Monck, Duke of Albemarle, &c. With Remarks upon his Actions* (London, 1671), p. 92.

[18] John Price, *The Mystery and Method Of His Majesty's Happy Restauration,
Laid Open to Publick View* (London, 1680), pp. 75-76.

[19] John Collins, "Mysteria Revelata," HMC *Report on the Manuscripts of F. W.
Leyborne-Popham, Esq. of Littlecote, Co. Wilts.,* ed. Mrs. S. C. Lomas (Norwich,
1899), pp. 198-239. For Mrs. Lomas' remarks, see pp. xiv-xvi. Collins, p. 232, describes his unsuccessful attempt to persuade Heylyn to write a "history of the late times"
and Restoration according to Collins' specifications.

ther than accidental Royalism, that the general did not intend to restore the King till circumstances forced his hand.

In examining the other histories belonging to the reign of Charles II we may begin with the remainder of those that appeared before Titus Oates's revelations plunged the monarchy into its greatest crisis since the Civil War. David Lloyd wrote several works relating to the history of the war, but we need only note his Royalist *Memoires of the Lives, Actions, Sufferings & Deaths of Those Noble, Reverend, and Excellent Persona- ges, That Suffered By Death, Sequestration, Decimation, Or otherwise, . . . In our late Intestine Wars* (1668), which includes a life of Charles I. Heylyn's *Cyprianus Anglicus* and *Aerius Redivivus* revived the contro- versies of the thirties to provide solid intellectual fare for thoughtful Roy- alists of the England of the Cabal and Danby. Sir Winston Churchill in his *Divi Britannici: Being a Remark Upon the Lives of all the Kings Of this Isle* (1675) [20] left a memorial of his delight in the English past, his love of country, and the vigor and feeling of his Royalism in a series of rhapsodic comments on the successive kings. In explaining the origins of the war he resorts to the idea of the surfeit of peace and mentions the dif- ficulties that Charles inherited from his father. Rather tactlessly, in this volume dedicated to Charles II he includes reflections on the ill luck of kings called "the Second." [21] The work is interesting chiefly for a few good literary passages, for the author's connection with a famous name- sake and descendant, and for the further light it throws on the varieties of seventeenth-century Royalism. George Meriton in his *Anglorum Gesta; Or, a Brief History of England* (1675; 2nd ed. 1678), which is profess- edly written for plain and busy people, says of Charles I's execution that "even his Enemies wept in private for what they had done in publick," and of Cromwell that "if his Cause had been Honourable and Just, he would have been as much Honoured by Posterity for his Vallour, as he is hated by all good Subjects for his *Disloyalty* and *Inhumanity* to his Sovereign Lord and Master the King." [22] *The Historians Guide* (1676), a convenient anonymous manual which went through a number of edi- tions, includes a chronology of the main events of the war. Francis Sand-

---

[20] This work is discussed in a pamphlet by C.R.H. Taylor, *The Churchill Book: The Curious Story of "Divi Britannici" written by Sir Winston Churchill more than two and a half centuries ago* (Wellington, N.Z., Whitcombe & Tombs Limited for The Friends of the Turnbull Library, 1942), and in A. L. Rowse, *The Early Churchills: An English Family* (London, Macmillan & Co Ltd., 1956), pp. 29-34, 113.

[21] Sir Winston Churchill, *Divi Britannici: Being a Remark Upon the Lives of all the Kings Of this Isle* (London, 1675), p. 252.

[22] George Meriton, *Anglorum Gesta; Or, a Brief History of England,* 2nd ed. (Lon- don, 1678), pp. 322, 324-325.

ford's handsomely printed *A Genealogical History of the Kings of England* (1677) also deals with the war but is weak in interpretation and meritorious mainly for its physical appearance and genealogical usefulness.

We come next to the history of the Civil War by the famous Sir William Dugdale, *A Short View of the Late Troubles in England* (1681), which, despite the misleading claim of its title, remains a good-sized folio even when one subtracts its appendix of documents on the Treaty of Uxbridge. Dugdale says in the preface that the *Short View*, which is known to have been in print by March 1681,[23] was *"long since compiled."* According to the continuator of his autobiography, he did not originally intend to publish it during his lifetime.[24] Conceivably the reason why he changed his mind and published it when he did, some five years before his death, was that he or his friends believed the book would prove useful in support of the monarchy during the succession crisis.[25] He is probably referring to its forthcoming anonymous publication when he writes in a letter to Wood:

I am not a little startled at what you tell me of the Booke in the presse at Oxford . . . I was promised all secresy therein, I pray you therefore use what meanes you can to divert the thoughts of those another way, who seeme to be so confident that I am the Author of it: for I know that the malice of that faction which finde themselves toucht, is so great, that they will endeavour to do what mischeif they can to any that detects them.[26]

This reference to enemies seems curious, even given the troubled conditions of the times, yet Dugdale's hatred for Puritans and rebels and belief in their malignity were so boundless it is not altogether surprising he should begin to daydream about these monsters menacing himself. Besides, a report mentioned by Wood that the Oxford Parliament of 1681 if it had sat two days longer would have had the book burnt and Wood's statement that Howard Lord Escrick said that the author and printer ought to be hanged suggest that there may have been some foundation, if only a very slight one, for Dugdale's apprehensions.[27]

[23] Anthony à Wood, *The Life and Times of Anthony Wood,* ed. Andrew Clark, 5 vols. (Oxford, 1891-1900), II, 533, 524. My present remarks on Dugdale are based on my more detailed study, "Sir William Dugdale As Historian of the English Civil War," *The Lakehead University Review* (Lakehead University, Canada), 2 (1969), 116-134.

[24] Dugdale, *SV*, preface, sig. A2v; Dugdale's autobiography in *The Life, Diary and Correspondence of Sir William Dugdale,* ed. William Hamper (London, 1827), pp. 37-38.

[25] The continuator of his autobiography hints at this explanation, *ibid.,* p. 38.

[26] Dugdale to Anthony à Wood, written or received Nov. 25, 1680, Bodleian MS Tanner 456a f. 24. See also letters of same to same, Dec. 9 and 30, 1680, *ibid.,* ff. 25-26.

[27] Wood, *Life and Times,* II, 533. This was the William Lord Howard who later

Despite these bad beginnings, the book seems to have pleased many contemporaries. A favorable reception as to sale is suggested by Dugdale's request, in a letter which may have been written as little as two months after the book's publication, for more material on the grounds that he thought the book would "come to another Impression." [28] It certainly found friends in the universities, for when the King and Queen visited Cambridge in September 1681, the vice-chancellor officially presented a copy to the Queen, and a scholar at Oxford, writing in November of the same year, describes the book as "much esteemed here." [29] As people read to have their prejudices reinforced as well as to be informed, it is understandable that the sulphurous Royalism of the *Short View* should have delighted the more inflamed sort of Tories.

In ideology and to some degree in its factual and grimly serious development of its subject, the history thus published is the kind one would expect from the fact that in his correspondence Dugdale praises "the learned and right orthodox" Heylyn's *Cyprianus Anglicus* and *Aerius Redivivus* but dismisses "honest Tom Fuller" as having "a great flaw in his pate." [30] The *Short View* is laudable for its generous supply of facts and especially for its firm insistence on the exact dating of events, but today it probably interests the reader mainly by making him wonder how a scholar as great as Dugdale showed himself to be in other fields could produce a history insensitive, as this one is, occasionally even to the point of obtuseness. Dugdale unreservedly defends the conduct of Charles I both before and during the rebellion. He just as unreservedly condemns the morals and motives of his principal opponents, including, of course, Cromwell, who, apart from a few allusions to his courage, is treated in the *Short View* with hardly a glimmer of respect or sympathy. Nor does Dugdale show in the least that he grasps the complexity of personality, of historical processes, and of the machinery of society, as he ruthlessly systematizes the events of the war to accord with his black-and-white picture of a guiltless king struggling in vain against a band of evil politico-religious conspirators. I have advanced the idea in a study of this history which I have published elsewhere that its insensitivity may have arisen because Dug-

---

gave evidence against his fellow Whigs in the prosecutions that followed upon the Rye House Plot; Clark incorrectly identifies him with his brother Thomas who died in 1678.

[28] Dugdale to (presumably) Anthony à Wood, May 14, 1681, Bodleian MS Wood F41 f. 144.

[29] Wood, *F,* II, 27; publisher's advertisement cited in *Dugdale,* ed. Hamper, pp. 496-497; Z. Isham to Edmund Borlase, Nov. 20, 1681, BM Sloane MS 1008 f. 325.

[30] Dugdale to Earl of Huntingdon, Sept. 15, 1673, in Bodleian MS Carte 78 f. 530, printed in F. M. Powicke, "Notes on Hastings Manuscripts," *HLQ,* I (1937-1938), 275; Dugdale to Dr. Johnston, June 16, 1668, Bodleian MS Top. Yorks c. 18, f. 104.

dale's mind was too rigidly set in the ways of the genealogical and anti-
quarian studies in which he excelled to deal successfully with the much
more complex subject of the Civil War.[31]

Dugdale adheres fiercely and inflexibly to a straightforward conspiracy theory of the rebellion, in which he assumes that certain Protestant radicals, who are never clearly defined in his pages, combined with more
politically oriented dissidents to carry out a carefully laid plot to overthrow the monarchy. The following passage is long, but expresses enough
of Dugdale's views on the genesis of the rebellion to deserve quoting in
full:

And having thus demonstrated, that the Principles, by which this sort of
men [the Protestant radicals] be unhappily guided, are most dangerous and
destructive to civil Government; I now descend to those their Arts and Devices; whereof, by the help and influence of a most subtile, corrupt, and
schismatical party in Parliament, they made use, in order to the raising this
late nefarious Rebellion: the consequence whereof; *viz.* the extirpating of
Monarchy here, was in their design long before; however it may be thought
by some, that *Necessity* and *Despair,* put them upon that bold Exigent, after
they had gone farther, than they thought they could (by any outward reconciliation or pardon) be safe: . . . the first, and indeed most fatal Artifices, was
the reducing his Majesty to Necessities, to the end he might be inforc'd to
betake himself unto such extraordinary means for supply, as would certainly attract the odium of his Subjects.[32]

Dugdale's Protestant radicals obviously have much in common with Heylyn's Puritans or Presbyterians. Unfortunately, these writers do not define
their villains clearly enough to enable us to be sure how closely they come
to coinciding. Rather oddly, Dugdale tries to trace the more mischievous
aspects of Scottish Presbyterianism and of his English Protestant radicalism to a supposed sixteenth-century migration of two shiploads of German Anabaptists to Scotland.[33]

Looking at the other Royalist histories published about the same time
as the *Short View,* we see little reflection of the crisis of the monarchy
which began with Oates's revelations in 1678. *Behemoth,* as we shall see,
probably slipped into print at the time of the Popish Plot agitation for the
same reason as a number of Parliamentarian works. One can speculate on
the political as well as the personal motives behind the issuance of Thomas
Frankland or Franklin's bulky folio called *The Annals of King James and*

[31] MacGillivray, "Dugdale," *The Lakehead University Review,* 132-134.
[32] Dugdale, *SV,* pp. 19-20. For his belief that the rebellion was premeditated, see
also *ibid.,* preface, sig. [A3]; pp. 19, 38, 40, 43, 59-61, 66, 92, 105, 374, 389, 402, 600;
cf. Dugdale's autobiography and diary in *Dugdale,* ed. Hamper, pp. 15, 96.
[33] Dugdale, *SV,* pp. 8-9.

King Charles the First (1681), which is a collection of documents linked by commentary covering English political events from 1612 to 1642. Frankland was a medical impostor who had been exposed a few years before. There is evidence that he took bribes as a member of the Royal College of Physicians and he is alleged to have forged a will, but his venomously Royalist history shows that disloyalty was not among his defects. He died in the Fleet prison in 1690.[34] Nalson's *Impartial Collection* is of course marked by the feelings of the Popish Plot and the succession struggle.

The Revolution of 1688 marked little change in the writing and publication of Royalist histories, though it may have facilitated the publication of Hacket's *Scrinia Reserata*. Richard Cox's lengthy *Hibernia Anglicana: or, the History of Ireland From the Conquest thereof by the English* (1689-1690), which is written from an English and Protestant point of view, contains a curious passage on the death of Charles I that should be included in any anthology of seventeenth-century English comments on the Irish. "Oh!," Cox laments, "that I could say, They were *Irish* Men that did that Abominable Fact, or that I could justly lay it at the Door of the Papists! But how much soever they might obliquely or designedly Contribute to it, 'tis certain it was actually done by others, . . . " [35] Sir Roger Manley's *The History of the Rebellions in England, Scotland and Ireland* (1691) is a concise, respectable Royalist history, part of which had been published in Latin a few years earlier. Manley shows a soldier's generosity in commending the courage of his Parliamentarian enemies and even shows some feeling for the greatness of the monster of wickedness, Oliver Cromwell. He discovers no connecting thread in the sequence of rebellions from 1637 to 1685 which he describes in his history, except, perhaps, that of the restless wickedness generally behind rebellion. Wood's *Athenae Oxonienses* and *Fasti* (1691-1692) deserve to be ranked among histories of the Civil War because of their biographies of so many of the participants. Wood's attitude to the literary task he set himself raises intriguing questions. Was the secluded, surly, and aging scholar trying to live vicariously through his mastery, as biographer, of the lives of others? What were the psychological origins of the malice and even hatred he so often shows towards these persons? He seems driven by a desire to destroy as well as to immortalize his subjects. His friend Aubrey's *Brief Lives,*

---

[34] For Frankland's life, see *DNB* s.v. Frankland; Wood, *AO*, IV, 289-290; Wood, *Life and Times*, II, 392-393; Sir George Clark, *A History of the Royal College of Physicians of London*, 2 vols. (Oxford, Clarendon Press, 1964-1966), I, 338, 338n.
[35] Richard Cox, *Hibernia Anglicana: or, the History of Ireland From the Conquest thereof by the English*, 2 Parts (London, 1689-1690), Part II, 206.

which are among the finest achievements of English biography, supplied material for Wood's use but remained unpublished as independent works till the first fragmentary edition appeared near the end of the eighteenth century. Lacking the sombreness and unhappiness of Wood's lives, they contain incomparable portraits of the world of the Civil War and, especially, the Restoration.

Sir Philip Warwick's *Memoires* (1701) [36] belong to a trend, discernible at the end of the seventeenth century among both Royalists and Parliamentarians, towards the publication of Civil War memoirs and similar personal documents: Baxter's autobiography, Ludlow's *Memoirs* (1698-1699) and the more limited accounts of Denzil Holles (*Memoirs,* 1699), Sir John Berkeley (*Memoirs,* 1699), and Fairfax (*Short Memorials,* 1699) had already been published, and Clarendon's *History* was shortly to appear. Internal evidence suggests that Warwick's *Memoires* were written between 1676 and 1677, though at least one passage, referring to Hobbes's *Behemoth,* may have been added as late as 1679.[37] Warwick's surviving correspondence shows that he circulated his *Memoires* and other writings in manuscript among his friends.[38] After Warwick's death Dugdale was anxious that Thomas Smith of Oxford University should publish the *Memoires* to prevent them from being "smothered," [39] but the publication was long delayed and Warwick had been dead some eighteen years when they finally appeared in print.

Warwick had a long official career in the service of the Stuarts,[40] but he was not drawn into partisan bitterness by it, and the tolerance with which he looks upon the history of the Civil War recalls Clarendon. Warwick had the highest reverence for Charles I's character and morals and presents probably the most convincing portrait of the King as a human being that is to be found in any seventeenth-century history, but he does touch on the King's weakness so far forth as to question whether this exemplary prince "had the rigid policies, that are necessary for a good Prince towards contumacious and innovating spirits: (for the spirit of

---

[36] Abbott, *Bibliography of Oliver Cromwell,* p. 148, mistakenly lists a first edition of 1681.

[37] Warwick, *M,* pp. 36-37, 103, 197 (mention of *Behemoth*), 374, 403. It is always possible that he saw a manuscript version of *Behemoth* rather than a printed copy of 1679 or later. He may allude, p. 84, to the Popish Plot which broke upon the public in the autumn of 1678.

[38] Warwick's letters in Bodleian MSS Smith 29 and 54; Thomas Smith to Warwick, Sept. 1678, Bodleian MS Smith 66 pp. 83-84.

[39] Dugdale to Anthony à Wood, May 22, 1684, June 3, 1684, and Nov. 8, 1684, Bodleian MS Wood F41 ff. 172, 174, 177.

[40] *DNB* s.v. Warwick and (for Warwick's interregnum activities) Clarendon, *L,* II, 237.

government may require of a good Prince the departing from his own good nature)." [41] Praising the good times before the war, he defends Charles and Laud, but hints at a doubt or two about the wisdom of Charles's policies and admits that Laud had an unfortunate character and pursued a dangerous policy in Scotland. Warwick pays much more attention to Puritanism than do many contemporary historians, but distinguishes between two kinds of Puritan that flourished in the pre-war days, "the Church-Puritan, (of which number there were very many knowing, learned, and probably good men)" and "the Knave-Puritan," and regrets that among the canonical clergy disputes between the more orthodox churchmen and the church Puritans gave the knave Puritans an opportunity to overthrow them both.[42] Despite his remarks on Puritanism, Warwick is not impressed by the nature or the extent of the opposition to the regime: "his Majestie's task," he says, "was more to curb the innovating humor of an ambitious sort of men, who made way for their own greatnes, by making Parliamentary authority rivall Regall, than to satisfie the Subject in generall." [43]

At this point in our discussion, one of the tenets outlined in another work of Warwick's, a treatise he wrote on government,[44] becomes relevant. He holds that the English monarchs are absolute but limited: they have the sovereignty without sharing it with anyone, but at the same time they have limited themselves by suspending a part of their power. This is the view of the English government that he falls back upon to explain in the *Memoires* what the dissidents of the time of Charles I wanted to do: they were struggling to break the King's monopoly of the sovereign power and to force him to share it with the Houses of Parliament.

Warwick gives a valuable description of the division of the country geographically into Royalist and Parliamentarian in the First Civil War.[45] The south and the east were under Parliamentarian control, because of the dominance of London, but they were all the same full of Royalist affections. The port towns of the west, because of Parliament's control of the sea, were Parliamentarian by interest as well as by inclination. He gives only fragmentary indications of economic factors in the division, but besides those implicit in the remarks above, he notes the economic ad-

---

[41] Warwick, *M*, p. 46; cf. p. 74.
[42] *Ibid.*, pp. 85-88.
[43] Warwick, *M*, p. 62.
[44] [Sir Philip Warwick], *Rules of Government: Or, a true Balance between Sovereignty and Liberty* (London, 1710), first published as *A Discourse of Government* (London, 1694).
[45] Warwick, *M*, pp. 215-219, 260-261, 268-269.

vantages on the Parliamentarian side, especially because of the vast wealth of London, and he alludes, interestingly and with regrettable brevity, to "rich Yeomen" sacrificing their personal interests to serve the King.[46]

His treatment of Cromwell, in which he closely anticipates the main features of Clarendon's famous character of the Protector, is surprisingly moderate. In this moderation he differs not only from many of his fellow Royalists but from the republicans Ludlow and Mrs. Hutchinson. "I have no mind to give an ill character of Cromwell," he declares, "for in his conversation towards me he was ever friendly; tho' at the latter end . . . finding me ever incorrigible, and having some inducements to suspect me a tamperer, he was sufficiently rigid." [47] He criticizes Cromwell's crimes, his "many wicked and flagitious acts," but admits that he filled his position of power with fitting majesty and can even find charity enough to describe Cromwell on his deathbed as "this poor Gentleman." [48] He appears to draw a line, sometimes but not always and never very explicitly, between the person of Cromwell, which he can regard with some mellowness and even praise, and his crimes, which he abhors. His description of the uncouth Cromwell of the early Long Parliament and his remarks on his later evolution into a figure of dignity deservedly form one of the best known passages of the *Memoires*. Of Cromwell's life he concludes, "that verily I believe, he was extraordinarily designed for those extraordinary things, which one while most wickedly and facinorously he acted, and at another as successfully and greatly performed." But the swift rise and abrupt fall of the House of Cromwell he compares to a "bonfire of straw," and he reflects sententiously on the mutability of that felicity which is not grounded on virtue.[49] Cromwell as an international figure he condemns for the assistance he gave to the rise of France.

2. *Thomas Hobbes*

Thomas Hobbes's history of the English Civil War, *Behemoth or the Long Parliament* (1679) is open to the reproach that it tells us more about Hobbes than about the war. Nevertheless, the work is valuable in both

---

[46] *Ibid.*, p. 219.
[47] *Ibid.*, p. 247. He reports, *ibid.*, p. 248, that "for six weeks together" he was a prisoner in Cromwell's "serjeant's hands, and dayly waited at Whitehall." In accordance with his usual practice in the *Memoires* of severely excluding material which has only a personal as apart from a historical significance, he does not state the reason for his imprisonment.
[48] *Ibid.*, pp. 389, 248, 389.
[49] *Ibid.*, pp. 247-248, 248, 395, 390.

respects and has been unjustly neglected.[50] It is true, of course, that *Behemoth* does not provide the wealth of detailed information on the war that one may find in some other contemporary histories of the subject, and it is true that much of the interpretation must be rejected. It is noteworthy, however, for the wayward brilliance of the interpretation, the superb prose, the revelation of what it was possible for a profoundly rationalistic thinker to conclude about the religious issues of the war,[51] and the interest of seeing this daring and powerful thinker, more fully than he has done elsewhere, apply his philosophy of the state to the catastrophe of the war.

The form Hobbes chose for *Behemoth* is the doctor and student dialogue, a traditional form he employs elsewhere in his writings. Though Hobbes identified himself more closely with the doctor A. than with the student B., the student, who is an eloquent Hobbesian, also speaks with profit, and his naive questioning enables the doctor A. all the more effectively to expose the bestiality of the rebels. B. is sometimes used to express views which A., more closely associated with Hobbes, hesitates to utter. The work is distinguished from the other seventeenth-century histories of the war principally by its dialogue form and wealth of ideas. A much smaller and less important difference, which is, however, significant of Hobbes's secular outlook, is that it omits the references to divine intervention which are so common in other histories of this period.

Hobbes's long life began at Westport, which is now a part of the Malmesbury from which he took his designation of Hobbes "of Malmesbury." The year was 1588, the year of the great Armada. His father, a clergyman, is described by Aubrey as "one of the ignorant 'Sir Johns' of queen Elizabeth's time," who "could only read the prayers of the church and the homilies; and disesteemed learning, . . . as not knowing the sweetnes of it." [52] Perhaps the father's rough and discreditable character, which

---

[50] An earlier version of this section on Hobbes appeared in the *Journal of the History of Ideas*, 31 (1970), 179-198. C. B. Macpherson discusses *Behemoth* in his *The Political Theory of Possessive Individualism* (Oxford, Clarendon Press, 1962), pp. 64-67, but I cannot agree with him in what he claims to find in *Behemoth*. Thomas Hobbes, *Behemoth or the Long Parliament*, ed. Ferdinand Tönnies (London, 1889), has been reprinted in a 2nd ed. (London, Frank Cass & Co. Ltd., 1969), with an introduction by M. M. Goldsmith. All subsequent references to *Behemoth*, unless otherwise identified, apply equally to the original Tönnies edition of 1889 and the 1969 reprint. Dietrich Braun, *Der sterbliche Gott oder Leviathan gegen Behemoth* (Zürich, Basler Studien zur historischen und systematischen Theologie, Band 2, 1963), is a study, not of *Behemoth*, but of Hobbes's doctrine of "Christ's kingdom."

[51] "Das Büchlein enthält vielleicht die erste rationalistische Betrachtung der neueren Geschichte, in dem Sinne, wie sie später durch Voltaire populär wurde: . . . " Ferdinand Tönnies, *Thomas Hobbes Leben und Lehre*, 3rd ed. (Stuttgart, Fr. Frommanns Verlag, 1925), p. 61.

[52] Aubrey, *BL*, I, 323.

resulted at last in his flight from Westport after striking a fellow clergyman, contributed to the markedly unfavorable view of clergymen found
in the son's writings. A wealthy uncle provided for young Hobbes's support at Oxford University. After graduation he became tutor and companion to William Cavendish, later second Earl of Devonshire. His association with the Cavendish family, first as employee and then as friend,
lasted with varying interruptions for the remainder of his life. In the
reigns of James I and of Charles I before the Long Parliament, he travell-
ed on the continent on several occasions in charge of persons to whom he
had become tutor, and at home was the friend or acquaintance of literary
men, scholars, and intellectuals, including Bacon, Ben Jonson, and Falkland; presumably, too, it was then that he became a friend of Edward
Hyde, the future Earl of Clarendon.[53]

The failure of Charles I's experiment in personal government and the
challenge of 1640 to his authority separate Hobbes's long years of dor-
mancy and incubation from his years of philosophical and literary achievement. Hobbes's development as a writer was remarkably late: had he
died in 1638 or 1639 at the age of fifty, posterity would have remembered
him, if at all, only as the translator of Thucydides. At the time of the
Short Parliament, if his own dating is correct, he wrote the treatise now
known under the title of *The Elements of Law.* "Of this treatise," he says,
"though not printed, many gentlemen had copies, which occasioned
much talk of the author; and had not his Majesty dissolved the Parliament, it had brought him into danger of his life." When the Long Parliament met he feared reprisals for his defense of the royal power and fled
to France, being "the first," he was later to boast with a certain insensitivity, "of all that fled." [54] In exile he enjoyed the intellectual compa-
nionship of Paris and wrote and published. He did not see England again
until after the publication of his greatest work, that "very wicked book,
with a very strange title," [55] the *Leviathan* (1651). Then he abandoned
Paris and the French intellectuals and exiled Royalists there and, returning home, made his peace with the Commonwealth.

[53] *Ibid.,* I, 331, 332, 365, 151; Edward Hyde, Earl of Clarendon, *A Brief View
and Survey of the Dangerous and pernicious Errors to Church and State, In Mr. Hobbes's Book, Entitled Leviathan,* 2nd impression (Oxford, 1676), p. 3; Sir Edward
Hyde to John Barwick, July 25, 1659, in Peter Barwick, *The Life Of the Reverend
Dr. John Barwick,* trans. [Hilkiah Bedford] (London, 1724), p. 430.
[54] Thomas Hobbes, "Considerations upon the Reputation, Loyalty, Manners, and
Religion, of Thomas Hobbes, of Malmesbury," IV, 414, in Hobbes, *The English Works
of Thomas Hobbes of Malmesbury,* ed. Sir William Molesworth, 11 vols. (London,
1839-1845), henceforth referred to as *Works*
[55] Burnet, *OTA,* I, 333.

The dangers or supposed dangers of his political and religious philosophy made him, after the publication of *Leviathan,* not only one of the most celebrated but one of the most vigorously abused Englishmen of his time. His beliefs being destructive of many received ideas, it became imperative for the defenders of orthodoxy to refute him. Whether or not the contemporary story that some of the bishops proposed not long after the Restoration to have him burnt as a heretic was anything more than a bit of fanciful gossip – and in the context of the England of Charles II, it does not sound in the least degree convincing – the fact that it existed is at least significant of his unpopular position. He lived in freedom and comfort, all opponents notwithstanding, a scandal but not a martyr and a seventeenth-century example of the English tolerance for unpopular ideas. He died, still in the patronage of the Cavendish family, at Hardwick in 1679.

Hobbes states that he wrote his history "circa annum aetatis suae octogesimum," [56] which would be about the years 1667 and 1668. It was not, however, immediately published. Hobbes presented a manuscript copy to Charles II, "and some days after," he says, "when I thought he had read it, I humbly besought him to let me print it; but his Majesty, though he heard me graciously, yet he flatly refused to have it published." [57] Whether or not we should believe the excuse, which the King is alleged at some time to have given, that he dared not license the work for fear of displeasing the bishops,[58] it is at least understandable that he should not want to sponsor a work which contained a slighting treatment of his orthodox clergy. Another reason for his refusal may have been that although Charles regarded Hobbes as a favorite, had given him a pension, and welcomed him whenever he came to court, he was unwilling to share the guilt of another political treatise by the most striking, but also most unpopular, thinker in his dominions.[59] Charles had, moreover, at all times an admirable disinclination to rake over the smouldering embers of the Civil War, a disinclination not all shared by some of the most fiercely

[56] Thomas Hobbes, "T. Hobbes Malmesburiensis Vita," I, xx, in Hobbes, *Thomae Hobbes Malmesburiensis Opera Philosophica Quae Latine Scripsit Omnia,* ed. Sir William Molesworth, 5 vols. (London, 1839-1845), henceforth referred to as *Opera.*
[57] Thomas Hobbes to William Crooke, June 19, 1679, printed in preface to Hobbes, "Considerations upon the Reputation," *Works,* IV, 411.
[58] John Aubrey to John Locke, Shrove Tuesday, 1672/3, printed in Maurice Cranston, *John Locke: A Biography* (New York, The Macmillan Company, 1957), p. 152.
[59] The extent of this unpopularity is represented in Samuel I. Mintz, *The Hunting of Leviathan* (Cambridge, Eng., Cambridge University Press, 1962), though some modifications are necessary in view of two articles by Quentin Skinner, "Thomas Hobbes and His Disciples in France and England," *Comparative Studies in Society and History,* 8 (1965-1966), 153-167, and "The Ideological Context of Hobbes's Political Thought," *The Historical Journal,* 9 (1966), 286-317.

loyal writers of his times. He may have thought that *Behemoth* probed needlessly into historical topics best left undisturbed. It is also possible that Charles resented the attacks on the Papists, toward whom he was already more than sympathetic, and even the attacks on the "Presbyterians" and other nonconforming Protestants, who were a possible counterweight to be used in any royal struggle with the dominant Church of England. But whatever the actual reasons for Charles's refusal, *Behemoth* proved to be submerged rather than totally suppressed. Aubrey mentioned in a letter of 1673 that a manuscript copy of the work could be seen at the shop of one of the London booksellers,[60] and copies surreptitiously printed were in circulation in 1679, some months before the author's death. Altogether four editions bear the date of that year.[61] An explanation of why *Behemoth* was published at that time can be found in the same circumstances which, as we have seen in chapter I, facilitated the publication of a cluster of Parliamentarian histories about the same time, namely, the partial collapse of the censorship and the aroused public concern for political and religious issues. Though Hobbes regretted the King's prohibition, he submitted quietly to it, and he regretted the publication in 1679. An improved text was published in 1682, but the authoritative text, containing corrections and some minor passages previously suppressed, did not appear until published by Ferdinand Tönnies in 1889.[62]

The tightly written *Behemoth* contains at least as much factual material on the war as the average contemporary history of the same length, yet Hobbes was more concerned with presenting a particular interpretation than with imparting factual information. Indeed, the work would have been improved if Hobbes had confined himself more exclusively to interpretation than he did. The later parts of the book are in some places a little tiresome with their reiteration of commonplace facts. B. indicates Hobbes's intention when he remarks:

I suppose, your purpose was, to acquaint me with the history, not so much of those actions that passed in the time of the late troubles, as of their causes, and of the councils and artifice by which they were brought to pass. There be divers men that have written the history, out of whom I might have learn-

[60] Aubrey to Locke, Shrove Tuesday, 1672/3, in Cranston, *Locke*, p. 152; cf. Hobbes, *Works*, IV, 411-412, VI, 164.
[61] Hugh Macdonald and Mary Hargreaves, *Thomas Hobbes: a Bibliography* (London, The Bibliographical Society, 1952), 64-66. Two of these editions consist of the same sheets with different title pages.
[62] Molesworth's text of *Behemoth* in Hobbes, *Works*, VI, is from the improved version of 1682. Tönnies produced his text from a manuscript in St. John's College, Oxford, but the differences between it and the 1682 text (despite Tönnies' claims in his preface, p. ix) are interesting rather than important.

ed what they did, and somewhat also of the contrivance; but I find little in them of what I would ask.[63]

Hobbes had unusual opportunities to gain information about the war, because of his special connection with the Cavendish family and his acquaintance with prominent Royalists of other families, but no trace of these special advantages appears in his narrative. The book of advice that William Cavendish, Marquess of Newcastle, wrote for Charles II shares some ideas with *Behemoth,* but presumably it was Newcastle who borrowed ideas from Hobbes rather than Hobbes from Newcastle.[64] Hobbes depended for his account of the actual hostilities or of the whole period 1642-1660 on "Mr. Heath's chronicle," [65] that is to say, on Heath's *A Brief Chronicle Of the Late Intestine VVarr* (1663). In opinions, as apart from facts, Heath's historical labors seem to have left no trace on *Behemoth's* pages. Hobbes handles factual information competently and, apart from much confusion of opinion with fact, includes only one gross mistake – his idea that at the end of the First Bishops' War the King went to Edinburgh and there yielded to the abolition of episcopacy in Scotland.[66] This idea had a basis in fact, for Charles did briefly contemplate such a trip to Edinburgh after the pacification, and Hobbes may simply have been betrayed by some treacherous memory of what he had heard the King intended to do. Heath, it may be noted, gets this matter right.

Hobbes's own previous writings provided a substantial body of commentary on the issues of the war, but it is necessary to ask what connection exists between the political doctrines of *Behemoth,* with its fierce Royalist loyalties, and the political doctrines of Hobbes's previous writings. For the *Leviathan* in some passages gave implied support to the government established after the execution of Charles, Hobbes was tactless enough to boast that he had reconciled a thousand gentlemen to that

[63] Hobbes, *Behemoth,* ed. Tönnies, p. 45; cf. pp. 119-120. M. Wren, "Of the Origin and Progress of the Revolutions in England," in *Collectanea Curiosa,* ed. John Gutch, 2 vols. (Oxford, 1781), I, 242-243, has a similar passage.

[64] This treatise is published without a title in *A Catalogue of Letters and Other Historical Documents Exhibited in the Library at Welbeck,* ed. S. Arthur Strong (London, John Murray, 1903); for notice of the similar ideas of Hobbes and Newcastle, see C. H. Firth's preface to the Duchess of Newcastle, *The Life of William Cavendish,* ed. C. H. Firth, 2nd ed. (London, George Routledge & Sons Limited, n.d.), pp. xxii-xxiii.

[65] Hobbes, *Behemoth,* ed. Tönnies, ep. ded. to Arlington.

[66] Hobbes, *Behemoth,* ed. Tönnies, p. 29; cf. p. 75. For Charles's intentions at this time, see Gardiner, *HE,* IX, 44, 46, Rushworth, *HC,* III, 944, and Clarendon, *HR,* I, 100 n., 162. Alexander Ross, *The History of the World: The Second Part, in Six Books: Being a Continuation of the famous History of Sir Walter Raleigh, Knight* (London, 1652), p. 645, also has the mistake about the King going to Edinburgh at this time, but I have not noticed it in any other seventeenth-century histories.

government,[67] and the Hobbesian view of government is at odds in a number of points with the orthodox Royalist view or views.[68] Is it possible, then, that *Behemoth* involves a retraction or reversal of views formerly expressed? In fact, this does not appear to be so. None of the views offensive to Royalists are recanted in *Behemoth*, though to be sure some are unobtrusively suppressed, and others, as might be expected, are brought out less blatantly than in works Hobbes wrote under other circumstances. No new views are brought forth though some are loudly expressed that with safety could only be implied before. The allegiance which Hobbes proposed in 1651 to give the Puritan Leviathan was, at any rate, dependent on the protection it was able to give him; but the Puritan government, whose mutability he emphasizes in *Behemoth*, was unable to protect even its own form and existence. It is always possible that *Behemoth* was intended as a defense and advertisement of the loyalty of a Royalist whose loyalty had been laid open to question by his own statements – not to mention his action, somewhat dubious in a Royalist exile, of seeking refuge in England under the Commonwealth [69] – but if so, this involved a shifting of emphasis rather than a reformulation of basic doctrines.

In *Behemoth*, Hobbes has applied to contemporary political events the conclusions of his political philosophy. This political philosophy, in turn, was not merely a creation of the recluse's study; it had its roots in the events of the philosopher's contemporary world. To understand *Behemoth*, knowledge of the main body of Hobbes's political philosophy is not essential, but there are a few passages which remain puzzling without the assistance provided by the political philosophy. It may be noted that reflections similar to those in this paragraph can be made on the relationship of Marx's three classic treatises on French political events to his political philosophy. These three treatises were Marx's *Behemoth*.

Behemoth satisfies the view of history Hobbes expresses in introducing his translation of Thucydides: the view that history is practical instruction

---

[67] Hobbes, "Six Lessons to the Professors of the Mathematics," *Works,* VII, 336.

[68] For a confrontation of Hobbesian and Royalist views, see Clarendon, *Brief View and Survey.* Though published earlier, it casts much light on *Behemoth.* J. Whitehall, *Behemoth Arraign'd: or, a Vindication of Property Against a Fanatical Pamphlet Stiled Behemoth* (London, 1680) is a sensible, unimportant attack from a Whig standpoint.

[69] Perhaps this is what Julius Lips, *Die Stellung des Thomas Hobbes zu den politischen Parteien der grossen Englischen Revolution. Mit erstmaliger Übersetzung des Behemoth oder das Lang Parlament* (Leipzig, Ernst Wiegandt 1927), p. 96, means when he says that "der 'Behemoth' war von ihm als Verteidigungsschrift gegen erhobene Angriffe gedacht." Cf. George E. G. Catlin, *Thomas Hobbes as Philosopher, Publicist and Man of Letters: an Introduction* (Oxford, Basil Blackwell, 1922), pp. 16-17.

for the affairs of life, including the life of man as a member of the state.[70]
The didactic intention of *Behemoth* is apparent from the work itself
throughout, but Hobbes expressly says in his epistle dedicatory to it that
"There can be nothing more instructive towards loyalty and justice than
will be the memory, while it lasts, of that war." The didactic view of history is familiar from the prefaces of seventeenth-century histories, where
its platitudes are endlessly repeated, but the didactic view, except perhaps
by accentuating partisanship, rarely had any effect in giving seventeenth-
century histories a form or appearance different from that of today. Yet
it is possible that *Behemoth* was one of the exceptions to the general
practice, and that the didactic function is part of the reason why Hobbes
chose the dialogue form.[71]

The title of the work requires consideration. "Behemoth," like "Leviathan", is a biblical animal or monster,[72] but what is the particular application of the name to a history of the English Civil War? Before answering this question, we must consider the possibility that Hobbes himself
did not use this name in the title, for it is not included in the titles of all
the early editions,[73] and in a letter of 1679 to Aubrey he writes that

I have been told that my book of the Civill Warr is come abroad, and am
sorry for it, especially because I could not get his majestye to license it, not
because it is ill printed or has a foolish title set to it, for I believe that any
ingenious man may understand the wickednesse of that time, notwithstanding
the errors of the presse.[74]

Perhaps Hobbes is simply complaining of the omission of the name
"Behemoth" from the title, but if so, "foolish" seems a remarkably harsh
word to apply to the plain, unassuming titles of those editions of 1679
which do omit it. Can he perhaps be complaining about the *inclusion* of
the name "Behemoth" in the title? Hobbes tells the reader in *Leviathan*
what significance he wants the name "Leviathan" to bear, but there is no
overt indication in the text (as apart from the title) of *Behemoth* what
significance the name "Behemoth" is to bear. Nor is the name applied

---

[70] "The History of the Grecian War Written by Thucydides. Translated by Thomas
Hobbes of Malmesbury," *Works*, VIII, iv, vi, vii. Cf. his "Thomae Hobbes Malmesburiensis Vita Carmine Expressa," *Opera*, I, lxxxviii.

[71] Whitelocke's annals are another exception, as chapter V below shows.

[72] Behemoth is described in Job chapter 40 (Revised Standard Version). The description of Leviathan in the following chapter of Job produces an obvious mental association of the two monsters.

[73] Macdonald and Hargreaves, *Thomas Hobbes: a Bibliography*, pp. 65-67, list
editions of 1679 to 1682.

[74] Hobbes to Aubrey, Aug. 18, 1679, in Aubrey, *BL*, I, 380-381 (also 342). Tönnies
in his preface to *Behemoth*, p. xi, tries to explain this complaint about the title but
does not open the possibility that Hobbes himself did not use the word "Behemoth."

specifically to the Long Parliament in the title of any printed edition until the edition published by Tönnies. The possibility that the name was applied to *Behemoth* by someone other than Hobbes, perhaps by a publisher searching for a word that would catch the attention of the public, is, however, if not dismissed at least much weakened by the St. John's College manuscript of *Behemoth* which Tönnies used for his edition, for there the title, like the text, seems to be in the hand of Hobbes's usual amanuensis, James Weldon.[75]

Various interpretations are possible for the meaning of "Behemoth" in this title. "Behemoth" has commonly been seen as an inferior monster, whose name indicates that the Long Parliament or the rebellious powers contrasted unfavorably with the ideals represented by "Leviathan." [76] A Victorian writer gives this interpretation a further twist by suggesting that the title contrasts Leviathan with "an aggregation of monsters" [77] ("Behemoth" is, etymologically, plural), and a recent writer similarly stresses the plurality represented in the word "Behemoth." [78] Hobbes himself, as is evident from a passage in his controversy with Bishop Bramhall, accepted the idea of unfavorable contrast between "Behemoth" and "Leviathan." He comments that Bramhall and others should not misspend their time by writing against his *Leviathan*, "but if they will needs do it, I can give them a fit title for their book, *Behemoth against Leviathan*." [79] The above interpretations are of course consistent with the possibility that someone other than Hobbes attached the name of "Behemoth" to his history.

An interpretation will now be advanced which attempts to give a more exact application of the word. Unfortunately because, as must be stressed, this interpretation remains very speculative, it is not possible to argue from the greater exactitude of the application that the word "Behemoth" is likely to have been the choice of Hobbes himself. To understand this interpretation, one must see the book in relation to Hobbes's doctrine of the 'kingdom of darkness' as described in *Leviathan*. The theme of the kingdom of darkness, which is developed so wittily and strikingly in *Leviathan*, is not repeated explicitly in *Behemoth*, but the material for the

[75] For information on Weldon and on the elderly Hobbes's need for an amanuensis, see Quentin Skinner in *Political Studies*, 13 (1965), 213-214. I am very grateful to Mr. Charles Morgenstern, Assistant Librarian of St. John's College, Oxford, for answering some questions about Hobbes's manuscript.
[76] Catlin, *Thomas Hobbes*, p. 17; J. W. N. Watkins, *Hobbes's System of Ideas* (London, Hutchinson University Library, 1965), p. 15.
[77] Sir James Fitzjames Stephen, "Hobbes's Minor Works," in his *Horae Sabbaticae*, 2nd series (London, 1892), p. 39.
[78] Braun, *Sterbliche Gott*, p. 196.
[79] Hobbes, "The Questions concerning Liberty, Necessity, and Chance" (1656), *Works*, V, 27.

concept is there; only the shaping and decorative metaphor of the kingdom is lacking. What is the kingdom of darkness? It is, Hobbes explains in *Leviathan*, "nothing else but a *confederacy of deceivers, that to obtain dominion over men in this present world, endeavour by dark and erroneous doctrines, to extinguish in them the light, both of nature, and of the gospel; and so to disprepare them for the kingdom of God to come.*" [80] Most, though not quite all, of what Hobbes means by this kingdom is simply clericalism and its consequences, broadly understood so as to include not only the more obvious manifestations of clerical ambition, but also such matters as the use of the universities to disseminate disloyal principles. During the times of which Hobbes wrote in *Behemoth*, the kingdom of darkness flourished exceedingly in England, with the Long Parliament presiding over it. The way, therefore, is open, by an obvious parallel, for Hobbes to refer to the Long Parliament as the devil, the ruler of the kingdom of darkness, and it may be suggested that he does so, by the device of calling the Long Parliament "Behemoth." The word "Behemoth" may have been intended by the biblical writer to refer to the hippopotamus, but it has also been applied to the devil.[81] The kingdom of darkness is not the only element that Hobbes sees in the English Civil War: it is only one part of a complex set of circumstances which he sees at work, but it is one which attracts a strikingly large part of the attention of this fierce Erastian.

The idea advanced here, that the Long Parliament is to be seen as the devil presiding over the kingdom of darkness, suffers, admittedly, from the same lack of evidence for its application as the other interpretations of the word "Behemoth," that is, from Hobbes's omission of any explanation of the meaning of the word in his history. It may or may not be significant that in the very first speech of his history there is a reference to the devil's temptation of Christ. It may or may not be significant as far as the title is concerned, though it is certainly interesting in other respects, that at the end of *Behemoth*, when Hobbes has B. explain that there has been "in

---

[80] Hobbes, "Leviathan," *Works*, III, 603-604.

[81] *Brockhaus Enzyklopädie in Zwanzig Bänden*, 17th ed. (Wiesbaden, F. A. Brockhaus, 1966—) or *New Catholic Encyclopedia*, 15 vols. (New York, McGraw-Hill Book Company, 1967), s.v. "Behemoth"; Martin Luther to George Spalatin, Sept. 9, 1521, *Luther's Works*, vol. XLVIII: *Letters I*, ed. and trans. Gottfried G. Krodel (Philadelphia, Fortress Press, 1963), p. 306 & n. For a useful contemporary discussion of the Biblical Behemoth, see Joseph Caryl, *An Exposition with Practical Observations Continued upon The Thirty-eighth, Thirty-ninth, Fortieth, Forty-first, and Forty-second (being the five last) Chapters of the Book of Job* (London, 1666), pp. 604-656. The interpretation of the word "Leviathan" (which also includes the idea of the devil) in Hobbes's time is outlined in John M. Steadman, "Leviathan and Renaissance Etymology," *Journal of the History of Ideas*, 28 (1967), 575-576.

this revolution a circular motion of the sovereign power," [82] he may be echoing one of the key passages in the treatment of the kingdom of darkness in *Leviathan*. But the problem of the title is, at any rate, of little importance compared with Hobbes's incisive analysis of the causes of the war.

At the beginning of *Behemoth*, A. describes the disaffection to the King in 1640 and B. asks, "But how came the people to be so corrupted? And what kind of people were they that could so seduce them?" A. in turn explains that the seducers were (1) Presbyterians, (2) Papists, (3) the future advocates of liberty of religion, or Independents and other sectaries, (4) men whose allegiance had been corrupted by the reading of the classics, (5) great towns, (6) adventurers and wastrels, and (7) lack of understanding of the nature of authority and obedience.[83] His careful examination of the causes of the war under each of these heads may safely be regarded as the most important part of *Behemoth*.

Hobbes sees the causes of the war and of the King's defeat, therefore, in a complex set of events, stretching well into the past, but all his causes of the war and defeat, however, whether mentioned in this list or elsewhere in *Behemoth*, can be summed up in one: the failure of all manner of men, Royalist and ostensibly loyal as well as seditious, to observe the strict subordination to the King which Hobbes expounds so forcefully in *Leviathan* and elsewhere. To grasp this universal failure is to grasp the key to his interpretation. Hobbes especially singles out for his censures the imperfect subordination of all religious matters to the interest of the King.

He traces the origins of the Presbyterians, the religious group he treats

---

[82] Hobbes, *Behemoth*, ed. Tönnies, p. 204. In "Leviathan," *Works*, III, 695-697, Hobbes notes that "as the inventions of men are woven, so also are they ravelled out; the way is the same, but the order is inverted," and he applies this reflection to the rise of the power of the kingdom of darkness and its undoing in England. In the end, he says, speaking of the conditions prevailing at the time of his writing *Leviathan*, with the fall of episcopacy and the Presbyterians "we are reduced to the independancy [sic] of the primitive Christians, . . . which, if it be without contention, and without measuring the doctrine of Christ, by our affection to the person of his minister, . . . is perhaps the best." Is the *Behemoth* passage, which deals with the return of the monarchy to the Stuarts, a sly attempt to restate what must have been for Hobbes, if anything in *Leviathan* was regrettable, one of that book's more regrettable passages? Perhaps the reason why Hobbes does not make his doctrine of the kingdom of darkness explicit in *Behemoth* is that he does not want to awaken memories of his previously having criticized episcopacy under this concept and to give the appearance of inconsistency as he uses this concept first, in *Leviathan*, to the disadvantage of the Stuart church and secondly, in *Behemoth*, to the disadvantage of the Protestant enemies of that church. Hobbes's use of the word "revolution" in the *Behemoth* passage cited above is illuminated by the material collected in Vernon F. Snow, "The Concept of Revolution in Seventeenth-Century England," *The Historical Journal*, 5 (1962), 167-174, which however, misses (p. 169) the *Behemoth* passage.

[83] Hobbes, *Behemoth*, ed. Tönnies, pp. 1-4.

most savagely, to the Marian exile. They succeeded early in establishing themselves in Scotland, but in England they did not win power till the Civil War, and then they were quickly supplanted by the sects. They took their ideas from the Presbyterian systems established at Geneva and elsewhere on the continent and attempted to establish a church government of synods and classes in England. It would be useful and interesting to have Hobbes's definition of a Presbyterian and his views on the relationship between Presbyterianism, Puritanism, and Calvinism in England before the meeting of the Long Parliament. Probably we should understand Hobbes's "Presbyterians" to be "Presbyterian" only in the loose, broad sense in which many contemporaries applied these terms to a wide-ranging collection of politically and theologically conservative English Puritans.[84] Though Hobbes does try to associate his "Presbyterians" with Presbyterianism in the correct and full sense of the term, Presbyterianism in the fullblown form exemplified in Geneva and Scotland, this may be taken as simply another attempt on the part of Hobbes to impute the worst possible motives and the greatest possible consistency to his enemies. It may be suggested further that there is no serious case for accusing Hobbes of dropping below his usual precision in the use of language. Even if he had private doubts about the uniform applicability of "Presbyterian" as a blanket term applied to a varied group of clergymen, these doubts must have been well assuaged by the thought that he was simply following common contemporary usage. Terminological purists like Baxter might protest the common misuse of the term "Presbyterian," but the convention of ordinary educated speech was on Hobbes's side. In the remainder of this section on Hobbes the term "Presbyterian" will be adopted as Hobbes used it, without trying to find an expression that comes closer to the reality to which he was pointing.

Hobbes describes the link between Presbyterian beliefs and political opposition to the monarchy. The Presbyterian clergy, during their period of unobtrusive but diligent burrowing into English society and the English structure of received ideas, won "the concurrence of a great many gentlemen, that did no less desire a popular government in the civil state than these ministers did in the Church." Eventually "the doctrine of the Presbyterians" became "the very foundation" of the Long Parliament's

---

[84] For the difficulties in the use of these terms, see the discussion of Baxter in chapter VI below and the very good passage in H. R. Trevor-Roper, *Religion the Reformation and Social Change and Other Essays* (London, Macmillan, 1967), p. 407. The various contemporary denunciations of the Presbyterians for having caused the war must be seen in the light of this difficulty of definition.

pretensions.[85] The Presbyterian clergy were motivated by self interest, for they preached up rebellion so

that the State becoming popular, the Church might be so too, and governed by an Assembly; and by consequence (as they thought) seeing politics are subservient to religion, they might govern, and thereby satisfy not only their covetous humour with riches, but also their malice with power to undo all men that admired not their wisdom.[86]

The defect in this account of the motives of the Presbyterian clergy is partly a psychological one – incomprehension could be carried little further – but Hobbes is by no means the only writer who has seen in the religion of the Puritan clergy a cloak for worldly motives. In his interesting and shrewd comments on the preaching methods of the Presbyterian clergy, he suggests lines of thought which later critics of religion have in their various fields carried further, especially in noting that the Presbyterians preached a morality conformable to the vices and ambitions of their bourgeois audiences and that they deftly exploited feelings of sexual guilt.[87]

Not discovered in the beginning of the troubles, but evident later, was another group of seducers of the people from their loyalty, the Independents and other sectaries. These had their origin in the Presbyterian preaching and in "the private interpretation of the Scripture, exposed to every man's scanning in his mother-tongue." [88] A. and B. therefore discuss the advisability of having the scriptures in English. Though B. presses, or seems to press, rather strongly against translation, expressing, perhaps, some uncertainty or reservation in Hobbes's own mind about the advisability of translation, A. concludes that the scriptures are so instructive of morality and faith that the reading of them cannot be forbidden to the people "without great damage to them and the commonwealth." [89] Hobbes shows, of course, no trace of perception of the spiritual treasures which later writers have praised in the Puritans, but he seems to regard the Independents and other sectaries as sincere, as he did not usually regard the Presbyterians, or at least he does not openly denounce this possibility.

Like the Presbyterians and like the Independents and other sectaries, the Papists are numbered by Hobbes among those who seduced the people from their allegiance; but throughout a long discussion, in which he traces

[85] Hobbes, *Behemoth*, ed. Tönnies, pp. 23, 82.
[86] *Ibid.*, p. 159.
[87] *Ibid.*, pp. 25-26.
[88] *Ibid.*, pp. 3, 22, 136.
[89] *Ibid.*, p. 53.

the history of the pretensions of the papacy and outlines his views on
heresy, he does not make clear exactly what the Papists contributed to
causing the war. He seems to realize his own failure properly to sub-
stantiate his accusation, when he refers lamely in conclusion to the Gun-
powder Plot and adds that

> the Papists of England have been looked upon as men that would not be
> sorry for any disorders here that might possibly make way to the restoring of
> the Pope's authority. And therefore I named them for one of the distempers
> of the state of England in the time of our late King Charles.[90]

Hobbes's real grievance against the Papists, though he could not wrest it
properly into the shape of a cause of the rebellion, was their refusal to
recognize the King's ecclesiastical sovereignty, that is to say, his complete,
undivided sovereignty; but on the basis of that grievance alone Hobbes
seems unreasonable and unfair in including them in his list.[91] But Hobbes's inclusion of the Papists becomes a little more understandable when it
is seen in the light of Hobbes's attitudes towards the Papists elsewhere in
his writings and of a particular treatment of the Papists found in the
works of certain other contemporary historians and observers of the war.
First, Hobbes's attitude to the Papists elsewhere in his writings is extremely hostile, and it is noteworthy that in an appendix to the Latin version
of *Leviathan* he blames the Papists for the war in a much more drastic
and uncompromising way than in *Behemoth*.[92] Secondly, we find, not
only in Hobbes but in some other contemporary historians and observers
writing about the war, a strong desire to expose the Papists as a cause of
this catastrophe, or at least to connect them with its origins and main
events sufficiently to establish good grounds for suspicion that they were
a cause.[93] The apparent failure of Hobbes's usual logic and clarity in
dealing with the role of the Papists may perhaps be accounted for simply
by his submitting too easily to a desire supported by powerful resentments
in himself and by a current of thought among his contemporaries. Hobbes

---

[90] *Ibid.,* p. 20.
[91] Hobbes's dislike of the Papists may have been sharpened by his observation of
lingering traits of Popery in the English Protestants. For these traits, see his "Leviathan," *Works,* III, 332; "Considerations upon the Reputation," *Works,* IV, 432;
Behemoth, ed. Tönnies, pp. 6, 24, 56-57, 89, 95, 135-136.
[92] Hobbes, *Opera,* III, 559.
[93] Examples are Heylyn and Nalson, whose ideas are discussed in the present
volume; [Thomas Frankland], *The Annals of King James and King Charles the First*
(London, 1681), preface and pp. 768, 865-866; and Richard Perrinchief, "The Life
of Charles I," in *Works* of Charles I, 2nd ed. (London, 1687), pp. 52, 61. Connected
with this are the many attempts by contemporaries to associate Richelieu with the
Scottish rebellion and to blame the Papists for the Great Fire of London in 1666.

was ordinarily too cool and detached a thinker to be easily overcome by contemporary opinion; but here his defenses were at their weakest, for he did share, if not entirely for the conventional reasons, in the fierce anti-Romanist passions of his time.

Along with such transparent ecclesiastical enemies as those already noted, the King had highly unsatisfactory ecclesiastical friends, and Hobbes does not hesitate to reprove Laud as one of them. B. suggests that Laud "was perhaps a very great politician," and A replies in a passage full of fine scorn:

That did not appear by any remarkable event of his counsels. I never heard but he was a very honest man for his morals, and a very zealous promoter of the Church-government by bishops, and that desired to have the service of God performed, and the house of God adorned, as suitable as was possible to the honour we ought to do to the Divine Majesty. But to bring, as he did, into the State his former controversies, I mean his squabblings in the University about free-will, and his standing upon punctilios concerning the service-book and its rubrics, was not, in my opinion, an argument of his sufficiency in affairs of State.[94]

For the busy, meddling, unsuccessful Laud, Hobbes must have had something of the contempt he expresses elsewhere in *Behemoth* for "those divinity-disputers" amongst whom "you will hardly find one in a hundred discreet enough to be employed in any great affair, either of war or peace." [95] He frees Laud from the charge of being a popish sympathizer, though if he had judged the Archbishop as harshly as he judged the Presbyterians, he might easily have affirmed the charge.

He takes a similarly unfavorable view of Laud's followers. Ambitious clergymen under his regime, he notes with some scorn, "fell to preaching and writing for free-will, to the uttermost of their power, as a proof of their ability and merit." [96] He criticizes the bishops of Charles I for their arrogance and rigidity in an erased passage, imperfectly restored by Tönnies, of the St. John's College manuscript. In his controversy with Bishop Bramhall he speaks of "the rebellion that followed the controversy here between Gomar and Arminius." [97] In *Behemoth* he does not attribute as much importance to the Arminian controversy as he seems to do here, but he has B. state it is "strange, that the state should engage in their parties, and not rather put them both to silence." This observation, it is

---

[94] Hobbes, *Behemoth*, ed. Tönnies, pp. 72-73.
[95] *Ibid.*, p. 144.
[96] *Ibid.*, pp. 62, 89; cf. p. 95.
[97] Hobbes, "An Answer to a Book Published by Dr. Bramhall," *Works*, IV, 329.

worth noting, is about the closest Hobbes gets in *Behemoth* to an open criticism of the policies of Charles I.[98]

If the Presbyterians failed in their duty to the monarchy by being conscious revolutionaries, and the party of Laud by their pedantry and egoism, and if the papists and the Independents and other sectaries were also guilty subjects, was there then a religious party in the church or out of it of which Hobbes could approve? The answer is apparently no, for just as the Presbyterians and the Independents and other sectaries preached up the rebellion, so the rest of the Protestant clergy, he says, "contented with their livings, preached in their parishes points of controversy, to religion impertinent, but to the breach of charity amongst themselves very effectual; or else elegant things, which the people either understood not, or thought themselves not concerned in." Hobbes does, however, grudgingly concede that "this sort of preachers, as they did little good, so they did little hurt." [99] It is not clear from this passage whether Hobbes is speaking of the actions of these preachers before the rebellion or during it; if he has the later period in mind, as the context seems to suggest, then he very badly slights the Royalist clergy, whose wartime sufferings were so loudly honored by their literary partisans throughout the second half of the seventeenth century. Probably Hobbes sees the remedy for the situation he has described in his suggested reform of the universities.

The universities produce even greater evils than these supine but (presumably) well meaning and technically loyal clergy. The two universities, he complains, have been to England "as the wooden horse was to the Trojans." [100] In the universities the clergy and laity learn to be seditious; "as the Presbyterians brought with them into their churches their divinity from the universities, so did many of the gentlemen bring their politics from thence into the Parliament." [101] Gentlemen, studying the classical authors in universities and elsewhere, are corrupted by the doctrines of liberty which they find in them and so become rebels.[102] Hobbes's notion about the power the classics exerted over their readers is oddly confirmed by the Conclusion of Burnet's *Own Time*. Without mentioning Hobbes and perhaps without recollecting what he had written, Burnet complains that the English gentry learn despotic principles in the universities and proposes that, to remedy this evil, "Plutarch's

---

[98] Hobbes, *Behemoth,* ed. Tönnies, p. 62.
[99] *Ibid.,* p. 159.
[100] *Ibid.,* p. 40.
[101] *Ibid.,* pp. 23, 55-56.
[102] *Ibid.,* pp. 3, 23, 43, 56, 158. For the bad effect of the classical languages upon the behavior of the clergy, see his "Considerations upon the Reputation," *Works,* IV, 434.

Lives, with the Greek and Roman history, ought to be early put in their hands." A modern author, shifting the problem to the statistical plane, has argued that Hobbes overstated "his case against the universities by making the courses of study the source of rebellion" and that a more convincing source can be found in the preparation by the universities of too many men for the available positions.[103]

In order to ensure greater loyalty and tranquility in the state, Hobbes accordingly recommends a reform of the universities: "The core of rebellion," he says, "as you have seen by this, and read of other rebellions, are the Universities; which nevertheless are not to be cast away, but to be better disciplined. . . ." [104] The reform is not in itself to be designed as a blood purge, but if the King is to carry it out without danger of resistance from sympathizers with disloyal elements in the universities, he should be backed by an army or at least by the financial means to raise one. In the universities thus reformed, doctrines of obedience, not, as heretofore, doctrines of sedition, are to be taught. When he speaks of the Roundhead purge of Oxford in 1648, he notes with approval the expulsion of the morally unworthy and censures the purge only faintly.[105]

Obedience, which is to be taught in the purified universities, is, Hobbes declares, "a science, and built upon sure and clear principles, and to be learned by deep and careful study, or from masters that have deeply studied it." [106] Among the seducers of the people from loyalty to Charles I, he includes the lack of understanding of the nature of authority and obedience, but in the England of Charles II ignorance on this question need not be pleaded. "The rules of *just* and *unjust* sufficiently demonstrated, and from principles evident to the meanest capacity, have not been wanting; and notwithstanding the obscurity of their author, have shined, not only in this, but also in foreign countries, to men of good education." [107] When the universities have thus been brought to inculcate Hobbesian principles of loyalty, the people can be instructed in loyalty by the clergy without fear of their incurring contamination from their teachers.

There was another institution and its results which one might expect to find included by this critic of the universities among the sowers of sedition. When the Marquess of Newcastle wrote his book of advice for

---

[103] Burnet, *OTR*, VI, 208-210; Mark H. Curtis, "The Alienated Intellectuals of Early Stuart England," *Past & Present*, No. 23 (November 1962), 40, 27.

[104] Hobbes, *Behemoth*, ed. Tönnies, p. 58.

[105] *Ibid.*, pp. 58 (cf. p. 56), 147-148.

[106] *Ibid.*, p. 159.

[107] *Ibid.*, pp. 39-40; Hobbes, "Six Lessons to the Professors of the Mathematics," *Works*, VII, 335.

Charles II, he identified schools and indeed widespread literacy itself among the causes of the war. But Hobbes does not so much as touch upon these ideas, and it can be argued that he did not share them from the fact that he attempted, late in his life, to found "a free-schoole." [108]

Hobbes also, in his examination of the causes of the rebellion, notes the part played by London and the other great towns of trade, which admired the prosperity of the Low Countries after their rebellion and thought that a similar rebellion would yield them similar prosperity. But for London, he says, "the Parliament never could have made the war, nor the Rump ever have murdered the King." [109]

Hobbes's treatment of the Parliamentary resistance to Charles I contains a recurrence of the psychological improbability which mars his treatment of the Presbyterians. He seems to believe that even years before the outbreak of the rebellion men with a "design of changing the government from monarchical to popular, which they called liberty" were leading or otherwise promoting the Parliamentary opposition to the King. Hobbes thinks, however, that the King's Parliamentary opponents "never would have ventured into the field, but for that unlucky business of imposing upon the Scots, who were all Presbyterians, our book of Common-prayer." [110] The Long Parliament seized the opportunity to force the King into resistance and England into rebellion. Referring to the year 1641, he remarks that "in the northern counties were quartered the Scotch army which the Parliament called in to oppose the King, and consequently their quarter was to be discharged." [111] The time at which Parliament "called in" this army, it will be recalled, was the summer of 1640, in the interval between the dissolution of the Short Parliament and the meeting of the Long Parliament. One can see what Hobbes means (if he is not simply mistaken in chronology or unusually careless in phraseology), but the assumption that a non-existent Parliament could call in an army is surprising in the rigorous dissector of Puritan logic. He himself detects a similar logical defect in the claims of the enemy.[112] Hobbes is not very explicit in his views about how the Parliamentary resistance of 1640-1642 was managed; he speaks of a cabal formed by "the most seditious of both Houses" during the King's absence in Scotland in 1641, to govern the House of Commons and put

[108] Newcastle in *Catalogue,* ed. Strong, pp. 185-186, 188-189, 192; Aubrey, *BL,* I, 342-343.

[109] Hobbes, *Behemoth,* ed. Tönnies, pp. 3-4, 126, 202.

[110] *Ibid.,* pp. 26, 28. For Parliament's pursuit of the sovereignty, see especially pp. 23, 26-29, 35-36, 75, 78-79, 83, 88-89, 97-98, 102, 119, 145.

[111] *Ibid.,* p. 86.

[112] *Ibid.,* pp. 120, 182.

the kingdom into rebellion; but he does not make clear what relation this cabal, dated so surprisingly late in its origin, bore to the previous machinations and ambitions he observes in this Parliament.[113]

He does not, of course, in his discussion of the origins of the rebellion, include misgovernment by Charles I as one of the causes, and it is possible to see what he thought about charges of misgovernment when he comes to discuss the contents of the Grand Remonstrance. He minimizes the misdeeds recited, flings back as much as possible the responsibility for misgovernment on the opponents of the King, and thinks it worthwhile to include the following curious quibble:

A. A second accusation was, that they endeavoured to suppress the purity and power of religion.

B. That is canting. 'Tis not in man's power to suppress the power of religion.[114]

Elsewhere he expresses contempt for Hampden's refusal to pay ship-money; [115] there is something perverse in his unwillingness to understand Hampden's motives, but certainly Hampden's refusal did conflict with Hobbes's teachings on the liability of subjects to provide financial support for the sovereign power.

The rebels were untrue to the King by rejecting their loyalty completely, but "the King's counsellors, lords, and other persons of quality and experience" were also defective in loyalty, for they had the

fault, which was generally in the whole nation, which was, that they thought the government of England was not an absolute, but a mixed monarchy; and that if the King should clearly subdue this Parliament, that this power would be what he pleased, and theirs as little as he pleased: which they counted tyranny.[116]

Hobbes of course did not share this fault, for he had proved in his political theory that the King is or ought to be absolute and that mixed monarchy is absurd. He notes with distaste that the King's principal declaration-writers were lawyers or pretenders to legal knowledge who had formerly ("if I have not been misinformed") been enemies of "ship-money and other extra-parliamentary taxes," and who had come over to the King's side only "when they saw the Parliament grow higher in

---

[113] *Ibid.*, pp. 78-79.
[114] *Ibid.*, p. 82. For the passage of the Grand Remonstrance to which Hobbes is referring, see S. R. Gardiner, ed., *The Constitutional Documents of the Puritan Revolution,* 3rd ed. (Oxford, Clarendon Press, 1906), p. 207.
[115] Hobbes, *Behemoth*, ed. Tönnies, p. 37.
[116] *Ibid.*, pp. 114, 116-117, 125.

their demands than they thought they would have done." [117] Hobbes
states in introducing his translation of Homer that the historian ought
not "to make himself an absolute master of any man's good name," and
he explains in *Behemoth* why he does not reveal the names of these
offending declaration-writers; in effect, his explanation seems to be that
he is willing to let bygones be bygones in matters of mere description,
which can add nothing of use to the lessons he is expounding.[118] Acrimonious though many passages in *Behemoth* are, his censures seldom
fall on particular persons. But we can easily guess at the names he con-
ceals: Hyde, Falkland, and Colepeper.[119] Hobbes believes that lukewarm
Royalists impeded the King's victory by taking the edge of the soldiers'
zeal and preventing the vigorous and even ruthless prosecution of the
war.[120]

Hobbes sees the death of the King after his military defeat as the
logical result of the plan of the Parliamentarians to wrest his authority
from him; and B. is made to wonder why Charles exchanged so many
messages with his enemies during the drift towards open warfare in
1642, when this ultimate murder should already have been evident to
him.[121] Though done by the Independents, the murder was the result
of "the folly and first treason of the Presbyterians, who betrayed and sold
him to his murderers," and Hobbes is inclined to blame the Presbyterians
the more heavily of the two.[122]

Hobbes's treatment of the greatest of the regicides lacks the bitterness
with which many other contemporaries assailed him. Despite Hobbes's
attribution of improbably deliberate, wicked, and lucid designs to the
Presbyterians and Parliamentarians, he does not emphasize Cromwell's
ambition. Even in early 1648 Cromwell still had so many obstacles to
face that Hobbes "cannot believe he then thought to be King; but only

[117] *Ibid.,* pp. 116-117, 125.
[118] Hobbes, *Works,* X, vi; cf. viii; Hobbes, *Behemoth,* ed. Tönnies, p. 117. William
Lilly, in his life of Charles I in his *Monarchy or No Monarchy in England* (London,
1651), p. 78, has some remarks, from his Parliamentarian standpoint, on lukewarm
Royalists; and Roger Coke, *A Detection of the Court and State of England during
The Four Last Reigns And the Inter-Regnum,* 3rd ed., 2 vols. (London, 1697), I,
279, has a similar passage from a Whig standpoint. Sir Edward Walker, who had
views on this question rather similar to Hobbes's, and who was in the Royalist army,
comments on Lilly's statement in his *Historical Discourses* (London, 1705), pp. 239-
240. See also Duchess of Newcastle, *Life of William Cavendish,* pp. 93-94; Warwick,
Rules of Government, p. 62; Warwick, *M,* pp. 197-198, 228, 230, 233.
[119] Warwick identifies Hyde, Falkland, and Colepeper with Hobbes's strictures on
the declaration-writers, *ibid.,* p. 197.
[120] Hobbes, *Behemoth,* ed. Tönnies, pp. 115-116, 131.
[121] *Ibid.,* p. 102.
[122] *Ibid.,* pp. 155, 165, and *passim.* Lips, *Stellung des Thomas Hobbes,* p. 96,
comments on Hobbes's sparing of the Independents at the expense of the Presbyterians.

by well serving the strongest party, which was always his main polity, to proceed as far as that and fortune would carry him." [123] He speaks through the mouth of B. with some approval of the proposal to make Cromwell king: "That was indeed a bold motion, and which would, if prosperous, have put an end to a great many men's ambition, and to the licentiousness of the whole army." Yet he suggests that it may, after all, have been made with the intention of ruining Cromwell.[124]

Hobbes again favors the established power in his account of Richard Cromwell's brief rule. B. expresses surprise that the members of Richard's Parliament, who had shown their recognition of his authority by meeting on his summons, should now dispute his authority; and A. seems to agree that they had fallen into an error of political theory. B. reflects that this Parliament had the same ill temper of all Parliaments since Queen Elizabeth's time and remarks that its members were "ignorant men." [125] But despite this last flickering show of sympathy for the Protectorate, Hobbes rejoices over the Restoration, the event with which he ends his book.

Did Hobbes, in his discussion of the Civil War, suggest that Parliament should be abolished or reduced in power? One may certainly draw from Hobbes's political philosophy the conclusion that in the Hobbesian state Parliament would be of very little importance, if it existed at all, but this attitude to Parliament is only barely hinted at in *Behemoth*. There he does of course attack particular Parliaments and particular groups of Parliament men, but except implicitly and very unobtrusively [126] he does not venture upon a more general criticism of the institution. Apart from whatever he may have implied about the continued freedom and existence of Parliament, Hobbes in *Behemoth* was following full in the paths of Royalist orthodoxy. Royalists, like their opponents, were deeply devoted to Parliament, and hints such as Heylyn's about the desirability of the destruction of Parliament are very rare in their writings. Hobbes must have been confirmed in his cautious handling of this point by the political prejudices of the upper classes that he knew through his Cavendish connection and otherwise.

Hobbes has sometimes been recognized as one of the prophets of

---

[123] Hobbes, *Behemoth,* ed. Tönnies, p. 147.

[124] *Ibid.,* p. 188. In the Molesworth text of "Behemoth," *Works,* VI, 388-389, B. asks "who had the supreme power" after Cromwell's dissolution of the Long Parliament in 1653, and A. replies, "If by power you mean the right to govern, nobody had it." This surprising denial of the claim of Charles II is apparently only a textual error; *Behemoth,* ed. Tönnies, p. 180, has a saving "here" after "nobody."

[125] *Ibid.,* pp. 192-193.

[126] E.g., *ibid.,* p. 56.

modern totalitarianism, and there are passages in *Behemoth* in which he seems to foreshadow some of its darker practices. His concern for the scouring of the universities, as a prerequisite for that controlling and even molding of English opinion which he advocates, and his desire for more uncompromising warfare may be cited. But how is one to interpret the notion he introduces of the mass murder of the Presbyterian ministers before the rebellion? [127] Is it a casual exercise in argument or a monstrous (though in its particular application, retrospective) suggestion? Richard Cromwell, he remarks in a passage which must be weighed in any attempt to answer the foregoing question, was advised to kill some officers plotting against him, "but he had not courage enough to give . . . such a commission." [128] But Hobbes was aware of the vigor and extent of the forces struggling against the monarchy, even though he was often wrong in his analysis of them, and was aware, as Clarendon apparently was not, that something of the same vigor and emancipation from convention was necessary to overcome them.

Yet despite this awareness in its author, *Behemoth* is not, after all, the work of a practical man of affairs. This brilliant historical essay is distorted by a defect fundamental to most of Hobbes's political philosophy – his failure or refusal to comprehend minds which were radically different from his own, that is to say, most minds. He attributes to the Presbyterians and Parliamentarians improbably deliberate, wicked, and lucid designs. Himself a highly unorthodox Royalist, he shows little understanding of or respect for the attitudes and motives of his fellow Royalists. While aware of the strength of the forces arrayed against the monarchy, and even aware to some extent of the impermeability of the human mind to reason, he retains, almost paradoxically, an excessive belief in the importance of theory and demonstration. It is revealing of Hobbes's conviction of the value of theory that he should place the exaggerated emphasis he does [129] on the declaration of royal right in the

[127] *Ibid.*, p. 95; cf. p. 72. He speaks, pp. 160, 164, about Parliamentarian plans for a massacre of the defeated Royalists. This idea also occurs in other contemporary Royalist writers, one of which, interestingly enough, speaks of the act as being "according to *Hobbes's* Doctrine then lately published." Barwick, *Life of John Barwick*, p. 163.

[128] Hobbes, *Behemoth*, ed. Tönnies, p. 192. Hobbes's remark, *ibid.*, p. 168, on the King's benefit by the Scottish defeat at Dunbar and his similar, more general, remark, p. 165, about the destruction of the King's enemies, seem cynical and heartless, but see the sentiments of Charles himself on Dunbar as reported by Clarendon, *HR*, V, 149, 170.

[129] Hobbes, *Behemoth*, ed. Tönnies, p. 204. B. H. G. Wormald, *Clarendon: Politics, History & Religion 1640-1660* (Cambridge, Eng., Cambridge University Press, 1951), p. 223, cleverly says that "Hobbes had all the doctrinaire's respect for the ideas of other people."

Militia Act of 1661. Possession of the militia power is equivalent to the possession of the sovereignty in Hobbes's political system,[130] but in view of the titanic conflict Hobbes has just described this emphasis on paper rights and paper victories is little better than ridiculous. *Behemoth* is marked by the radical misunderstanding of the minds and actions of men as they play their parts in the political world that Clarendon observes and censures in his reply to *Leviathan*.

3. *John Hacket*

The *Scrina Reserata* [131] of John Hacket (1592-1670) is superficially a bizarre book. Hacket writes in an eccentric and highly individual prose style and sows his pages thick with innumerable learned quotations and much curious illustrative information. Yet the oddity of the work should not be allowed to detract from its merits. The *Scrinia Reserata* is a distinguished artistic achievement with many passages of great charm and beauty and is a detailed and perceptive historical source. As the biography or life and times of John Williams, Bishop of Lincoln and Archbishop of York, it deals with many aspects of the political and ecclesiastical history of England during the reigns of James I and Charles I. Hacket's historical judgments are seldom in themselves bizarre, despite the strange appearance they sometimes acquire from the prose in which he clothes them, nor do his eccentricities of expression seem to have corresponded to any eccentricities of his character. He led the conventional life of a successful clergyman, was a friend of Selden and Usher,[132] and had sober religious and political principles. He was devoted to the Church of England and little influenced by Puritanism, however sharp a critic he was of the Laudian regime, and was devoted, with only a few reservations, to Charles I.

[130] Hobbes, "Leviathan," *Works*, III, 166; Hobbes, *Behemoth*, ed. Tönnies, pp. 102, 145.

[131] Coleridge's comments on *Scrinia Reserata* in S. T. Coleridge, *Coleridge on the Seventeenth Century*, ed. R. F. Brinkley (Durham, N.C., Duke University Press, 1955), pp. 208-222, are important; see also Sir James Fitzjames Stephen's essay on *Scrinia Reserata* in his *Horae Sabbaticae*, 1st ser., (London, 1892), pp. 286-308. The standard life of Hacket by Thomas Plume, published in John Hacket, *A Century of Sermons Upon Several Remarkable Subjects*, ed. Plume (London, 1675), is conveniently reprinted with notes as Plume, *An Account of the Life and Death of ... Hacket*, ed. Mackenzie E. C. Walcott (London, 1865). The biographical data below on Hacket, unless otherwise identified, are drawn from *Scrinia Reserata*, Plume, or the life of Hacket in the *DNB*.

[132] For these friendships, see Hacket, *SR*, Part I, 69; Hacket to William Dillingham, June 4, 1656, BM Sloane MS 1710, f. 196; Plume, *Account*, ed. Walcott, pp. 42, 66, 104, 134. Hacket is said to have assisted Ben Jonson in translating Bacon's *Essays* into Latin. Wood, *AO*, II, 615.

In his book, the principal standard Hacket brings to the making of his historical judgments is the welfare of Williams. Though he is not willing to defend Williams' morality at all times,[133] he generally praises or condemns events and men and institutions as they favored or harmed his hero. In the many instances in which this very limited standard does not apply, he finds another standard in his own conventional Royalist and Anglican principles. Observance of these two standards causes him to blunder into confusion and contradiction or near contradiction when he discusses the character and the regime of Charles I.

With the man on whom the first of these standards is based, Bishop Williams, Hacket had a long and apparently intimate acquaintance. Hacket was the son of a senior burgess of Westminster; notwithstanding his father's being of Scottish descent, Hacket shows no particular sympathy for the Scots in his history. Both his parents are said to have been much devoted to the Church of England. Young Hacket was educated at Cambridge University. Shortly after Williams became Lord Keeper in 1621, he made Hacket his chaplain, "whom of all his Chaplains," we are told, "he ever most loved and esteemed." [134] Hacket says that from the time of that appointment

till thirty Years expired with his Life, I trespass not against Modesty if I say, I knew his Courses as much, and saw them at as near a distance, as any Man beside. I have as much Intelligence from an Eye-witness Information, and from his familiar Conference with me, as can be expected from any Writer of the Memorials of a great Statist: . . .[135]

It is probable from this and other passages that much of the information about events at court reported in *Scrinia Reserata* came from Williams himself. Hacket's source, unfortunately, is no guarantee of the reliability of his information, for we learn from a passage in Clarendon that the Bishop was one of those persons who invent conversations, complete with answers and replies, and retail them as if they had really taken place. Williams did so, Clarendon notes, even upon matters "of great moment." [136] Hacket maintained his familiarity with Williams during the Bishop's imprisonment in the Tower from 1637 till 1640, when he emerged to enjoy his short lived prominence in the Long Parliament. In 1642 Williams left Westminster to join the King in the north and,

---

[133] See, for example, his candor about Williams' defense of the wicked Mr. Lamb and his admission of Williams' faults of pride, ambition, and anger. Hacket, *SR,* Part I, 36-38, Part II, 63, 229.

[134] Plume, *Account,* ed. Walcott, p. 18.

[135] Hacket, *SR,* proem, p. 2.

[136] Clarendon, *HR,* I, 464-468.

Hacket says, "I never saw him more to confer with him; from whom before I learnt all things in effect that I knew." [137] It will be noted that this statement does not absolutely exclude the possibility of future meetings, but that it does indicate the end of their conversations: they never met again *to confer*.

Hacket was deprived during the war of his living of St. Andrew's, Holborn, but he managed to retain another of Williams' benefactions, the little benefice of Cheam in Surrey, being still established there when Charles II returned in 1660. On one occasion, apparently while he was still at St. Andrew's, he was threatened, according to his contemporary biographer Plume, by a soldier with a pistol while he was officiating in his church; but "the Doctor smiled at his insolency in that sacred place, and not at all terrified, said *he* would do what became a Divine, and he might do what became a soldier." We are told by the same authority that after Hacket's removal to Cheam he was taken prisoner by the Earl of Essex' army and released only after warm solicitations to change sides and that as a result of the King's execution (which Hacket remembers with a remark about "the day that they crucified Christ upon the Cross again") he had an aversion to visiting the guilty city of London but set it aside when the Earls of Holland and Norwich requested his spiritual assistance in view of their expected execution.[138]

He wrote *Scrinia Reserata* during his years of eclipse at Cheam. The title is evidently an allusion to the printed collection of documents called the *Cabala: sive Scrinia Sacra* (1654) which he uses among his sources. He states that he completed the writing of the book on February 17, 1657/8; [139] at least a few additions were made later and he was still searching for information in 1660,[140] but substantially the book is a document of the period of Puritan rule, deeply and movingly stamped with its author's anguish over the disastrous consequences of the Civil War. When he began writing is harder to say. As he mentions that having

[137] Hacket, *SR*, Part II, 184.

[138] Plume, *Account*, ed. Walcott, pp. 64, 66-67, 68-69; Hacket, *SR*, Part II, 224. Some letters from Hacket to William Dillingham in BM Sloane MS 1710 ff. 182-202, belong to the period 1653-1661 but do not mention his composition of the history.

[139] I.e., as Hacket dates the year, in "1657." Hacket, *SR*, Part II, 229.

[140] He speaks, *ibid.*, Part II, 139, of the Long Parliament lasting nineteen years till its final suppression, and alludes, Part II, 198, 196, to Matthew Wren's *Monarchy Asserted* (1659) and Samuel Butler's *Hudibras*, Part I (1663). William Dolben in a letter to Lady Grace Wynn, Dec. 11, 1660, summarized in *Calendar of Wynn (of Gwydir) Papers 1515-1690 in the National Library of Wales and Elsewhere* (Aberystwyth, The National Library of Wales, 1926), p. 362, speaks of Hacket's desire to gain information for his history about Williams' actions in the affair of Conway Castle. I am grateful to the National Library of Wales for supplying me with a copy of the full letter.

reached that point in his narrative at which he spoke of Williams taking his seat in the Long Parliament he interrupted the writing "for above two years," [141] he must have been at work before 1656. He is unlikely to have begun his writing before Williams' death in 1650.

His criticisms of Charles and Laud are in themselves quite sufficient to explain why his manuscript long remained unpublished. He also shows in *Scrinia Reserata* and in his letters a resentment of the excesses of the press which suggests that a personal distaste for the press may have been a further hindrance to his appearance there with a controversial work. But there can be no doubt at all from the work itself that he meant it to be read and thus presumably – one cannot be more positive, in view of the seventeenth-century practice of circulating works in manuscript – to be published. Plume does not mention the work in his life of Hacket, but he had the manuscript of it in his possession some years later, in 1686, when Archbishop Sancroft borrowed it from him,[142] and he may have been the editor of the published edition which appeared (hastily issued, the publisher claimed, to forestall a surreptitious edition) in 1693. Lest any reader of the present study wonder whether a work of such early origin should be studied as a work later than Hobbes's *Behemoth*, he should be reminded that in the present study Civil War histories are considered, whenever possible, by dates of publication rather than by dates of composition; to this may be added that Hacket himself, unless he had some original intention of publishing *Scrinia Reserata* under a continuing Puritan regime, can hardly have seriously thought of publishing it much earlier than the date at which it finally did appear.

Hacket was guided in writing it by a desire to commemorate his dead friend and patron and perhaps by an urge to fill the idle hours at Cheam with some activity more substantial than mere study, but he puts his purpose on a more theoretical footing by explaining in the proem that his purpose is didactic. He intends, he says, *"in the Narration of one Life, to insert Rules for any,"* and he cites with approval the belief of Isaac Casaubon that *"A right History is a System of Exemplary, or Practick Philosophy."* [143] Hacket only rarely deviates into open moralizing; he is content for the most part to let the events he narrates preach

---

[141] Hacket, *SR*, Part II, 139.

[142] Archbishop Sancroft's receipt of Nov. 9, 1686, Bodleian MS Tanner 30 f. 137. Hacket in his will (preserved at Somerset House) left Plume "two Bookes of my Sermons" but does not mention *Scrinia Reserata*. Walcott in his edition of Plume, *Account*, p. 151, says that the manuscript of *Scrinia Reserata* is in Trinity College Library, Cambridge, but it is not there now, and after various enquiries I have been unable to find any trace of it.

[143] Hacket, *SR*, proem, pp. 3-4; Part II, 63.

their own instructive sermon. Nor does he make Williams a standard moralist's hero; one is not at all aware in reading *Scrinia Reserata*, as one is in reading Burnet's lives of Hale and Bedell, that the subject of the biography is being held up as a pattern of behavior. Hacket may not have been sufficiently content with all the moral aspects of Williams' personality and career to represent him as an exemplary as well as a great man. Hacket's intention was to use the history of one career to inculcate the wisdom of practical life and to encourage awareness of the actions of God in human affairs. His innumerable learned quotations are intended to instruct the reader in a more general way, serving the educative purpose of an anthology.

Hacket's later years were dignified, if not much eased, by his elevation in 1661 to the bishopric of Lichfield and Coventry. Plume states that when Hacket arrived at Lichfield and found his war-damaged cathedral "lying in the dust," he on "the very next morning . . . set his own coach-horses on work, together with other teams to carry away the rubbish." [144] This anecdote well illustrates Hacket's devotion to the church and the warm, impetuous feelings he seems to have had, but it needs to be qualified with the observation that the reconstruction of the cathedral was under way even before Hacket's arrival. He subsequently plunged with great zeal into the work and became an accomplished campaigner for the necessary money and a generous contributor himself.[145] At Lichfield he was troubled by a quarrel with the dean, Thomas Wood. Totally uncooperative and monumentally parsimonious, an ally of Nonconformists and resolutely determined to perform as few as possible of his ecclesiastical duties, Wood had the unanswerable merit of influence at court. His career included the twin distinctions of excommunication by Hacket and suspension from his bishopric (for he succeeded Hacket as bishop of Lichfield and Coventry) by Archbishop Sancroft, but he survived both to become an episcopal pillar of the Revolution of 1688.[146] Hacket extols Williams and Plume extols Hacket, and readers who tire

---

[144] Plume, *Account*, ed. Walcott, p. 80.

[145] For Hacket's labors in restoring the cathedral, see M. W. Greenslade, ed., *A History of the County of Stafford*, III (London, The Victoria History of the Counties of England, 1970), pp. 175-176.

[146] Plume does not mention the Wood affair. It is described in the life of Wood in R. E. C. Waters, *Genealogical Memoirs of the Extinct Family of Chester of Chicheley* (London, 1878), II, 488-506, and in Greenslade, ed., *County of Stafford*, III, 177-178. For the excommunication of Wood, see Hacket to the Archbishop of Canterbury, Jan. 20, 1667/8, in Bodleian MS Tanner 131 f. 18, and Pepys's diary under date Jan. 31, 1667/8. A report of the same month held that Wood had also excommunicated Hacket; Charles Bertie to Sir Thomas Osborne, Jan. 30, 1667/8, HMC, 14th Report, Appendix, Part IX (London, 1895), p. 370.

of the excess of episcopal virtue may reflect upon the unapostolic but by no means unresourceful figure of Thomas Wood.

There is no need to repeat the account Hacket gives in *Scrinia Reserata* of Williams' rise in the world, but we should note his opinions on James I, under whom Williams enjoyed his rise and years of prosperity. Hacket is said to have "long intended to write" James's life, abandoning the plan only when his books and manuscripts were lost on the sequestration of his living at Holborn.[147] We must distinguish between the praise Hacket bestows on James's reign and the praise be bestows on James as a person. To that reign he looks back, amid the wreckage of the war, as to a golden age, but he is aware that James himself, though excellent, was not quite without flaw. He speaks in confident defense of James's political theories and political practice:

Some thought that the good King studied to Enthral the people; far from his mind God wot. But his speculation was, that Northern Nations love not a Yoke upon their Necks, and are prone to Anarchy; that they will ruin themselves, if they be not held down to a good temper of Obedience; and that, by too much Liberty, Liberty it self will Perish. . . . But as King *James* did rather talk much of free Monarchy, then execute it: So no people did ever live more prosperously then we did under him, . . .[148]

He goes on to praise the wealth and peace that existed under James and utters the heartfelt cry, "Let them keep silence with shame enough, that Ball aloud, we were corrupted by them; whose Fault was that? Therefore God hath taken them away from us, . . ." [149] Hacket alludes here probably to the contemporary idea that the war was a divine punishment for the abuse of peace and plenty and conceivably even to the contemporary idea that a surfeit of peace and plenty can produce civil war. He objects to Heylyn's assault on the wisdom of King James and calls upon his own memories of the court to reassure the reader of James's devotion to learning. But he concedes, all the same, the weakness of James's character, admitting that

He submitted himself to be ruled by some, whom he should have awed with Authority; but he wanted Courage to bow them to his own Bent. A Prince that preserves not the Rights of his Dignity, and the Majesty of his Throne, is a Servant to some, but therein a Friend to none, least of all to himself.[150]

---

[147] Plume, *Account,* ed. Walcott, p. 26; cf. p. 26 n., p. 148.
[148] Hacket, *SR,* Part I, 224.
[149] *Ibid.,* Part I, 224. See my Appendix to the present work for the idea of the surfeit of peace and plenty.
[150] Hacket, *SR,* Part I, 138, 226-227, quotation from Part I, 167.

The allusion here must be to Buckingham, who was first Williams' patron and later his enemy. James preserved Williams as Lord Keeper even against the malignity of the overweening favorite, but with the death of James "the Day of the Servant's Prosperity shut up, and a Night of long and troublesome Adversity followed." [151]

Hacket relates with great sorrow and stateliness the fall of Williams from power and his subsequent persecution at the hands of the government. It is interesting to notice, as an example of the theological interpretation of historical events, that when Hacket has to explain why Williams could never find his peace and prosperity again when once he had lost them, he places the blame chiefly on his sins, the chief sins being pride, ambition, and anger.[152] He uses the same interpretation later at the expense of Williams' enemies, when he discusses the Court of Star Chamber, in which Williams had been convicted. He says that "God was offended at the Court, which over-drip't so many with its too far spreading Branches of Arbitrary and Irregular Power," and that "God spared not to dig up this burdensome Tree by the root." [153] The theological interpretation does not necessarily abolish the need for secondary causes to work God's will, and Hacket accordingly criticizes the human agents involved in Williams' misfortunes and does not fail to criticize both Laud and Charles.

Laud is presented in dark colors in Hacket's pages. The hero of Heylyn's writings is the villain of *Scrinia Reserata*. As Hacket tells the story, Williams was set on by Buckingham to obtain for Laud his first bishopric, that of St. David's. James was unwilling to accede to Laud's elevation, and on being pressed by Williams declared that

the plain Truth is, that I keep Laud back from all Place of Rule and Authority, because I find he hath a restless Spirit, and cannot see when Matters are well, but loves to toss and change, and to bring Things to a pitch of Reformation floating in his own Brain, which may endanger the steadfastness of that which is in a good pass, God be praised.

Williams' plea won out, but Laud repaid this and other favors with the grossest ingratitude.[154] As soon as he saw that Williams was under the displeasure of Buckingham, "he would never acknowledge him more,

---

[151] *Ibid.*, Part I, 228.

[152] *Ibid.*, Part II, 63; cf. 229.

[153] *Ibid.*, Part II, 132, 133. See also Part II, 126, where he criticizes it but looks forward to a revival of the Court in a better form. For his criticisms of the Court of High Commission, see Part I, 97-98. For his view of sin as a cause of the war, see Part II, 142, and Plume, *Account*, ed. Walcott, p. 74.

[154] Hacket, *SR*, Part I, 63-64; cf. Gardiner, *HE*, IV, 138-139.

but shunn'd him, as the old Romans in their Superstition walk'd a loof from that Soil, which was blasted with Thunder." Laud's enmity is attributed to his ambition.[155] Laud worked to undermine Williams further with Buckingham, and Laud was the cause of the long persecution of Williams which included his imprisonment.[156] Hacket confesses that he believes Laud "was better than he was commonly thought" but insists that he meets "with him in his worst Action that ever he did, and cannot shun it." As to the source of his power, Hacket says that "Whether he had little or sufficient insight into Government, is disputable, but he knew how to govern the King: . . ."[157]

Hacket admits that Charles favored the persecution of Williams, and, more surprisingly, he declares that Charles kept bad faith with Williams. He accuses the King only indirectly when he says of Williams, that "Having delivered up the Great Seal, from the first day that he removed to *Bugden*," his episcopal residence, "all Promises were broken, which gave him Assurance of Countenance and Safety"; but he accuses the King directly when he says that "The Faults of the Blessed *Charles* were small, yet some he had; who having assured *Lincoln* he should never be question'd again about the matter brought against him by *Lamb* and *Sibthorp* [principally charges of betraying Privy Council secrets], yet remitted it to the *Star-chamber*."[158] It was Laud, Hacket declares, who "made his Soveraign break his word with his Subject."[159] In these passages Hacket is expressing a view of Charles which would have seemed untrue to most of his fellow Royalists. Parliamentarians were free to believe that Charles was a violator of his word, but it is surprising to find their conclusion or prejudice confirmed by a voice from the Royalist ranks. Elsewhere in the same work, wherever Hacket can consider Charles apart from the authorship of Williams' misfortunes, his views turn a somersault and Charles becomes "the greatest Saint that ever ruled our Nation."[160]

Hacket reviews the ecclesiastical history of the Stuart period to 1640 from the standpoint of moderate Anglicanism. He regrets that the triumphant Arminians caused heartburning and emulation by preferring only those of their own opinion and neglecting others. Williams, he observes, followed the example of the great English prelates of the past, who

---

[155] Hacket, *SR,* Part I, 108, 64, Part II, 19, 86.
[156] *Ibid.,* Part II, 19, 65-66, 85, 129.
[157] *Ibid.,* Part II, 65, 86.
[158] *Ibid.,* Part II, 62, 114.
[159] *Ibid.,* Part II, 115.
[160] *Ibid.,* Part II, 183.

preferred men indifferently without respect to their opinions on the controverted points of the Arminian theological disputes and did not promote unfamiliar ceremonies in their dioceses. He seems to avoid deciding whether the ceremonialism which came in with Arminianism was an innovation or not.[161]

Like his friend Fuller, Hacket observes that the definition of a Puritan became dangerously widened in the reign of King James. Though long, the passage is important and should be quoted in full:

> The Old Non-conformists were call'd by the Nick-Name of Puritans in Queen *Elizabeth's* days. I know not who impos'd it first, whether *Parsons* the Jesuit, or some such Franion: I know it grew not up like Wild Oats without Sowing. But some Supercilious Divines, a few years before the End of K. *James* his Reign, began to Survey the Narrow way of the Church of *England* with no Eyes but their own, and measuring a Right Protestant with their streight line, discriminated, as they thought fit, sound from unsound, so that scarce ten among a Thousand, but were Noted to carry some Disguise of a Puritan. The very Prelates were not free from it, but, *Tantum non ni Episcopatu Puritani*, became an Obloquy.[162]

Elsewhere he remarks that Williams, because he preached much during his period of official disgrace, was censured for Puritanism:

> For the good Office of Preaching, perform'd often by a Bishop, was call'd Puritanism by some in those times, that fomented such a Faction, that made the Name of Puritan the very Inquisition of *England*. Not using it, as formerly, to preserve the good Order, and Discipline of the Church; but to cast any Man out of Favour, that was so innocent, as not to be able to be charged with any thing else. Thrust a worthy Man between the first and second Censure, and how hard did we make it, by such uncharitable Traducings, to live evenly in the indivisible Point of Protestantism? [163]

He shrewdly suggests that if the bishops had preached more diligently, they would not have fallen under suspicion of being popishly inclined.[164] Hacket takes a moderate attitude to the people who were Puritans in the ordinary rather than the extended sense of the term, and his bitterness against the King's enemies in the war is directed against them as rebels, not Puritans. Laud, he observes, was determined to suppress the Puritan leaders or drive them out of England, but Williams perceived

---

[161] *Ibid.*, Part II, 42, 45, 86. He speaks, Part II, 45, of "the new Wine, which other Prelates [i.e., other than Williams] broach'd: or call it their Pregnancy to revive old things, which had long laid still."

[162] *Ibid.*, Part I, 95. He calls Fuller, Part I, 207, "my industrious Friend," and refers to his *Church History* several times in *Scrinia Reserata.*

[163] *Ibid.*, Part II, 39.

[164] *Ibid.*, Part II, 39.

that these violent methods made the Puritans more violent and "that the cutting of some great Boughs made the Under-woods grow the faster." Williams followed gentle policies in his own dealings with Puritans, having the design of winning them over through mildness.[165] Unlike Heylyn, Hacket does not, so far as one can detect from any passage of *Scrinia Reserata*, believe that the overthrow of Charles was the result of a long-established Puritan or Presbyterian plot.

When he speaks of the Scots' resistance to the Prayer Book, he unsympathetically remarks that Laud "had entangled himself in his own Webb, nay, the King, and all *England* and *Scotland* with him." For the King, however, he has full sympathy. "Let all Ages remember," he says, that this rebellion "sprung from no other occasion, but that the King invited them to prayer in publick, in such a Form of Liturgy as himself used, putting no greater burden upon their Conscience than upon his own." [166] This argument could be used to justify the persecution of Christians by a heathen ruler or of Protestants by a Roman Catholic ruler or any attempt by one person to force another to commit an immoral act, but Hacket does not notice the difficulty. He is convinced that the King could have defeated the Scots in the First Scottish War "if he had not been more desirous of Quietness than Honour and Victory." [167]

In his eagerness to defend Charles, Hacket writes in a way that conflicts with his tale of the persecution of Williams. He thinks that Charles's break with Parliament from 1629 to 1640 was politically unwise but declares that while it lasted "we could not say that we wanted Justice, Peace, and Plenty, much less the true worship of God." But despite this brave boast about justice, he admits that Williams' "troubles" during this period occurred "for want of a Parliament to keep him from Maleficence," and he mentions that Williams, sometime before the Long Parliament met, appealed to the next meeting of Parliament against his persecutors in the Court of Star Chamber.[168] Hacket complains of Charles's enemies in the early Long Parliament, "and yet they would trust him with nothing: An Affront of deep Indignity! Dare they not trust him that never broke with them? And I have heard his nearest Servants say,

---

[165] *Ibid.*, Part II, 86. On the question of Hacket's own tolerance as a bishop, see opposing views in Walter G. Simon, *The Restoration Episcopate* (New York, Bookman Associates, Inc., 1965), pp. 141, 151-152, 158, and Greenslade, ed., *County of Stafford*, III, 119.

[166] Hacket, *SR*, Part II, 137, 141.

[167] *Ibid.*, Part II, 142.

[168] *Ibid.*, Part II, 84-85, 134-135; *Calendar of State Papers, Domestic Series, of the Reign of Charles I. 1638-1639*, ed. John Bruce and William Douglas Hamilton (London, 1871), p. 219.

That no man could ever challenge him of the least Lye?" [169] And yet this passage was written by a man who insisted, earlier in the same biography, that Charles broke faith with Williams! After reading Hacket's account of the manner in which the processes of the judicial system were used or abused to ruin Williams, what is to be thought when Hacket writes of the Five Members as follows?

... How far those five were guilty, I have nothing to say, because plain Force would not let them come to a Tryal. But if they were innocent, why did they not suffer their Practices to see the Light? It had been more to their Honour to be cleared by the Law, than to be protected against the Law:...[170]

There is pathos in Hacket's inability to reconcile fully in his writings what he was emotionally committed to believe about Williams with what he was emotionally committed to believe about the martyr King.

Without trying to give a complete and well developed account of the origins of the Civil War, Hacket deals with some aspects of the problem. He says of the first Parliament of Charles I, that of 1625, that "Here was the Foundation laid of all the Discontents that followed" and that peace might have been preserved "if the People in that, or in any Parliament, had been as good as the King." [171] In a long passage dealing with the approach of civil war in 1642 but also apparently with the causes of the war, he complains of the Presbyterians, who "had wrought a great distast in the Commons at the King, and at all that had his ear and favour"; of impudent scholars; of the corruption resulting from long peace; of wastrels and others, often from good families, who hoped to profit from upheavals; of the ambition of "the Parliament, our continual Hectick," to reduce the King to a shadow of sovereignty; of London, "the Epitome of *England*," which "marr'd all *England*"; and of the French, who did all they could to fan the fires of discord in England.[172] When we compare this list with the corresponding remarks on the factors in the rise and development of the war made by other seventeenth-century writers we can find nothing in it that is singular, but it does show that Hacket has some apprehension of the complexity of society and of historical events. He spares the King, however, for he believes that the Parliament began a war in which "the King was involved without any Fault of his." [173]

---

[169] Hacket, *SR*, Part II, 191. Hacket variously terms Charles "Holy King *Charles*," "a thrice-honour'd King, a most pious Saint, a patient and a crowned Martyr," and "a Prince so pious, so admirable in his Ethicks." *Ibid.*, Part II, 85, 225, 142.

[170] *Ibid.*, Part II, 177.

[171] *Ibid.*, Part II, 9.

[172] *Ibid.*, Part II, 182-183. He repeats his charge against the French, Part II, 223; cf. 216.

[173] *Ibid.*, Part II, 187, 187-188.

Among his remarks on the period of military operations, it is worth noting his views on the King's Army, which, he declares

consisted of as valiant and brave Men, as ever march't upon *English* Ground. If there were somewhat of the Libertine among them, there was nothing but the Hypocrite among the Enemy; whose Sacriledges, Robberies, and Spoils I defer alittle to spread open, and the Foxes skin shall never be able to cover all the Lion. Few Soldiers in the heat of their Blood, in their Hunger and Watchings, in their Necessities, and revengeful Executions make perfect Saints.[174]

However, he does not really concede the charges of debauchery; he praises the daily diligence of the Royalist soldiers at Common Prayer and their great loyalty and service under adversity and suggests that the worst debauchees were "Some scores" of men who were driven into the King's camp by the oppressions of the Parliament but had no real zeal for the King. Even David, he remembers, was defended by men of dubious character when he needed them. Charles's Army failed, not because of riotous living, but because of "neglect of Duties for want of pay" and too much confidence that a cause so just could not fail. "The Law was behind the Parliamentarians," he explains with a touch of irony, "fight, or hang." [175]

Hacket's hero Williams was made Archbishop of York in 1641, but the war proved in most respects merely a continuation of his previous misfortunes. "Was not the Ship well built?" Hacket asks in admiration. "Were not the Ribs of it heart of Oak, which endured a Storm of twenty five Years? and in that long time never enjoy'd a calm Sea?" [176] After arriving at Oxford in January 1645, the prescient Williams, Hacket says, found occasion to warn the King against Cromwell as the most dangerous of his enemies, as a man who "*would climb higher*" and who had "*the properties of all evil Beasts.*" Hacket also represents Williams as advising the King at Oxford sometime later in the first half of the same year to submit to the Parliament but with the preservation of his crown and person and the indemnity of his adherents.[177] Hacket does not mention the kinship Williams has sometimes been supposed to have had with Cromwell, but then perhaps he had not heard of it. He includes the embarrassing tale of his patron's collaboration in the Parliamentarian

---

[174] *Ibid.*, Part II, 194-195.
[175] *Ibid.*, Part II, 203-204.
[176] *Ibid.*, Part II, 4.
[177] *Ibid.*, Part II, 212, 214-215.

capture of the royal fortress of Conway Castle.[178] Williams had acted on good grounds and after considerable provocation, but the event was disastrous to his reputation, at least among those whose emotional commitments did not predispose them to believe, as Hacket did, that "From his Fidelity to his Majesty he never went back an inch." [179]

Warm in his zeal for his two heroes, Hacket was capable also of hatred. His account of Cromwell is the usual Royalist abuse, distinguished only by the high literary quality of the vituperation and by a surprising proposal. He describes Cromwell in the following words:

> that Imp of Satan, compounded of all Vice and Violence, and *Titan*-like Courage, devoid of all Pity and Conscience, the greatest of the Souldiery, and by his Arts greater than them all, waxen to be a *Colossus*, between whose strides the Seas flowed, his Countenance confess'd him to be a Tyrant, . . . He regarded not Parliament, Courts of Law, Patents, Charters, much less any Canons which Holy Church had ever appointed, no, nor the Scriptures of God, in comparison of some new Light shining in the Lanthorn of his own Head: But his way was to govern three Kingdoms by his Armies, the Armies by the Agitators, and the Agitators by himself, whom he shot dead upon the place, if they cross'd his Will; . . . If I had ever met with a more odious Passage than that in St. *Basil*, . . . I would afford it him, . . . *a Morsel fit for the Devil's Stomach.*[180]

He wonders why none of the kings of Europe has avenged the death of Charles and declares boldly that someone ought to assassinate Cromwell. However, "The Cattive Cannibal *Cromwell* lives, and is mighty, cockers his Genius, and abounds in Luxury," and Hacket can only reflect that at least his conscience will afflict him.[181] As the incitement to assassination was written during Cromwell's period of rule, it must have required a certain mild courage, even if the offending passage was intended to remain for the time undisturbed among the author's private papers, but it seems strange in the mouth of this learned and fanciful scholar.

---

[178] *Ibid.*, Part II, 218-221. Cromwell signs his letter to Williams of Sept. 1, 1647, as "cozen," but the relationship is probably imaginary. B. Dew Roberts, *Mitre & Musket: John Williams Lord Keeper, Archbishop of York 1582-1650* (London, Oxford University Press, 1938), pp. 125, 255.

[179] Hacket, *SR*, Part II, 220.

[180] *Ibid.*, Part II, 223-224.

[181] *Ibid.*, Part II, 224-225. This particular advocacy of assassination probably does not conflict with his earlier denunciation of assassination, Part II, 80-81, in his treatment of the murder of Buckingham.

CHAPTER IV

RUSHWORTH AND NALSON

John Rushworth's *Historical Collections* appeared in successive folio volumes over a period of more than forty years. Bibliographical details are tedious, but as certain problems about the publication and content of the *Historical Collections* have to be examined, the following outline may be given. The First Part, without volume number or part number, appeared under the date 1659. Volumes two and three (1680) constituted "The Second Part," volumes four and five (1692) constituted "The Third Part," and volumes six and seven (1701) constituted "The Fourth and Last Part." The work ends with the death of the King in 1649, though Rushworth had once intended to carry it at least as far as the breaking of the Long Parliament in 1653.[1] Rushworth also issued *The Tryal of Thomas Earl of Strafford* (1680), based on shorthand notes he took during this famous trial; though not correctly belonging to the *Historical Collections,* it is sometimes catalogued by librarians as a volume of them.

We need not search long to discover the intellectual origins of the *Historical Collections.* Rushworth's name is perpetuated by the most famous of all printed collections of Civil War documents, but he was not the first in the field either with a printed collection of documents on the war or on other subjects in English history. Edward Husbands' two volumes of ordinances and other documents of the Long Parliament (1642, 1646) and Henry Scobell's two volumes of acts and ordinances of that Parliament and its successors (1651, 1658) had already appeared. The *Cabala: sive Scrinia Sacra* (1654) and the *Ephemeris Parliament-*

---

[1] Rushworth, *HC*, II, preface, sig. B2ᵛ. The British Museum has a printed prospectus dated March 27, 1699, for the Fourth Part, which purports to give information on the number of copies printed of the first three parts. The *Historical Collections* are numbered and paginated in four parts, not in seven volumes, but I refer to the separate volumes by the numbers they would bear if numbered separately. As variations of text exist, at least in the first volume, I should add that I make all my references to the British Museum Reading Room set shelfmarked 2072 f.

aria (1654), which has a preface by Fuller, supplied documentary material for the period of the war's gestation. Among still earlier printed collections of documents were the many editions of statutes issued since the early days of English printing.[2] Since the beginning of the Long Parliament, historical documents, printed and unprinted, had proliferated. The interest of the public in seeing them is suggested by the practice of seventeenth-century historians in reprinting in their histories the more important of those which had already been published. It is interesting to ask whether Rushworth was influenced by the example of the great collection of tracts which his publisher and friend George Thomason was making and whether there is truth in the report that he drew on these tracts in compiling the *Historical Collections*.[3] Unfortunately for the state of our knowledge about an interesting historical connection, evidence to answer these questions seems to be lacking. Rushworth may have relied on printed sources collected by himself rather than by Thomason.

Rushworth (1612?-1690) showed an obsession with public affairs from an early age. With motives that are now hard to determine, he was busy making observations and "collections" long before the fall of the despotism of Charles I. Later, his gatherings of these years provided some of the material for the *Historical Collections*. He says that he "did personally attend and observe all Occurrences of moment" in the eleven years interval of Parliament, whether in the Star Chamber, Court of Honor, the *"Exchequer-Chamber,* when all the Judges of *England* met there upon extraordinary Cases," or "at the Council Table, when great Causes were heard before the King and Council." [4] During this period he *"took with his own Pen* verbatim *(as near as he could)"* his own transcript of the ship-money hearings in the Exchequer Chamber.[5] As convulsions began to shake the monarchy and "matters were agitated at a greater

---

[2] For a survey of these pre-war editions of statutes, see *The Statutes of the Realm. Printed by Command of His Majesty King George the Third. In Pursuance of an Address of the House of Commons of Great Britain,* 11 vols. (London, Dawsons of Pall Mall, 1963), I, xxi-xxiii.

[3] For this report, see J. Granger, *A Biographical History of England, from Egbert the Great to the Revolution,* 4th ed., 4 vols. (London, 1804), IV, 65n. There is a little information on the connection of Rushworth with Thomason in Fortescue's preface to the *Catalogue* of the Thomason Tracts, ed. G. K. Fortescue, 2 vols. (London, For the Trustees of the British Museum, 1908). Lois Spencer, "The Politics of George Thomason," *The Library,* 5th ser., 14 (1959), 24-25, attempts to compare the approaches to the past taken by Rushworh and Thomason.

[4] Rushworth, *HC,* I, preface, sig. [b4]ᵛ. The best life of Rushworth and appraisal of his work is by Firth in the *DNB.* Except where I otherwise indicate, I draw on Firth for biographical information about Rushworth in this chapter.

[5] Rushworth, *HC,* II, preface, sig. Bᵛ.

distance, I was there also," he says, "and went on purpose out of a curiosity to see and observe the passages at the Camp at *Berwick,* at the Fight at *Newborn,* at the Treaty at *Rippon,*" and "at the great Council at *York.*" [6] He was also, though he neglects to make the fact explicit in the *Historical Collections,* a witness of the Marquess of Hamilton's proceedings during Hamilton's first visit to Scotland as commissioner in 1638.[7]

The assembling of the Short and the Long Parliaments provided him with exciting new speeches to listen to and opened a career for him in public affairs. He was made clerk assistant to the House of Commons in the Short Parliament and was used as a messenger by the Long Parliament. When the New Model Army was formed, he became secretary to Sir Thomas Fairfax (his kinsman [8]) and to the council of war. Rushworth's letters written to the Speaker of the House of Commons and to Fairfax's father during the period of his association with the Army contain detailed accounts of military affairs and show the matchless opportunity Rushworth had to observe his beloved public affairs. In the same period, letters written to Rushworth show by their respect and deference how influential the secretary was considered to be. It is a further tribute to his importance that suspicions (presumably unfounded) developed about his possible complicity in the King's execution.[9] When Fairfax resigned his commission rather than invade Scotland, Rushworth continued for a few months as Cromwell's secretary. When his first volume was published, it contained a dedication (later deleted [10]) to Richard Cromwell, written in an avuncular tone, encouraging him to respect the law and to rule with the aid of Parliaments. This advice probably indicates Rushworth's attitude to the government throughout the protectorate. The despotic and unparliamentary aspects of Oliver's rule must have depressed him. He was elected to Parliament in 1657 and, again, to Richard's Parliament in 1659.

---

[6] *Ibid.,* I, preface, sig. c.

[7] Manuscript prospectus for the Second Part of *Historical Collections,* preserved at Longleat House, Coventry Papers, II, f. 119. Cf. Rushworth, *HC,* II, preface, sig. B2, where an allusion to this visit may be concealed by careless phrasing.

[8] Rushworth's autobiographical sketch in Aubrey, *BL,* II, 207.

[9] For a circumstantial account of his supposed complicity, see the statement by Alice Thornton in Thomas Comber, *Memoirs of the Life and Writings of Thomas Comber* (London, 1799), pp. 401-402.

[10] A copy of volume I in the British Museum (1326.k.11) has, in addition to the dedication, a warmly complimentary passage in the preface in which Rushworth addresses "my good and worthy Friends of the Army." This passage may have been added after the fall of Richard. A difficulty in tracing the bibliography of volume I is that it was apparently surreptitiously reprinted with the original date unchanged in the reign of Charles II; see my chapter 1, note 1, above.

During these last years of the Puritan regime, the first volume of his *Historical Collections* was completed. The Puritan authorities revealed some interest in its preparation, for on October 27, 1657, the Council arranged for the establishment of a committee "to read a collection or history compiled by John Rushworth, and give their opinions on it." [11] Whatever the committee may have done, Bulstrode Whitelocke is recorded in the printed edition of his *Memorials* under the date January 1, 1657/8, as saying that "I having lent Mr. *Rushworth* some Manuscripts, he attended me to shew me his Historical Collections, as his Highness had ordered." [12] The relations of Whitelocke and Rushworth are recorded in more detail by Wood:

When the author was fitting this book for the press he made use of certain manuscripts in the hands of Bulstr. Whitlock one of Oliver's lords, and when it was finished he presented it to the view of Oliver himself, but he having no leisure to peruse it, he appointed the said Whitlock to do it Jan. 1657 [i.e., 1657/8], and accordingly running it over more than once, he made some alterations in, and additions to, it. [13]

C. H. Firth in his life of Rushworth in the *Dictionary of National Biography* takes a middle position between these statements. Citing Whitelocke as his authority, he says that Whitelocke "assisted Rushworth by the loan of manuscripts, and supervised the volume before it was sent to press." It will be noticed that the assertion of Whitelocke's *Memorials*, on which Wood may have relied and Firth did rely, is the most favorable to Rushworth's independence of authorship of any of the three. Whatever Whitelocke may have done with the manuscript, the words of the *Memorials* are perfectly compatible with the possibility that nothing happened but an interview of a few minutes in which Whitelocke, a busy man, may have glanced over a few sections of a bulky manuscript. But it must also be noted that Whitelocke's words as reported in the *Memorials* are inconsistent with another account of the same day's events he has given elsewhere. In a manuscript journal of Whitelocke's which has never been published, Whitelocke includes the following entry under the date January 1, 1657/8, the date of his supposed interview with Rushworth: "Letters from Mr Rushworth to Wh. to appoint a time for him to attend

---

[11] *Calendar of State Papers, Domestic Series, 1657-8, Preserved in the State Paper Department of Her Majesty's Public Record Office*, ed. M. A. E. Green (London, 1884), pp. 142-143.

[12] Bulstrode Whitelocke, *Memorials of the English Affairs: ... King Charles the First, to King Charles the Second* (London, 1732), p. 666. Whitelocke's manuscript annals in the British Museum, which form the basis of the printed *Memorials,* break off before this passage is reached.

[13] Wood, *AO,* IV, 282.

Wh. to shew him his Historicall Collections (as his H⁵ had ordered) and thanking Wh. for some manuscripts wᶜh he had lent to Rushworth." [14]

In view of this last statement, we cannot even be positive that the interview took place, much less be positive about what Whitelocke did with the manuscript of Rushworth's book. The passage in the *Memorials* describing the interview may be the careless or mistaken reconstruction of an editor rather than the statement of Whitelocke himself. But even assuming for the sake of argument that Whitelocke did make a reasonably careful examination of the manuscript, its consequences for the content of the manuscript are likely to have been insignificant. In view of the staunchly Parliamentarian – if not strictly, perhaps, Cromwellian – sympathies of Rushworth, and the fact that this early volume of the history only carried the narrative as far forward as the somewhat remote date of 1629, it is unlikely that it ever contained material offensive to the government. Similarly, if Whitelocke made additions to the manuscript, as Wood claims, it is unlikely, in view of Whitelocke's barely Parliamentarian sympathies, that these made it more decidedly Parliamentarian than it was before.

In preparation for examining the interpretation of events expressed in this First Part, it is necessary to understand the mechanics of the expression of opinion in the *Historical Collections*. Rushworth's interpretation must be squeezed out of his selection of documents, the reflections he makes in his prefaces, his scanty commentary on documents and events, and the colorless narrative with which he ties together the various elements of his collection. "The Province I have undertaken," he says,

is to consign to Posterity *Overt-Acts, (Facta, Scripta, Dicta, prout facta, scripta vel dicta sunt)* without either judging of their Qualities, or diving after the secret Reasons of them, in assigning which, Authors many times relate their own *Conceits,* rather than the *true motives* which induced the Actors to such Resolutions.[15]

While he is not quite as sparing of interpretation as these words would suggest, it is usually necessary to hunt and conjecture to see more than

---

[14] This is the diary or journal described in HMC, 3rd Report (London, 1872), p. xiii, Appendix p. 202, as two volumes of "Annals of English affairs from 1605 to 1675." In my chapter V below on Whitelocke I refer to it as Whitelocke's "shorter annals." It has no pagination.

[15] Rushworth, *HC,* VI, 1. Rushworth, *ibid.,* I, preface, sig. [b3]ᵛ, c, professes his impartiality, and, II, preface, sig. A-Aᵛ, says that he will provide the evidence but let the reader act as judge of it. In the latter place he says that the reader is left *"to read to himself his own improvement, Lectures of Prudence, Policy, and Morality."* It thus appears that, as might have been expected, Rushworth adheres to the common didactic view of history.

the broad outline of his views. He is clearly for the Parliamentarian side in the great controversy of course. Whether the religious element in the Parliamentarian cause interested him as well as the political does not transpire, but one may suspect from his relative lack of preoccupation with religious issues that they did not press with much weight upon his mind. There is no parallel in his espousal of the Parliamentarian cause to the Royalist fury of his counterpart Nalson. In his language if not in the more subtle workings of his bias, Rushworth really does try to be neutral with respect to the two contending parties of the war. Only occasionally, very occasionally, does he choose words that reveal his partisan position, as, for example, in his reference – if it is indeed his and not the interpolation of an editor – in his final volume to "The Popish and Malignant Party." [16] His carefully studied pose of neutrality was itself offensive to Royalists; to be neutral was to deny that the guilt of the rebels was self-evident. To please Royalists, Rushworth would have had to go beyond mere treacherous neutralism. One of his contemporary or near contemporary critics complains "that any of his great Admirers may be defied to produce one single Passage, expressing the least Remorse or Penitence for his abetting and concurring in those wicked and impious Actions." [17] The very existence of the *Historical Collections* as a great body of documents edited by a man deeply involved in the Parliamentarian cause hinted that the claims of this cause could be safely exposed to the revelations of documentary evidence.

The First Part was more forthright than the following volumes in its criticisms of the royal government. Moreover, material from the period it covered was by its nature more embarrassing to Royalists than material of a later period after, say, 1637. Rapin observes, perhaps with a

[16] *Ibid.,* VII, 1106.

[17] Arthur Charlet (1655-1722), in his undated notes on *HC,* in *OPH,* XXIII, Appendix p. 226. Charlet, p. 227, gives a backhanded testimony to Rushworth's popularity: "Any Man may easily guess the Tendency of his Books, by the Principles and Actions of his Admirers, who are unanimously all the Dissenting and Republican Party; who, upon all Occasions, appeal to them as an Apology for their past and future Actions; yet it cannot be denied but, thro' the Diligence of the Faction, and the Popularity of his Pretences to write without Remark or Reflection, several unthinking, otherwise honest, Persons have been prevailed upon to give too much Credit and Countenance to Books that deserve neither Praise nor Regard upon any Respect:...." The manuscript prospectus for the Second Part of *Historical Collections* at Longleat House, Coventry Papers, II, f. 118, speaks vaguely of the lack of encouragement Rushworth experienced after the issuance of his first volume, but the problem to which it alludes seems not to have been one of lack of readership. Presumably, too, Rushworth is the well received historian mentioned by Gilbert Burnet, *The Memoires of the Lives and Actions of James and William Dukes of Hamilton and Castleherald* (London, 1677), preface, sig. aᵛ. Cf. Rushworth's commendation of this book of Burnet's, *HC,* II, preface, sig. B2.

touch of exaggeration, that had Rushworth "begun his Collections no higher than with the affairs of the Parliament, of *November* the 3d 1640, the King's friends would doubtless have readily forgiven him. But the Papers of the twenty foregoing years are too hard of digestion, . . ." [18] This volume showed that the war was not groundless, by revealing that misgovernment and cause for suspicion had existed from a time long before the outbreak of warfare, and it revealed the existence of these things in a period in which the opponents of the monarchy were not as yet sufficiently prominent for their misdeeds to divert attention from or to account for the misdeeds and errors of the monarchs. Perhaps not injudiciously, Nalson began his *Impartial Collection* with the Scottish rebellion and contributed only flashbacks to the history of the preceding period.

From Rushworth's own explanation of his starting point it appears that he did originally intend to begin at the date Rapin mentions, but was forced to move his narrative back to 1618 in order to produce a complete rather than fragmentary treatment of the Civil War.[19] Presumably he believed that a historian had to go back that far to uncover at least the more open and evident of the causes of the rebellion. In 1618, too, appeared the great blazing-star and in this phenomenon – though he avoids being explicit – he seems to see political significance.[20] Despite this idea that 1618 is a critical or at least important date in the movement towards the Civil War, Rushworth nowhere attempts systematically to account for its origins. Of course, it is possible to argue that he intended to do so in the later parts but was prevented by the Restoration, which made his old political opinions dangerous to him. It is unlikely, however, that he ever had any such intention: it would be hard to reconcile with his plan to refrain as much as possible from commentary and one suspects also – admittedly, one can do little more than suspect – that he was not a man to whom theoretical expositions of historical events much appealed. His interests like his narrative seem to have been severely and narrowly concentrated on the actual procession of events.

In accordance with these remarks, the First Part of *Historical Collections* is deficient in theory and interpretation, but it does contain, in its earlier pages, an indictment, though largely an indirect one, of the personality and policies of King James. Rushworth pictures in his commentary and in his documents James's unworthy subservience to Spain.

---

[18] Paul de Rapin-Thoyras, *The History of England,* trans. N. Tindal, 2nd ed., 2 vols. (London, 1732-1733), II, 349.
[19] Rushworth, *HC,* I, preface, sig. [b3]-[b3]ᵛ.
[20] *Ibid.,* I, preface, sig. [b3]ᵛ; pp. 8, 10.

We are told that the Spanish marriage was the King's "Darling-Design," that he studied "all the wayes of rendring himself acceptable to *Spain*," that "The Wall of this Island, the English Navy," was allowed to decay in order, if rumor spoke truly, to conciliate Spain, that when Frederick was being dispossessed of the Palatinate, there was only "slender aid from the King of Great *Britain*, to preserve his Childrens Patrimony," and that Raleigh was executed to please Gondomar. James was unstable, Rushworth hints, in his attachment to Protestantism. Being, in addition, "jealous of uncomptrolled Soveraignty, and impatient of his Peoples intermedling with the Mysteries of State," he "had fallen into a great dislike of Parliaments." Rushworth even prints the letter which was sent to Pope Clement VIII in 1599 signed by James and which James blamed on the presumption of a secretary of state.[21]

Rushworth's unflattering picture of Charles I is also found mostly in his First Part. He prints the letters which Pope Gregory XV sent to Charles and Buckingham when they were in Spain, Charles's reply, and the private articles of the Spanish and French marriage treaties. He does, however, confess the constancy of Charles to his religion while he was in Spain. In referring to the directions given by Charles for levying a thousand German horse, he says, "The supposed intent of which German Horse was, as was then feared, to inforce the Excise which was then setting on foot." [22] Thus he makes a suggestion, based upon conjecture at the time of the event, which could not but reflect upon the reputation of Charles.

In the First Part similarly appears an unflattering picture of Laud and the Arminian school. Rushworth says that the Arminian way "in common judgment was inclined to Popery" and that while Laud lived in Oxford he was suspected of inclining to Popish tenets; this latter statement is supported by the quotation of one of Laud's own letters sent in complaint to his patron Neile. Rushworth prints, for the first time, Archbishop Abbot's narrative of his own fall, with its strictures on the ambitious Laud.[23]

One of the passages in this part of *Historical Collections* gave rise to a controversy which seems to vindicate Rushworth by the very diversity of evidence turned up by his critics. Rushworth had printed the text of the speech King James delivered to Parliament on January 30, 1621, but Thomas Frankland, in his *Annals of King James and King Charles the*

[21] *Ibid.*, I, 3, 15, 4-5, 9, 1, 20, 162-163.
[22] *Ibid.*, I, 78-83, 88-90, 169 (cf. 152), 83, 474; Gardiner, *HE*, VI, 222-225, discusses the German horse and the excise proposal.
[23] Rushworth, *HC*, I, 62, 434-457.

First (1681) took issue with a passage in the text which seemed to make the monarchy itself one of the traditional three estates in Parliament or at least to ignore the claim of the clergy to be one of the estates in Parliament. Frankland dismissed Rushworth's text as "a Hodge-podge of the *Collectors*," and printed a version he regarded as authentic, in which the estates were safely restored to their state of Royalist orthodoxy. Nalson also, in turn, took issue with Rushworth's text of the speech and its treatment of the three estates but printed a text of the speech which he regarded as more authentic than that used by Frankland. Then Roger Coke, in his *Detection of the Court and State of England during The Four last Reigns And the Inter-Regnum* (1694; 3rd ed., 1697), referred to the charge against Rushworth with respect to this speech, noted the existence of three different versions of the speech – Rushworth's, Frankland's, and Nalson's – and observed that these all differed from yet another version, that in *"the Record of Parliament."* [24] The difficulty of recovering the accurate substance of speeches and proceedings in the early Stuart Parliaments is well known, and it is unlikely that Rushworth was guilty of the deliberate misrepresentation Nalson suspected. A student of Rushworth's collection might, of course, wonder how, among the various accounts of the speech, the Parliamentarian compiler happened to print one that was especially favorable to his political allegiances. He might also wonder whether, if Rushworth abridged the speech from some longer original text as Nalson suggests, he accurately represented the thought of the original.

Rushworth did not issue the next installment of *Historical Collections* till more than twenty years later. Doubtless the delay was at least partly owing to the unfavorable political climate after the Restoration. Though Rushworth was a member of the Convention Parliament, he did not reappear in the Cavalier Parliament. If he felt the lack of his old closeness to public affairs, it must have gratified him to become secretary to the Lord Keeper, Sir Orlando Bridgeman, in 1667. He was also a member of the three last Parliaments of Charles II, which met in the storm-charged atmosphere of the Popish Plot and the Exclusion crisis. At this time the Second Part of his *Historical Collections* was published.[25]

---

[24] *Ibid.*, I, 21-23; [Thomas Frankland], *The Annals of King James and King Charles the First* (London, 1681), preface to reader, sig. [b2]; pp. 47-50; Nalson, *IC,* I, introd., vi-xiv; Roger Coke, *A Detection of the Court and State of England during The Four Last Reigns And the Inter-Regnum,* 3rd ed., 2 vols. (London, 1697), I, "An Apology to the Reader," p. 8.

[25] The two volumes of this part were in print by Feb. 17, 1679/80, for Wood in a letter to (presumably) Ralph Sheldon of that date says that they have "lately come to this place." Bodleian MS Tanner 456 f. 22.

C. H. Firth states in his life of Rushworth in the *Dictionary of National Biography* that "Certain passages of the manuscript" of this part "were suppressed to satisfy the scruples of the secretary of state." Such suppressions were desired by the government, but they do not appear to have been made. On July 19, 1677, Rushworth sent the last papers of the Second Part to Secretary of State Coventry.[26] The attitude taken by Coventry can be read in a letter of September 6, 1677, written by Rushworth to Thomas Thynne, M. P. Rushworth says that Coventry has returned his papers and "excepted against nothing but some passages in the beginning of the Parlament the 3ᵈ of Novembᵉʳ 1640, not but that he knew the passages mentioned were spoken by the Lord Digby, Lo: Faulkland, Culpeper Hide &c. Some reflecting upon the Bishops, others upon the Judges, others upon Projects &c." Rushworth thereupon agreed with Coventry to omit these offending passages and to break off his narrative before the meeting of the Long Parliament.[27] There can be little doubt, however, that the Second Part as actually published does contain those very passages to which Coventry objected. The publication does not break off, as Rushworth's words indicate it would, before his narrative reaches the Long Parliament. The title page accurately states that in the Second Part the story is carried as far as the beginning of the Long Parliament and includes "some Remarkable Passages therein during the first Six Months."

Towards the end of this part, accordingly, a longish section composed of speeches delivered in the early and undivided Long Parliament is included. One finds Hyde speaking against the Court of the President of the North and against the ship-money judges; [28] Digby and Culpeper against various grievances, including ship-money and monopolies; [29] Falkland against abuses in the church; [30] and other persons against vari-

---

[26] Rushworth to Sir Henry Coventry, July 19, 1677, Coventry Papers at Longleat House, II, f. 115; there is a summary of this letter in HMC, 4th Report, Part I (London, 1874), p. 231. The manuscript prospectus for Rushworth's Second Part at Longleat House, Coventry Papers, II, f. 118, says that Rushworth "hopes to perfect" this part "in, or before Hilary Terme next 1676" and that some persons have already contributed financially towards it. Rushworth's receipt of May 29, 1676, for a contribution or subscription payment towards the Second Part is in the Victoria and Albert Museum, Forster MS 462.

[27] BM Add. MS 32095 f. 36; this letter is summarized in HMC, 5th Report, Part I (London, 1876), pp. 317-318, and is printed at length in my article, "Note on a Case of Seventeenth Century Censorship," *N & Q*, 211 (1966), 262-263, on which the present discussion of the censorship of the Second Part is based.

[28] Rushworth, *HC*, III, 1336-1337, 1340-1341. See also III, Appendix pp. 238 and 235 (correctly 244-245) for Hyde against the ship-money judges.

[29] *Ibid.*, III, 1337-1338.

[30] *Ibid.*, III, 1342-1343. Presumably it is to these speeches that Charlet alludes, *OPH*, XXIII, Appendix pp. 229-230.

ous abuses including those of the bishops. Marginal notes identifying most of the speakers draw the reader's attention to the fact that they either accompanied the King at Oxford during the hostilities or (as in the case of Denzil Holles and others) otherwise served the Stuarts at some stage of their career. These notes could hardly have avoided annoying Royalists who read the Second Part, reviving, as they did, one of the scandals of the Royalists – that they had shared in the attack of the Long Parliament on the abuses of the government of Charles I. Even Clarendon, when he wrote his *History* and *Life*, could not bring himself to face this scandal directly. Whether the pointed notes were part of the material presented to Coventry for his scrutiny may be doubted, but the passages to which they are attached fit Rushworth's description in the letter above of the passages to which Coventry objected.

Assuming, then, that the identification is established, the question arises: why did Rushworth change his intention and print material to which official objection had been made and which he had agreed to suppress? According to Rushworth's statement, twice made in this part of the *Historical Collections*, when he first came to the press with this part he intended to terminate it with the meeting of the Long Parliament.[31] Had he done so, he would of course have been acting in accordance with the letter above. The explanation he gives for carrying his story into the proceedings of the Long Parliament is somewhat cloudy, but the thoughts entangled in the prose seem to be that the early actions in the Long Parliament are intimately connected with the events that preceded it and are useful to elucidate those events.[32] The explanation at any rate in no way disposes of the agreement with Coventry. Perhaps for some reason Coventry changed his mind and a new agreement was reached. Perhaps some other circumstances intervened. It is most likely, however, that Rushworth simply took advantage of the lapse of the Licensing Act and the distraction of the government in the midst of the furore of the Popish Plot and Exclusion Crisis to print material which the government no longer had complete power to suppress and to print it, moreover, adorned with provocative notes.

The Second Part of the *Historical Collections* proved to be the last Rushworth lived to see in print. His later years make an unhappy story. Wood says that "After the dissolution of Oxford parliament, he lived

---

[31] Rushworth, *HC*, II, preface, sig. B2v, III, 1334. In a letter to Sir Harbottle Grimstone, May 7, 1681, printed by S. R. Gardiner, *N & Q*, 6th ser., 5 (1882), 325, Rushworth says that he "hudled upp" the passages dealing with proceedings in the Long Parliament "of a suddaine into" his Second Part.
[32] Rushworth, *HC*, II, preface, sig. B2v, III. 1334.

very retiredly and obscurely within the city of Westminster." [33] Dugdale, who received financial and other aid from Rushworth towards the publication of his *Monasticon* during the Interregum and seems, despite their sharply varying politics, to have retained some kindness for him, reports on his status in a letter of November 8, 1681. "I confesse," he says,

I have an antient acquaintance wth M[r] John Rushworth; but have not seen him this Twelve months; nor had I then, but that I casually met him in S[t] Margarets Churchyard at Westm[r]. For though I was many times at his lodging, early and late, they always denyed him. I doubt he is now very poore, w[ch] is the reason y[t] he thus doth abscond.[34]

Wood says that he was eventually committed as a prisoner for debt to the King's Bench Prison and that he was a prisoner for "the six last years (or thereabouts) of his life"; his commitment probably can be dated in 1683 or 1684.[35] Rushworth's poverty seems to have aroused the disapproval of Wood, who sternly notes that he twice had an opportunity to enrich himself, first as secretary to Fairfax and afterwards as secretary to Bridgeman.[36] Perhaps Rushworth simply failed to live up to the degree of villainy Wood expected in a Parliamentarian. Despite all misfortunes, Rushworth continued his work as a historian: in a letter of 1687 he mentions that he is "perfeting" his account of the First and Second Civil Wars – probably he simply means all the unpublished portion of the *Historical Collections* – "but the times favors not the comeing of it forth." [37] A little less than two years later Aubrey wrote that "Yesterday I saw Mr. Rushworth: which was a great mortification. He hath quite lost his memory with drinking brandy. . . . His landlady wiped his nose like a child." [38] When death had ended these degradations, it also prevented the bestowal of a gift which the Duke of Newcastle – son of the Royalist general – had intended for Rushworth. A pathetic letter from Rush-

---

[33] Wood, *AO,* IV, 282.

[34] Sir William Dugdale to (presumably) Anthony à Wood, Bodleian MS Wood F41 f. 148. Perhaps Dugdale was Wood's informant for the above statement about Rushworth's retired life.

[35] Wood, *AO,* IV, 282, 284. Six years of imprisonment would suggest 1684 as the date of committment, but Dugdale in a letter to Wood, May 1, 1683, contradicting a report that Rushworth has died, says that he is "a prisoner (as I heare for debt) in the Marshalsie, or Kings Bench." Bodleian MS Wood F41 f. 163. Rushworth may have been committed more than once, so the exact dating of his misfortunes remains speculative. For an allusion to still earlier financial difficulties of Rushworth's, see Andrew Marvell to Sir Henry Thompson, Jan., 1674/5, *The Poems & Letters of Andrew Marvell,* ed. H. M. Margoliouth, 2nd ed., 2 vols. (Oxford, Clarendon Press, 1952), II, 316.

[36] Wood, *AO,* IV, 281, 282.

[37] Aubrey, *BL,* II, 208. It appears from Rushworth's letter of 1681 cited in note 31 above that Rushworth was then at work on the Third Part and hoped "to haue it made publique, in (if not before) Michaelmas Tearme next 1681."

[38] Aubrey, *BL,* II, 209.

worth's daughter Katharine begs the Duke for charity on behalf of herself and her sisters. "When your servant by your Grace's order," she writes, "came to bring your second present, my father was newly dead, which he said he would acquaint your Grace withal and also where we his children live, but did not leave any money, ..." [39]

The Third and Fourth Parts of the *Historical Collections*, appearing after his death, carried on their title pages the assurance that they had been "Fitted for the Press in his Life-time," but Rushworth's prefaces, which had been the most intimate of his contacts with the reader in the previous parts and included his interesting reflections on historical method, were now continued without distinction by some anonymous hand or hands. The absence of Rushworth's own prefaces casts some doubt on whether he really did wholly prepare these volumes for the press and deprives us of a further view of his personality. In the prefaces only did one gain an impression of Rushworth as a human being – rightly or wrongly, the impression being that of a competent and masterful man, sardonic and well acquainted with the world's deceits, who knew public events well and felt perfectly at home wherever they were taking place. The problem of whether the remaining contents of the Third and Fourth Part are fully Rushworth's or not need cause little trouble in attempting to recover Rushworth's interpretation of the war, for these parts contain little explicit interpretation in their treatment of either men or events. Their colorlessness is no argument against the authenticity of these parts as products of Rushworth's labor, for Rushworth imposed a self-censorship after the Restoration and apart from his use of the annotated speeches by Hyde and others and some comments on Laud and other matters in the preface, his Second Part is as politically unassertive as the Third and Fourth.

In dealing with the hostilities and their outcome, the Third and Fourth Part preserve a studied neutrality. About Rushworth's views on Cromwell we can conclude almost nothing. We are told on one occasion that "indeed it may well be presumed" that Cromwell "was not like to be behind-hand in Artifices for removing of those that would have removed him," [40] but it is impossible to base any idea of what Rushworth thought about Cromwell on isolated remarks such as this. Once Monck is called "the famous Instrument of King *Charles* the Second's happy Restau-

---

[39] Katharine Rushworth to Duke of Newcastle, April 16, 1691, in HMC, 13th Report, Appendix, Part II, i.e., Portland II (London, 1893), pp. 164-165, or original on deposit in British Museum (Portland MSS, "Cavendish Papers 1661-1695," f. 499).

[40] Rushworth, *HC*, VI, 3.

ration," [41] but again it is impossible to depend on such slight evidence, though there is nothing unlikely in the idea that this observation did represent Rushworth's genuine opinion both at the time of the Restoration and later.

John Nalson (1637-1686) [42] seems almost a caricature of the frenzied Tory clergyman of the reign of Charles II. During his childhood and his university years at Cambridge he experienced the life of a country torn by Civil War and deprived of its accustomed monarchical government, but whatever his observations then did to mold him his ideas most clearly bear the mark, not of the Civil War, but of the political and religious struggles of the latter part of the reign of Charles II. In his great debt to this period he contrasts with all the other Royalist historians considered in this study, but the contrast involves no greater understanding on his part; he was simply up to date in his prejudices. In the second half of the 1670's he became a pamphleteer on the side of the government. While carrying on an acrimonious pamphlet warfare against Whigs and Dissenters, he was punished by the House of Commons for one of his publications. His zeal in the good cause of monarchy and church is indicated by his declaration in his *Impartial Collection* that the rebels and dissidents of the time of Charles I had the *"Great Design of overthrowing the best Monarchy, and Extirpating the most Apostolical Church in the whole World."* [43] He further insists that

Rebellion, . . . is a Crime so black and horrid in the sight of God and all good Men, that no excuses can Palliate or Extenuate, nor any Circumstances of Hardships or Oppressions, Injustice or Wrongs can justifie; since it is utterly inconsistent with not only all the Rules of Christianity, which teaches us not to resist the Powers which are ordained of God, under a penalty of Damnation, which is a danger and a loss of so vast Extent, as that the loss of Liberty, Goods, and even Life it self, which are the utmost we can suffer from unjust Men, are but trifles if compared with it. . . .[44]

---

[41] *Ibid.*, V, 303.

[42] The best life of Nalson and study of his work is by C. H. Firth in the *DNB*. For Nalson's date of birth as established by his date of baptism, see *The Registers of the Parish Church of Leeds, from 1612 to 1639: Third and Fourth Books*, ed. George Denison Lumb (Leeds, The Publications of the Thoresby Society, vol. III, 1895), p. 217. There is a work by Roger Coke called *Treatises of the Nature of Man. . . . Also the History of the Life of Sir Edward Coke. With Remarks upon it. And Reflections upon the Impartial Collections of John Nalson L. L. D.* (London, 1685), but the promised material on Nalson is missing from the only two copies of it, both incomplete, which I have been able to trace (one owned by The Library Company of Philadelphia and the other on deposit in The John Rylands Library) and possibly was prevented from appearing by some accident which left the printing of the work unfinished.

[43] Nalson, *IC*, II, ep. ded. to Charles II, sig. A^v-A2.

[44] *Ibid.*, II, 560.

In another of his works, *A True Copy of the Journal of The High Court of Justice* that tried Charles I (1684), he puts his hatred for the Dissenters of Charles II's time in the form of a political aphorism with the declaration that "*Rebellion* with its portentous Retinue, is as naturally included in *Separation* as Fire in a Flint." [45] Despite this hatred, one feels that the Dissenters were an object of morbid fascination to him, that he was the kind of persecutor who is attracted, with dread, loathing, and a perverted kind of love, to the very thing he crusades against. But the Church of England, he found, shared none of the treasonable possibilities of the Dissenters. In the same work, more than a little incongruously in view of the events that were to follow a few years later, he informs James, the Duke of York, to whom the volume is dedicated, that the Church of England "*hath not the least blemish of Disloyalty in Her Beautiful Face.*[46]

The two bulky folio volumes of his *An Impartial Collection of the Great Affairs of State* (1682, 1683, respectively),[47] contain a vast amount of information but share enough of the spirit of his pamphlets to tempt one to regard them as simply further products of his pamphleteering. The purposes of the *Impartial Collection*, as summarized by himself, are to counteract "Partial and False Accounts of the late Tragical Revolutions," to assist posterity in shunning rebellion, and, above all, to vindicate the government and servants of Charles I.[48] In addition to or underlying all of these is the simple desire to provide a counterwork to Rushworth. He contends "That Mr. *Rushworth* hath concealed Truth, endeavoured to vindicate the prevailing Detractions of the late Times as well as their Barbarous Actions, and with a kind of rebound Libel'd the [present?] Government at second hand." [49] Rushworth, he finds, has been misleading in his selection of texts to print and in his abridgment of his texts. Indeed, he may even have made additions to them in order to support his Parliamentarian doctrines. He has suppressed loyal speeches but has been sedulous to print speeches that deal with grievances in order "to insinuate into the Credulous and Unwary, that the heavy Complaints

---

[45] John Nalson, ed., *A True Copy of the Journal of The High Court of Justice, for the Tryal of K. Charles I.* (London, 1684), p. 125.

[46] *Ibid.,* ep. ded. to James, Duke of York, sig. [A2].

[47] The first volume was in print by Jan. 14, 1681/2, as the Earl of Longford in a letter of that date to the Duke of Ormonde says, "There is a book lately come out written by one Nalson which detects Mr. Rushworth of very great partiality and untruths in his last [sic] collections. I have read but very little of it, . . ." HMC, Ormonde n.s. VI (London, 1911), p. 293. Despite the statement of Longford, Nalson was not specifically replying to Rushworth's Second Part and tends to direct his criticism instead against the First Part.

[48] Nalson, *IC,* I, introd., pp. ii-iii.

[49] *Ibid.,* I, introd., p. v.

of Grievances were *Vox Populi* and the universal and just Cry of the Nation; and by Consequence, That the King, his Ministers and Government were wholly unjust, oppressive, cruel and tyrannical." [50]

Nalson departs very sharply from Rushworth's principle of avoiding interpretation. His collection abounds in wordy and bitter expressions of his political convictions and in his opinions about the successive events and documents he deals with. As he says, "I have not tied my self strictly to the Rules of a Bare Collector, but indulged my self in the Liberty of an Historian." [51] Accordingly, his views on the war, so far as the abortive nature of his work permits him opportunity to express them, are easily recovered. He intended to continue the collection to the death of Charles I [52] but died before he was able to publish more than his two volumes, leaving the narrative suspended at a point a little beyond the attempt on the Five Members.

He begins his narrative proper with the Scottish rebellion of 1637 but reaches further back, without regard for the limits set by this opening date, to include a long exposition of the origins of the English Civil War. To the familiar theme that it was principally caused by Protestants disaffected to the Church of England he adds the twist that their disaffection to this church was originally encouraged by Papists. In order to discuss the Protestant movement that Nalson has in mind, the present writer has adopted the rather awkward terms, "Protestants disaffected" and "Protestant disaffection." Nalson himself speaks variously of "the Nonconforming-Puritans," "the Dissenters," "the Non-conformitans," "the Dissenting Protestants," "the Reforming, or as they were then called, The Puritanical Party," "the Schismatical Party of *Puritans, Presbyterians, Independents, Anabaptists,* &c.," and, referring to the period of the early Long Parliament, "the Factious and Nonconforming Party, who then went under the common Name of *Presbyterians,* though Composed of all the Differing Sects of *Independents, Anabaptists, Brownists, Antinomians,* &c." [53] Despite this profusion of names – the list is not exhaustive – it is not clear precisely what people he is talking about; he seems to have a comparison with the Dissenters of the reign of Charles II constantly in mind and to some degree he probably projects his image of the Dissenters back into the days before the outbreak of hostilities.

---

[50] *Ibid.,* I, introd., p. xxv.
[51] *Ibid.,* I, introd., p. ii.
[52] Title pages of both volumes of *IC.* The OPH, XXIII, Appendix pp. 232-240, prints Nalson's description of the intended contents of the next volume which will, he says, p. 232, deal with "the four Years Civil War."
[53] Nalson, *IC,* I, introd., pp. xxxviii, xlviii, lii, lviii, lxi, lxxviii, lxiv.

The Marian Exiles, according to his interpretation, on their return home began to instil their doctrines, not only into the populace, but into the nobility and gentry. Then the Papists, seeing an opportunity to ruin the Reformation, entered "in at the back-door of Schism and Separation" and "joyned hands with the Nonconforming-Puritans, to bring Ruin and Desolation upon this Church and Kingdom." [54] He relates two long entertaining stories to show that the Papists, in the early years of Elizabeth's reign, followed a deliberate policy of encouraging Protestant disaffection to the Church of England.[55] At the end of the second of these stories, he remarks that "From this Narrative we may observe, that the chief Rise and Original of our unhappy Divisions and Separations is to be fetcht from the devilish Policy of the Papists, counterfeiting a Design to advance the Reformation of the Protestant Religion to a greater Purity," and he draws the moral that in the interest of preserving Protestantism the contemporary Dissenters should return to the Church of England.[56]

This last observation may seem to betray its author. Is he then only expounding his theory and narrating his unlikely stories to make a glib case against the Rome-hating Dissenters? The answer is in all likelihood no. The theme of a connection between Protestant disaffection to the church and Popery appears too frequently in his writings to be a mere pretense. Whatever private reservations he may have had, there can be little doubt that the connection was one on which he had brooded. He is fond of finding similarities between Presbyterians and Papists. We learn that both believe that no faith is to be kept with heretics, that both are cruel and believe in "propagating Religion by Fire and Sword," and that Presbyterians and Jesuits "agree in placing the ultimate Sovereignty in the People." [57] After referring to the association he believes Richelieu had with the rebellions in Charles's three kingdoms, he proposes to give posterity

some Reason to suspect that there may be dangerous Confederacies even between the Pretenders to Reformation, and the greatest Papists though for different Ends, the Reformers to secure themselves from Justice by embroyling the Nation, and the Popish Ministers of Foreign Nations, to keep us busie at home.[58]

[54] *Ibid.,* I, introd., p. xxxviii.
[55] *Ibid.,* I, introd., pp. xxxix-xlviii.
[56] *Ibid.,* I, introd., p. xlviii.
[57] *Ibid.,* II, 682, 539; I, 495 marg. note. Cf. his *High Court of Justice,* p. 124.
[58] Nalson, *IC,* II, 897. He professes, I, 262, to suspect that some of those belonging to the confederacy against Charles I in Scotland were intending to introduce Popery there.

His pamphlet *Foxes and Fire-brands* (1680), in which he first published his two stories about the Papists encouraging Protestant disaffection in the early years of Elizabeth's reign, deals with the connection between separation and Popery. In the same vein his pamphlet *A Letter from a Jesuit at Paris, to His Correspondent in London; Shewing the most effectual way to ruine the Government and Protestant Religion* (1679) reveals the similarity of the tactics of Whigs and Popish conspirators.

The Papists having thus helped to establish English Protestant disaffection to the church, the disaffected vigorously cultivated the movement. They gained converts high and low and at length began to oppose Queen Elizabeth in the House of Commons.[59] They continued their opposition under the Stuarts and at last entered into open warfare with the monarchy in 1642. Nalson asserts that "the Reforming, or as they were then called, The Puritanical Party, Combined with the Popular and Discontented, were all along ever since the times of Queen *Elizabeth*, the Occasions of all the Disturbances, and Convulsions of State, the perpetual disturbers of the Peace of the Kingdom." To advance their ends, they used the charges that the government intended to introduce popery and arbitrary power; though extremely effective, these charges were of course without foundation.[60]

Nalson stresses the importance of religion in the origins of the war more strongly than most seventeenth-century English historians of the war. He has little opportunity to speak of its role in the ensuing period of actual warfare because of the abortive nature of his *Impartial Collection*. He does, however, mention that the cry of Popery, which had been the support of the rebellion, cost the lives of Charles and Laud, and that

to the shame of the Common Christianity, even Religion was with violence dragged into the Field, and as the *Turks* treat their miserable *Asapi,* posted in the front of Rebellion, to take off the edge of those Loyal Swords which were drawn in the Defence of Her and Royal Property.[61]

What Nalson thought about the sincerity of the religion of the rebels is not clear; he is of course profoundly unsympathetic to them and aware of their selfish motives – he points out the personal poverty and financial desperation of Oliver Cromwell and other members of the popular party

---

[59] *Ibid.*, I, introd., pp. xlviii-xlix.
[60] *Ibid.*, I, introd., pp. lxi, lxxviii. Cf. the similar passage, p. lxxviii, in which he blames "the Discontented, Ambitious and Popular Men, striking in with the Schismatical Party of *Puritans, Presbyterians, Independents, Anabaptists,* &c." for the war.
[61] *Ibid.*, I, 467, 1.

before their rebellion [62] – but he does not follow the practice of many of his fellow Royalists in raging at the rebels as hypocrites.

Despite the furious loyalty he expresses in his writing of the non-documentary parts of the *Impartial Collection*, Nalson has a curious habit of making statements that betray the Royalist position at certain points. Does he do so deliberately or by accident? It is always possible that he worked a little too swiftly to consider his statements carefully in all their aspects; the great lengths of his sentences and the anger with which he so often writes suggest the impetuous rather than the considered writer. His passage on the origins of Charles's levies of ship-money, though not explicit,[63] suggests that he was not convinced of their legality; probably had he been convinced he would not have left his opinion in doubt. But his passage on the state of the nation at the assembling of the Long Parliament in 1640 is explicit and rather surprising on a number of subjects including ship-money:

It [the Parliament] was assembled to redress the grievances of the Subjects, to compose the differences between the two Nations of *England* and *Scotland* and prevent a War, to reform Religion, to ease the People of the illegal Pressures and Exactions by Projects Monopolies and Shipmoney, and to do all those great and glorious things which are in the Power of a Parliament towards the Establishment of Religion, Liberty and Peace. . . .[64]

These hopeful prospects were blasted by the activities of "the Fermenting Party" and England instead underwent a Civil War. At this time "The Nation was big to be delivered from the Pressures of those then exclaimed against illegal and arbitrary Impositions, but, they found *Rehoboam's* harsh Counsel practised upon them and the little finger impositions turned into Loins, the Rods into Scorpions, ..." [65] Though he exclaims against the popular fiction, used as a propaganda device by the enemies of the monarchy, that the government was popishly inclined, the following passage reveals the presence of popish (apparently Jesuit) troublemakers at the court. He speaks of

the secret influence, which Cardinal *Richelieu* and the Jesuits gave both to the *Scotish* Commotions and *English* Rebellion. For these Serpents who in disguise crawled both about the Court and Country mutually exasperated them one against the other; animating the King against his Subjects, as Designing against his Crown and Dignity, and the Subjects against their Prince, as aiming at the Subversion of their Laws, Liberties and Religion.[66]

[62] *Ibid.*, II, 510.
[63] *Ibid.*, I, 656-659.
[64] *Ibid.*, I, 480.
[65] *Ibid.*, I, 480-481.
[66] *Ibid.*, I, 467.

The idea that secret agents had been at work, creating trouble between monarch and people, gains support from Charles I himself, who alluded mysteriously in his scaffold speech to *"ill Instruments between"* King and Parliament, who had been *"the chief Cause of all this Bloodshed"*; [67] it is possible that Nalson has this speech in mind, but if he has, the passage still suggests that Charles was over-easy to deceive and unduly tolerant of popish influences in high places.

Though Nalson defends the decorum fostered in the church by Laud (it was intended "to avoid those Divisions which the Papists had sown among us, and from which they hoped to reap a plentiful harvest in our Ruine") and venerates episcopacy, yet he says that Falkland, Digby, and Grimstone, who opposed the Root and Branch movement in the House of Commons, "were of the King's Mind for Reformation not Extirpation." [68] Again, this opinion can be thrust back upon Charles himself, for the *Eikon Basilike* seems to say, in its opening passages, that the King was convinced of the need for reforms in the church, and Nalson does not doubt the authenticity of the *Eikon*. But whether Nalson was thinking of the *Eikon* or not, the remark is a larger concession to the enemies of Laudianism than purists of the Heylyn stamp could be expected cheerfully to accept. Even the clergy of the Convocation which met with the Short Parliament are not spared one of Nalson's criticisms, as he speaks of "the future Loyalty and sufferings of most of that Convocation, though they will not warrant their proceedings from mistakes, or Justifie every thing in those Canons, even since, by a moderate and healing Parliament not thought fit to be confirmed." [69]

Surely Nalson is only writing carelessly, however, when he says that the lives of Charles and Laud were brought "to infamous and untimely Ends." [70] Admittedly, this usage has some logical support – it is possible to die a glorious death at the hands of enemies so cruel as to use means of execution that are *usually* shameful – yet after all, the usage is little better than slovenly: "infamous" cannot be the right word to express Nalson's meaning in this passage. That he could fall into such a solecism casts doubt upon whether he means what he seems to say in some of his other surprising passages. However, there is no doubt that most of these passages are too elaborate to be mere slips. The exposure is an exposure of thought, not just a slip of words. Perhaps Nalson in the laborious historical researches about which he complained was led to deviate somewhat

[67] Rushworth, *HC,* VII, 1429
[68] Nalson, *IC,* I, 519, 773.
[69] *Ibid.,* I, 667.
[70] *Ibid.,* I, 467.

from the extremer Royalist views of the rebellion and to adopt opinions inconsistent with the constant Royalist fury of his writing. Perhaps he simply began his historical research and writing from a more moderate standpoint than one would at first suspect from a survey of his vehement expressions.

Nalson gives space to the criticisms of the government offered in the early Long Parliament by later Royalists such as Falkland – he is very warm in his commendation of Falkland, "that Excellent Man" [71] – and he does not fall into the assumption of some Royalist writers that an embarrassing stage in the career of many prominent Royalists never existed. He quotes Falkland against ship-money, against Finch, and against episcopal abuses; Digby for triennial Parliaments; and (for a Royalist of less perfect allegiance) Sir Edward Dering on religious and political abuses.[72] Speaking earlier of the Short Parliament, Nalson admitted that "the Presbyterian Faction . . . had drawn in a great Party of Loyal Gentlemen with their fair pretences." [73] He takes the part of the King in the attempt on the Five Members and believes that the King had evidence to prove his charges, but that the evidence was stifled when the King's papers were captured after the Battle of Naseby. All the same, he confesses that the attempt caused dismay even among the King's supporters. Once he remarks that the attempt "did not escape odd Interpretations, even from those who professed themselves his Friends." [74] Thus he seems, for a moment, to touch upon that dislike of lukewarm or imperfect Royalists which is found in Hobbes and certain other Royalists, but generally he is content to pass over Royalist criticism of the monarchy without trying to censure it. There is, in any case, a streak of servility in Nalson which suggests that he was not likely to be very severe on members of the upper classes or question their superior comprehension of state affairs so long as they redeemed their passing errors with ultimate loyalty.

Probably Nalson needed less of a struggle against his Royalist prejudices to deal in a moderate and fairminded way with the Irish rebels. He could have the satisfaction of feeling that he was being decent to people that Puritans especially loathed. While he agrees that the Irish rebellion was cruel and outrageous, he thinks that its cruelty has been overstressed by partial writers and he notes that nothing is usually said about the cruelty exercised on the Irish by the English governors who ruled Ireland

[71] *Ibid.*, I, 654.
[72] *Ibid.*, I, 654-656, 725-726, 768-771, 729-732, 516-517.
[73] *Ibid.*, I, 341.
[74] *Ibid.*, II, 820, 829, 841.

after Strafford's departure for the Scottish wars and English politics.[75] Besides the cruelty of the governors, which inflamed the disturbances once they had begun, the causes of the Irish rebellion were fear of the English Puritans, the example of the rebellion in Scotland (in accordance with his interest in the connections between Protestant disloyalty and Popery, he suggests that Argyle was in conspiracy with the Irish), the removal of Strafford, and the desire of shaking off the supremacy of the English crown.[76] He notes the wickedness of the Irish rebels in giving rise to reports that they had the approval of the King for their deeds and the great impression that these reports "made in the minds of the Common People of *England*." [77]

In view of what has been said about Nalson's historical views on the war, it appears that the *Impartial Collection* cannot be regarded as a mere Royalist diatribe unintelligently expressing High Tory opinions. Though Nalson no doubt intended the work to be in considerable part a tract for the times against the Dissenters and Whigs, he did not grossly oversimplify issues, though he often misunderstood them, and he was capable of accepting the validity of some of the criticisms of the government of Charles I. Compared with the Royalist diatribe of the great Sir William Dugdale, which establishes an uncompromising antithesis between rebels and King, the *Impartial Collection* appears as a relatively responsible attempt at historical understanding.

In preparing this work, Nalson was allowed to copy and even borrow official papers, but it is difficult to be certain of the exact relationship in which he stood to the government. Addressing Charles II, he says that "*Your Majesties Gracious Incouragement gave the first Life and Being to this Work,*" [78] but one would read too much into this statement by taking it as a declaration that the *Impartial Collection* had official sponsorship and support. The title pages declare it to be published by the King's "Special Command," but there is, of course, a difference between publication and writing. The following pleas suggest that Nalson did not receive regular financial support from the government for his historical labors.

Proud of what he had done as a pamphleteer and historian, he longed for suitable encouragement in the form of church preferment, asking, at various times, for the mastership of Trinity College, Cambridge, for the

---

[75] *Ibid.*, II, introd., pp. vi-viii.
[76] *Ibid.*, II, 536-539, 560.
[77] *Ibid.*, II, 894-895.
[78] *Ibid.*, II, ep. ded. to Charles II, sig. A.

deanery of Worcester, and for prebends at Ely and Westminster.[79] In a
letter of 1683 to the Archbishop of Canterbury he broadly hints that he
would like to share in the rumored "distributions of his Maties Bounty"
and asserts that

A little Oyle will make y[e] Wheels go Easy, w[ch] truly hitherto, w[th]out
complaining, I haue found a very heauy draught. My Lord, pardon me I
beseech yo[r] Grace according to yo[r] accustomed goodness, if I say it is some
discouragem[t] to see others, who I am sure haue not outstript me in y[e]
Race of Loyalty & hearty indeauours to serue y[e] King & Church, carry
away the prize.[80]

A letter written by Nalson about a year later to the same recipient abuses
Rushworth soundly and gives a curious insight into how seriously Nalson
took himself and how seriously he took the idea of a historian and a
clergyman. He says that Rushworth sometimes makes such errors "as
may giue one that is very serious y[e] temptation to Smile, both at his Folly
& confidence in publicacon." One can read his self-importance and self-
pity, perhaps his diligence, and even a faint threat that he will give up
his task altogether if he is not rewarded, in his words in the same letter
that

I haue filld' the pages of my Rushworth wth correccons & Supplements, &
if it please God to giue me life & health, & the Gouernm[t] think it worth y[e]
while to haue those matters more fairly & truely rep[re] sented to posterity;
It shall not stick at my part, if it be not done.[81]

Within a month he is writing to the Archbishop advancing his claim to a
certain "Sine Cura" that has taken his eye and assuring the Archbishop
that "it is not great things I seek, but something that may make me Easy,
& inable me to do some good while I am in y[e] World." [82] The authorities
do not seem to have been very responsive to his pleas for advancement,
but he did at least get the prebend at Ely.

Yet these revelations do not touch upon the whole of Nalson's personality and accomplishment. A more attractive, if still self-pitying, side
becomes evident in his edition of the journal of the trial of Charles I. He

[79] Nalson to the Archbishop of Canterbury, Aug. 14, 1680, July 21, 1683, Sept. 13,
1683, Bodleian MSS Tanner 37 f. 117, Tanner 34 ff. 79, 135; Nalson to Charles II,
n.d. (copy only), Bodleian MS Tanner 103, f. 247.
[80] Nalson to the Archbishop of Canterbury, July 14, 1683. Bodleian MS Tanner 34
f. 80.
[81] Nalson to the Archbishop of Canterbury, June 9, 1684, Bodleian MS Tanner 32
f. 65.
[82] Nalson to the Archbishop of Canterbury, July 7, 1684, Bodleian MS Tanner 32
f. 84.

has toiled, he writes there, in the slow and heavy work of the *Impartial Collection*, which he wishes had fallen on abler shoulders, "with such Assiduity and Zeal, as hath not been extreme propitious either to my Health or Estate." Nevertheless, he finds that

such is the multiplicity of the swelling Matter; so great is the Difficulty of sifting out Truth, notwithstanding the little distance of Time; and the Materials for Composing those Collections are to be drawn together from so many remote and distant Quarters, that it cannot be rationally expected by others, I am sure from former tryal, it is not to be hoped by my self, that a Work of that Nature and Proportion should be finished without the assistance of a considerable time.

This extended time is all the more necessary, he adds pathetically, because in his desire to complete the work he is obliged "to play the good Husband with the Oyl of both my Lamps of Life and Fortune, since if either of those happen to be burnt out, the other will not light the Work to its Journeys End." [83] And in fact he died about two years later without publishing any more volumes of the *Impartial Collection*. It is hard to believe that Nalson was a man of much common sense – in addition to their violence, his writings bear a trace of eccentricity – but he seems at least to have discovered that the task which he had perhaps somewhat rashly and lightheartedly undertaken could be successfully carried out only through long and hard work.

[83] Nalson, *High Court of Justice*, to the reader.

CHAPTER V

WHITELOCKE

The usefulness of Bulstrode Whitelocke's *Memorials of the English Affairs: or, An Historical Account of what passed from the Beginning of the Reign of King Charles the First, to King Charles the Second His Happy Restauration* (1682; enlarged edition, 1732) has been generally recognized, but there have been varying estimates over the years as to their accuracy. James Wellwood, writing a little more than a generation after Whitelocke's death, declared that the *Memorials "will be a lasting Monument of his Fidelity and exactness, and when he Relates any Matter or Transaction of his own Knowledge, He may be intirely depended upon."* [1] It will be noticed that this assertion contains a limitation: an area is indicated in which he cannot be so fully depended upon as elsewhere. The editors of the *Old Parliamentary History*, while severely criticizing Rushworth, found Whitelocke *"very exact"* but Clarendon *"much less so."* They were aware, however, that Whitelocke, like Clarendon, made many chronological errors.[2] Charles Morton, the eighteenth-century editor of two of Whitelocke's works, spoke of the *Memorials*, "the candor, accuracy, and usefulness of which ... are so universally allowed." [3] But J. L. Sanford, who was one of the founders or revivers of accurate knowledge of the Civil War in the nineteenth century, spoke

---

[1] In his "To the Editors Of the following Memorials," in Bulstrode Whitelocke, *Memorials of the English Affairs, From the Suppos'd Expedition of Brute to this Island, to The End of the Reign of King James the First* (London, 1709), henceforth cited as Whitelocke, *Memorials Brute to James*. This work must be distinguished from Bulstrode Whitelocke, *Memorials of the English Affairs: or, An Historical Account of what passed from the Beginning of the Reign of King Charles the First, to King Charles the Second His Happy Restauration* (London, 1732), henceforth cited as Whitelocke, *Memorials*.

[2] *OPH*, I, "The Preface to the First Edition," p. viii; XXIII, Appendix p. 216; IX, introd., pp. iv-v.

[3] In his ep. ded. to Lord Lumley in Bulstrode Whitelocke, *A Journal of the Swedish Ambassy*, ed. Charles Morton, 2 vols. (London, 1772), I, sig. aᵛ. For my references to the journal itself I have used the edition, Whitelocke, *A Journal of the Swedish Embassy*, ed. Henry Reeve, 2 vols. (London, 1855).

of the *Memorials'* "thorough untrustworthiness." [4] A greater man who devoted part of his life to the same study was more generous and more cautious. Ranke recognized the derivative nature of some of Whitelocke's material but recognized the utility of the *Memorials* and declared it "true beyond a doubt" that they were "more trustworthy than Clarendon's History." [5] C. H. Firth, however, in his definitive judgment on Whitelocke's *Memorials*, says that the value of this history "was greatly overestimated by whig writers of the next generation, who opposed it to Clarendon's 'History of the Rebellion' as being more truthful and impartial" and that it "swarms with inaccuracies and anachronisms." [6]

The *Memorials* present an unusual problem, because they are, for most of their length, merely an abridgment of an unpublished longer work. This longer work exists in the British Museum in the form of five folio volumes of manuscript "annals" in which Whitelocke gives a highly detailed, journal-type account of his life from his birth to April 2, 1656.[7] Possibly Whitelocke continued the annals to the Restoration and possibly he continued them beyond that event. The portion of the printed *Memorials* which deals with events between the point at which the annals in the British Museum break off and the Restoration may have been compiled from a part of the annals now lost.[8] But however that may be, Whitelocke did at least complete the record of his life in another form. In a shorter version of the annals, now owned by Lord Bute,[9] his whole life is again described from his birth and is continued to a final

---

[4] J. L. Sanford, *Studies and Illustrations of the Great Rebellion* (London, 1858), p. 324n.

[5] Leopold von Ranke, *A History of England Principally in the Seventeenth Century,* 6 vols. (Oxford, 1875), VI, 28.

[6] Firth's life of Whitelocke in *DNB*. For criticism of a document in the *Memorials,* see Ralph C. H. Catterall, "A Suspicious Document in Whitelock's 'Memorials'," *EHR,* 16 (1901), 737-739.

[7] BM Add. MSS 53726, 37343, 37344, 37345, 4992. These volumes will be referred to below as "Annals," I, II, III, IV, V, respectively. When a passage is cited in the annals, the page number of the same passage in Whitelocke, *Memorials,* if it exists there, will follow in brackets. Thus the reference Whitelocke, "Annals," II, f. 160 (30) means Add. MS 37343 f. 160; Whitelocke, *Memorials,* p. 30.

[8] The Rev. Ph. Stubbs, writing to the Earl of Oxford about Whitelocke's manuscripts, Nov. 16, 1713, speaks of a manuscript "Diary from 1605 to 1660." HMC, Portland V (Norwich, 1899), p. 359, or original on deposit in British Museum (Portland MSS, Harley Papers, XXXI). It is difficult to base any conjecture on this slight remark, but it is some evidence for the continuation of the annals to 1660. Of course Stubbs may have been wrong about the date or he may have been referring to some work other than the annals now in the British Museum.

[9] Described in HMC, 3rd Report (London, 1872), p. xiii, Appendix p. 202. I am most grateful to Lord Bute for permitting me to read the two volumes of these shorter annals when they were on deposit in the British Museum and to Miss Catherine Armet, archivist to Lord Bute, for her helpfulness in making these volumes accessible to me. As the shorter annals have no pagination, I cite passages by date only.

entry on July 21, 1675, one week before his death. This work, which we may call the "shorter annals," is especially useful for its account of Whitelocke's life after the Restoration. The 1682 edition of the *Memorials* is said by Wood to have been "published by" Arthur Annesley, the Earl of Anglesey.[10] It is easier to believe that Annesley wrote the preface than that he undertook the huge task of reducing the manuscript annals to their printed form. As practically nothing is known about the circumstances under which the *Memorials* were prepared from the annals, it is impossible to say whether Whitelocke himself had any share in selecting the material to be published. He does say in some remarks directed to his children that he does not intend the world beyond his family to have any share in the annals,[11] but perhaps he changed his mind; an author's distaste for print is always suspect. The new edition of 1732 was enlarged by the addition of further material taken, at least up to the point at which the British Museum manuscript breaks off, from the annals. The identity of the editor or editors is not revealed. In the following pages I base my conclusions about Whitelocke as a historian of the Civil War on the basic manuscript work, the annals, as far as it continues, but for Whitelocke's historical treatment of the remaining period, from 1656 to 1660, I am forced to rely, though with imperfect confidence in the authenticity of the text, on the printed *Memorials*.

The relationship of the printed edition of 1732 to the manuscript may be further defined as follows: (1) The printed version simply omits all material before the accession of Charles I, that is, everything for a period covering 1605 to 1625. This material mostly relates to Whitelocke's personal life, and the historical as apart from the autobiographical loss is small. (2) Throughout the remainder of the printed version, material of merely personal interest not directly related to the political history of the times has been severely cut. This has had the unfortunate result that in the suppression of many autobiographical passages some of the most interesting material of the manuscript has been lost to the reader of the printed version. (3) The narrative has been made more impersonal for the printed versions by deleting words which show that in many passages Whitelocke is addressing his children rather than the general reader. (4) Many small changes in phraseology and occasional larger adjustments in the narrative have been introduced in the printed version, mostly to accommodate the narrative to the cutting described above. (5) It must

[10] Wood, *AO*, III, 1045.
[11] Whitelocke, "The Preface and Dedication to his Children," in his "Annals," V, f. 2; Whitelocke, "The Preface" to the annals, BM Add MS. 37341 ff. 2, 2ᵛ.

be said in defense of the anonymous editor or editors, that the cutting and rewording have been done very carefully and conscientiously, so that the printed version gives almost precisely the same view of Whitelocke's political opinions and his judgments on the war as the manuscript. (6) His religious preoccupations are less evident in the former than in the latter, owing to the reduction of merely personal matters, but are accurately, if concisely, indicated in the printed version. The reader of the printed version only fails to realize, through the emphasis of repetition and the sheer number of pages devoted to the subject how much religion mattered to Whitelocke. (7) The scrappiness of the printed version, which reads like a series of jottings, is also a quality of the original and is not a result of the method by which the printed version was compiled. This scrappiness, it will be noted, is characteristic of other works by Whitelocke. (8) In the manuscript, Whitelocke seems almost as colorless as he does in the printed version; the addition of a considerable amount of autobiographical material does little to make him more vivid as a person.

Comparison of the manuscript, the 1682 edition, and the 1732 edition, throws some light on the problem of how this latter, enlarged edition was prepared. Wherever the text of the 1682 edition deviates from the manuscript, the deviations have generally been preserved in the 1732 edition. It seems likely, then, that a copy of the 1682 edition was used as a basis for preparing the text of the 1732 edition, and that the additional material from the manuscript which this latter edition contains was copied into or added in some other way to this copy to produce the text for the 1732 edition.

That Whitelocke turned to the writing of history is hardly surprising in view of the keen interest in the whole course of English history which he betrays throughout the annals. He assures the reader that he has studied English history since his early years, being encouraged by the precedent set by his father who was learned in this subject. In a curious letter to Lord Ashley,[12] which he drafted towards the end of his life, he says that he has "thoughts of writing the History of England, which is not so well written as those of other Countries," [13] but that he "held it not

---

[12] Whitelocke to Lord Ashley, Feb. 22, 1671/2, BM Add. MS 32094 f. 265 (draft only).

[13] For complaints in Whitelocke's lifetime and earlier about the poverty of English historical writing, see David Nichol Smith, ed., *Characters from the Histories & Memoirs of the Seventeenth Century with an Essay on the Character and Historical Notes* (Oxford, Clarendon Press, 1918), pp. x-xiii, xxi, and Herschel Baker, *The Race of Time: Three Lectures on Renaissance Historiography* (Toronto, University of

fitt for me to engage in this buisnes without his M^{tyes} command & encouragement." He adds that "The frownes of the world & particular injuries haue brought me & my numerous family into greater streights then I am willing to mention." Accordingly, he desires Ashley, who was then a member of the Cabal, to move Charles II to approve the project and "to graunt me some allowance, (what he pleaseth will content me) for my pains & necessary charge heerin." He will "theruppon," the old lawyer and ex-rebel says hopefully,

lay aside the practise of my profession to applye my selfe wholly to this worke so as I hope may be pleasing to his M^{ty} & for the good of future times ... the extreame violence of my distemper of the stone confines me to my house & study, where yett I hope to liue to serue his M^{ty}. ...

From the description, this proposed history seems not to be the annals, though possibly the annals were to contribute to it.

In contrast with the publicly-minded motives advanced in this letter are the paternal and domestic motives of the annals. With a certain egocentricity but without complacency or vanity, Whitelocke frequently pauses in the annals to warn his children of lessons they may learn from his life; the annals are didactic history with a vengeance. The didactic view of history in the seventeenth century rarely contributed in any way to making seventeenth-century historical writing different from that which appears today when the didactic view is practically dead, but Whitelocke's annals are in this respect an exception to the general practice. Occasionally the didacticism becomes a little ridiculous, as when he warns his children that I "doe not aduise you" to follow his example in exploring a cave.[14] Whitelocke's children would have ended up a mouse-like lot if they had taken all his cautions seriously.

Psychologically the annals are poor, for they reveal little of the inner workings of Whitelocke's mind and less of the workings of other people's minds. The contrast with the psychological richness of Clarendon's writings is striking. At the same time, Whitelocke does not fail as a psychologist by caricaturing the minds of other people as Hobbes does in *Behemoth*; he fails simply by calmly and unobtrusively ignoring all the complexities of their mental makeup. All the emotions and states of mind represented in Whitelocke's annals are stylized and simple – the sort of

Toronto Press, 1967), pp. 73-79. Statements similar to those they cite can also be found in Francis Osborne, Sir William Temple, William Penn, Bolingbroke, and Dr. Johnson.
[14] Whitelocke, "Annals," I, f. 38; cf. ff. 40^v, 56^v. He specifically states his didactic purposes, I, f. 111^v.

emotions and states of mind one would expect to find in a moralistic book written for children. This reliance on basic emotions and states of mind is all the more surprising because Whitelocke himself was obviously a man of complex personality – a personality reflected rather than revealed in the annals and even more dimly reflected in the *Memorials.* One of the most obvious, least subtle aspects of his complexity is that the timorousness and old-maidishness often evident in the annals contrast with the daring and adventurousness he often shows in his life; it is a little surprising to find that he carried away his second wife by threatening her attendants with a sword and that he got most of his teeth knocked out while fighting in one of the early skirmishes of the war.[15]

Part of the reason for the psychological simpleness of the annals may be merely that Whitelocke was writing for his children and did not as a parent want to expose himself unduly to them. Despite the warm protective affection with which he regards them, he never leaves the role of a father: they are not, he gently reminds them at one point, "to be seuere Judges of your fathers actions." [16] The psychology of himself that Whitelocke reveals, except between the lines, is the sort of simplified psychology of ourselves that we generally reveal to large numbers of acquaintances rather than the more intimate psychology we reveal to a few friends, and as Whitelocke addresses his children he tends to take on the mask of a man addressing a crowd. He is an extraordinary man, but the image he puts before the crowd tells only a part of the truth and all that is most complex in the truth has been left out. Perhaps if Whitelocke's children had been a little less numerous – there were 16 of them alive at the Restoration and his child-begetting achievements aroused the merriment of a contemporary pamphleteer [17] – he would have been able to put off the role of a seventeenth-century father a little further in the interests of intimacy. It is, however, unlikely that he would ever have equalled Clarendon in self-depiction, or wanted his children to follow the principle of his contemporary Sir Hugh Cholmley, who in a curiously twentieth-century abdication of the paternal role asked his sons to add to his memoirs, when they would come into their hands, "any remarkable

[15] *Ibid.,* II, ff. 8ᵛ-9, 253-253ᵛ, 255.
[16] *Ibid.,* I, f. 96; cf. also his "The Preface" to the annals, BM Add. MS 37341 f. 3ᵛ.
[17] For the number, see his *Whitelockes Notes uppon the Kings Writt for Choosing Members of Parlement XIII Car. II Being Disquisitions on the Government of England by King Lords and Commons,* ed. Charles Morton, 2 vols. (London, 1766), I, ep. ded. to Charles II; for the merriment, see the anonymous *My Lord Whitlocks Reports on Machiavil; or His Recollections For the use of the Students of Modern Policy* (London, 1659), p. 2. Whitelocke himself made a joke on the number of his children in his conversations with Queen Christina. Whitelocke, *Embassy,* ed. Reeve, II, 100.

infirmities" of his that he neglected to include.[18] Reticence about himself almost necessarily bound Whitelocke to reticence about others, for one can rarely discuss others with any vividness or depth without revealing a good deal about oneself.

The annals are not in any way a political defense, either of Whitelocke personally or of his successive parties and attachments. He seems barely if at all convinced of the rightness of his own side during much of the twenty years of war and revolution. In its political tone, so far as it has one, the work is not Royalist, yet neither does it reflect the ideas of the other side sufficiently to deserve the term "Parliamentarian" except for the reason it is called "Parliamentarian" in this study – that is to say, because its author was a former Parliamentarian and is not known to have explicitly renounced the cause. Perhaps the word "quietistic" suits it best. Whitelocke tacitly accepts the Restoration and the monarchy, is singularly lacking in the desire for political self-vindication, but above all stresses the need for his children and the country to avoid in the future such disasters as he has described. All this is true of the *Memorials* as well as the annals, though the *Memorials*, because of their clipped state, speak in this, as in much else, with a muted voice.

Whitelocke's political career shows his extraordinary ability to survive in politics and therefore provides some clues – and some puzzles – about his character.[19] He was born in 1605, the son of the judge Sir James Whitelocke (1570-1632), and followed his father in the profession of the law. The elder Whitelocke had been identified with the opposition to James I and his wife was a Puritan or inclined to Puritanism: Bulstrode, therefore, did not need to break fully with family traditions when he became a Parliamentarian in the Civil War. During the period of Charles's personal rule Bulstrode may have become identified to a limited extent with the opposition to the government. At any rate, his kinsman John Hampden consulted him about ship-money,[20] and complaints were

---

[18] Sir Hugh Cholmley, *The Memoirs of Sir Hugh Cholmley, Knt. and Bart. Addressed to His Two Sons. In Which He gives some Account of his Family, and the Distresses they underwent in the Civil Wars; and how far he himself was engaged in them* (n.p., 1787), p. 33.

[19] The only full length biography of Whitelocke in print at the time of writing is R. H. Whitelocke, *Memoirs, Biographical and Historical, of Bulstrode Whitelocke, Lord Commissioner of the Great Seal, and Ambassador at the Court of Sweden, at the Period of the Commonwealth* (London, 1860), which should be supplemented with the life of Whitelocke by C. H. Firth in the *DNB*. Except where I have otherwise indicated, I base my biographical account of Whitelocke on these, the annals, and the shorter annals owned by Lord Bute. Miss Ruth Spalding is writing a new biography of Whitelocke.

[20] Whitelocke, "Annals," II, f. 142ᵛ-143 (25). He also identifies himself, "Annals," II, ff. 270, 239ᵛ, 261, 262ᵛ (66) as a kinsman of Hampden and Ferdinando Lord Fairfax.

brought against him for his failure to suppress nonconformity at Abing-
don, where he was recorder.[21] According to himself, however, he rejected
solicitations on behalf of the Covenanters at the time of the First Bishops'
War and "perswaded his friends not to foment, these growing publique
differences, nor to be any means of incouraging a forein Nation, proud
& subtle against our natural Prince, & feared great & euil consequences
therof." [22] Following up these convictions with deeds, he gave the Earl
of Holland "as a present" a pair of fine horses to be used in the campaign
of 1639 against Scotland. He observes with apparent pleasure that the
gift pleased the King.[23] But as a member of the Long Parliament he
shared in the prosecution of Strafford and he remained with the Parliament after the outbreak of war. Both in the House of Commons and in
the Westminster Assembly, of which he was also a member, he opposed
the Presbyterian extremists.[24] He kept on good terms with the Army
leaders and escaped Pride's Purge but refused to take any part in the
trial of the King; he did, however, become a member of the Council
of State of the republic. He is principally remembered as a politician as
one of the commissioners of the great seal. First appointed a commissioner in March 1648, he served, though not continuously, under the
Long Parliament and the two Cromwells, and severed his connection
with the great seal for the last time when Monck caused the Long
Parliament to be restored in 1659. Meanwhile, he had served as ambassador to Sweden in 1653-1654 and had taken part in the attempt to
make Cromwell king.

His relations with Cromwell seem to have been outwardly amicable.
Contemporary allegations that he was one of the members especially
attacked by Cromwell at the breaking of the Long Parliament in 1653 [25]
receive no support in the annals or in the shorter annals owned by Lord
Bute and seem incompatible with his relations with Cromwell as described elsewhere in these writings. However, it is probable that privately
Whitelocke felt considerable mistrust of Cromwell and the formidable
power he wielded.[26] He supported Richard Cromwell in pursuance, it is

---

[21] Whitelocke, "Annals," II, ff. 5-7 (23). Even as early as this conflict (it appears
in his annals under his 30th year) he was, he says, "much for liberty of conscience."
For his later attachment to religious toleration, see "Annals," III, ff. 125-125ᵛ, V, f.
123ᵛ (284, 625).
[22] Whitelocke, "Annals," II, f. 160 (30).
[23] Whitelocke, "Annals," II, f. 160ᵛ.
[24] *Ibid.*, ff. 315-316ᵛ, III, ff. 12-12ᵛ, 71 (99-100, 170, 229).
[25] For these allegations, see C. H. Firth, "The Expulsion of the Long Parliament,"
History, 2 (Oct., 1917), 133, and Firth's life of Whitelocke in *DNB*.
[26] I base this statement on Whitelocke, *Embassy*, ed. Reeve, I, 100, 17-19, 28-29,
321-324, II, 233, 455, 457, 463, and the astonishing passage, II, 145.

said, of a promise he made to Oliver.[27]

The Restoration brought trying days for Whitelocke. He writes under the date of the last day of May, 1660, in the shorter annals that he "was full of trouble in the midst of" the "jollity in others"; while the nation celebrated the Restoration, Whitelocke wondered what would be "the issue of this buisnes as to himselfe." Whitelocke had his whole political career since 1640 to live down. He had also committed the especial offence of warning the Common Council in November, 1659, of Monck's design to bring in the King. In view of Whitelocke's previous dexterity in political survival, one feels that he had at last miscalculated badly in arriving at the Restoration in so defenseless a position and with so little claim to the King's gratitude. It appears from his own account, however, that he only narrowly missed an opportunity to be one of the architects of the Restoration, for in December of 1659, at the urging of several of his Parliamentarian colleagues, he represented to Fleetwood the desirability of anticipating Monck in adopting the policy of restoring the King. Whitelocke accepted the proposal that he himself should go to Breda to make the necessary arrangements with the King. Unfortunately, Fleetwood was soon reminded of an inconvenient engagement which bound him to inaction till Lambert's consent could be obtained, and so hesitated and was lost.[28] In pressing this course of action upon Fleetwood, Whitelocke was not entirely in the throes of a last minute conversion: he had earlier advised Oliver Cromwell to restore Charles II. Whitelocke escaped exception from the Act of Indemnity, though perhaps with some difficulty,[29] and was reconciled to Charles II. It has been claimed, apparently on the basis of family tradition, that he paid Charles an immense fine or bribe,[30] but there is no evidence in the annals or in the shorter annals owned by Lord Bute of any such payment. He did, however, have to spend a good deal of money on other persons. A gift of £250 to his old friend Clarendon facilitated or at least accompanied the passing of his pardon under the great seal.[31]

---

[27] R. H. Whitelocke, *Bulstrode Whitelocke*, p. 427, reports a family tradition that Whitelocke "gave a solemn pledge to uphold Richard to the best of his power."

[28] Whitelocke, *Memorials*, pp. 690-691.

[29] Thomas Langley to Sir Richard Leveson, June 16, 1660, HMC, 5th Report (London, 1876), Appendix p. 207.

[30] R. H. Whitelocke, *Bulstrode Whitelocke*, pp. 451-452, 446-447, names the sums demanded and actually paid. Firth in his life of Whitelocke in the *DNB* is doubtful of what he calls this "family tradition."

[31] Whitelocke's shorter annals owned by Lord Bute, entry for June 21, 1660. See also the entries for June 13, 1660, April 26, 1661, for more general remarks on his expenses in securing his safety, and the latter entry for a particular instance of payment.

Whitelocke lived on till 1675, ill, excluded from office, and to all appearances intensely discontented. Perhaps the complaints of an aging and unhappy man should not be taken at full face value, but it appears from his record of his last years in the shorter annals owned by Lord Bute that his relations with some of his children were badly troubled. The good advice that he poured out in his annals must have fallen on deaf ears. To a Royalist, these domestic misfortunes no doubt would have seemed poetically just. The man who had rebelled against his King faced rebellion in his own family, when his sententious teachings were ignored by his own flesh in favor of the apparent amoralism of his political career. For Whitelocke, relief remained to be found in his religion, learning, wide intellectual interests, and industriousness. Drawing on all of these, he turned, as Clarendon did, his years of enforced political inactivity to good account by diligent writing – historical, religious, and political. Had fate, the Stuarts, or his fellow rebels brought him to a worse end, one can imagine that he would have spent the last hours before his execution penning, in his neat handwriting, page after page of laborious prayers to be preserved by his children.

Whitelocke's career suggests a supple politician of no very strong political convictions. Indeed, it is not easy to form any distinct conception of his mind and character. In his actions and writings he seems to slip agilely between clearly defined positions, escaping all easy categorization. His motives for initially adhering to the Parliamentarian side in the war against Charles I may be treated separately from his motives for pursuing his later career under Parliamentarian and Cromwellian auspices, and on the first set of motives Clarendon has stated his opinion.

Clarendon had good opportunity to understand Whitelocke, for the two men were friends, apparently close friends, before the rebellion. In his annals Whitelocke includes letters written to him at that time by Edward Hyde. As he mulls over these letters one feels that he regards them and is putting them forward as evidence – but evidence of what? Of his past respectability? Of Clarendon's betrayal of an old friendship? Behind the veiled defensiveness so common in Whitelocke's autobiographical writings, the argument, whatever it was, is lost. In referring to Whitelocke's participation in the Treaty of Uxbridge, Clarendon says that

Whitlocke, who from the beginning had concurred with them [the Parliamentarian leaders] without any inclination to their persons or principles, had the same reason still not to separate from them: all his estate was in their quarters, and he had a nature that could not bear or submit to be undone: yet to his friends who were commissioners for the King he used his old openness, and professed his detestation of all their proceedings, yet could not leave them.[32]

But elsewhere he offers a more lenient judgment which may even be based on a belief or half-belief that Whitelocke, if misguided, was nevertheless sincere in his actions. Though Maynard and Whitelocke, he says,

did ... bow their knees to Baal, and so swerved from their allegiance, it was with less rancour and malice than other men: they never led, but followed; and were rather carried away with the torrent, than swam with the stream; and failed through those infirmities which less than a general defection and a prosperous rebellion could never have discovered.[33]

Whatever may be the truth of the first judgment, and whatever the pliable Whitelocke may have told his old friends at Uxbridge, there seems to be no objection to assuming the truth of the second, since Whitelocke repeats essentially the same judgment, complete with another water metaphor. Reflecting in a passage dated July 31, 1649, on the troubles that had befallen the Parliamentarian party, especially the divisions and dissensions among the victors in the war, he warns his children:

that there is neither safety nor discretion for any who can auoyd it, to ingage in matters of this nature.

We who were ingaged in those before mentioned, were unexperienced in [these] things, & in the consequences of them, slipt into them by degrees, & before many of us were aware of them, & being once in, were by little & little plunged farther in, & knew not how to gett out agayne.[34]

And he reflects that his children will be "inexcusable" if, with the examples of the sufferings of this Civil War before them, they "ingage in such affayres." Similarly, he concludes his account of the breaking of the

---

[32] Clarendon, *HR,* III, 497.

[33] Clarendon, *L,* I, 55-56. Clarendon's statements as quoted above probably reflect beliefs about Whitelocke held in the Royalist headquarters at Oxford. See HMC, 13th Report, Appendix, Part I, i.e., Portland I (London, 1891), p. 602. See also Whitelocke, "Annals," II, ff. 265v-266, for the anecdote about the fiery Royalist physician Dr. Turner, who treated Whitelocke when the latter fell ill at Oxford when he was there as a Parliamentarian commissioner in 1643. Turner said, "thou art an honest fellow, drawne in too farre by the rogues att Westminster." Whitelocke merely replied, "I prithe D^r doe not speake so of them to me." *Ibid.,* II, f. 266. Perhaps there were stronger elements of duplicity in Whitelocke's character than appear on the surface of the annals, and perhaps he accordingly took pains to retain an interest in the enemy camp. In "Annals," I, ff. 106-107, 71-73v, is a revealing anecdote of how in an attempt to escape violence at the hands of French mariners he called himself and his companions "Catholiques" – which they of course were in the strict sense, but not in the sense in which the Roman Catholic mariners understood and were intended to understand the term – and an account of his sharp practice with respect to his father's will. I do not consider that any of the evidence for Whitelocke's "duplicity" is sufficient to make me qualify my following assertion that Whitelocke was sincere in his religion.

[34] *Ibid.,* III, f. 333v (417).

Long Parliament by Cromwell with the observation that his children may be instructed

> How God makes use of strange and unexpected means, to bring his purposes to passe, & what daunger there is, in joyning with such people, & in such affayres as they undertooke, wherin your father was too suddeinly & too farre plunged, & aduiseth you to be warned by his harmes, to auoyd the like unto your selues.[35]

Always a moderate and perhaps always a monarchist, Whitelocke was only a timid and unhappy revolutionary.

We should also consider how far his religious convictions can be included among his reasons for entering the war on the Parliamentarian side and for adhering to the successive revolutionary governments. His Puritanism was Erastian and dry, but what he lacked in emotion, he made up in scholarship: learning was of immense importance in Whitelocke's religion. The religious aspects of Whitelocke's character seem hard to reconcile with the rest of his character. When one has assembled in evidence all the visible aspects of Whitelocke's character, one feels that there is a little too much evidence to be reconcilable into a character for one human being. It is almost as if the evidence for one man's religion had got mixed in with the total evidence that has been assembled for the depiction of another man's character. Whitelocke's religion, important though it was to him, seems easily detachable from all the rest of him, and when the editor or editors of the *Memorials* did detach it, by leaving out of the printed text most of the religious material that appears in the annals, all the remainder of Whitelocke's character seemed just the same as before. None of this should be taken as being in the least degree argument that Whitelocke was in any way insincere in his religion: he was not. It is, however, hard to be confident of the connection between his religion and his political actions. His experience of drifting into the rebellion as described by Clarendon and verified by himself seems to account to so large an extent for his entry into the war on the Parliamentarian side as to leave little need of calling in his religion as evidence, though one may suppose that his religion did at least ease the process of rebellion for him and that it gave him some ideological commitment to the Parliamentarian side, both at the beginning of hostilities and throughout the whole ensuing period to 1660. It is also probable that in the early 1640's his religious convictions did not sufficiently differ from pre-Laudian Anglicanism to urge him very forcefully into radical courses

---

[35] Whitelocke, "Annals," IV, f. 271ᵛ. Omitted almost wholly in his *Memorials*.

and were for the most part of a kind that reconciled him to the early Parliamentarians rather than a kind that severed him from the Royalists. There is, in addition, something private about Whitelocke's religion that suggests he preferred to keep it as much as possible out of the public arena.

Another influence on Whitelocke was the English law. Without going so far as to present him as entirely a self-sacrificing patriot, it is plausible to suggest that his devotion to the law and his belief that it must be maintained for the common good were important, possibly even highly important, in persuading him to persist in his public duties under most of the various governments that ruled between 1649 and 1660. In deciding whether or not to accept his appointment as one of the commissioners of the new great seal which had been made after the execution of the King, "The most considerable particulars," he says, "were, that I was already very deeply ingaged with this party, that the buisnes to be undertaken by me was the execution of law & justice, without which, men could not liue, one by another, a thing of absolute necessity to be done." [36] He relates a verbal defense of his profession which he addressed to Fleetwood in May 1656, after Fleetwood had represented to him that his enemies at Cromwell's court had objected to him as a lawyer. Whitelocke asserted that the Long Parliament and men of former ages had a good opinion of his profession,

but if the present Age were wiser than our Ancestors, it was because they had 200000 [sic] Men in Arms to prove them so; and if they disliked the Profession of the Law, it was because the Law is the only Opposer of unlimited Will and Arbitrariness, which did not love to be curbed. . . . in time it will be understood that the Law was a good Bulwark for the Defence of the Rights of the People of *England*.[37]

In his words one may detect hostility to the men of armed violence who surrounded him. Perhaps it was a desire to uphold his profession against the claims of the soldiery which makes him remind the reader of the annals several times that Ireton had legal training. It is noteworthy that when he explains why he accepted a position on the Committee of Safety appointed by the officers in October 1659 after the renewed expulsion of the Rump, one of his reasons is that he wanted to frustrate designs against the laws. For all the political athleticism with which he survived a course of revolutions and upheavals, he did surrender his commissionership of

[36] Whitelocke, "Annals," III, f. 257 (378).
[37] Whitelocke, *Memorials,* p. 644. As the corresponding portion of the annals is missing, it is impossible to tell whether the surprising figure of two hundred thousand is Whitelocke's or someone else's. The shorter annals cast no light on this matter.

the great seal in 1655 rather than accept certain reforms in the Court of Chancery.

To discover his views on the reign and person of James I, it is necessary to have recourse to another of his works, his general history of England called *Memorials of the English Affairs, From the Suppos'd Expedition of Brute to this Island, to The End of the Reign of King James the First* (1709). As the title of this work is confusingly similar to that of the Civil War *Memorials*, we may refer to it, for convenience' sake, as the *Memorials Brute to James*. It seems to be mostly a series of notes drawn from the historians he has used and has little value except as a convenient manual of basic facts. Almost certainly it is not the history he proposed in the letter to Ashley to write under Charles II's patronage. Probably it is identical with a certain "Abridgement of the whole History of England" which he describes himself in the annals as having written; he says that though this abridgment "were made & finished" at "seuerall times, yet a good part of it was in" his twentieth year.[38] Despite this early date (James's death took place in this year) the section on the reign of James draws on works of a later date including Arthur Wilson's life of James (1653) and Archbishop Spottiswoode's *History of the Church of Scotland* (1655). Nevertheless, a treatment of events so recent is unlikely to have been based entirely on printed sources – in fact, this is practically impossible – and one may assume that Whitelocke's account of James owes something to personal observation and perhaps to information derived from his father the judge.

Whitelocke's account of James is unfavorable and occasionally verges on the scandalous. He remarks that James "went a Journey into *Scotland*, Hunting, and Revelling by the way," that he informed Gondomar of Raleigh's intended expedition to the New World, that "he once intended to lay by *Parliaments*, as making King's less, and Subjects more than they are," and that he was "disgrac'd in foreign Countries." He borrows a phrase from Wilson to censure Rochester, who, "though plung'd in Lust, is held up by the Chin in the glories of the Court," and he notices the Essex divorce case very unfavorably. Though he admits that James was not involved in the death of Overbury and concludes his account of James's reign by saying that "yet was he a good Man, and a good King," [39] there is no doubt that James is treated much more harshly in this volume than his son in the annals or other *Memorials*.

[38] Whitelocke, "Annals," I, f. 12ᵛ. Despite his stated intention to insert this abridgment "intirely in this place," it is absent from the manuscript of the annals.
[39] Whitelocke, *Memorials Brute to James*, pp. 296, 297, 299, 302, 292, 295, 310;

Whitelocke gives only an unrewarding factual account in the annals or *Memorials* of the early struggles of Charles I with his Parliaments and he gives an account of the subsequent personal rule of Charles that is only slightly more full. Convinced, but in an offhand and unimpassioned way, that the government acted illegally in this pre-war period, he speaks in the section of his annals devoted to his twenty-fourth year of the Attorney-General Sir Robert Heath as "a fitt instrument for those times," says that Sir Edward Coke in Parliament "earnestly opposed" the "illegal actions" of the court, and shows that he considers ship-money to have been illegally collected.[40] He never criticizes Charles personally. In his account of Archbishop Laud and ecclesiastical affairs, he makes clearest his disapproval of government policies.

Whitelocke had personal connections with Laud. Laud was his father's friend, and when young Whitelocke was a student at St. John's College, Oxford, Laud, who was then the President of the College, took an especial interest in his education. Laud treated him with great kindness and hospitality when they happened to meet in 1632 or 1633. In a passage which recalls one in *Cyprianus Anglicus* in which Heylyn describes being Laud's dinner guest, Whitelocke describes being, on this occasion, Laud's supper guest.[41] About two years later Whitelocke fell foul of Laud when he married a woman of noble family without the official permission required by an order of the King – an order unknown, he says, to him. Whitelocke's subsequent interview with Laud showed Laud's tactlessness and bad temper, and Whitelocke felt much resentment at the manner in which he had been treated. Whitelocke reports a conversation he had on this subject with Dr. Bayly, Laud's successor as President of St. John's College:

> D^r you were alwayes wont to haue a puritannicall jerke
> att the Church.
> Wh I hope that I am as much one of the Church, as
> any man that weares a canonicall coate or a silke
> girdle.
> Dr This comes uppon the same straine, & you will not
> leaue your puritan perswasions.
> Wh. I shall begin to thinke it better to be a Puritan,
> then a proud & angry Prelat.

Arthur Wilson, *The History of Great Britain, Being the Life and Reign of King James the First* (London, 1653), p. 65.

[40] Whitelocke, "Annals," I, ff. 52^v, 111, 110^v, II, f. 139^v (13, 23, 22-23, 24).

[41] Whitelocke, "Annals," I, ff. 73^v-75; R. H. Whitelocke, *Bulstrode Whitelocke*, pp. 76-80.

Whether or not this conversation as recorded in the annals represents the exact words or exact sense of what was spoken – it sounds a bit over bold – it does reflect Whitelocke's opinions as revealed elsewhere in the annals. Afterwards Laud handsomely effected a reconciliation,[42] and it is likely that Whitelocke totally forgot his old resentment: he shows little evidence of ever being vindictive. He later returned the kindness Laud had shown him at St. John's by avoiding taking any part in the Archbishop's trial, though it does not appear that he did anything to save Laud. Perhaps that was not to be expected, in view of Whitelocke's sensitivity to perilous situations and skill in avoiding them. Whitelocke's ecclesiastical friends also included Bishop Williams, the hero of *Scrinia Reserata*, and Bishop Juxon, who in Whitelocke's younger days introduced him to the pleasures of hunting.

Whatever the precise nature of Whitelocke's private feelings about Laud, his portrait in the annals and *Memorials* of Laud as a public figure is unflattering. He regards Laud as having acted disingenuously in launching the prosecution of Prynne for *Histriomastix*.[43] Bastwick was prosecuted, Whitelocke notes – he is referring to Bastwick's prosecution of 1635, not of 1637 – but "a booke in defence of the popish religion, & of the Church of Rome, auerring it to be a true Church," was dedicated to Laud and patronized by him.[44] He says that Laud

was more buisy in temporal affayres, & matters of state then his predecessors of later times had bin, your Grandfather [Judge Whitelocke] who was an-tiently & throughly acquainted with him, & knew his disposition, would say, he was too full of fire, though a just & good man, & that his want of experience in state matters & his too much zeale for the church, & heate, if he proceeded in the wayes he was then in, would sett this Nation on fire.[45]

As one might expect in a common lawyer of Puritan convictions, Whitelocke shows resentment of the ambitions and presumption of the pre-war clergy. He speaks grumpily under his twenty-seventh year "of the expectation & temper of the Clergy in that time." He notes with disapproval that at the sentencing of Bastwick in 1635 the bishops then present denied that they had their jurisdiction as bishops from the King,

---

[42] Whitelocke, "Annals," II, ff. 11-13; quotation from f. 11ᵛ.

[43] *Ibid.*, I, f. 80 (18). See also I, f. 109ᵛ (22), where he seems to mean that Laud lied to Prynne at a later stage in the prosecution. Prynne proposed Whitelocke's exception from the Act of Indemnity in 1660, so Whitelocke cannot be supposed to be prejudiced in his favor.

[44] Whitelocke, "Annals," I, ff. 109ᵛ-110 (22).

[45] Whitelocke, "Annals," II, f. 201ᵛ, I, f. 52 (34, 13). In his *Memorials Brute to James,* p. 302, he detects, anachronistically, Laud's baneful influence on official policy in the reign of James.

and he reflects on what discomfiture this position might have caused
them if they had taken it in the reigns of Henry II, Edward III, or
Henry VIII. He includes a vaguely expressed slur on Arminianism in the
Memorials Brute to James [46] but makes only a few neutral remarks about
the theological and ceremonial aspects of the Laudian regime in the
annals and *Memorials*.

Whitelocke does not try to trace the origins of the Civil War. He does
not declare what relation the character and administration of James, the
illegal practices of the following years, and the actions of Laud and his
clergy had to the ensuing war. We are not even told that Laud did set
the nation on fire – only that Judge Whitelocke feared he would. Whitelocke gives a noncommittal account of the beginning of the troubles in
Scotland as a result of the imposition of the Prayer Book. The following
passage on the attitude of the English people at the time of the Second
Bishops' War shows Whitelocke's disapproval both of the English enemies
and of the English friends of the Covenanters:

> The discourses of the Scottish warre, were very various, those who fauour-
> ed the popish & prelaticall wayes, did sufficiently inveigh against the Couen-
> anters, butt generally, the rest of the people fauoured & approued their
> proceedings, & there was a strange spirit of diuision in the opinions &
> wishes of most men in these affayres, too many not only fauouring butt
> joyning with & assisting the proceedings of the Scotts Couenanters.[47]

In his account of the events which next took place he does not give a
comprehensive explanation of how the Parliament and the King broke
into open warfare, but his opinion of the general mechanism of the
process may be gathered. To the statements already noted concerning his
experience of being plunged involuntarily into war, must be added a
corresponding passage of wider application in a speech which he reports
himself to have made in the summer of 1642. According to the annals,
he said that

> It is strange to note how we haue in sensibly slid into this beginning of a
> Ciuill war by one unexpected accident after another, as waues of the sea,
> which haue brought us thus farre, & we scarce know how, butt from paper
> Combates by Declarations, Remonstrances Protestations, Votes, Messages
> Answears & replies, we are now come to the question of raysing forces, &
> naming a Generall & officers of an Army.[48]

---

[46] Whitelocke, "Annals," I, ff. 63v-64, 110 (17, 22); Whitelocke, *Memorials Brute
to James,* p. 302; cf. p. 293.
[47] Whitelocke, "Annals," II, f. 205v (36).
[48] Whitelocke, "Annals," II, ff. 251v-252 (60).

It is of course impossible to place the fullest reliance on a statement dated so early, when the future still had so much to unfold and so many people held opinions which were to be drastically changed by events. Yet this picture of men, overwhelmed by circumstances, plunging helplessly into an unintended war agrees so closely with the general tone of the annals that one can hardly doubt that when he wrote them it seemed to White-locke historically well based as an account of what had happened early in the rebellion. Like so much else that appears in his writings, it shows that he shared, in whatever degree, Clarendon's perception of how men can be mastered against their intentions by the swirling complexity of the events about them.

Whitelocke emphasizes the sufferings caused by the war. He sees these as the sufferings of people rather than as the evil caused by a particular party, and instead of using them as a text for declaring against the Royal-ists he prefers to draw the conclusion of the necessity of avoiding such misfortunes in the future. This necessity is one of the lessons that he out-lines most strenuously to his children. He notes the cruelties shown by both sides to the women at the siege of Colchester in 1648 and the at-tempts of the besieged to obtain flesh from a dead horse in the face of the enemy fire and says,

Lett these passages deterre you from all occasions which may tend to the fomenting of any such troubles heerafter, & lett them incite you to thank-fullness for the present peace, & freedom from such miseries, to which (blessed be God) we are now strangers, & may this Nation neuer feel the like againe.[49]

He constantly reveals his dread of the brutality of the common soldiers, who are, he emphasizes, as likely to injure persons belonging to their own side as to the other. Even when he describes the plundering of his house by the Royalists in 1642 he concludes without partisan bitterness:

And this (my children) is remembred to you, that you may know your fathers sufferings which were not smalle, and that it may rayse in you, a constant hatred of any thing that may in the least tend to the fomenting of such unhappynes & misery, from which I charge you uppon too much ex-perience to keep your selues cleer.[50]

The war which thus brought suffering to the people failed to bring security to the nominal victors. Whitelocke stresses this failure and again

---

[49] Whitelocke, "Annals," III, ff. 186v-187 (331).
[50] Whitelocke, "Annals," II, f. 259v (65).

enunciates precepts of caution for the guidance of his children. Under the date of July 2, 1646, he declares:

> Thus you see (my children) that euen after almost a Conquest, yett they [the triumphant Parliamentarians] apprehended no safety, such are the issues & miseries of a Ciuill War, that the victors are full of feares from those whom they haue subdued, no quiet, no security, O lett our prayers be to God neuer to haue such calamitous times againe.[51]

Under the date of April 10, 1648, speaking of the conflict of the Parliament with the Army and of both with the insurrectionary apprentices, he says, "Thus we were in continuall perplexities & daungers, & so will it be with all who shall ingage in the like troubles." And again he notes, under the date of November 6, 1648, that the condition of the victors in this Civil War was "to be continued full of fears, and daungers to themselues," and that their misfortune should be a lesson to his children to oppose such troubles. Similarly (July 31, 1649) he complains that in this war "the Conquered were ruind, & the Conquerors, did therby butt create to themselues new warre & troubles." [52]

With all his dread of civil disorders, which recalls that of Hobbes, and his repeated assertions to his children about the desirability of avoiding such misfortunes in the future, he never follows Hobbes into expounding any political theories or principles for maintaining the peace in the future. He confines himself to simple exhortation to avoid trouble without dealing with the theoretical aspects of the problem of how a citizen should comport himself under the rule of an oppressive king. Thus a vital piece in his children's instructions in the annals is lacking. A Royalist might suggest that peace could be best maintained by a policy of strict obedience to the King in most matters and by a total abandonment of all theories that justify resisting an oppressive king under any circumstances whatsoever, but Whitelocke, for all his unhappy and unsettling experiences, never expresses any such conclusions in the annals. It is difficult to be certain of his intentions, but it is a good guess that he does not intend his warnings against rebellion to be an absolute and unconditional prohibition of rebellion under all circumstances. In any case, he bases himself on grounds of expediency, not of morality. He says that the consequences of rebellion are bad, not that it is wicked in its own right. We are probably not far wrong in reconstructing Whitelocke's thought on future rebellions along the following lines. While he admits that a further rebellion may be justifiable at some time, he holds that it should not be undertaken

---

[51] Whitelocke, "Annals," III, ff. 56-56ᵛ (214).
[52] Whitelocke, "Annals," III, ff. 144ᵛ, 215ᵛ, 333 (299, 347, 417).

except in case of dire necessity and with a sober recollection of the consequences of rebellion as they were exemplified to his own generation, and
that even under these circumstances his children should keep out of it if
they possibly can and leave its turbulent fortunes to be undergone by
others. Altogether, Whitelocke's reflections on rebellion seem directed to
the preservation of his family and country, not of the monarch. No one
could draw the conclusion from them that his children ought to *resist*
rebels. It would be almost ridiculous to call Whitelocke's annals a seditious work, but they do at least show that Whitelocke, for all his dismay
at what had happened and for all his pliability, has not allowed himself,
in his role as historian, to be pushed into an open and humiliating advocacy of the ideology of the enemy.

If Whitelocke thus, as seems likely, refuses to abandon completely the
right to rebellion, the reader nevertheless looks into the pages of the annals
or the *Memorials* in vain for any reasoned justification of the Parliamentarian war against Charles I. Whitelocke, who does not rant against the
Royalists and can on occasion even speak of them with sympathy and is
remarkably impartial in his treatment of the two sides in the war, is
generous or guarded in his treatment of Charles both in that King's
political or personal aspects. Whitelocke says that his second wife "was
much unsatisfyed with the Kings proceedings, butt more with the finall
proceedings ag^t him," [53] and this mild statement represents about the
greatest degree of political resentment against the King that can be found
in Whitelocke himself by a reader determined to make him seem as indevoted to Charles as possible. Even when one gives full weight to his
criticisms of the royal government as it existed before the meeting of the
Long Parliament, it is not really clear that he was "much unsatisfyed"
with what Charles had done. He is sometimes capable of treating Charles
as a person with surprising favor. Speaking of the treaty for peace at
Oxford in 1643, he says:

> In this Treaty, the King manifested his great parts & abilities, strength
> of reason, and quickness of apprehension, with much patience in hearing
> what was obiected against him, wherin he allowed all freedome, & would
> himselfe summe up the arguments, & giue a most cleer judgement uppon
> them.

And he adds the customary complaint, which contemporaries so often
repeated about Charles, "that he had a better opinion of others judge-
ments then of his owne though they were weaker then his own," and

---

[53] Whitelocke, "Annals," III, f. 296^v.

gives an example of this diffidence in the King at the time of this treaty.[54]
With the same view of the King in mind, Whitelocke complains under
date October 2, 1648, about the current activities of the King's chaplains.
Motivated, he implies, by their self-interest, they dissuaded the King from
coming to terms with his victorious enemies, yet perhaps, Whitelocke
suggests, the King's superior judgment was not fully convinced by their
arguments.[55]

Whitelocke relates that on the day of the King's execution he stayed
at home at his "prayers, that this dayes worke might not so displease God,
as to bring prejudice to this poore afflicted nation," [56] and he seems
surprised that others were so easily led into taking part in the King's trial.
"It was indeauoured," he says,

> to haue putt the buisnes wholly uppon the Army that if they would haue the
> thing done, they should doe it them [selves] as most proper for such an ir-
> regular & unheard of buisness to be done in an irregular way, & [by] such
> irregular men, butt they were subtle enough to see & auoyd that, & to make
> those whom they left sitting in the Parlem^t to be their stales, & to doe their
> most durty worke for them, many of whom they found & perswaded to be
> strangely forward to ingage in it.[57]

It is always possible, however, that what is found here is the distaste of
the lawyer rather than the man; it does not appear from the annals, the
shorter annals owned by Lord Bute, or from any aspect of Whitelocke's
subsequent service to the Commonwealth and Protectorate that he felt
that peculiar horror of regicide which many of his fellow countrymen
felt or professed to feel.

Whitelocke had abundant opportunity to observe Cromwell, not only
in his public actions but in his intimacy, when Cromwell would make
verses and smoke tobacco with Whitelocke and other associates,[58] but his
mildly unfavorable treatment of Cromwell is unrevealing. No doubt this
reticence is in keeping with Whitelocke's character; to say more about

---

[54] *Ibid.*, II, ff. 267-267^v (68-69).

[55] Whitelocke, "Annals," III, f. 199 (340). The whole sentence in the printed text
at this point beginning "But the prelatical Party" is not in the annals. Whitelocke also
complains of the success of the bishops in persuading the King against his better judgment, III, f. 110^v (269).

[56] Whitelocke, "Annals," III, f. 254 (376).

[57] Whitelocke, "Annals," III, ff. 237^v-238 (363). The 1732 (but not the 1682)
edition inserts the words "as to bring a sovereign Prince to a publick Trial by his own
Subjects," after "unheard of Business."

[58] These convivial meetings are mentioned by Whitelocke, *Memorials*, p. 656. S. R.
Gardiner, *History of the Commonwealth and Protectorate*, 4 vols. (London, Longmans,
Green, and Co., 1903), III, 73n., justly scoffs at the belief expressed by Whitelocke,
Memorials, p. 551 ("Annals," IV, f. 243^v) that Cromwell sent him to Sweden to
remove him as an impediment to Cromwell's "ambitious Designs."

the terrible master in whose service he unenthusiastically but diligently labored would be to contribute to the definition and labelling of himself, and from that he always shied away. But among the more memorable passages of the whole annals is his description of Cromwell's early soldiers, with its unexpectedly Victorian flavor; for a moment, the Roundhead of the nineteenth-century imagination flashes across the stage. Cromwell, he says,

had a braue Regiment of Horse, of his Countrymen, most of them freeholders & freeholders sons & who upon matter of conscience ingaged in this quarrell & under Cromwell.

And thus being well armed within, by the satisfaction of their own Consciences, & without by good iron armes, they would as one man, stand firmely, and charge desperately.[59]

He is inclined to regard Cromwell as having acted disingenuously in countenancing the stirrings of the officers against the Long Parliament under the republic; [60] on the dissolution of this Parliament in 1653 he makes the following observations:

Thus was this Great Parlem^t which had done so great things wholly att this time routed by those whom they had sett up, & that tooke their Com^{ns} & authority from them, nor could they in the least justify any action they had done or one drop of blood they had spilt, butt by this authority.

Yett now the seruants rose ag^t their Masters, & most ingratefully & disingeniously, as well as rashly & imprudently, they dissolued that power, by which themselues were created officers & soldiers, & now they tooke what they designed, all power into their own hands.

All honest & prudent indifferent men, were highly distasted att this unworthy action.[61]

Whitelocke even seems disgusted that no member of the House offered to draw his sword against Cromwell at this dismissal. He notes sympathetically the surprise of some that the members of the Barebones Parliament would "take uppon them, the supreame authority of this Nation, considering how little authority Crom. & his officers had to giue it, or these gentlemen to take it." [62] Though Whitelocke in the annals attacks Cromwell only occasionally and mostly (one could almost say wholly) indirectly, there is little in the predominantly factual account of Cromwell there to shield that statesman from the criticisms levelled against him by

[59] Whitelocke, "Annals," II, f. 272^v (72).
[60] Whitelocke, "Annals," IV, 217-217^v, 261^v (541, 552). See "Annals," II, f. 346 (117) for reference to Cromwell's carrying "on his designe more actiuely, of making way for his own aduancement."
[61] Whitelocke, "Annals," IV, f. 271 (554).
[62] Whitelocke, "Annals," IV, f. 281^v (559).

contemporary Royalists and republicans. But at this point it is helpful to remember the distinction between a Parliamentarian proper and a Cromwellian; though Whitelocke served both the Long Parliament and Cromwell, his primary allegiance – never perhaps very fervent – was to the former rather than the latter.

Two further aspects of Whitelocke's thought which are visible in the annals but have not yet been discussed in this chapter may now be considered.

After the manner of thinking of his time, Whitelocke sees divine intervention in the war at various times and in various ways, but religion itself as a mover of human affairs did not attract his attention except rarely and usually very faintly. Firth's complaint that Clarendon wrote the history of a religious revolution while leaving out the religious element is equally applicable to Whitelocke. In the annals or *Memorials,* Whitelocke does not try to define Puritanism or to give more than a few disconnected observations on its development, and although he is somewhat fuller on the relatively alien topic of the development of Scottish Presbyterianism, his normal practice is to deal with events of religious significance only occasionally and in a haphazard manner. He does go so far as to include religion among the causes for which the Parlimentarians fought,[63] but in doing so he may be only remembering the catchphrases of the war. In this exclusion of religion from political history, there may be a reflection of Whitelocke's personal practice of keeping his religion isolated in its own compartment of his life. Whether he was really convinced, as Clarendon may have been, that religion simply was not at any time a force of major importance in the English rebellion does not transpire.

Whitelocke was as far from being a democrat as most of his fellow members of the propertied classes. His aloof, mildly suspicious attitude to the common people is basically conventional in terms of the ideas of the day. It would be unreasonable to expect anything more favorable from someone whose autobiographical writings are marked by aloofness from the human race in general, a mild but persistent misanthropy, and a brooding, self-pitying dislike of a vice that seems to have particularly oppressed his feelings – ingratitude. He describes how he was reviled in November 1644 by a Royalist mob at Oxford, "part of that body" for which he was making sacrifices and efforts; [64] this is a curious passage and revealing for the insight it imparts into the relation which a Parlia-

---

[63] Whitelocke, "Annals," II, f. 280 (76).
[64] Whitelocke, "Annals," II, f. 338 (112).

mentarian statesman felt he had to the common people of the realm. Whitelocke in turn was by no means incapable of a hard and self-centered attitude to the common people, as is shown in his unintentionally ironic and amusing account of the clamor of "Diuers widdowes of soldiers, & creditors of the Parlem^t" at the door of the House of Commons. Though the women professed to be on the point of starvation, Whitelocke chooses to regard them as ungrateful.[65]

It will be apparent from the foregoing examination of Whitelocke's views that he does not provide any effective defense of the Parliamentarian side in the war. To sum up: Whitelocke is troubled by misgivings about his own part in the war; he does not try to blame the war on the enemy (nor, for that matter, does he blame it on his own side) and treats it as a national misfortune of a sort to be sedulously avoided in the future; he refrains from criticizing Charles I, apart from the indirect criticism involved in his recognition of the illegalities of Charles's government and the exorbitances of Laud's behavior; and he shows no special allegiance to either republic or Cromwell. In fact, a fairminded seventeenth or eighteenth-century reader of Royalist convictions might well be pardoned if he rose from his study of the *Memorials* with the firm conclusion that they offered more ammunition for support of the Royalist cause than for support of the Parliamentarian cause. If this hypothetical reader then went on to read the annals too, there would be no need for him to alter his conclusion, for the annals only enlarge our view of Whitelocke as a man without altering in any significant way our view of his interpretation of the war.

Because their careers were so similar and because they both described the war at enormous length, the historian with whom one most readily links Whitelocke is Clarendon. Yet when one compares Whitelocke's annals and Clarendon's *History*, it is evident that the annals fall far short of the literary and psychological richness and sociological insight of the *History*. Whitelocke does not share Clarendon's zeal for character-painting, though one may guess that similar motives underlie Clarendon's characters and the dialogue-type reports of conversations that Whitelocke occasionally includes. These reports are compatible, as Clarendonian characters are not, with Whitelocke's psychological reticence. Whitelocke's treatment of Cromwell is especially disappointing. Even without bothering about psychology, he could have given a magnificent portrait of Cromwell and his adherents if he had simply described them in the annals with the wealth of external detail with which he describes Queen

---

[65] Whitelocke, "Annals," III, ff. 34-34v (186).

Christina and her court in his brilliant *Journal of the Swedish Embassy*. Clarendon's portrait of Charles I is equally drab, but there was less worth saying about Charles than about Cromwell. A further contrast between Whitelocke and Clarendon, one which does not put Whitelocke at a disadvantage, is geographical. Their histories complement each other, as Whitelocke describes events as seen by someone stationed at the center of Parliamentarian activities, that is, at Westminster, and Clarendon describes the same events as seen from one of the several shifting centers or foci of Royalist activities.

BAXTER

In his autobiography the *Reliquiae Baxterianae: or, Mr. Richard Baxter's Narrative of The most Memorable Passages of His Life and Times* (1696) Richard Baxter has left us a vivid picture of an incident in his life as a young Puritan clergyman in the obscure corner of provincial England where he lived when war was beginning in 1642. Parliament had ordered the destruction of popish statues and images in churches or on churchyard crosses. The churchwarden of Baxter's church in Kidderminster, "an honest, sober, quiet Man," set about to remove a crucifix from the cross in the churchyard. Finding his ladder too short, he went in search of another, and in his absence "a Crew of the drunken riotous Party of the Town (poor Journey-men and Servants)" formed to defend this and other threatened artifacts. Baxter was then walking almost a mile out of the town. Otherwise, he supposes, "I had there ended my days," for the mob, thinking him responsible for the churchwarden's activities, was soon in hot pursuit of Baxter. Whether the threat was as great as Baxter imagined is at this distance of time an unanswerable question. Certainly Baxter, who throughout his life was courageous in resisting unjust authority, was nervous and timid in facing dangers of a more conjectural sort. When he saw a danger clearly, he was not afraid, but his imagination constantly made a coward of him. But perhaps in this case the danger was real enough. Though neither he nor the church-warden had the misfortune actually to encounter the mob, Baxter says that it severely injured two other men. Returning from his walk after the dispersal of the mob and still unaware of the danger he had undergone, Baxter heard "the People Cursing at me in their Doors." On the follow-ing Sunday he publicly reproved his erring parishioners and offered to leave them if they wished. The threat was sufficient and, by now re-pentant, they wished him to stay. But the growing tensions of the country continued to be felt in the streets of Kidderminster, and before the end of the year Baxter had twice left town to escape from the "Fury of the Rabble," egged on, as they were, by their Royalist social superiors.[1]

The account of these troubles illustrates one of the merits of the *Reliquiae Baxterianae* as a history of the Civil War. In this history the Civil War is described as seen from deep in provincial England.[2] The best of English literature has dealt extensively with rural and provincial England, but the best of English history has largely neglected this aspect of the national life. Seventeenth-century historians of the Civil War did of course describe the actions of armies in the countryside, but they rarely paid attention to the environment and daily lives of the ordinary people who lived there. A similar complaint may be made about those historians who did describe events as they took place at some fixed point in provincial England: they were in provincial England, but they were rarely of it. Mrs. Hutchinson described the war as seen from the provinces, yet one finds little about provincial life in her pages beyond tales about the local politicians with which her husband wrangled. Maintaining themselves aloof from the common people, as was appropriate to and practically unavoidable for members of the privileged classes, the two Hutchinsons remained national or metropolitan in their interests. The north was, Mrs. Hutchinson says, "a formidable name" to the London ladies she knew when she was a young bride,[3] and the Hutchinson *Memoirs* or her autobiography give little hint that she ever absorbed any of its particular flavor. Perhaps Baxter was able to record the war all the more effectively in terms of the outlook of provincial England simply because he was, both in his social origins and in his clerical employment, so close to its lower orders and because, as a largely self-educated man, he never took on any degree of sophistication or polish to sever himself from the outlook of simple people of limited horizons. For all his intellectual power and all his intellectual self-discipline, he always retained a touch of the embarrassing crudity of the self-educated man.

The origins of Baxter's political outlook are illustrated in his life history.[4] He was born in a village in Shropshire in 1615 and raised in

---

[1] Baxter, *RB*, Part I, 40, 42.

[2] I developed this point earlier and with additional material in my article, "Richard Baxter: a Puritan in the Provinces," *Dalhousie Review,* 49 (1969-1970), 487-496.

[3] Mrs. Lucy Hutchinson, *Memoirs of the Life of Colonel Hutchinson,* ed. C. H. Firth, new ed. (London, George Routledge & Sons, Ltd., 1906), p. 54.

[4] The *Reliquiae Baxterianae* is the principal source for Baxter's life. The standard scholarly biographies are G. F. Nuttall, *Richard Baxter* (London, Nelson, 1965) and two volumes by Frederick J. Powicke, *A Life of the Reverend Richard Baxter 1615-1691* (London, Jonathan Cape, Ltd, 1924) and *The Reverend Richard Baxter under the Cross (1662-1691)* (London, Jonathan Cape, Ltd, 1927), which, despite their misleading titles, are really the first and second volumes of a single biography. The

the same county. His father had merely "the Competent Estate of a Freeholder, free from the Temptations of Poverty and Riches." [5] Like his father before him, this Baxter was addicted to gambling in his youth, but he was recovered for a religious life in time to be a good influence on his son. In his father's home and neighbourhood, young Richard early observed how men of religious inclinations were hated and opposed by their neighbours. The religiously minded elder Baxter, though wholly conformable to the church, "was reviled commonly by the Name of *Puritan, Precisian* and *Hypocrite*." [6] Baxter paints a dismal picture of the ecclesiastical squalor of the districts that he knew as a child, where much of the pastoral function was discharged by men, some of them Baxter's early teachers, who liberally revealed the Old Adam in their ignorance, drunkeness, and indifference. Baxter's education included, somewhat surprisingly, a year and a half at Ludlow Castle, then an important administrative center, and a month at the court, where the prevailing bias against Puritanism disgusted him. When the Long Parliament met he was back in his rural retreats, serving as assistant to the clergyman at Bridgnorth in his native county. Though he did not conform to the church in some respects – he did not, for example, wear the surplice – he had not come into any conflict with the ecclesiastical authorities.

The most provincial and deeply buried stage of his life was almost over, for the war brought a progressive widening of his horizons. In 1641 he

Powicke volumes will be referred to here under the titles respectively of *Life of Baxter* and *Baxter under the Cross*. All details of Baxter's biography in this present chapter, unless otherwise identified, come from one or more of these four volumes. Studies of Baxter that I have found illuminating are the observations of S. T. Coleridge on the *Reliquiae Baxterianae* in his *Notes on English Divines*, ed. Derwent Coleridge, 2 vols. (London, 1853), II, 5-119, and in *Coleridge on the Seventeenth Century*, ed. R. F. Brinkley (Durham, N.C., Duke University Press, 1955), pp. 321-359; Sir James Stephen's essay "Richard Baxter" in his *Essays in Ecclesiastical Biography*, 2 vols. (London, Longmans, Green, and Co., 1907), II, 1-42; and Richard Schlatter's introductory essay, "Richard Baxter, Puritan Conservative," to his volume of Baxter writings, *Richard Baxter & Puritan Politics* (New Brunswick, N.J., Rutgers University Press, 1957). [Samuel Young?], *Vindiciae Anti-Baxterianae* (London, 1696) and Thomas Long, *A Review of Mr. Richard Baxter's Life* (London, 1697), are attacks on the *Reliquiae Baxterianae* by a Nonconformist and an Anglican respectively. Something that is badly needed in Baxter studies is a psychological examination of him such as Frank E. Manuel has provided for Newton.

[5] Baxter, *RB*, Part I, 1. He says in his *Richard Baxter and Margaret Charlton: a Puritan Love-Story . . . Being the Breviate of the Life of Margaret Baxter*, ed. John T. Wilkinson (London, George Allen & Unwin Ltd., 1928), p. 67, that his father was "a mean freeholder (called a Gentleman for his ancestors' sake, but of a small estate, though sufficient)." Baxter in his youth sometimes undertook the menial labor of plowing, but perhaps only for the reasons of health he mentions; the relatively patrician Whitelocke also "held the plough for health." Baxter, *RB*, Part I, 6; Whitelocke's shorter annals owned by Lord Bute, under dates Sept, 15, 1666, Oct. 6, 1666.

[6] Baxter, *RB*, Part I, 3.

began his celebrated ministry at Kidderminster; later he served as chaplain in the Parliament's Army, where he struggled against the political and religious radicalism which he was alarmed to find growing there. Politically and theologically conservative, Baxter reveals lingering doubts in the *Reliquiae Baxterianae* and elsewhere about the rightness of his involvement in the war.[7] He describes the reaction of himself and the people, or at least the godly people, of Kidderminster to the Army's perversion of the Parliamentarian cause:

Though we had judged the Parliaments War to be lawful and necessary, to save themselves and us from the *Irish* and their Adherents, and to punish Delinquents in a Course of Law, while we believed that nothing was intended against the King or Laws; yet as soon as ever we saw the Case changed, and *Cromwell's* Army enter into a Rebellion against King and Parliament, and kill the King, and invade the *Scots,* and fight against the King that should have succeeded, *&c.* we openly disowned them, and on all just occasions exprest our abhorrence of their Hypocrisie, Perjury, and Rebellion; . . .[8]

Throughout the Commonwealth and under the Protectorate Baxter was in political opposition, though he admits that at last he was inclined to be sympathetic to Richard's claim.[9] Meanwhile, he grew to national fame through his writings and his attempts at ecclesiastical reorganization while remaining solidly based at provincial Kidderminster. In April 1660 he came to London, at least partly in compliance with the wishes of his admirer the Earl of Lauderdale – not yet transmogrified into the monster of Charles II's Scottish administration – to confer with him.[10] This migration marks the severing of his roots in provincial England, for he was never able to resume his old pastoral role at Kidderminster and henceforth made his home almost entirely in or near London. Though he faced the prospect of the Restoration with despondency and realized that the godly clergy would suffer,[11] he never seems to have doubted the moral rightness of restoring the lawful King. He rejected the offer of a bishopric made by the restored monarchy and, failing in his hopes of winning the

---

[7] *Ibid.,* Part I, 40, 119; Richard Baxter, *A Holy Commonwealth, or Political Aphorisms, Opening The true Principles of Government* (London, 1659), p. 486.

[8] Baxter, *RB,* Part I, 90.

[9] *Ibid.,* Part I, 100.

[10] The passage in which Baxter relates why he came to London was condensed and mangled in the printed version of *RB,* Part II, 215, but has been restored in *The Autobiography of Richard Baxter Being the Reliquiae Baxterianae Abridged from the Folio,* ed. J. M. Lloyd Thomas (London, J. M. Dent & Sons Ltd., 1925), pp. 142-143.

[11] Schlatter, "Richard Baxter, Puritan Conservative," *Richard Baxter,* pp. 18-19, and the letter Schlatter prints in which Baxter indicates his feelings at this time, *ibid.,* pp. 140-141; Baxter, *RB,* Part I, 71, 136, Part II, 216.

triumphant restored church to a compliance with the conscientious scruples of the more moderate Puritans, he took up his role as a Nonconformist clergyman.

There is no need to dwell upon the subsequent conflicts of Baxter with church and state. Though the greatest man among the Nonconformist clergy, he frequented Anglican as well as Nonconformist services and his measure of compliance, both in theory and in practice, with the established church won him the resentment and criticism of many of his fellow Nonconformists. He lived long enough to be the subject of a famous trial presided over by Judge Jeffreys in the reign of James II and to write a tract in defense of the Revolution of 1688.[12]

The religious opinions which Baxter professed and on which the religious interpretations of the *Reliquiae Baxterianae* are based provide difficulties of definition. He has been called a "Baxterian" and his views "Baxterianism." [13] These terms indicate the very personal quality of his views and his refusal to conform to the more standard religious groupings of textbooks and denominational loyalties, but they do not indicate his doctrines. His abridger Thomas correctly says that "Often the chief spokesman of the Presbyterians, he was, for all that some historians and others say, never a Presbyterian. He died as he lived, a moderate Episcopalian." [14] Baxter himself states what he disliked in the Presbyterians.[15] What is meant by saying that Baxter was a moderate episcopalian is that he approved of what he conceived to be the primitive form of episcopacy but not of the contemporary English Protestant episcopacy. In the statement of his religious position which he composed in 1672 when applying for a preaching license under the Declaration of Indulgence, he declared that "My judgement of Church-government is for that Form of Episcopacy which is described in Ignatius and Cyprian, and was the usage then of the Christian churches." [16] Powicke says that he held a "(nearly always) intermediate position between strict Calvinists and extreme Arminians"; by Schlatter he is defined as "an exponent of the covenant or federal theology." [17] Baxter insisted that "My Religion is meerly Christian" and that "The Church which I am a member of is the Universality

---

[12] This tract, written shortly before his death, was published for the first time in Schlatter, *Richard Baxter,* pp. 157-178.
[13] Stephen, "Richard Baxter," *Essays,* II, 28; Powicke, *Baxter under the Cross,* pp. 64, 234.
[14] Baxter, *Autobiography,* ed. Thomas, p. xxvii.
[15] Baxter, *RB,* Part II, 142-143.
[16] Baxter, *Autobiography,* ed. Thomas, p. 293, where the statement is printed in full.
[17] Powicke, *Baxter under the Cross,* p. 64; Schlatter, "Richard Baxter, Puritan Conservative," *Richard Baxter,* pp. 22-23.

of Christians, in conjunction with all particular churches of Christians in England or elsewhere in the world, whose communion according to my capacity I desire." [18] He was tolerant enough of the religious opinions of other Christians when he was writing the *Reliquiae Baxterianae* to be convinced that Roman Catholics were capable of salvation and to have a good word even for Anabaptists.[19] Nalson summed up Baxter's ability to transcend narrowly sectarian differences and to stand forth as the representative of a wide variety of Nonconformist opinion with the complaint that he was "the whole Schisme in *Epitome*." [20]

When Baxter died in 1691, the task of publishing the *Reliquiae Baxterianae* fell on his friend and fellow Nonconformist minister Matthew Sylvester, who says that Baxter intended the work to be published and that he once considered publishing it himself before his death.[21] The composition of the bulk of the work is assignable to the years 1664, 1665, and 1670, as years were calculated in seventeenth-century England, but Baxter made later additions to bring it up at last to the events of 1685.[22] Lacking the unity of a completed literary work, it has the untidy immediacy of a diary.

Apart from Baxter's occasional inaccuracy as to facts, there is a self-confessed element of distortion in the *Reliquiae Baxterianae*. He says at one point that he has "purposely omitted almost all the Descriptions of any Persons that ever opposed me, or that ever I or my Brethren suffered by, because I know that the appearance of *Interest* and *partiality* might give a fair excuse to the Readers incredulity." To this he adds that he has been "more free" in describing and censuring "the *Cromwellians* and Sectaries" because, as they were ready to support and benefit him, no one can suppose he has been self-interested in his criticisms of them.[23]

---

[18] In his statement of 1672 in Baxter, *Autobiography,* ed. Thomas, p. 293. He says in Baxter, *RB,* Part III, 102, that he sought a license at this time "on condition I might have it without the Title of *Independent, Presbyterian,* or any other Party, but only as a *Nonconformist.*"

[19] *Ibid.,* Part I, 131, for his views on the salvation of Roman Catholics; Part I, 133, Part II, 140-141, for his views on the Anabaptists.

[20] John Nalson, ed. *A True Copy of the Journal of The High Court of Justice, for the Tryal of K. Charles I.* (London, 1684), introd., p. ix.

[21] Sylvester in Baxter, *RB,* preface to the reader, sig. [c3]-[c3]ᵛ. Sylvester's relationship to Baxter may have been of a nature that would have been trying to a more forceful and self-confident man than Sylvester, as the example of Baxter's wit recorded by Sylvester, *RB,* ep. ded., sig. [A2]ᵛ, suggests.

[22] For these dates, see "A Breviate of the Contents" in Baxter, *RB,* sig. d2-[d4]ᵛ, and Part II, 448, Part III, 1, 141, 177, 200. Edmund Calamy says in his *An Historical Account of My Own Life, with Some Reflections on the Times I Have Lived in. (1671-1731),* ed. J. T. Rutt, 2 vols. (London, 1829), I, 380, that he drew up this breviate.

[23] Baxter, *RB,* Part I, 136.

Despite the period of years over which the *Reliquiae Baxterianae* was written, there is probably no reason to suppose that this principle was not followed throughout the work, and assuming that it was, one must ask what degree of distortion such an unhistorical principle introduced. In reply, it is probably safe to say that the greatest distortion is found in his treatment of events after the Restoration, during the period in which the enemies of himself and the other Nonconformists were triumphant. It must further be noticed that even though the Cromwellians and sectaries were willing to befriend Baxter, his personal feelings towards them were highly antipathetic. He was not, therefore, by his sympathies ideally prepared to be an impartial judge of them. Moreover it is simply unlikely that Baxter felt much interest in describing individuals. He does say that "the true Description of Persons is much of the very Life of History, and especially of the History of the Age which I have lived in," and he regrets that the need to appear impartial prevents him from giving characters of the participants in the Savoy Conference,[24] in which he played a prominent part, but these stirrings of interest in character-painting seem merely freakish. How well Baxter could paint character when he set his mind to doing so is shown by his fine account of Cromwell's personality, mind, and motives, but generally his accounts of the minds and personalities of individuals whether friends or otherwise, are brief and unrevealing; he almost never describes physical appearances. His interest seems to have inclined towards the description of groups of men rather than individuals: he obviously enjoys expounding in elaborate detail the opinions of the conflicting political and religious groups of his time.

Baxter's skill in such description of groups depends on an aspect of his mind which makes him especially impressive as a historian – his passion for rigorous definition and painstaking analysis. Dowden says that "The union in Baxter of the indefatigable pastor and the inquisitive and restless schoolman of Protestant theology is perhaps his distinguishing characteristic. His intellect pursued logical distinctions and subtleties with an almost morbid curiosity; . . ." [25] Baxter himself says that he came early in life to study the schoolmen

because I thought they narrowly searched after Truth, and brought Things out of the darkness of Confusion: For I could never from my first Studies endure *Confusion*! Till *Equivocals* were *explained*, and *Definition* and

---

[24] *Ibid.*, Part I, 136, Part II, 363.
[25] Edward Dowden, *Puritan and Anglican: Studies in Literature*, 3rd ed. (London, Kegan Paul, 1910), p. 216. Burnet, *OTA*, I, 320, says that Baxter "was most unhappily subtle and metaphysical in every thing."

Distinction led the way, I had rather hold my Tongue than speak! and was never more weary of Learned Mens Discourses, than when I heard them long wrangling about unexpounded Words or Things, and eagerly Disputing before they understood each others Minds;. . . . I never thought I understood any thing till I could *anatomize* it, and see the *parts distinctly*, and the *Conjunction* of the parts as they make up the whole.[26]

He notes that the doctrinal controversies between Arminians and anti-Arminians and "our Doctrinal Controversies with the Papists themselves" have been much troubled by the use of imprecise or ill defined ideas, arguments, and words.[27] In the following pages his application of his analytical powers to the elucidation of the terms "Puritan" and "Presbyterian" and to the nature of the division of England into two sides in the war will be especially noted.

Connected with these precision-loving and analytical qualities of Baxter's mind, but indebted also to his position as a member of a vigorously denounced religious party, is his skeptical attitude to history. No attempt will be made here to trace the development of this attitude – presumably there was some kind of development – but some principal consequences of it will be noted. He complains that

Many of the Malignant Clergy and Laity, especially *Le Strange* the Observator, and such others, do with so great Confidence publish the most Notorious Falshoods, that I must confess it hath greatly depressed my Esteem of most History, and of Humane Nature. If other Historians be like some of these Times, their Assertions, when-ever they speak of such as they distaste, are to be Read as *Hebrew*, backward; and are so far from signifying Truth, that many for one are downright Lies.[28]

He says in the account of his intellectual development which he gives in the *Reliquiae Baxterianae* that "I am much more cautelous [*sic*] in my Belief of History than heretofore," and he goes on to discuss truth and falsehood in history and the standards by which his own history is to be judged; and he more than once elsewhere calls himself "a Hater of false History." [29] It is interesting to note that his historical skepticism has led

[26] Baxter, *RB*, Part I, 6.
[27] *Ibid.*, Part II, 141. The *Reliquiae Baxterianae* contains many other examples of Baxter's fondness and aptitude for careful analysis. See, for example, his account of his intellectual development, Part I, 124-138, his account of the contending religious parties of the Civil War, Part II, 139-146, and his account of the Conformists and Nonconformists in the reign of Charles II, Part II, 386-429.
[28] *Ibid.*, Part III, 187.
[29] *Ibid.*, Part I, 135-136; Richard Baxter, *Church-History of the Government of Bishops and Their Councils Abbreviated. Including the chief part of the Government of Christian Princes and Popes, and a true Account of the most troubling Controversies and Heresies till the Reformation* (London, 1680), title page; Richard Baxter, *Richard Baxter and Margaret Charlton,* to the reader, p. 64, where he calls himself "a vehement hater of false History."

him to take a sympathetic view of the ancient heretics – his sympathy is of course not unqualified – who have been denounced but whose writings have been allowed to perish, so that they cannot speak in their own defense.[30] He sees that he himself and the English Nonconformists may similarly suffer an unjust verdict in history.[31] Even the histories of honest men, he finds, are to be treated with reserve:

Conscionable men's Histories are true; but if they be also wise, they tell us but some part of the truth, concealing that which would do harm, and which the depraved world cannot bear without abusing it. But we that are less wise, tell all the truth, too little regarding how men will receive it. And hence comes all History, which hath not evidence equal to natural, to be of less credit than most men think; while bad men lie, and good men leave out so much of the truth as makes the rest to be as another thing than altogether it would appear.[32]

In view of his awareness of the problem of historical accuracy, it is a little disappointing to see in the *Reliquiae Baxterianae* some surprising examples of gullibility. Though these may be in part excused by an appeal to the habits of thought of the time, there can be little doubt that Baxter was, as Burnet noted in recalling his acquaintance with him, "credulous." [33]

After these remarks about Baxter's cultivation of definition and analysis and his historical skepticism, it will seem paradoxical to confess that his account of events before the meeting of the Long Parliament is, like Ludlow's, confused. In Baxter's case, a likely explanation for the confusion is that he is recollecting events as they appeared to a young student and clergyman in provincial England, far from the centers of power and politically significant events and ill supplied with accurate, much less firsthand information. In the sphere in which the young and obscure Baxter moved after leaving the court in 1634, state policy, even in religious matters, can hardly have been a common topic of conversation or thought. Thus we find him saying that the Etcetera Oath,

---

[30] Baxter, *RB*, Part I, 135.
[31] *Ibid.*, Part I, 136, for himself; Baxter, *Church-History*, "What History is Credible, and what not," sig. [a4]v, for the Nonconformists. In this preface he describes, as its title indicates, means by which the reader can be guided in distinguishing true history from false.
[32] Baxter, *Richard Baxter and Margaret Charlton*, to the reader, pp. 61-62.
[33] See his accounts of "strange Providences" occurring in the Civil War and his lurid stories about heresy in New England, Baxter, *RB*, Part I, 46-47, 75; "(Burnet's Autobiography)," in Gilbert Burnet, *A Supplement to Burnet's History of My Own Time*, ed. H. C. Foxcroft (Oxford, Clarendon Press, 1902), p. 463.

which was imposed on us for the unalterable subjecting of us to Diocesans, was a chief means to alienate me, and many others from it [the form of episcopacy used in England]. For now our drowsie mindlesness of that subject was shaken off by their violence; and we that thought it best to follow our business, and live in quietness, and let the Bishops alone, were rowzed by the terrours of an Oath to look about us, and understand what we did.[34]

Rather vaguely, Baxter observes that "it fell out that at the same time when we were thus rowzed up in *England*" by the Etcetera Oath, "or a little before, the *Scots* were also awakened in *Scotland*." And with similar vagueness, after describing the tumults in Scotland and the formation of the National Covenant, he says that "It fell out unhappily that at the same time while the *Scots* were thus discontented, the King had imposed a Tax here, called *Ship-money*, as for the strengthning of the Navy." [35] And yet the Scottish revolt began almost three years before the Etcetera Oath was imposed and the first writ extending the collection of ship-money to the whole of England was issued two years before the Scottish revolt began. Baxter does manage to give an account of the ship-money dispute full enough to dispel some of the impression of confusion given in the statement just quoted about its origin, but in his account of the First Bishops' War he goes from bad to worse: "The *Scots* came with an Army, and the King's Army met them near *Newcastle*; but the *Scots* came on till an Agreement was made, and a Parliament called; and the *Scots* went home again." [36] As might be expected from the foregoing, Baxter has little to say about Laud's policies, though he does allude, among his remarks, to "*prelates, who were reducing us so near* Rome *as* Heylin *in the Life of Laud describeth*." [37]

If Baxter is thus uncertain in his account of public events in the years immediately before the meeting of the Long Parliament, he is lucid in his account of the term "Puritan." In the accustomed manner, he traces English Puritanism back to the days of the Marian exile. The division between "the Diocesan Party" and their opponents then initiated continued through the years. Speaking of the "Nonconformists" – he is here using the word in the sense of Puritan pre-war clergymen who were unwilling to conform to all the requirements of the church – he says:

The name *Puritan* was put upon them, and by that they were commonly known: when they had been called by that name awhile, the vicious Multitude of the Ungodly called all *Puritans* that were strict and serious in a Holy

---

[34] Baxter, *RB*, Part I, 16.
[35] *Ibid.*, Part I, 16.
[36] *Ibid.*, Part I, 17.
[37] *Ibid.*, Part III, 41; cf. Part I, 18.

Life, were they ever so conformable! So that the same name in a Bishops mouth signified a Nonconformist, and in an ignorant Drunkards or Swearers mouth, a godly obedient Christian. But the People being the greater number, became among themselves the Masters of the Sense. And in *Spalatensis's* time, when he was decrying *Calvinism,* he devised the name of *Doctrinal Puritans,* which comprehended all that were against *Arminianism.* Now the ignorant Rabble hearing that the Bishops were against the Puritans, (not having wit enough to know whom they meant) were emboldened the more against all those whom they called Puritans themselves, and their Rage against the Godly was increased: and they cried up the Bishops, partly because they were against the Puritans, and partly because they were earnest for that way of Worship which they found most consistent with their Ignorance, Carelesness, and Sins.[38]

Fuller and Hacket offer explanations of the term "Puritan" which contain a similar realization that the meaning of the term was extended in the reign of James I, but neither writer draws Baxter's distinction between the term as used by the ecclesiastical authorities and the term as used by the rabble.

In accordance with these observations on the hostility of the rabble to the godly, and basing himself presumably on his own acquaintance with the countryside, Baxter sees a kind of popular, anti-moral revolt, a boiling up of the Royalist or blindly conventional dregs of society, in the earlier stages of hostilities in the Civil War. The rabble and their brethren the Royalist common soldiers attacked the godly in the interests of the King and his party. Baxter is inclined to exempt the King from personal responsibility for the outrages, but he comments that some of the gentry patronized them.[39] Rather surprisingly, he finds that most of the men who composed the anti-Puritan rabble at Kidderminster went into the King's army and were killed.[40] The Parliament, however, he holds, gained strength from the fact that the rabble and Royalist common soldiers would not let the religious people live in peace and so drove them into active adherence to the Parliament.[41] He does not mention any corresponding activities of the pro-Parliamentarian rabble, presumably because their activities did not come within his own experience, but if he had joined his fellow historian and (after a manner) Puritan Arthur Wilson in venturing into the scenes of disorder Wilson describes in his autobiography, he would almost certainly have reacted with equal disgust

---

[38] *Ibid.,* Part I, 32-33.
[39] *Ibid.,* Part I, 44, 40-44. He says in his *Holy Commonwealth,* p. 457, "The Warre was begun in our streets before the King or Parliament had any Armies."
[40] Baxter, *RB,* Part I, 42, 86.
[41] *Ibid.,* Part I, 44.

to these exorbitances of the pro-Parliamentarian rabble.[42] Baxter was simply hostile to any impertinences on the part of the lower orders.

Baxter's analytical and clearly discerning mind, which produces this valuable definition of the term "Puritan," is again valuable when he comes to deal with the ghost-like and evasive term "Presbyterian." Probably no word connected with the Civil War has been so much abused. Baxter himself has been inaccurately called a Presbyterian. In the *Reliquiae Baxterianae* he clears the Presbyterians of the calumny of having caused the war. He says:

> But that great Lie that the *Presbyterians* in the English Parliament began the War, is such as doth as much tempt men that know it, to question all the History that ever was written in the World, as any thing that ever I heard spoken: Reader, I will tell it thee to thy admiration. When the War was first raised, there was but one *Presbyterian* known in all the Parliament; . . .[43]

He describes a similar want of Presbyterians among the Lords Lieutenant to whom the Parliament committed the militia and among Essex' officers. And, surprisingly, he declares that

> The truth is, *Presbytery* was not then known in *England,* except among a few studious Scholars, nor well by them. But it was the moderate Conformists and Episcopal Protestants, who had been long in Parliaments crying out of Innovations, Arminianism, Popery, but specially of *Monopolies*, illegal taxes, and the danger of Arbitrary Government, who now raised the War against the rest whom they took to be guilty of all these things: And a few Independents were among them, but no considerable Number.[44]

Abandoning for the moment our examination of events in strictly chronological order, we should look at other accounts by Baxter in the *Reliquiae Baxterianae* of the erroneous popular use of the term "Presbyterian" so that we may more clearly understand his views on the association of Presbyterians and the war. He says, speaking of his attempts at ecclesiastical reorganization during the Interregnum:

> But the greatest Advantage which I found for Concord and Pacification, was among a great number of Ministers and People who had addicted themselves to no Sect or Party at all; though the Vulgar called them by the Name of *Presbyterians*: And the truth is, as far as I could discover, this was the

[42] Arthur Wilson, "The Life of Mr. Arthur Wilson the Historian . . . which he calls, 'Observations of God's Providence, in the Tract of my Life.' Written by himself," in *Desiderata Curiosa*, ed. Francis Peck, 2 vols. (London, 1732-1735), II, Lib. XII, pp. 23-25. Cf. Clarendon, *HR,* II, 318-319.

[43] Baxter, *RB,* Part III, 41, 149.

[44] *Ibid.,* Part III, 41. In his preface to his *The Second Part of the Nonconformists Plea for Peace* (London, 1680), sig. a, a2, he defends the Presbyterians from the charge of having begun the war, which he regards as begun between two conforming parties of the Church of England.

Case of the greatest number of the godly Ministers and People throughout *England*. For though Presbytery generally took in *Scotland*, yet it was but a stranger here: . . . .[45]

Similarly, speaking of the time immediately after the Restoration, he says:

And here you may note by the way, the fashion of these Times, and the state of the Presbyterians: Any Man that was for a Spiritual serious way of Worship (though he were for moderate Episcopacy and Liturgy), and that lived according to his Profession, was called commonly a *Presbyterian*, as formerly he was called a *Puritan*, unless he joyned himself to *Independents*, *Anabaptists*, or some other Sect which might afford him a more odious Name.[46]

Baxter realizes that there are real Presbyterians, though these are apparently rare, and that there are those who are only miscalled Presbyterians, and among such is himself.

Baxter's attempt to show that the rebellion was entered upon on the Parliament's side not by Presbyterians but by certain other persons who (a few exceptions apart) were conforming and even episcopal Protestants proves on examination to be ingeniously resourceful but logically complicated and troublesome. As Baxter was never a Presbyterian himself, he is, paradoxically, shifting blame for the rebellion from a group to which he never belonged to a group (that of conforming and episcopal Protestants) to which he once belonged. He is taking advantage, consciously or unconsciously, of the public confusion of terminology to exculpate himself and his associates by showing that a religious group they supposedly belonged to was innocent but that a religious group the older of them had once belonged to was not. One aspect of the quest for self-justification which gave rise to these difficulties was his logic-chopping desire to show his "prelatist" enemies that they had much more in common with the rebels than they supposed, that the rebels were really, in some sense, substantially people of their own kind. Carrying this desire to an extravagant length, he dumfounded his opponents at the Savoy Conference, according to a story he tells about himself, by offering to cite to them no less a conformist than an archbishop who had supported the Parliament against the King. When they gave up the riddle, he named Archbishop Williams.[47]

A further difficulty in Baxter's use of the word "Presbyterian" occurs

[45] Baxter, *RB*, Part II, 146.
[46] *Ibid.*, Part II, 278. He also draws attention to misuse of the term "Presbyterian," *ibid.*, Part II, 284, 375-376. In Worcestershire, he says, Part I, 97, he knew of only one Presbyterian at the time of his Worcestershire Association.
[47] *Ibid.*, Part II, 339-340; cf. Part III, 149.

in his account of the Restoration. "What the Presbyterians did to preserve and restore the King," he says, "is a thing that we need not go to
any Corners or Cabinets to prove!" He supports this statement by citing
evidence ranging from "The Votes for Agreement upon the King's Concessions in the *Isle of Wight*" to

> the Gratulations of General *Monk* in *England*, the Concurrence of the
> *Londonners*, and the Ministers there, the Actual Preparations of the Res-
> tored Members of the Long Parliament, and the Consent of the Council of
> State left by them, and the Calling in of the King hereupon by the next
> Parliament, without one contradicting Voice, and finally the Lords and
> Gentlemen of the King's old Party in all Countreys [i.e., districts], addressing
> themselves to the Parliamentarians, and the King's grateful Acknowledg-
> ments in his Letters, and his Speeches in Parliament, ...[48]

This is a most puzzling argument. How have the Presbyterians, once too
thin on the ground to support a rebellion, now become numerous enough
to play a major, perhaps decisive,[49] part in restoring the King? Most
likely Baxter has simply fallen in with the imprecise popular language
and sometimes speaks of Presbyterians in the restricted sense, which he
recognizes to be the only true one, and sometimes in the loose, enveloping
popular sense. Nevertheless, in dealing with so difficult a question of
definition one cannot be absolutely certain and must concede that perhaps somehow Baxter dexterously and perfectly reconciled all his uses of
"Presbyterian."

Though Baxter thus holds that the Presbyterians, properly so called,
did not begin the war, he gives, as has been seen, only an unsatisfactory
account of events before the meeting of the Long Parliament, and he
becomes a competent reporter of political events only from the meeting
of the Long Parliament. He recognizes the existence in the early and
undivided Long Parliament of a coalition of those who opposed political
illegalities and those who opposed ecclesiastical illegalities and innovations. The first breach among the members arose on the issue of the
death of Strafford. He elaborately describes the state of opinion at this
time among those of the Parliament who stood for reconciliation with
the King and those of the Parliament who stood apart from this policy.
Baxter says, "whether any designed the subduing of the King, and the
change of Government, at that time, I cannot tell: For I then heard
of no notable *Sectary* in the House but young Sir *Henry Vane*." After
this survey of Parliamentary opinion he includes a list of the things which

---

[48] *Ibid.*, Part II, 215, 215-216, 229.
[49] *Ibid.*, Part II, 229.

heightened former displeasures into a civil war, a list in which he sees persons on both sides contributing by their actions to its outbreak.[50]

In this list he places especial emphasis on "the terrible Massacre in *Ireland,* and the Threatnings of the Rebels to Invade *England.*" He describes the fear which the reports of the Irish rebellion aroused in England and adds that when "the poor People," thus alarmed, "saw the *English* Papists join with the King against the Parliament, it was the greatest thing that ever alienated them from the King." One of the purposes as he understood them of the Parliament's war was "to save themselves and us from the *Irish* and their Adherents." He says that when evidence came to light in the reign of Charles II of Charles I's complicity in the Irish Rebellion it reassured the former Parliamentarians of the rightness of their cause.[51] Whether or not the Irish rebellion struck the English people as forcefully as Baxter supposed – he seems to stress more heavily than most of his contemporaries its importance as a cause of the following English war – there is no doubt that it deeply impressed him. In his political treatise called *A Holy Commonwealth* (1659) he says that even if the King had been victorious in the war, "His impious and popish Armies" would have turned against him, just as the Parliament's Army turned against its masters, and he hints that the result would have been a reproduction in England of the horrors of the Irish massacre.[52] These gory horrors were well suited to appeal to Baxter's combination of credulity, timorousness, and anti-papal feeling. Along with his desires to be fair to the Papists and to avoid the promotion of cruelty to anyone, even members of this detested sect, Baxter had deep-seated apprehensions of their "Power and Malice." [53] He examines in the *Reliquiae Baxterianae* with some tendency towards believing it the evidence for supposing that the Papists set the Great Fire of London in 1666, he thinks that they made later attempts at a new firing, and he suspects that they had a hand in the King's execution.[54]

Baxter analyzes the division of England into two sides in the First Civil War. The King was supported by part of the nobility and gentry, most of the tenants of these Royalists (or at least most of the tenants of the gentry portion of them), and most of the rabble. Parliament was sup-

[50] *Ibid.,* Part I, 18-19, 24-29; quotation from Part I, 25.
[51] *Ibid.,* Part I, 26, 29, 90; Part III, 83.
[52] Baxter, *Holy Commonwealth,* pp. 478-479. See also the revealing passage, pp. 49-50, of the autobiographical verses in his *Poetical Fragments: ... Written Partly for himself, and partly for near Friends in Sickness, and other deep Affliction* (London, 1681).
[53] Baxter, *RB,* Part II, 217, 374.
[54] *Ibid.,* Part III, 18, 180-185 (correctly 184-185), Part II, 373-374.

ported by its share of the nobility and gentry "and the greatest part of the Tradesmen and Free-holders, and the middle sort of Men; especially in those" places that depended "on Cloathing and such Manufactures." [55] Just as the molestations of the Royalist rabble and common soldiers drove godly men to support of the Parliament, so conscience led men to support it:

> But though it must be confessed, That the Publick Safety and Liberty wrought very much with most, especially with the Nobility and Gentry, who adhered to the Parliament, yet was it principally the differences about Religious Matters that filled up the Parliaments Armies, and put the Resolution and Valour into their Soldiers, which carried them on in another manner than mercenary Soldiers are carried on.[56]

And he gives an elaborate account in which he expounds, without rancor and with a painstaking regard for the complexity of the subject, the opinions of the Parliamentarians in defense of the stand which they took in the conflict.[57]

Unfortunately, the reasonable principles of conscientious Parliamentarians did not prevent their course from ending in disaster, and the account of the war in the *Reliquiae Baxterianae* reflects Baxter's disgust with the Army's betrayal of the original Parliamentarian cause. In his remarks on the Second Civil War he is sympathetic to the defeated side.[58] After Pride's Purge, he says, the House of Commons consisted of "the *Vanists*, the Independants, and other Sects, with the Democratical Party," who were intended by Cromwell "to do his Business under the Name of the Parliament of *England*." [59] Baxter speaks of the King's execution as follows:

> And before his own Gate at *Whitehall* they erected a Scaffold, and before a full Assembly of People beheaded him: Wherein appeared the Severity of God, the Mutability and Uncertainty of Worldly Things, and the Fruits of a sinful Nation's Provocations, and the infamous Effects of Error, Pride and Selfishness, prepared by Satan to be charged hereafter upon Reformation and Godliness, to the unspeakable Injury of the Christian Name and Protestant Cause, the Rejoicing and Advantage of the Papists, the Hardning of Thousands against the Means of their own Salvation, and the Confusion of the Actors when their Day is come.[60]

---

[55] *Ibid.*, Part I, 30.
[56] *Ibid.*, Part I, 31.
[57] *Ibid.*, Part I, 34-38.
[58] *Ibid.*, Part I, 61.
[59] *Ibid.*, Part I, 63.
[60] *Ibid.*, Part I, 63.

For all this disapproval of the execution, Baxter provides no grounds in the *Reliquiae Baxterianae* for believing that he ever experienced the shock many Royalists professed to feel at this deed. For the King he does not reveal any especial feeling and it is noteworthy that he does not attempt to praise or defend him. Neither, admittedly, does he present any indictment of him, unless one insists on regarding a few scattered remarks as an indictment, and for this refusal or failure several reasons may be cited, including his conservatism, the fact that he formed his Parliamentarian convictions during the period in which the King was still generally exempt from personal attacks by the Parliamentarians and did not support the Parliamentarian cause beyond that period, and, perhaps most important of all, the special nature of his recollections. His hazy picture of events before the meeting of the Long Parliament suggests that the period in which Charles's misdeeds were most evident and most difficult to defend did not loom very large in his consciousness and that, therefore, neither did those misdeeds. Cromwell is by contrast with the remote, shadowy figure of the King a well developed figure in the autobiography, and it is perhaps a further hint of coolness in Baxter's attitude to the King that he is able to describe [61] so plausibly what he supposes to have been Cromwell's reasoning as he defended the King's execution in his own mind.

Though the great Puritan divine joins Royalists and republicans in condemning the great Puritan statesman, Baxter's views on Cromwell have a subtlety and discrimination rare in contemporary treatments of Cromwell. His reflections on Cromwell are a detailed study of the intertwining of good and evil in a single life.[62] Here it is worthwhile to remember that Baxter's judgment had been sharpened by the exhaustive practice of pastoral inquisition into human motives. No doubt the errors and limitations of Baxter's account of Cromwell, like his failure to speak as a friend and admirer of Cromwell even after the opportunities which their meetings offered him to get a better understanding of the statesman, must be attributed in part to a grave difference between their temperaments. The highly intellectual Baxter, as Powicke has pointed out, was unable to share Cromwell's mysticism: *"He* was no mystic." [63] In his psychological reconstruction of Cromwell, Baxter states his belief that

---

[61] *Ibid.*, Part I, 99.
[62] *Ibid.*, Part I, 98-100.
[63] Powicke, *Life of Baxter,* p. 126. Powicke's series of articles entitled "The Rev. Richard Baxter's Relation to Oliver Cromwell," *Transactions of the Congregational Historical Society,* 10 (1927-1929), 122-144, 167-182, 212-227, 250-266, reprints the relevant sections of the *Reliquiae Baxterianae* with notes.

Cromwell "having been a Prodigal in his Youth, and afterward changed to a zealous Religiousness, . . . meant honestly in the main, and was pious and conscionable in the main course of his Life, till Prosperity and Success corrupted him." Cromwell and the pious men he chose to be his early soldiers began to be corrupted after their successes in Lincolnshire and at Marston Moor.[64] Baxter may believe that Cromwell was in some degree sincerely religious to the end of his life; he certainly believes that he retained some of his old piety, despite his wrongful actions, in the earlier years of his greatness. He reproduces for the reader the reasoning by which he supposes Cromwell in his own thoughts justified many of his misdeeds.[65] Though the more intelligent people saw through the devices of Cromwell's rise, "the Simpler sort believed that he designed nothing of all that came to pass; but that God's Providence brought about all, without his Contrivance or Expectation." [66]

Though Baxter disliked the Protectorate of Oliver Cromwell and cautiously opposed it, he bears witness to the good results of the Protector's religious policy and the opportunity it offered for even greater religious advances than were made. Speaking of his own contemporary observations of the Protector, Baxter says:

as he kept up his approbation of a godly Life in the general, and of all that was good, except that which the Interest of his Sinful Cause engaged him to be against; so I perceived that it was his design to do good in the main, and to promote the Gospel and the Interest of Godliness, more than any had done before him; except in those particulars which his own Interest was against: And it was the principal means that hence-forward he trusted to for his own Establishment, even by *doing good*: That the People might love him, or at least be willing to have his Government *for that Good*, who were against it, as it was *Usurpation*.[67]

Baxter describes his own complex attitude to this strange government. He felt that his duty included disowning the usurper's sin, encouraging his good actions, and approving "of *no Evil* which is done by any, either Usurper or a lawful Governour." [68] He contrasts the liberty which he enjoyed to preach the gospel under a usurper whom he opposed and the miserable state of himself and other godly clergymen under the rule of their rightful King. "Sure I am," he says, "that when it became a matter of Reputation and Honour to be Godly, it abundantly furthered the

[64] Baxter, *RB*, Part I, 98.
[65] *Ibid.*, Part I, 98-100.
[66] *Ibid.*, Part I, 72.
[67] *Ibid.*, Part I, 71.
[68] *Ibid.*, Part I, 71-72.

Successes of the Ministry"; before the war authority and its ally the rabble discountenanced piety.[69] Baxter realizes that there was an apparent contradiction between his disaffection to the Protectorate of Oliver Cromwell and the benefits he and godliness in general received from it, but for him his moral obligation to uphold the legitimate monarchy justified his disaffection and he gives no sign in the *Reliquiae Baxterianae* of repenting of it.

Though Baxter's evidence indicates that Richard Cromwell enjoyed a popular support his father never possessed,[70] Richard was soon overthrown and Charles II set on the way to being restored. In a pedantic analysis of the Restoration, Baxter attributes it to the efforts of "The Ministers of *England* and *Scotland*, and all the sober People who regarded them," in reviving, through their opposition to the usurpation, the overwhelmed strength of Cavaliers, Scots, and Army.[71] It appears from the context that the English branch of these clergy and followers was Puritan. In this way he gives an extraordinary importance to his own group in bringing about the Restoration. His theory does not arise merely out of a desire to prove that the monarchy and established church missed an opportunity for gratitude. It reflects his inflamed opinion of the importance the Puritan clergy enjoyed or deserved to enjoy during their period of freedom. Thus when he speaks of the Army leaders who overthrew Richard, he complains "That they should so proudly despise not only the Parliament, but all the Ministers of *London* and of the Land, as to do this, not only without advising with, and against their Judgments; but in a factious Envy against them, lest they should be too much countenanced: . . ." [72] Similarly in speaking of an earlier event, the execution of the Puritan divine Christopher Love in 1651, he says that "This Blow sunk deeper towards the Root of the New Commonwealth, than will easily be believed; and made" the leaders of the Commonwealth "grow odious to almost [all] the Religious Party in the Land, except the Sectaries." [73] One wonders whether there is not in Baxter's emphasis on the importance of the ministers in ending the Roundhead regime a late recurrence of his provincialism, a reflection of how large his fellow ministers loomed in his thoughts in Worcestershire and how remote from him

---

[69] *Ibid.*, Part I, 84, 86-87.
[70] *Ibid.*, Part I, 100.
[71] *Ibid.*, Part I, 65.
[72] *Ibid.*, Part I, 101.
[73] *Ibid.*, Part I, 67. Does he imply here that Fairfax resigned his commission because of this execution?

at the same time seemed the political events of Cromwellian and early post-Cromwellian London. More conventionally, and without in any way contradicting his views as outlined above, Baxter believes that God used the turbulent officers to restore the King against their intentions.[74]

---

[74] *Ibid.,* Part I, 101, 105, Part II, 214.

CHAPTER VII

PARLIAMENTARIAN AND WHIG HISTORIANS FROM THE RESTORATION TO 1702

1. Survey of the Historians

Edmund Ludlow and Mrs. Lucy Hutchinson differ from all the other Parliamentarian historians of the Civil War who are known to have written in the period from the Restoration to 1702 through the fierceness of their advocacy of the Parliamentarian cause or, more particularly, of the republicanism to which their Parliamentarianism led them. We have seen that in the same period Rushworth expresses his Parliamentarian views only weakly, Whitelocke is close to being a repentant Parliamentarian, and Baxter condemns much of the outcome of the Parliamentarian cause.

While it is not surprising that few Parliamentarian histories were published between the Restoration and the Revolution of 1688 and that those were lukewarm in the defense of the Parliamentarian cause, it is surprising that so few Parliamentarian and Whig histories were published from the Revolution to the end of our period in 1702 and even more surprising that most of those were similarly lukewarm. There must at this time have been few manuscript Parliamentarian histories awaiting publication. And even at this late date, it would seem, potential writers on the war were still so impressed by the Royalists' case that they could not bring themselves seriously to challenge it.

The Parliamentarian demoralization appears in an acute form in Dudley North, fourth baron North, the father of the four North brothers of the famous *Lives of the Norths*. The work that North wrote as a repentant Parliamentarian, called *A Narrative of Some Passages in or Relating to the Long Parliament* (1670), may have increased his readers' understanding of the mentality of the more moderate members of the rebellious Long Parliament, but it is unlikely that it increased anybody's respect for them or for the logic of the Parliament's cause. North observes with surprise that he has "consulted the Histories of several Nations, to see, if I could meet with any thing running paralel to the raising and issue of this War; but I have absolutely failed of doing it." He seems baffled by the problem of finding causes of the war but speaks of discontent over some faults in the government of church and state and troublemakers who poured complaints into "the ears of the generality, whereby they incensed them so far, as thereby they found means to raise a power against their Sovereign." He refers to the state of affairs during the Interregnum as "that Anarchy," and acknowledges in the conventional manner "the miraculous way of Divine providence, in" effecting the Restoration.[1]

If North's work reflects the disasters of the forties and fifties, *The History Of the Execrable Irish Rebellion* (1680) by Edmund Borlase, a Chester physician with literary ambitions, reflects the political and religious tensions of England in the seventies. Borlase as a historian is hostile to the Irish and vaguely favorable to the Parliament. His large and ill written volume is interesting almost entirely for the two following reasons. First, a collection of his papers in the British Museum allows us to follow the history of its publication and reception in a degree of detail rare in the study of the English histories of the century.[2] Secondly, Borlase borrowed freely from a manuscript version of Clarendon's then unpublished *History of the Rebellion and Civil Wars in Ireland,* printing patches of Clarendon's prose as his own while making occasional small verbal alterations to eliminate Clarendon's Royalist bias. Borlase may not have known the name of the author he thus mistreated.[3] It is a curious fact that Clarendon made his historian's debut in the world under the uncouth disguise of Borlase's *History* of the Irish rebellion.

The London bookseller Nathaniel Crouch, who used the pseudonym of Richard Burton, was by contrast with Borlase a writer of workman-

---

[1] [Dudley North, fourth baron North], *A Narrative of Some Passages in or Relating to the Long Parliament* (London, 1670), pp. 88, 8-9, 86-87.

[2] BM, Sloane MSS 1008, 1015, Stowe MS 82, Add. MS 22548 f. 93. The present discussion of Borlase is based on my article, "Edmund Borlase, Historian of the Irish Rebellion," *Studia Hibernica,* 9 (1969), 86-92, in which I discuss Borlase, his *History,* and his manuscripts in the British Museum.

[3] He never identifies the author in any source that I have seen. Significantly, it appears from a letter of the Earl of Anglesey to Dr. Sall, March 22, 1679/80, that Anglesey, who was in a better position than Borlase to know the author's name, was ignorant of it. BM Stowe MS 82 ff. 161-162, or Stowe MS 83 f. 114v. The authorship seems to have been equally unknown to Sir Robert Southwell, whose comments on Borlase's intention of printing a narrative of the Irish rebellion (presumably Clarendon's) have already been reported in my chapter I, note 2, above. However, Nalson knew the name of the author and notes Borlase's use of him with considerable scorn. Nalson, *IC,* II, introd. p. viii.

like, journalistic plainness. The series of competent, popular histories he wrote included *The Wars in England, Scotland and Ireland* (1681), which is a history of England from 1625 to 1660 with special attention to events up to the King's execution, and, more importantly, his very fair-minded *The History of Oliver Cromwel* (1692). In both of these he wrote about the Civil War in a neutral or almost neutral spirit. Simply by refraining from the familiar Royalist denunciation of the Parliamentarians, he suggested that there was, after all, something to be said for them.

At the beginning of the latter book he sums up the difficulties, as he sees them, of discussing Cromwell. *"There have been few Persons,"* he says, *"upon whose actions so many different Sentiments have passed, . . ."* Cromwell has been both praised and condemned extravagantly. Burton observes, somewhat doubtfully, that some have attributed all his greatness to hypocrisy and ambition, and he is openly skeptical about the more extreme theories about Cromwell's long designed plan for his own rise. He sensibly recalls that *"It is a Maxim, That great Virtues have been often mixed with great Vices in many great men in the World,"* and he indicates that his portrait of Cromwell will conform to this maxim. However, his purpose is not to defend or to criticize but only *"to give a plain and Impartial Account of Matters of Fact . . . without Reflections on Parties."* [4]

In practice, this means that as Burton proceeds through his account of Cromwell's life he avoids deciding in detail about the good and the ill of his actions by passing over controversial events with a brief, factual narrative. He can thus seem impartial, but at the expense of being superficial and hasty. The first edition has practically no personal information about Cromwell, who remains only a military and political figure. Later an appendix on "His Character" was added in which Burton attempts to weigh the good and bad in Cromwell but seems to find more of the latter. The result of this appendix is to leave the reader with a poorer opinion of Cromwell than he gains from reading the first edition alone. Burton's *Cromwel* is a transitional work. He has gone beyond the familiar Royalist attitude that Cromwell was a monster who happened to possess a few undeniably princely qualities and points, however uncertainly, toward the nineteenth-century view of him. One can imagine that his book persuaded some readers to be skeptical about Cromwell's supposed

---

[4] R. B[urton], *The History of Oliver Cromwel:* . . . . *Relating only Matters of Fact, without Reflection or Observation* (London, 1692), "To the Reader," sig. A2-[A2]v.

wickedness, but he does not try to force skepticism on the reader by argument or scholarly use of evidence. Instinct and personal sympathy rather than knowledge and intellect inform his book.

After the Revolution of 1688, a number of Whig works appeared. *The Secret History, of the Four last Monarchs of Great Britain* (1691), published anonymously, is a popular history of no scholarly or intellectual value. Its treatment of James I is hostile, its treatment of Charles I neutral except for a jeer at his religion in the preface. D. Jones's *A Continuation of the Secret History of White-Hall; . . . . Together with the Tragical History of the Stuarts* (1697) contains a sensational history of the Stuarts but shuffles over the rise of the Civil War in one page. While hinting very strongly that Charles II arranged the murder of the Earl of Essex in the Tower in 1683, it treats Charles I mildly.

Its author was a friend of Roger Coke, who wrote the ambitious and relatively important Whig history called *A Detection of the Court and State of England during The Four last Reigns, and the Inter-Regnum* (1694; 3rd ed., 1697). Coke is highly critical of the Stuart kings but dislikes the war against Charles I and condemns his execution. His treatment of Cromwell is harsh: Cromwell, as Coke saw him, was a bloody handed usurper at home and injured the interests of England abroad, especially by assisting the rise of France. Coke's *Detection* is a reminder of how little there was in the Whig creed that could induce a man to be sympathetic to Cromwell, but he does manage, with a painful effort at fairmindedness, to include a survey of Cromwell's good deeds (which Burton's *Cromwel* reprints in its later editions) reduced into six points. Perhaps the most unexpected aspect of his book is his marked and very modern concern for economics.

John Seller's faintly Whiggish *The History of England* (1696) was, like Coke's *Detection*, a long work which went through several editions. Seller speaks harshly of James I but has a word of praise for the private character of Charles I and condemns his execution. If Charles had not, he says,

given too much heed to *Buckingham, Laud,* and some other flattering Parasites and Courtiers, who were continually Buzzing into his Ears nothing but Absolute and unlimited Power, putting him upon Dissolving his Parliaments, and then raising Money, and Ruling without them, as appear'd by his Twelve Years interval of Parliaments, *viz.* from *Anno* 1628, to 1640. whereby he lost the Love of his People; he had never been brought to that dismal Catastrophe, but might have Liv'd and Dy'd a Happy Prince.[5]

---

[5] John Seller, *The History of England. Giving a True and Impartial Account of the most Considerable Transactions . . . from the coming of Julius Caesar into Britain* (London, 1696), p. 601.

Seller can find things to praise as well as to condemn in Oliver Cromwell: he was courted and feared by the continental powers and made England renowned throughout the world, he had "singular Courage and Resolution," and his army was admirably well disciplined and free from the usual military vices of swearing, drunkenness, and profaneness. "In short," Seller finds, "had he not been a *Usurper*, he might have been compar'd with the best of our Princes: but his Usurpation, and the indirect means he used to obtain his Power, spoil'd all his Good Qualities." [6]

The Whig spirit is stronger in the *Memoirs Of the Most Material Transactions in England, for The Last Hundred Years, Preceding the Revolution in 1688* (first three editions, 1700), by James Wellwood, a Scots physician who had settled in England. Wellwood praises Queen Elizabeth and holds that with her "dy'd in a great part the Glory and Fortune of the *English* Nation." When the unsatisfactory reign of James ended he was little lamented, and he left a doleful legacy of troubles to his son.[7] While Wellwood notices that the seeds of rebellion were already germinating in James's reign, he also finds that later mismanagement of public affairs helped produce it. The fall of the monarchy and hierarchy was "in great part" owing to Laud's "indiscreet Zeal." Charles's "*Immoderate Desire of Power*, beyond what the Constitution did allow of, was the Rock he split upon." Whatever persons advised the King to make the attempt on the Five Members "are justly chargeable with all the Blood that was afterwards spilt; for this sudden Action was the first and visible Ground of all our following Miseries." [8] "No Age," he generously remarks in discussing the early undivided Long Parliament, "ever produc'd Greater Men than those that sat in this Parliament." Even future Royalists joined in the Parliament's attacks on the misgovernment of the reign. Remarking on the difficulty of determining which side began the war, he suggests that both sides drifted into "a *Fatal and Bloody War*; which, it's reasonable to believe, was never design'd at first by either Side," by making military preparations without thinking realistically about their consequences.[9]

Oliver Cromwell, he holds, was a great man who would have been justly honored by posterity if he had not killed the King and violated his

[6] *Ibid.*, pp. 614-615.
[7] James Wellwood, *Memoirs Of the Most Material Transaction in England, for The Last Hundred Years, Preceding the Revolution in 1688*, 3rd ed. (London, 1700), pp. 18, 20, 42.
[8] *Ibid.*, pp. 42, 92, 68.
[9] *Ibid.*, pp. 50-51, 69-71.

country's liberties. Probably Cromwell intended to restore the King after his removal from Holmby House in 1647 but was forced to change his mind and destroy the King to preserve his own position when information about his intentions of restoring the King was in danger of coming to light. After Cromwell's death, the *"Natural Byass"* of the English led them back to monarchy. Cool though he is towards many aspects of the character and regime of Charles II, Wellwood approves of the institution of monarchy ("Our Ancestors had wisely settled themselves upon that *Bottom*"), as was fitting for a good Whig to do.[10]

2. Edmund Ludlow and Mrs. Lucy Hutchinson

The *Memoirs* of himself written by Edmund Ludlow (1617?-1692) and the *Memoirs of the Life of Colonel Hutchinson* written by the Colonel's wife Lucy Hutchinson (1620-1681 or 1681/2), will be treated together, because they have so much in common in origin, form, and interpretation that any attempt to treat them separately cannot avoid an appearance of repetition.

These writers were born to good families. Mrs. Hutchinson occasionally reveals her sense of rank by expressing scorn for the socially inferior in the *Hutchinson Memoirs*, and one can even find limited evidence of Ludlow's similar attitude to the socially inferior in his *Memoirs*. This sense of rank was not inconsistent with the revolutionary yet often aloof and aristocratic English republicanism of their time, but in practice, if applied to daily affairs, it must have caused difficulties. It is therefore not surprising to find Ludlow repudiating it sufficiently on one occasion to admit that although Hewson and Pride had been (so he reports) a shoemaker and a drayman, yet "had they driven no worse trade, I know not why any good man should refuse to act with them." [11] His own father was a Wiltshire knight who brought notice – or simply infamy – upon himself by declaring in the Long Parliament as early as May 1642 that Charles was not worthy to be King of England. Mrs. Hutchinson was the daughter of a lieutenant of the Tower of London and sister of a prominent Royalist, Clarendon's friend Sir Allen Apsley the Younger.

---

[10] *Ibid.*, pp. 107, 115-116, 118.
[11] Edmund Ludlow, *The Memoirs of Edmund Ludlow Lieutenant-General of the Horse in the Army of the Commonwealth of England 1625-1672*, ed. C. H. Firth, 2 vols. (Oxford, 1894), II, 32; cf. I, 139, II, 275, and Firth's introd., I, xxvi. Cf. Mrs. Lucy Hutchinson, *Memoirs of the Life of Colonel Hutchinson Governor of Nottingham*, ed. C. H. Firth, new ed. (London, George Routledge & Sons, Ltd., 1906), pp. 45, 64, 71, 105, 227.

Entering the Civil War in 1642 as a member of the Earl of Essex' bodyguard, Ludlow became a devoted and valuable servant, first of the Parliament and then afterwards of the republican idea.[12] During the struggle against Charles I he served in a series of military engagements, most notably his defense of Wardour Castle in which he showed in military action some of the stubbornness which was later to characterize his political career. He was elected to Parliament in 1646. He sided with the Army in its quarrel with the Parliament, assisted in Pride's Purge, and served as a regicide judge and as a member of the Council of State of the Commonwealth. In 1650 he became lieutenant-general of the horse in Ireland, and after the death of Ireton he held the supreme command in Ireland for almost a year. As a republican he opposed the rule of the two Protectors with great firmness. In the political commotions which followed upon Richard's fall Ludlow fought energetically against the ambition and treachery which were undermining the possibility of a stable republican government and against the slide of political power back into the possession of the House of Stuart.

The avalanche proved impossible to resist, and Ludlow describes with disgust the ceremonies and debaucheries which accompanied the return of Charles II to London. ". . . it was," he says, recalling the scenes he witnessed,

a strange sight to me, to see the horse that had formerly belonged to our army, now put upon an employment so different from that which they had at first undertaken; especially, when I consider'd that for the most part they had not been raised out of the meanest of the people, and without distinction, as other armies had been; but that they consisted of such as had engaged themselves from a spirit of liberty in the defence of their rights and religion: but having been corrupted under the tyranny of Cromwel, and kept up as a standing force against the people, they had forgotten their first engagements, and were become as mercenary as other troops are accustomed to be.[13]

He scorns the pageantry with which the King was received – ceremonies of any kind seem to arouse Ludlow's resentment, and he often shows his disrespect for them in the *Memoirs* – and he notes that "The dissolution and drunkenness of that night was so great and scandalous, in a nation

---

[12] The chief sources of information about Ludlow's life are his *Memoirs* and C. H. Firth's introduction to his edition of the *Memoirs* and his life of Ludlow in the *DNB*. E. S. de Beer in *N & Q*, 207 (1962), 223, adds a little information on Ludlow's life as an exile. All biographical data above on Ludlow, unless otherwise identified, come from these sources.

[13] Ludlow, *Memoirs*, II, 274-275.

which had not been acquainted with such disorders for many years past," that the new King was forced to issue a proclamation against drinking of healths to placate the Presbyterian dupes who "had betray'd all into his hands." [14] Mrs. Hutchinson, who thought "it was a wonder in that day to see the mutability of some, and the hypocrisy of others, and the servile flattery of all," shows that her husband, Ludlow's fellow regicide John Hutchinson, was sufficiently shaken by this crisis or catastrophe of the republican cause to ask himself if his course of political action had been justifiable. He concluded after careful re-examination of the evidence that the answer was yes,[15] but it is hard to imagine the stolid Ludlow even asking the question.

The remaining thirty-two years of Ludlow's life were spent mainly as an exile in Switzerland, where he escaped plots against his life engineered by the adherents of the Stuarts and wrote his *Memoirs*. His recollections were his principal source of information in writing; probably he destroyed his personal papers before he left England. He did, however, use among other sources a manuscript of the then unpublished *Memoirs of Sir John Berkley* (1699), which had been "left in the hands of a merchant at Geneva," [16] and printed accounts of the trials of the regicides. How faithful the existing printed text of Ludlow's *Memoirs* is to what Ludlow actually wrote remains at the present date of writing uncertain, as the manuscript has long been lost except for a portion of it covering the period from "the eve of the Restoration" to 1676, which reappeared recently to be sold at Sotheby's.[17] In discussing Ludlow in the present chapter, I have assumed, somewhat hesitantly, that the printed text gives an adequate picture of his views, but I have tried not to stress any statement from its pages unless it was confirmed by other passages or consistent with the apparent general tenor of his life and personality.

The life of Mrs. Hutchinson – to turn now to her – is closely interwoven with that of her regicide husband, whose career had much in common with that of Ludlow.[18] She had the good fortune to receive a

[14] *Ibid.*, II, 275.
[15] Hutchinson, *Memoirs*, pp. 322, 331.
[16] Ludlow, *Memoirs*, I, 153.
[17] See the catalogue of the sale of June 23, 1970, for a description of the manuscript.
[18] The chief sources of information about Mrs. Hutchinson's life are the *Hutchinson Memoirs*, Firth's introduction to his edition of these *Memoirs* and his life of Col. and Mrs. Hutchinson in the *DNB*, and Mrs. Hutchinson's "The Life of Mrs. Lucy Hutchinson Written by Herself," printed with the *Hutchinson Memoirs*. "S.R." (probably Sydney Race) in *N & Q*, 174 (1938), 39, sheds new light on the date of Mrs. Hutchinson's death with the information that she was buried in "1681," probably in October. All biographical information above about Mrs. Hutchinson, unless otherwise identified, comes from these sources.

far more thorough education than most women of her time and class and grew up under the influence of a Puritanical mother. The grave child of her short, uncompleted autobiographical sketch, who tired out her fellow children "with more grave instructions than their mothers" and who used to turn the "idle discourses" of her mother's maids to "good subjects," [19] reappears in the *Hutchinson Memoirs* as the reserved young student John Hutchinson married in 1638. The courtship which preceded this event gives rise to one of Mrs. Hutchinson's vigorous pieces of writing and has been a comfort to readers who have felt a need to demonstrate to themselves that even the Puritans were human. Readers untroubled by this need will suspect the presence of romantic exaggeration. Hutchinson became governor of the town and castle of Nottingham for the Parliament during the war, a Member of Parliament, a regicide judge, and a member of the Council of State of the Commonwealth, but he opposed the personal rule of Cromwell. Mrs. Hutchinson was in close contact with the troubled events of these times, especially during the period of her husband's governorship. The fierce and narrow intolerance with which she regards the opinions and failings of so many members of her own side as well as of the Royalists in the *Memoirs* may reflect an embitterment of her feelings following the Restoration and the failure of the Parliamentarian cause, but it is hard to avoid a suspicion that it also reproduces the spirit in which she lived through the war.

Her husband managed to escape death at the Restoration, partly because of his servile submission to the new authority, but he was arrested in 1663 on suspicion of being involved in a plot and died, still a captive, in squalid surroundings at Sandown Castle on the Kentish seacoast in the following year. In a passage of magnificent defiance that makes one forget she was not an eyewitness of the proceedings, Mrs. Hutchinson describes the return of his body to Owthorpe in his native Nottinghamshire for burial:

The next day after they had gotten out the body, they brought it with a handsome private equipage to Canterbury, and so forward towards London, meeting no affronts in their way but at one town, where there was a fair, and the priest of the place came out, with his clerk in his fool's coat, to offer them burial, and to stop their hearse laid hold on the horses, whom when the attendants put by, the wicked rout at the fair took part with them, and set upon the horsemen; but they broke several of their heads, and made their way clear, having beaten off all the town and the fair, and came on to London. They passed through Southwark, over the bridge, and through the whole heart of the city, to their lodging in Holborn, in the day time, and

[19] Hutchinson, "Life ... Written by Herself," *Memoirs,* p. 15.

had not one reviling word or indignity offered them all the way, but several people were very much moved at that sad witness of the murderous cruelty of the men then in power.

From London he was brought down to Owthorpe, very seriously bewailed all the way he came along by all those who had been better acquainted with his worth than the strangers were among whom he died, and was brought home with honour to his grave through the dominions of his murtherers, who were ashamed of his glories, which all their tyrannies could not extinguish with his life.[20]

The little that is known about Mrs. Hutchinson's subsequent life hints at misfortune and unhappiness and an exile in the bosom of her country as dark as ever we can imagine Ludlow's being, especially if we place emphasis on her complaint, belonging apparently to this period, that "my infirmities and imperfections, ioynd with my outward ill successes have much weakend my authority, and made it of no force with all persons." [21] Yet it was in this period, presumably between her husband's death in 1664 and 1671,[22] that she wrote the *Memoirs* and immortalized herself and him. Her information came principally from her recollections, but she also knew Thomas May's histories.[23] Various writers have adhered to the belief that she took the Duchess of Newcastle's *Life* (1667) of the Duke of Newcastle in either its manuscript or printed form as her model, but I have shown elsewhere [24] that this belief is based on speculation, not evidence. There is nothing improbable in the idea that someone as intellectually active as Mrs. Hutchinson, who had occasion to mention the Duke of Newcastle a number of times in her history, would read the *Life* of the Duke when it appeared in print. It is, however, hard to believe that she could have felt much esteem for the fanciful Duchess. Nor, for that matter, is Mrs. Hutchinson, who was very far from being a feminist and expresses her views very strongly on the due subordination and the inferiority of women to the stronger sex,[25] likely to have approved very warmly, if she approved at all, of the decision of the Duchess to follow a literary career.

[20] Hutchinson, *Memoirs*, p. 382.

[21] Mrs. Lucy Hutchinson, *On the Principles of the Christian Religion, Addressed to Her Daughter; and on Theology* (London, 1817), introd., p. 1. This book is discussed by Elizabeth Braund, "Mrs. Hutchinson and Her Teaching," *The Evangelical Quarterly*, 31 (1959), 72-81.

[22] Firth's introd. to Hutchinson, *Memoirs*, pp. xi-xii.

[23] *Ibid.*, p. xiii; Hutchinson, *Memoirs*, p. 78.

[24] R. MacGillivray, "The Upham Thesis and the Literary Debts of Mrs. Lucy Hutchinson," *Revue de l'Université d'Ottawa*, 40 (1970), 618-630. This article is a reply to A. H. Upham, "Lucy Hutchinson and the Duchess of Newcastle," *Anglia*, 36 (1912), 200-220, and other writers cited in my article.

[25] Hutchinson, *Memoirs*, pp. 72, 278; Hutchinson, *Principles*, p. 6.

The Duchess is all charming affectations and simpering femininity, but Mrs. Hutchinson writes with a hardheaded aggressiveness well suited to the defeated but uncrushed enemy of an entire political order. This contrast is illustrated by a statement the Duchess could not possibly have penned. Describing in the *Memoirs* her husband's waiting before the doors of authority on a certain occasion after the Restoration, Mrs. Hutchinson says, "But at last, *parturiunt montes*! and out comes Secretary Bennett!" [26] The *Memoirs* are not only an account of the Colonel for his children, to whom they are addressed, not only a vindication of the righteous (how pitifully few in number!), but a defiant story of survival and triumph in a world of little men, though what survived was neither a man nor a cause, but the greatness of Colonel Hutchinson, which he carried triumphantly with him unscathed through the world to his grave.

Her opinions throughout the *Memoirs* are impressed on the reader by a style of exceptional clarity, expressiveness, and rhetorical force. The more unattractive aspects of her strong character are shown by the fact that it is so often unpleasant emotions or others not far different from them that provide the occasions for her best prose passages. Some verses she wrote about the garden of her house at Owthorpe,[27] in which she laments for her husband as the gardener who will never return and touches on the theme of the irreversibility of human life (the garden may flourish under the influence of "Another gardener and another spring," but her loss has left her an irremediably defective person) carry traces of her habitual severity yet reveal at the same time the gentle, non-political emotions which she might have brilliantly cultivated in print in an age less tortured by politics.

Though the *Ludlow Memoirs* were published at the end of the seventeenth century, within a decade of their author's death, the *Hutchinson Memoirs* remained in manuscript till 1806, when the Reverend Julius Hutchinson published them, trimmed of what he considered superfluous material – mostly, it must be confessed, to the artistic benefit of the book – and with many small stylistic alterations. In a proud but timorous preface, this descendant of the Colonel's half brother demonstrated nervously that if the Colonel were then alive he would be an Anglican or at the worst a very moderate Dissenter and would be a firm upholder of

---

[26] Hutchinson, *Memoirs*, p. 353.

[27] I am grateful to the City of Nottingham Public Libraries for letting me examine the manuscript of these verses and for providing me with a xerox copy of them. A portion of them is printed in Christopher Hill, "Colonel John Hutchinson, 1615-1664: a Tercentenary Tribute," *Transactions of the Thoroton Society of Nottinghamshire*, 69 (1965), p. 87. See Hutchinson, *Memoirs*, p. 376, for a passage on planting and gardens which may throw light on their origins.

the Hanoverian settlement.[28] All the existing editions of the *Memoirs* are based on the defective text of the first editor, but the most important of the omitted passages have been printed in *Notes and Queries* from the manuscript, now preserved in the City of Nottingham Museum and Art Gallery at the Castle, Nottingham.[29] All quotations from the *Memoirs* in the present chapter are from the printed text, but they have been checked against the manuscript to ensure that they reproduce exactly the thought and exactly or almost exactly the words of Mrs. Hutchinson.

Since the religious opinions of few seventeenth-century historians of the Civil War can be ignored in a close examination of their historical views, the religious opinions of Ludlow and Mrs. Hutchinson should be considered. Ludlow was accused of being an Anabaptist, and Firth concludes that he "was in sympathy with the extremer sectaries." [30] There is little evidence of religious feeling and no description of his own theological tenets in his *Memoirs*, but this need not necessarily be attributed to faintness of interest in religion; it is his practice to omit facts, such as the date of his birth and marriage, which have only personal significance. It is by no means impossible that an intense personal religion was one of the keys to Ludlow's life and largely explains its strange and troubled course. The *Memoirs* may simply be deceptive as to the importance of religion for him, just as the printed *Memorials* of Bulstrode Whitelocke are deceptive as to its importance for Whitelocke. A religious interpretation of Ludlow's career would help to explain how a man who seems, to the casual eye, a born receptacle for conservative and conventional ideas ended up so determined a revolutionary. But whatever his most intimate convictions may have been, one aspect of Ludlow's religious outlook is sufficiently clear in the *Memoirs* – his anticlericalism. The

[28] His fear of being mistaken for a republican is ridiculed in *The Edinburgh Review*, 13 (1808-1809), p. 25.

[29] I am grateful to the Corporation of Nottingham, which owns this manuscript, and to the Museum and Art Gallery for allowing me to study it and obtain a microfilm of it. A valuable series of articles by Sydney Race, *N & Q*, 145 (1923), 3-4, 26-28, 165-166; 183 (1942), 166; 197 (1952), 32-33; 199 (1954), 160-163, 202-204, contains information on manuscripts and other matters pertaining to Mrs. Hutchinson and prints some of the omitted passages of the *Memoirs*.
BM Add. MSS 39779, ff. 42-47v, 46172N, 25901, contain part of an early draft of the *Memoirs*; the abovementioned Museum and Art Gallery has a further leaf of this draft. For a discussion of this draft, see Firth's introd. to Hutchinson, *Memoirs*, and Sydney Race, "The British Museum MS. of the Life of Colonel Hutchinson, and Its Relation to the Published Memoirs," *Transactions of the Thoroton Society*, 18 (1914), 35-66.

[30] Firth's introd. to Ludlow, *Memoirs*, I, xxviii; Baxter, *RB*, Part I, 74, says that Ludlow "headed the Anabaptists in *Ireland*." W. T. Whitley, "General Ludlow's Baptist Comrades," *The Baptist Quarterly*, n.s., 11 (1942-1945), 39-45, casts no further light on Ludlow's religious opinions.

principal matter appertaining to religion in the book is his expression of dislike and suspicion of the clergy, without any apparent distinction as to their doctrines. Typical of his attitude to the clergy are his suggestions, referring to the year 1659, that the clergy have other interests to promote than that of the whole commonwealth, and are "a distinct party from the people," and his complaints that they resist reformation of their abuses, and that "the corrupt interests of the lawyers and clergy" were espoused by the restored Rump Parliament.[31] He does, however, make exceptions for individuals so far as to show marked respect for Robert Balsum, a minister who accompanied him during his stand at Wardour Castle.[32] Mrs. Hutchinson shows a far wider interest in the religious concerns of her time than Ludlow but shares his anticlericalism. The various clergymen who appear in her narrative almost all encounter her strong disapproval, and she is fond of an unmistakably scornful use of the word "priest" to designate some of the Puritan clergy. She describes the conversion of her husband and herself to Anabaptist tenets during the war.[33]

While Ludlow and Mrs. Hutchinson develop their interpretations of the war within a similar framework of political attitudes, their differing tastes and opportunities for observation produce considerable differences in approach. The *Ludlow Memoirs* are more important than the *Hutchinson Memoirs* as a source of factual information about national political events during the period of the war, partly because Ludlow played a more prominent part in national political life than Colonel Hutchinson. On the other hand, the *Hutchinson Memoirs* reveal the activities of a human being much more fully than the impersonal *Ludlow Memoirs,* which are devoted mostly to political and military topics, and they contain a much wider and much more reflective view of the origins of the war. These writers' interpretations coincide most sharply in dealing with events after the end of the First Civil War.

At the beginning of his *Memoirs* Ludlow gives a short and confused account of the origins of the war. He recounts various grievances against the government of Charles I, including what he considers Charles's betrayal of the Protestants of Rochelle, the advancement of a superstitious clergy, various religious abuses, and ship-money and other irregular

---

[31] Ludlow, *Memoirs,* II, 161, 133. For other criticisms of clergy and lawyers together, see *ibid.,* I, 365, 368, II, 356, and of lawyers alone, *ibid.,* I, 333-334.

[32] *Ibid.,* I, 74-75. He includes "two or three more religious men" with Balsum in this commendation but does not make clear that they were clergymen.

[33] Hutchinson, *Memoirs,* pp. 242-243. She speaks of "the ill-humours of the factious committee-men and priests," "the mouths of all the priests and all their idolaters," "Palmer the Priest," "a coachful of presbyterian priests." *Ibid.,* pp. 182, 211, 231, 256.

sources of revenue. No doubt he assembled this list from memory, for it contains many errors. He supposes, for example, that Charles went to war with France *after* the dissolution of the Parliament of 1628-1629 and that the Etcetera Oath was imposed some years before 1640. He censures the clerical supporters of the King, "whose influence upon the King was always greater than could well consist with the peace and happiness of England," but he hardly seems aware of the presence of a Puritan opposition to the official religious policies.[34]

In Ludlow's view, Charles was determined to establish a personal despotism. James, too, had this ambition but chose to advance it by fraud rather than violence; Charles, "having taken a nearer view of despotick government in his journey to France and Spain, tempted with the glittering shew and imaginary pleasures of that empty pageantry, immediately after his ascent to the throne" showed he intended "to make the Crown absolute and independent." [35] The ambitions of the King and his clergy led to the attempt to force a Prayer Book on the Scots. Ludlow says:

> Prerogative being wound up to this height in England, and the affairs of the Church tending to a conjunction with the See of Rome; before any farther progress should be made therein here, it was thought expedient, that the pulse of Scotland should be felt, and they perswaded or compelled to the like conformity.[36]

Then followed the Bishops' Wars, the Short Parliament, the Long Parliament, and the Irish rebellion, news of which, Ludlow says, "(as I have heard from persons of undoubted credit) was not displeasing to the King." Charles rejected the Nineteen Propositions because he presumed that "if reduced to the last extremity" he could obtain terms equally good, "and that if his arms succeeded according to his hopes, his will might pass for a law, pursuant to the opinion of those who thought no way so likely to render his authority absolute, as the making of a war upon his people." [37] Thus the English people fought to preserve their liberty from an aggressive King.

Mrs. Hutchinson's reflections on the origins of the war possess a comprehensiveness which not only marks her off from Ludlow, whose remarks on this question amount to little more than a loose collection of notes, but from most other seventeenth-century historians of the war. She not only discusses the standard grievances against James I and Charles

[34] The content of this paragraph comes from Ludlow, *Memoirs,* I, 9-13, the quotation from I, 10.
[35] *Ibid.,* I, 9-10.
[36] *Ibid.,* I, 13.
[37] *Ibid.,* I, 20, 34.

I, but includes a wide-ranging discussion of pre-war Puritanism and traces the socio-economic origins of the war back into the Middle Ages and Reformation period in accordance with the theories associated with the name of James Harrington. Her Harringtonian passage is long but deserves to be quoted in full:

The nobility of the realm having at first the great balance of the lands, and retaining some of that free honourable virtue, for which they were exalted above the vulgar, ever stood up in people's [MS of the *Memoirs* has: "the peoples"] defence and curbed the wild ambition of the tyrants, whom they sometimes reduced to moderation, and sometimes deposed for their mis-governments; till, at length the kings, eager to break this yoke, had insensibly worn out the interest of the nobility by drawing them to their courts, where luxuries melted away the great estates of some, others were destroyed by confiscations in divers civil wars, and others otherwise mouldered with time. While the kings were glad to see the abatement of that power, which had been such a check to their exorbitancies, they perceived not the growing of another more dangerous to them; and that when the nobility shrunk into empty names, the throne lost its supporters, and had no more but a little puff of wind to bear it up, when the full body of the people came rolling in upon it. The interest of the people, which had been many years growing, made an extraordinary progress in the days of King Henry the Eighth, who returning the vast revenues of the church into the body of the people, cast the balance clear on their side, and left them now only to expect an opportunity to resume their power into their own hands; and had not differences in religion [MS has: "which had not the different interests of religion"] divided them among themselves, and thereby prolonged the last gasps of expiring monarchy, they had long since exercised it in a free commonwealth.[38]

Mrs. Hutchinson does not mention the name of Harrington or explain how she came into contact with these views. It was not necessary that they be derived from Harrington himself or his writings; there was a community of ideas, for example, between Harrington and Henry Neville, Hutchinson's colleague in the Council of State, and Harringtonian ideas appear in other writers of the times, even making a slight, unstressed appearance in Ludlow's pages.[39] But Mrs. Hutchinson made or adopted one minor but shrewd emendation of the Harringtonian doctrines as

[38] Hutchinson, *Memoirs*, pp. 61-62.
[39] For the community of views between Neville and Harrington, the prevalence of Harringtonian ideas at the time of the Protectorate, and Ludlow's Harringtonian ideas, see H. R. Trevor-Roper, *The Gentry 1540-1640* (The Economic History Review Supplements, 1, n.d.), pp. 45-47; cf. Ludlow, *Memoirs*, II, 59. Neville is mentioned in Hutchinson, *Memoirs*, pp. 352, 358, 359, but not in connection with his ideas. Firth's introd. to Hutchinson, *Memoirs*, does not mention Mrs. Hutchinson's debt to Harringtonian ideas; it is, however, noted without additional comment in Christopher Hill, *Puritanism and Revolution: Studies in Interpretation of the English Revolution of the 17th Century* (London, Secker & Warburg, 1958), p. 310.

expounded in *Oceana*. Why did not the people sooner take advantage of the shift in property and decay in the real power of the monarchy and take political power into their own hands? Harrington attributes the prolongation of the monarchy to the lack of an occasion by which "the *people* not apt to see their own strength, should be put to feel it." [40] Mrs. Hutchinson finds the reason in religious differences. Her suggestion, it will be noted, accords better with the fact of the Restoration than does Harrington's.

Mrs. Hutchinson's view of James I who thus, according to her belief, inherited a decaying monarchy, is scathing. "The honour, wealth, and glory of the nation," she says, "wherein Queen Elizabeth left it, were soon prodigally wasted by this thriftless heir." James hated the godly people of England and Scotland for their treatment of his mother and desired, in some way consistent with his cowardice, to have revenge on them. His court "was a nursery of lust and intemperance" which corrupted the gentry of the land.[41] The rise of Buckingham was attributable to "no merit but that of his beauty and prostitution." [42] The modern concept of homosexuality had not in Mrs. Hutchinson's time yet taken form in the English mind, though of course the basic element for at least the concept of male homosexuality existed in the realization that men sometimes had sexual relations with others of their own sex. Hacket seems to feel that some explanation is necessary for James's habitual attachment to favorites, but he comes up with no better explanation than "the sweetness of this King's Nature." [43] But other contemporaries were franker, more cynical, or better informed about James or human nature, and Mrs. Hutchinson doubtless merely echoes contemporary report instead of relying on any secret information or on speculations of her own.[44]

---

[40] James Harrington, *James Harrington's Oceana,* ed. S. B. Liljegren (Heidelberg, Carl Winters Universitätsbuchhandlung, 1924), p. 49.
[41] Hutchinson, *Memoirs,* pp. 64-65.
[42] *Ibid.,* p. 68, cf. pp. 65, 69; cf. Hutchinson, *Principles,* pp. 273, 277.
[43] Hacket, *SR* (London, 1693), Part I, 39; cf. Part II, 36.
[44] [Francis Osborne], *Historical Memoires on the Reigns of Queen Elizabeth and King James* (London, 1658), Part II, 128, says that James's treatment of his favorites in public "prompted many to Imagine some things done in the Tyring-house, that exceed my expressions no lesse then they do my experience." Cf. [Sir Balthazar Gerbier?], *The None-Such Charles His Character* (London, 1651), pp. 20-21, 30. Yet perhaps the seventeenth-century reticence on the subject of James's sexual behavior, even among writers by no means sympathetic to the Stuarts, is more remarkable than any of the seventeenth-century comments on it. Wallace Notestein, *Four Worthies* (London, Jonathan Cape, 1956), p. 70, remarks that "It is hard in the literature of the time to find allusions to the matter, except in a cipher diary where we learn that the students of Gray's Inn were less reticent."

King Charles, in contrast to his father, was, she admits, "temperate, chaste, and serious." Under him "the fools and bawds, mimics and catamites, of the former court, grew out of fashion." But he was also "a prince that had nothing of faith or truth, justice or generosity, in him," and "was the most obstinate person in his self-will that ever was, and so bent upon being an absolute, uncontrollable sovereign, that he was resolved either to be such a king or none." [45] She speaks of his apparent approval of the poisoning of his father by the Duke of Buckingham and his countenancing of the Irish rebellion,[46] and records as well the more pedestrian grievances against him – the breaking of Parliaments, the betrayal and neglect of foreign Protestants, ship-money and other illegal exactions, romanizing prelates, the influence of Henrietta-Maria, and the suppression of Puritans.

Her remarks on the Puritans are illuminating. She traces the history of the Puritans from the early days of the Reformation, with occasional glances at continental religious struggles. In the reign of James, she complains in a longish, vigorously worded passage,[47] the term "Puritan" was used to asperse anyone who opposed or refused to share the wickedness of the court and other privileged elements in society. Though she does not make an explicit contrast between this use and the earlier uses of the term, the passage is clear enough to enable us to place Mrs. Hutchinson among those writers – Fuller, Hacket, and Baxter have already been noted as such – who saw an extension of the term in the reign of James I.

The "Puritan party," as she calls it, found its enemies not only in the government and the ungodly, but in false professors within its own ranks. Some persons joined the Puritan party for reasons of frustrated ambition; some joined to enrich themselves from their devotees; some tried to advance the Puritan party by skulduggery at court; and the party received unhealthy accessions as persons were driven into it by the violence of the Puritans' opponents.[48] She seems also to find fault with those Puritans who were sincere, for she says that of the gentry who were not plunged "in the mire of sin and wickedness," there were but few "that had not

---

[45] Hutchinson, *Memoirs*, pp. 69-70. She sees the English monarchy as historically a "bounded monarchy" which ambitious princes had from time to time tried to convert into an absolute monarchy. Hutchinson, *Memoirs*, pp. 61-62; "Life . . . Written by Herself," *ibid.*, p. 4.

[46] Hutchinson, *Memoirs*, pp. 68, 70, 77, 78.

[47] *Ibid.*, pp. 65-66. She holds, pp. 66-67, that the Papists "wanted not industry and subtlety to blow the coals between" the Puritans and their opponents.

[48] *Ibid.*, p. 67.

natural and superstitious follies, that were in some kind justly ridiculous and contemptible." [49]

These views on the origins of the war and on Puritanism are more striking than her views on the progress of hostilities. On that subject, she is hardly richer in ideas than Ludlow, and her account has both the advantage and the disadvantage of being strongly personal as she follows her husband through the minutiae of Nottinghamshire politics and warfare. While her narrative no doubt grows tedious to most readers who are not themselves Nottinghamshire people, it does recapture impressively the uncertainties, gambles, rivalries, and personal conflicts of a minor garrison.

In the account Ludlow gives of the hostilities in his *Memoirs,* we find complaints about the untrustworthiness shown by so many of his fellow Parliamentarians. These complaints are colored by one of Ludlow's favorite themes, that of betrayal. Betrayal seems to be his explanation for the ruin of the Parliamentarian and republican cause.[50] His distrust for Manchester and Essex and indeed for the nobility in general is marked. Speaking of the year 1644, he says that "by this time it was clearly manifest that the nobility had no further quarrel with the King, than till they could make their terms with him, having, for the most part, grounded their dissatisfactions upon some particular affront, or the prevalency of a faction about him." [51] Others, too, among the Parliamentarians badly lacked public spirit. Some made private agreements with the King; some who had acquired estates in the service of the Parliament next adhered to the King in order to preserve their gains; some whose real inclination was always to the King sat in Parliament during the fighting only to preserve their estates, which lay in the Parliament's territory and aided the King by their votes; and some, of course, "were contented to sacrifice all civil liberties to the ambition of the Presbyterian clergy," to which Ludlow was thoroughly opposed.[52] In the *Hutchinson Memoirs* the idea of betrayal exists only unobtrusively; no doubt Mrs. Hutchinson had too flexible an intelligence to be as much absorbed by it as Ludlow.

After the fallings off from the cause which Ludlow has described came the execution of the King. It is difficult to find evidence for Guizot's assertion, in his helpful and perceptive essay on Ludlow, that remem-

[49] *Ibid.,* p. 56.
[50] His views on the successive betrayals are conveniently summed up in his report of the account of the Civil War which he gave to the senators of Bern. Ludlow, *Memoirs,* II, 355-357. Cf. the opening sentence of the *Memoirs* with its complaint of betrayal.
[51] *Ibid.,* I, 105, II, 355-356.
[52] *Ibid.,* I, 135-136, 146-147.

brance of this act can be detected in the *Ludlow Memoirs* as "a source of regret and disquietude to" Ludlow. It is true that Ludlow's failure to dwell long upon the execution might be explained by saying that "he did not dare to relate in detail the death of the king," but it can be better explained by saying that the execution made little impression on this man of inflexible mind and unemotional temperament. Unless the passage is the interpolation of an editor, it is significant that he describes Juxon's ministrations to the King a few days before the execution with severe irony.[53] Mrs. Hutchinson contemplates the death of the King without enthusiasm and without regret and explains and justifies her husband's action with moderation in a passage which is a striking depiction of the motives, fears, and uncertainties of a great historical moment.[54] She mentions the apprehension of some persons that if they did not punish the King, "God would require at their hands all the blood and desolation which should ensue by their suffering him to escape"; while she does not mention what attitude Colonel Hutchinson took to the idea of divinely resented blood-guilt, the idea is accepted in the *Ludlow Memoirs*.[55]

Ludlow and Mrs. Hutchinson speak with warm praise of the government of the republican Parliament after the act of regicide. Their sentiments may be summed up in the statements of Mrs. Hutchinson, who speaks of "that glorious parliament" and asserts that it "restored the commonwealth to such a happy, rich, and plentiful condition, as it was not so flourishing before the war." [56] In the grave indictment these republicans present of Cromwell, the destruction of the republican Parliament is a major charge, and their sentiments about the Parliamentary disruption of 1653 are expressed in the statement of Ludlow that the nation was

likely to attain in a short time that measure of happiness which humane things are capable of, when by the ambition of one man the hopes and expectations of all good men were disappointed, and the people robbed of that liberty which they had contended for at the expence of so much blood and treasure.[57]

An early critic of Ludlow's *Memoirs* thought that Ludlow was inconsistent because he condemned Cromwell's action of 1653 but approved of

[53] *Ibid.*, I, 218-219; F. P. G. Guizot, *Monk's Contemporaries. Biographic Studies on the English Revolution*, trans. Andrew R. Scoble (London, 1851), p. 57. This work also contains a good essay on Mrs. Hutchinson.

[54] Hutchinson, *Memoirs*, pp. 271-272.

[55] *Ibid.*, p. 271, cf. pp. 270, 322; Ludlow, *Memoirs*, I, 135, 207, cf. 185.

[56] Hutchinson, *Memoirs*, pp. 305, 319, 292, cf. p. 273; Ludlow, *Memoirs*, I, 349-350, II, 231.

[57] *Ibid.*, I, 343-344, cf. II, 356; Hutchinson, *Memoirs*, pp. 291-293.

Pride's Purge.[58] Ludlow of course does not worry about the inconsistency; for him it was resolved by his pursuit of the English republic. Mrs. Hutchinson, with greater consistency, describes Pride's Purge as "this insolent force upon the house," even though it was directed against her husband's opponents, and says that Colonel Hutchinson "infinitely disliked" it.[59]

In these authors' criticism of Cromwell, there is little trace of sympathy. Ludlow's views on Cromwell, who is the arch-betrayer in his history, may be summed up in his comment that Cromwell died manifesting

so little remorse of conscience for his betraying the publick cause, and sacrificing it to the idol of his own ambition, that some of his last words were rather becoming a mediator than a sinner, recommending to God the condition of the nation that he had so infamously cheated, and expressing a great care of the people whom he had so manifestly despised.[60]

This passage suggests that Ludlow was unconvinced of the sincerity of Cromwell's religion and he speaks elsewhere of Cromwell "deluding the simple with a shew of religion," [61] but unfortunately, in keeping with Ludlow's usual reticence in religious matters, he does not expand these remarks into an examination of Cromwell's religion. It would be interesting to have a dissection of the religion of the greatest of the Puritan revolutionaries from the pen of this fellow regicide and political and religious radical. Ludlow traced his evidence of Cromwell's ambitions for supreme power back to some criticisms of the Parliament which Cromwell made to him in 1646 or 1647. "This text," Ludlow says, "together with the comment that his after-actions put upon it, hath since perswaded me, that he had already conceived the design of destroying the civil authority, and setting up of himself; . . . ." [62] Ludlow sees Cromwell as founding the Protectorate in alliance with the corrupt clergy and lawyers. Mrs. Hutchinson's criticisms of Cromwell's character and career similarly stress his ambition and injury to the republican cause; interestingly enough, she occasionally goes beyond the conventional objections to Cromwell's political actions to describe the personal experience her husband had of Cromwell's duplicity. She describes in detail how Cromwell

---

58 [Anon.], *A Modest Vindication of Oliver Cromwell From the Unjust Accusations of Lieutenant-General Ludlow in His Memoirs* (London, 1698), p. 39; cf. Burnet, *OTA*, I, 78-79, for another, similar inconsistency in the *Memoirs*. For Ludlow's views of 1653 on the dissolution of the Parliament, which were more tolerant than those he held later, see Ludlow, *Memoirs*, I, 356-357, and Firth's introd., I, xxxiii-xxxiv.
59 Hutchinson, *Memoirs*, p. 269.
60 Ludlow, *Memoirs*, II, 44-45.
61 *Ibid.*, II, 356.
62 *Ibid.*, I, 144-145.

cheated her husband out of a regiment and how he engaged in a discreditable attempt to oust the governor of Hull. But she also appeals to her husband's eyewitness experience to disprove the allegation that Cromwell undermined Fairfax when the invasion of Scotland was being contemplated in 1650.[63] Without imitating the Royalists who contrasted Cromwell's worldly might with the damnation that could reasonably be expected to be his lot in the next world she does follow a somewhat similar line of thought in remarking that after "Oliver's mutable reign" his vast ambition and cruel designs ended in "the narrow compass of a grave." [64]

Paradoxically, these writers agree in their good opinion of a man often condemned along with Cromwell, his son-in-law and intimate Ireton.[65] This apparent inconsistency in the treatment of two closely linked politicians and supposed conspirators provoked the early critic of Ludlow's *Memoirs* already mentioned to conclude that "*Ludlow* was no other then a thick-skull'd Officer of Horse." In accordance with a belief mentioned by Clarendon, Mrs. Hutchinson regards Ireton as an obstacle to Cromwell's ambition. Ludlow had of course served under Ireton in Ireland, and Colonel Hutchinson, according to his wife, was Ireton's kinsman.[66]

Ludlow took an active part in the events that intervened between the death of Cromwell and the Restoration, but his views on them can be summed up briefly. Many of the officers had by Cromwell's example been "corrupted with the horrid vices of ambition and treachery." The Army was reluctant to overthrow Richard, but was all too easily persuaded to expel the Rump anew.[67] Finally Monck and the Royalists profited from the divisions among the Parliamentarians – if they can still be honored with that name at so late a date – and the King was restored by the Convention, though Ludlow, as a die hard republican, argues that the Long Parliament was never legally dissolved. Like Mrs. Hutchinson, he censures the dishonesty and treachery of Monck; in his interpretation, Monck completes the cycle of betrayal.

3. Gilbert Burnet

The views of Gilbert Burnet (1643-1715) on the Civil War carry less weight than his views on a later period when he was personally involved

---

[63] Hutchinson, *Memoirs*, pp. 260-262, 275-276, 278.
[64] *Ibid.*, pp. 296,303.
[65] *Ibid.*, pp. 94, 289; Ludlow, *Memoirs*, I, 294-296.
[66] *Modest Vindication*, p. 31; Clarendon, *HR*, V, 265; Hutchinson, *Memoirs*, pp. 79, 94, 247, 273, 290, for the kinship of Ireton and Hutchinson.
[67] Ludlow, *Memoirs*, II, 137-138, 357.

in public affairs. As a historian of the war, however, he took care to obtain valuable information and he shows a valuable detachment from the passions of the various factions. He is also the only historian covered in our study who shows, except in insignificant matters, development of opinion in his historical writings on the war. When he first wrote as a historian about the Civil War, he was a Royalist who was able to sympathize with some of the grievances of the Scottish rebels. Later he wrote civil war history as a Whig who was hostile to Charles I but without any strong partiality for either the Scottish or English rebels. He saw the war then in the light of the misgovernment of the restored Stuarts, the Revolution of 1688, and his own modified political beliefs.

Something must be said about his life [68] and first of all about his Scottish origins. He was born in Edinburgh in 1643, the year of the formation of the Solemn League and Covenant. His father was a lawyer of moderate episcopalian views who deplored the rashness and violence of the Scottish bishops; he never took the Covenant and was forced three times to leave the kingdom because of his opposition to the dominant Presbyterian rebels. Gilbert's mother, the sister of no less a Presbyterian than Johnstone of Warriston, was, in her son's words, "most violently engaged in the Presbiterian way." Through her he gained, he tells us, an early acquaintance with the Scottish Presbyterians which immunized him against harsh thoughts of them.[69] At the same time, he insists, he did not sympathize with them. The influence of his mother and her associates, together with the realization that Presbyterianism was the national religion of Scotland in a peculiarly intimate and expressive way, must have subtly set Burnet out of sympathy with the more dogmatic forms of Anglicanism, episcopalianism, and anti-Puritanism for the rest of his life. Though he was eventually to be a bishop in the English church, one does not need to be a Jacobite sympathizer to feel that he always remained something of an intruder there. Yet whatever the influence of his mother, he did avoid her ideas in their fuller form, whereas we find him in adult life holding like his father to episcopacy and ecclesiastical moderation.

For young Gilbert, the Restoration almost coincided with the beginning of adult life. It was only a year or so later, before he reached the age of

---

[68] The biographical material for Burnet is extensive. The principal lives are his own autobiography, printed as "(Burnet's Autobiography)" in Burnet, *A Supplement to Burnet's History of My Own Time*, ed. H. C. Foxcroft (Oxford, Clarendon Press, 1902), pp. 451-514; T. E. S. Clarke and H. C. Foxcroft's *A Life of Gilbert Burnet Bishop of Salisbury* (Cambridge, Eng., Cambridge University Press, 1907), and Osmund Airy's life of Burnet in the *DNB*. The above biographical data, unless otherwise identified, come from one or the other of these sources.

[69] Burnet, "Autobiography," *Supplement*, ed. Foxcroft, pp. 459-460.

eighteen, that he passed through his trials as a preacher in the Scottish Kirk. After taking up his first parish duties a few years later, he made a distinguished career for himself as a Scottish cleric. In Scottish politics he had influential friends. While himself loyal to the episcopal settlement imposed on Scotland at the Restoration, he counselled moderation in dealing with the downtrodden but still resilient Presbyterians. From 1674, having fallen into disfavor with his former friend and patron Lauderdale, he lived in England rather than Scotland. His cordial relations with James the Duke of York gave way to James's hostility, and a few months after James's accession to the throne Burnet prudently went abroad. In 1688 he landed with William of Orange at Torbay. Burnet's subsequent career as the prominent and much maligned Whig Bishop of Salisbury was marked by his defense of the Revolution, of Whig interests, and of liberty of conscience.

Greatly though his life was occupied with the more public and practical aspects of religion and politics, Burnet was also a prolific and successful writer who deals with or touches upon the Civil War in four historical works: his *Memoires* of the Hamiltons, a product of his years in Scotland, his lives of Sir Matthew Hale and Bishop William Bedell, and, the most important of all his writings, his *History of His Own Time*. As his *History of the Reformation of the Church of England,* important as it is in other respects, is not concerned with the Civil War, its existence need only be mentioned here to show that Burnet had also penetrated as a historian into the historical background of his troubled age.

In these four historical works dealing with or touching upon the Civil War, the didactic view of historical writing is found. At the end of the *Hamilton Memoires* he avows a didactic purpose in writing the book – though presumably this purpose was only one among a number – and in the preface he speaks of the didactic usefulness of history.[70] The didactic view of history lurks behind the *Life of Hale* and the *Life of Bedell*; it would be evident that Burnet is holding Hale and Bedell up as examples, even if he did not explicitly state that he is doing so.[71] In the *Own Time*, he says, he wrote "with a design to make both my self and my readers wiser and better, and to lay open the good and the bad of all sides and parties." [72] He says that his "chief design . . . was to

[70] Gilbert Burnet, *The Memoires of the Lives and Actions of James and William Dukes of Hamilton and Castleherald* (London, 1677), p. 436, preface, sig a, [a4].
[71] Gilbert Burnet, *The Life and Death of Sir Matthew Hale* (London, 1682), preface; [Gilbert Burnet], *The Life of William Bedell* (London, 1685), pp. 218-219. All references to Burnet, *Hale,* are to the 8vo edition.
[72] Burnet, *OTA,* I, preface, p. xxxii. He says that this was his purpose when he began to write the *Own Time,* but evidently he means it still to be his purpose.

give such a discovery of errors in government, and of the excesses and follies of parties, as may make the next age wiser, by what I may tell them of the last." [73] A more theological turn of mind appears in his statement of intention in the last paragraph of his preface to his *Own Time*, where he says

> And now, O my God, the God of my life and of all my mercies, I offer up this work to Thee, to whose honour it is chiefly intended; that thereby I may awaken the world to just reflections on their own errors and follies, and call on them to acknowledge thy providence, to adore it, and ever to depend on it.[74]

Obviously the detection of his didactic view of history does not exhaust the question of his motives for writing history – these were no doubt a mixed lot – but it does show one approach which he took when he wanted to justify his historical writing.

The *Hamilton Memoires* or *The Memoires of the Lives and Actions of James and William Dukes of Hamilton and Castleherald* (1677), which were written some years before their publication,[75] were the first to appear of Burnet's historical works. This solid contribution to the history of the Civil War was well received [76] and, apart from his reflections on the Scottish bishops, has escaped the opprobrium piled on the *Own Time*. It had as its foundation the private papers of the Hamilton family, which were opened to Burnet by the then Duke and Duchess of Hamilton.[77] In the first draft or drafts of the work, Burnet merely quoted from these papers, but in a later draft he adopted the advice of his friend Sir Robert Moray *"to insert most of the Papers at their full length"* [78] and so turned the *Memoires* into what is as much a collection

[73] Burnet, *OTR*, VI, 183. He speaks, VI, 210, 213, 217-218, of the role history should play in the education of the gentry and nobility.
[74] Burnet, *OTA*, I, preface, p. xxxv.
[75] The dates of the ep. ded. to the King and of the licensing letter printed in the volume are in October and November of 1673. Burnet, *OTA*, II, 24, 27, 37, describes among the events of 1673 his successful attempts to get the book licensed. Foxcroft in Clarke and Foxcroft, *Life of Burnet*, p. 150, says "The appearance ... had been unaccountably postponed," but C. H. Firth in his introduction to Clarke and Foxcroft, *Life of Burnet*, p. xiv, offers some explanations for the delay. This introduction is reprinted in Firth, *Essays Historical & Literary*, ed. Godfrey Davies (Oxford, Clarendon Press, 1938). For these *Memoires* see also Robert Dewar, "Burnet on the Scottish Troubles," *The Scottish Historical Review*, 4 (1907), 384-398, and H. C. Foxcroft, "An Early Recension of Burnet's Memoirs of the Dukes of Hamilton," *EHR*, 24 (1909), 510-540.
[76] Firth's introd. to Clarke and Foxcroft, *Life of Burnet*, p. xiii; Burnet, *OTA*, II, 106.
[77] *Ibid.*, I, 531; Burnet, "Autobiography," *Supplement*, ed. Foxcroft, p. 479; Burnet, *Hamilton Memoires*, preface, sig. [a4].
[78] *Ibid.*, preface, sig. [a5].

of documents as biography. This alteration enhanced their usefulness and perhaps their popularity: readers were anxious to gain the accurate and intimate information about the war that documents provided. The writing presented the difficulty that the Hamilton brothers, of which Burnet had become the official biographer, were remembered, with whatever respective degree of justice, for their defective loyalty to Charles I. Sir Philip Warwick, who praises Burnet as the "master of a very good pen," also says that he represented the elder Hamilton "by a light, which few others either of his own Nation or ours discovered him by." [79] A further difficulty in writing the *Memoires* was that the actions of Charles I and Charles II in Scottish affairs would not all comfortably bear the light of public exposure. Burnet vindicated the loyalty of the Hamilton brothers, interpreted the elder Hamilton as a moderate among immoderate men, and quietly suppressed material discreditable to Charles I and Charles II.

In this work Burnet does not attempt a complete account of the Civil War or its origins. Even in dealing with Scottish matters his scope is limited. He admits that having found no relevant material in the Hamilton papers, he has not dealt with the plan of Charles I for the resumption of tithes or with the Balmerino prosecution, though he realizes that these things were connected with the origins of the Scottish rebellion.[80] He treats men and events predominantly with a guarded neutrality, only rarely breaking it with the denunciations so common in the pages of the other seventeenth-century historians of the Civil War.

The most striking element in the work, apart from his rehabilitation of the Hamiltons, is his inclusion of criticisms of the Scottish bishops of Charles I. These criticisms annoyed Dugdale, who cited them as evidence for supposing that Burnet was unfit to write the history of the English Reformation.[81] Burnet describes the imprudence, ambitions, and reckless aggression of the bishops before the rebellion, mingling his own criticisms with reports of the criticisms of others.[82] Despite their preceding

---

[79] Warwick, *M,* pp. 103-104.
[80] Burnet, *Hamilton Memoires,* preface, sig. a4-[a4]ᵛ. For his view that the Scots were "punished with a tract of bloody Civil Wars" for their sins, see *ibid.,* p. 85
[81] Sir William Dugdale to Sir John Cotton (copy only), Dec. 20, 1677, BM Add. MS 4162 f. 224.
[82] Burnet, *Hamilton Memoires,* pp. 29-31. Cf. pp. 160, 183, for criticisms of the Scottish bishops in exile at London after their downfall in Scotland, and 408 for the elder Hamilton's unfavorable views about the behavior of the Scottish bishops in their time of power. Burnet, *Bedell,* pp. 141-144, criticizes Maxwell, Bishop of Ross. Here, as in his criticisms of Sydserff, Bishop of Galloway, in *Hamilton Memoires,* p. 31, Burnet draws a contrast between the man's immoderate behavior as a bishop and his good qualities otherwise.

indiscreet behavior, "that which heightned all to a *Crisis* was, their advising the King to introduce some Innovations in the Church by his own Authority." [83] Here Burnet is thinking principally of the Scottish Prayer Book of 1637. Burnet does not extend his criticisms from the Scottish bishops to the English bishops, and he speaks well of Laud. Speaking of the elder Hamilton in 1638, when that Hamilton was commissioner of Charles I in Scotland, he says:

> with my Lord of *Canterbury* he kept a constant and free Intercourse; and whatever that Archbishop might have been formerly in *Scotish* Affairs, being abused by persons who did not truly represent them to him, he was certainly a good Instrument this year, which appears from his Letters to the Marquis, with the Copies of his Returns, which are extant.[84]

Is Burnet reproaching the Scottish bishops here for misinforming Laud? Burnet is not led by his critical attitude to the Scottish bishops into a defense of the Covenanters. Though he speaks of them without rancor, he recognizes them throughout the book as the King's enemies.

Despite the great concession Burnet made towards a Parliamentarian interpretation of the war in his views on the Scottish bishops, these views are apparently nothing more innovating and radical than those held by his father and the elder Hamilton, and he is impeccably orthodox in his treatment of Charles I. He even speaks of "the great Piety and strictness of Conscience that Blessed Prince carried along with him in all his Affairs." [85] Yet it appears from his own words elsewhere that Burnet was led by his perusal of the Hamilton papers to views on Charles quite different from this and that he suppressed evidence that supported an unfavorable interpretation. For he says in his *Own Time*:

> I did indeed conceal several things that related to the king. I left out some passages that were in his letters; in some of these was too much weakness, and in others too much craft and anger. And this I owe to truth to say, that by many indications that lay before me in those letters, I could not admire either the judgment and understanding, or the temper of that unfortunate prince. He had little regard to law, and seemed to think that he was not bound to observe promises or concessions, that were extorted from him by the necessity of his affairs. He had little tenderness in his nature; and probably his government would have been severe, if he had got the better in the war.[86]

---

[83] *Ibid.*, p. 30; cf. p. 31.
[84] *Ibid.*, p. 52.
[85] *Ibid.*, p. 379; cf. p. 93.
[86] Burnet, *OTA*, I, 531-532. The contrast between these views of Charles and the views in the *Hamilton Memoires* is noted, 531, n. 1.

And Burnet goes on to describe Charles's fondness for violent counsels. Research for the *Hamilton Memoirs*, he says in his autobiography, carrying the history of the transformation of his opinions about Charles a step further, "brought the character of King Charles the first very low with me, but the Earl of Clarendon's History sunk it quite." [87]

The *Hamilton Memoires* are colorless, as one would expect of a heavily documentary history, but *The Life and Death of Sir Matthew Hale* (1681) and *The Life of William Bedell* (1685) are literary achievements of considerable merit in which Burnet brings his heroes convincingly to life. One senses that Burnet is now writing with a confidence born of a greater experience of writing and of the world.

In these biographies a certain view of the war and of its issues is implied in the two people who are held up for the reader's admiration. Hale was a neutral in the Civil War and served as a judge under Oliver Cromwell (he refused a renewal of his authority by Richard Cromwell). Though loyal to the Church of England, he had a kind eye for the Nonconformists and their sufferings,[88] and notes by Baxter, based on his friendship with Hale, appeared in a later edition of Burnet's book. Bedell, a pious and diligent bishop, "was a *Calvinist* in the matter of Decrees and Grace" and opposed to the Laudian ceremonial innovations and, like Hale, was a strict observer of the Sabbath.[89] To a fervent Royalist, the career and sympathies of Hale must have seemed dubious and the opinions of Bedell must have seemed not above reproach. It may be suggested that these biographies, with their moralistic tone and exemplary heroes, were intended to appeal to a middle class audience, Anglican and otherwise, of somewhat puritanical tastes. Perhaps some light is thrown on Burnet's reading public by his remark in the letter of reproof of January 1680 which he sent to Charles II: "Your majesty may perhaps justly think, that many of those that oppose you have no regard for religion, but the body of your people consider it more than you can imagine." [90] One of the things that make these biographies refreshing reading is that in them Burnet broke with the uncompromising antithesis between non-Puritan Anglicans and Puritans, as this antithesis was understood and maintained by so many of the partisans, clerical and otherwise, of his day, and implied that neither camp had a monopoly of virtue and truth.

[87] Burnet, "Autobiography," *Supplement,* ed. Foxcroft, p. 479. Firth in his introduction to Clarke and Foxcroft, *Life of Burnet,* p. xv, observes that Burnet makes concessions of silence with respect to Charles II also.

[88] Burnet, *Hale,* pp. 31-33, 35-37, 49, 65-68.

[89] Burnet, *Bedell,* pp. 26-28, 146-147, 174, 229; Burnet, *Hale,* p. 76.

[90] In "The Life of the Author, by the Editor, Thomas Burnet, Esq.," in Burnet, *OTR,* VI, 273.

In the three historical works already examined, Burnet may be seen stirring uneasily within the intellectual framework of a Royalist interpretation of the war. In the *Own Time* he has completed his break with this old restricting framework. He is still a staunch monarchist who is convinced of the impossibility of establishing a permanent "commonwealth" in England,[91] but he is now an open critic of Charles I and his adherents.

In this work, the war is discussed in the first book and in scattered passages elsewhere. In the first book he professes to deal with events in Scotland from the beginning of the troubles to the Restoration, but he also includes some account of English affairs. He makes no attempt to include a complete history of the rebellion in either country. He follows the practice of stating information that has been hitherto unprinted or little known rather than information, however important, that is generally known. He appeals to the advice of Schomberg to excuse himself for not meddling in the narration of military affairs.[92] Conversation with his acquaintances contributed to his information in his strongly anecdotal account of the war, but he also consulted some of the principal printed historians of the war. He mentions Rushworth's *Historical Collections,* Whitelocke's *Memorials,* Heylyn's *Cyprianus Anglicus,* and the first volume of Clarendon's *History,* which, he says, "gives a faithful representation of the beginnings of the troubles, though writ in favour of the court, and full of the best excuses that such ill things were capable of." [93]

Burnet began writing his *Own Time* in 1683, but he later made extensive revisions. As late as 1711 or 1712, he revised the part that deals with events up to the death of Charles II and therefore includes the first book. In accordance with his expectation that he would continue to retouch and polish the work as long as he lived, he may have made alterations at any time up to his death in 1715.[94] Portions from the earlier drafts have been printed separately in a collection edited by H. C. Foxcroft.

The great work came forth in two volumes (dated 1724, 1734 respectively), meeting, it appears, with considerable public interest. Calamy, speaking of the first volume, says that "as it was long expected with great impatience before it appeared, so has it been read with as much eagerness as any book published in the present age." [95] The bitter nonjuror and antiquary Hearne says of the second volume that

[91] Burnet, *OTA,* I, 79.
[92] *Ibid.,* I, 84.
[93] *Ibid.,* I, 53, 64, 86.
[94] *Ibid.,* I, preface, pp. xxxiv-xxxv, II, 474; Foxcroft's note in Burnet, *Supplement,* pp. 1-2.
[95] Edmund Calamy, *An Historical Account of My Own Life,* ed. J. T. Rutt, 2 vols. (London, 1829), I, 44-45. A contemporary says, " 'Tis the present run of reading,

Learning is sunk so very low, that I am most certainly informed, that nothing is now hardly read but Burnett's romance or Libel, ... 'Tis read by men, women and children. Indeed it is the common table Book for Ladies as well as Gentlemen, especially such as are friends to the Revolution Scheme.[96]

Perhaps Burnet had tapped the audience of young ladies for which Macaulay was to yearn a few generations later!

In this history Burnet gives a rather fragmentary account of the origins of the rebellion in Scotland. His account includes discussion of two topics he omitted from consideration in the *Hamilton Memoires* – the plans of Charles I for the resumption of tithes and the Balmerino prosecution. On the other hand, he does not repeat the detailed description of political events in Scotland which he gives in the *Hamilton Memoires*; for that, the reader is referred to the earlier work. Though he opposed the Scottish Presbyterians in the *Hamilton Memoires*, he did not pile reproaches on them as he does in the *Own Time*, where he represents the ministers as "generally proud and passionate, insolent and covetous," censures their meddling in affairs of state, and indicates their decline from piety and an exemplary way of life during the war.[97] In the *Own Time* he also censures the Scottish bishops of James I and Charles I severely. While in the *Hamilton Memoires* he was able to speak, as has been seen, with a certain sympathy for Laud, in the *Own Time* he represents Laud as urging on the Scottish bishops and censures the violence of his proceedings in England. Burnet is never lacking in zeal for true religion, as he understands it, and in respect for what he believes to be deep and real piety, but as the views we have just been examining suggest, there is a strong flavor in the *Own Time* of what can only be called anticlericalism – directed not only against Scottish clerics but also against his own present-day fellow clergy in the Church of England.

In his unfavorable description of James I, Burnet sees him in his role as ruler of England rather than ruler of Scotland. He represents James as a favorer of Popery in his actions, censures his ill conduct of the defense of his son-in-law in Germany and his sending Prince Charles on his trip to Spain, and argues that his extravagance and generosity weakened the

but I have not heard one speak well of it"; another suggests that the Burnet brothers, sons of the bishop, have been so teased about this first volume that it will be long before they publish the second. E. Southwell to Lord –, Nov. 26, 1723, HMC, 7th Report (London, 1879), p. 513; Thomas Ward to unnamed correspondent, Jan. 9, 1723/4, HMC, 13th Report, Appendix, Part IV (London, 1892), p. 496.

[96] Thomas Hearne, *Remarks and Collections of Thomas Hearne,* ed. C. E. Doble, D. W. Rannie, H. E. Salter, and others, 11 vols. (Oxford, 1885-1921), XI, 317, 325 (entries for March 19, 1733/4, April 9, 1734).

[97] Burnet, *OTA,* I, 57, 54, 72, 273-274, 58.

monarchy. Like Mrs. Hutchinson, he contrasts James's "inglorious" reign with the "glorious and happy" reign of Elizabeth. "It is certain," he comments, that "no king could die less lamented or less esteemed than he was."[98]

For Charles he has a similar lack of sympathy. He observes that "he died greater than he had lived," and says:

His reign, both in peace and war, was a continued series of errors: so that it does not appear that he had a true judgment of things. He was out of measure set on following his humour, but unreasonably feeble to those whom he trusted, chiefly to the queen. He had too high a notion of the regal power, and thought that every opposition to it was rebellion. He minded little things too much, and was more concerned in the drawing of a paper than in fighting a battle. He had a firm aversion to popery, but was much inclined to a middle way between protestants and papists, by which he lost the one, without gaining the other.[99]

There is little reason to suppose from his narrative that he thought the execution of Charles worthy of much lamentation, and he rather coldly observes that the consequence of putting Strafford, Laud, and Charles to death was the enhancement of their reputations.[100] He includes an account, most of which has already been quoted, of his formation of unfavorable views of Charles while studying the Hamilton papers. When Burnet's views on Charles I are added to his preceding criticisms of James and to his comparison of Charles II to Tiberius,[101] it will be seen how unsympathetic his *Own Time* is even to the ostensibly Protestant Stuart kings.

Burnet says little about the events of the war in England. Delivering purely narrative history of events in which he took no part or about which he had no special information was not a part of his self-imposed task. Such comments of value to an interpretation of the war as he has to make can be expressed in the following jottings. Only by making concessions, he says, at the time of the undivided Long Parliament, was Charles able to divide England and make a party for himself. He sees Montrose's success as "very mischievous, ... the ruin of the king's affairs," by preventing a compromise peace. He speaks of the Cavaliers at the Restoration returning, after a show of zeal for liberty, "to their old principles for a high prerogative and absolute power." He seems to see the great service done by Monck as being merely the ensuring that Charles II was

---

[98] *Ibid.,* I, 15, 18-23.
[99] *Ibid.,* I, 80-81.
[100] *Ibid.,* I, 84-87. For Burnet on Laud, see also Burnet, *OTR,* VI, 202.
[101] Burnet, *OTA,* II, 470.

returned *without* conditions. "To the king's coming in without conditions," he thinks, "may be well imputed all the errors of his reign." But he does not regret the Restoration: "In the year 1660," he says, "we came again to our wits, and all was set right again." [102]

Though Burnet was too young during the Protectorate to have any personal knowledge of Oliver Cromwell, he appears to have felt a keen interest in his character and career. Burnet was an outsider in English society and therefore in some respects better prepared than most English historians to sympathize with such a national outcast as Cromwell, and Cromwell's religious fervor must have appealed, unconsciously if not consciously, to Burnet as the possessor of a warm strain of devotion. Burnet's kindness for Cromwell remains highly qualified, but in view of the frequent vilification of Cromwell, the kindness seems more significant than the qualifications. He sums up Cromwell's character in the following words:

The enthusiast and the dissembler mixed so equally in a great part of his deportment, that it was not easy to tell which was the prevailing character. He was indeed both; .... He was a true enthusiast, but with the principle ... from which he might be easily led into all the practices both of falsehood and cruelty: which was, that he thought moral laws were only binding on ordinary occasions, but that upon extraordinary ones these might be superseded. When his own designs did not lead him out of the way, he was a lover of justice and virtue, and even of learning, though much decried at that time.[103]

Burnet, we find, holds views somewhat similar to those of Baxter in the *Reliquiae Baxterianae* about Cromwell's strange mixture of good and bad. Baxter does not set down Burnet's exact views about Cromwell not believing that the moral laws were binding on all occasions, but he approaches them in his psychological scrutiny of Cromwell, as when he says that after the execution of the King Cromwell thought "that the End being good and necessary, the necessary means cannot be bad," and that "he thought Secrecy a Vertue, and Dissimulation no Vice, and Simulation, that is, in plain English a Lie, or Perfidiousness to be a

---

[102] *Ibid.*, I, 49, 64-67, 126, 161-162; Burnet, *OTR*, IV, 339; cf. VI, 209.
[103] Burnet, *OTA*, I, 142-143, 78. In an early draft of his *Own Time*, Burnet expresses similar views on Cromwell, representing him as a man who mingled good and evil in his character and who believed that "in extraordinary cases men were dispensed with, even from the laws of God, which he thought were rules only for ordinary cases." Burnet, *Supplement*, ed. Foxcroft, pp. 230, 241. The reference, p. 242, to "the two lawful kings that have come since" seems to date in the reign of James II at least part of the treatment of Cromwell in this early draft. Firth in his introduction to Clarke and Foxcroft, *Life of Burnet*, p. xxvi, gives the date as "about 1687."

tollerable Fault in a Case of Necessity." [104] The chief difference between Burnet and Baxter's views on the question of how Cromwell justified his wrongful acts to himself seems to be that Burnet thought that Cromwell rested on a definite religious principle which his religious intoxication had rendered plausible to him, whereas Baxter thought he was simply self-deceived in the way that almost anyone might be self-deceived without the aid of any private, plausible, morally disastrous "principle." Among Burnet's other remarks on Cromwell, we need only note that he speaks of Cromwell's success in making England feared and honored abroad and of the peace and prosperity of Scotland under the Protectorate.

[104] Baxter, *RB,* Part I, 99, 71.

CHAPTER VIII

CLARENDON[1]

The following discussion of Clarendon differs somewhat in scale from the studies of historians in preceding chapters. Clarendon is so much more important as an authority on the war than most of the other leading historians and is so comprehensive in his discussion of the war that an examination of him on the scale already established in this book would hardly be possible at less than book length and would distractingly emphasize one man in a work which has most emphatically been written as a study of a group. Fortunately, Clarendon is also one of the best known historians of the war, and on the assumption that most persons reading these pages are likely to have some knowledge of his works and the principal scholarly opinions about him, I have taken the liberty of considerable condensation or, as some of my readers will perhaps say, of incompleteness. I give the broad outline of his interpretation, as I understand it, stress some aspects of his interpretation which have not, in my opinion, been sufficiently considered by other writers on him, and at the end consider him from what is, I hope, an unfamiliar angle by comparing him with the other English language historians of the war who wrote before the publication of the first volume of his *History*.

In his *Life* he gives a charming account of his days as a young London lawyer (the offspring of a good gentry family) in the peaceful England before the war and of "the friendships and conversation he had still been used to, of the most excellent men in their several kinds that lived in that age." [2] All his life he made a cult of friendship, emphasizing the immense

---

[1] Some of the material of this chapter appeared in my article, "Clarendon among the Pre-Clarendonians," *The Humanities Association Bulletin,* 20, No. 3 (Fall, 1969), 9-19.

[2] Clarendon, *L*, Part I, quotation from I, 27. The principal printed sources for Clarendon's life are his *History* and *Life.* The best full length biography is still T. H. Lister, *Life and Administration of Edward, First Earl of Clarendon; with Original Correspondence, and Authentic Papers Never Before Published,* 3 vols. (London, 1837-1838), which should be supplemented with the life of Clarendon by Firth in the

value and importance of steadfast friends ("if indeed we abound with
such Treasure")[3] and celebrating his own friendships in particular. In
this spirit he tries to reduce the great figures of English history to the
rank of companions in good fellowship by his habit of affectionately
referring to kings as "Harry" when their name is Henry. Even when
he describes Cromwell's career, he quirkishly notes how devoid Cromwell's rise was of the aid of disinterested friendship.[4] But among all his
early friends and acquaintances – and these read like a roll call of the
intellectual elite of early Caroline England – he especially cherished Lord
Falkland, who gathered a famous circle of scholars and intellectuals
about him and is commemorated in a famous passage of the *History*.
These happy early scenes survived in Clarendon's mind as the picture of
a private utopia existing before the blight of war came upon England
and before he was elevated into the rough new world of politics and
savage personal rivalries.

As a member of the Short Parliament and of the Long Parliament,
he cooperated with the popular party. He led the attack on the Earl
Marshal's court, took part in the proceedings against the judges and in
the proceedings for Strafford's trial, and may have voted for the bill of
attainder which took away Strafford's life.[5] With the deepening of the
national crisis, however, he began to separate himself from the popular
party and to oppose their measures and entered unofficially into the
service of the King. The question of whether he changed sides or changed
his party depends on the meaning one wants to assign to words. The
essential fact seems to be that he saw himself as a man who remained
consistent in his opinions while others revealed themselves as more radical
opponents of the monarchy than they had seemed to be at the beginning
of the Long Parliament. After fighting a delaying action at Westminster

---

DNB. B. H. G. Wormald, *Clarendon: Politics, History & Religion 1640-1660* (Cambridge, Eng., Cambridge University Press, 1951), despite its evasive language and
playing with words (e.g., calling Hyde a "Parliamentarian" not a "Royalist," pp. 83,
120, 154, 233-235), contains valuable observations on Clarendon's life and historiographical achievement. It should be used in the light of the criticisms offered by
Godfrey Davies in his review of it, *EHR*, 67 (1952), 271-275.

[3] Edward Hyde, Earl of Clarendon, "Reflections Upon Several Christian Duties,
Divine and Moral, By way of Essays," *The Miscellaneous Works of the Right Honourable Edward, Earl of Clarendon, . . . Being a Collection of Several Valuable Tracts,
written by that Eminent Statesman. Published from His Lordship's Original MSS,*
2nd ed. (London, 1751), p. 98.

[4] Clarendon, *HR*, V, 278; cf. V, 282, VI, 91.

[5] Clarendon himself is silent on this point. Lister, *Life,* I, 94-95, believes that he
did not vote against the bill but hints that he may have abstained from voting. Firth
in his life of Clarendon in the *DNB* finds it "hardly possible to doubt that he voted
for that measure."

against the radicals as long as he could, he abandoned the Houses in May 1642 to join the King at York.

For the next quarter of a century he was a devoted servant of the monarchy. During the years of his attendance on Charles I he was equalled or overshadowed by other advisers, but in the court of the exiled Charles II, from the time of the King's return from England after the catastrophe at Worcester, he was the principal adviser. In 1643 he became Chancellor of the Exchequer, in 1658 Lord Chancellor. The Restoration began his period of dominance in English politics, but his position as Lord Chancellor, Earl of Clarendon, and father-in-law to the heir to the throne, James the Duke of York, proved insufficient to support his greatness. In 1667, having incurred the hostility of the House of Commons and the King, he fled into his second exile. He died, still in exile, at Rouen seven years later.

Clarendon's method of composing his *History* and *Life* and the sources of information available to him have been described in great detail by C. H. Firth.[6] As Firth's writings on this subject are readily accessible and are reasonably well known, his conclusions need not be dealt with here except to emphasize the relationship in time of these works to other contemporary histories of the war. Hyde first applied himself to the task of writing a history of the war during the years 1646 to 1648 and resumed the task in his second exile in 1668. The *History* contains material from both these periods of writing while the *Life* is wholly the product of the latter. This is perhaps the best place to add that whereas Clarendon's account of his career after the Restoration is sometimes referred to as a separate work under the title of the *Continuation,* I always refer to it, I hope with greater logic and consistency, as a part of the *Life.*

Unlike the *Life,* the *History* gives a comprehensive account of the rebellion, but this account is nevertheless uneven because Clarendon has allowed himself to be so much affected by his geographical position at the time of the events he is dealing with. For events up till the outbreak of fighting in 1642, his narrative is national in scope, apart from that geographical and social bias in favor of London which is usual in national histories of England or Britain. From the outbreak of fighting till he accompanied the Prince of Wales into the west in 1645, his interest tends to follow the activities of the King and the Royalist armies. With the

---

[6] In his three articles called "Clarendon's 'History of the Rebellion'," *EHR,* 19 (1904), 26-54, 246-262, 464-483. He gives a brief account of the composition in his life of Clarendon in the *DNB* and in his important essay on Clarendon in his *Essays Historical & Literary,* ed. Godfrey Davies (Oxford, Clarendon Press, 1938), pp. 114-115, 119-120.

beginning of his frustrating western experience, the unevenness of his treatment of the war begins to be a historical and literary flaw in the narrative; the activities in the west, simply because he knew so much about them and lacked personal experience of so many important things that were happening elsewhere, tend to be unduly emphasized. In discussing the period after his departure from the mainland of Britain into the Scilly Isles in 1646, a period which contains his residence in Jersey and continental exile, he tries to sustain a competent account of affairs in England and in particular at Westminster, but he suffers from a lack of personal knowledge and an understandable tendency to dwell upon the activities of the exiled Royalists. His narrative of his embassy to Spain in the company of Cottington is a charming digression but out of place, at least at such length, in a history of the rebellion. As the *History* progresses, one index of its author's increasing alienation from the centers of revolutionary and therefore of national activities is the fading away of the "characters" or pen-portraits which he so freely gives of the major figures in the early events of his narrative. In dealing with events in England, he does make occasional efforts to give characters of the new men who had come on the scene – there is, for example, a brief one of General Harrison – but for the most part he can only describe the activities of people who were, increasingly, strangers to him.

Clarendon includes no single comprehensive account of why the rebellion occurred, but he raises the problem a number of times, most notably at the very beginning of his *History,* and he touches on it repeatedly throughout his narrative in the *History* and *Life.* His sense of the complexity of historical events, of the machinery of society, and of the human mind, is so highly developed that any attempt to construct a simple list of the principal causes and facilitating circumstances which, as he understood events, had produced the rebellion, must seem on the surface somewhat crude, but in this case surface appearances deceive. These principal causes and facilitating circumstances can be separated quite clearly and without the need for elaborate qualifications from the complex narrative of which they are a part. One is simply divine judgment. The hand of God was active behind the great disaster which fell, unhappily but justly, on the dominions of Charles I. Connected with this is the idea that Charles's subjects had surfeited of too much peace and prosperity. To this he adds the working of the natural defects of human psychology: the weakness, vanity, self-delusion, irrationalism, blindness, and so forth, which can make men contribute, knowingly or unknowingly, to a national drift to disaster. Finally, there were real grievances against the government of Charles I before the meeting of the Long Parliament and he often mishandled men and events afterwards.

Passing over for the moment Clarendon's views on divine intervention (which will be considered later in connection with another problem) we may begin with his views on the surfeit of peace and plenty. Almost at the beginning of the *History* he says that the present miseries (he was writing in 1646) "have been brought upon us, from the same natural causes and means which have usually attended kingdoms swoln with long plenty, pride, and excess," and he associates these natural causes and means with the idea of a divine judgment behind the rebellion and with his views on psychology.[7] Further on we learn that another but less important surfeit had taken place earlier, back in the last years of James I. Then the people were "naturally enough inclined to" Charles and Buckingham's war against Spain because they had "surfeited with the uninterrupted pleasures and plenty of twenty-two years peace," because they were "in a surfeit of a long peace."[8] Clarendon refers, as historians contemporary to him do, to the peace and prosperity of England before the rebellion, but like some of them he sees these happy times as containing the germs of their own destruction. Charles's kingdoms were "flourishing in entire peace and universal plenty, in danger of nothing but their own surfeits," but their danger was not resisted, Scotland being the first that "threw off wantonly its own peace and plenty."[9]

The third of the causes or facilitating circumstances listed above as having produced the rebellion is the working of the natural defects of human psychology. One of the most important differences between Clarendon and the other seventeenth-century English language historians of the war is his stronger emphasis on and superior grasp of psychology. In saying this, it must also in all fairness be said in favor of these other historians that even they are often richly perceptive and are seldom really obtuse in their understanding of psychology. A reader may well feel that the Restoration dramatists often grossly oversimplify and misrepresent the human mind, but the general psychological perspicacity of these historians is one of the reasons why they may still be read, one after an-

---

[7] Clarendon, *HR*, I, 2. See also I, 51, 95, 96, 194, II, 81, 478, and the Levellers' petition, VI, 69; Clarendon, *L*, I, 61; Clarendon, "Contemplations and Reflections upon the Psalms of David. Applying those Devotions to the Troubles of the Times," *Miscellaneous Works*, pp. 520, 522, 524-525, 554, 725; Clarendon, *Religion and Policy and the Countenance and Assistance Each Should Give to the Other*, 2 vols. (Oxford, 1811), I, 279.

[8] Clarendon, *HR*, I, 4, 48. After the Restoration, the people soon grew "weary of that happiness they were possessed of." Clarendon, *L*, I, 269. In this case, however, Clarendon seems to find straightforward political reasons for the discontent.

[9] *Ibid.*, I, 66; Clarendon, *HR*, VI, 2.

other, without developing in the reader any sense of boredom or repetition. Clarendon's concern for psychology is best known through his famous "characters," but he also relies on his understanding of people's motives to explain why the rebellion developed as it did. He is well aware of how inadequately people understand their own motives and how easily they are led into courses unexpected by them and to consequences which they would, at the beginning of their action, have angrily rejected. Some people desire one thing and some another; some deceive their fellows and some are deceived by them, and most, perhaps, both deceive and are deceived; some knowingly do wicked acts and others, who disapprove, assist these acts by doing nothing to oppose them; and amid all the complexity of events and motives arises a pattern which is (under God) the work of men and yet, paradoxically, has not been planned by them. Clarendon's handling of psychology is not uniformly dexterous: he is more impressive in dealing with individuals, such as Essex and Hampden, and with society as a whole, than with intermediate groups. Grave examples of his feebleness and lack of insight in dealing with intermediate groups are his treatments of the Puritans, of the group of leaders in the Long Parliament in every respect except their skill in influencing others, and of the persons, seen as a collectivity, who dominated the counsels of foreign governments.

Fourthly, among the circumstances giving rise to the rebellion Clarendon includes misgovernment. His stressing of the good times before the war is perfectly consistent with his discussion of the grievances against the government of Charles I in church and state. These grievances should not have existed, but they were not serious enough to justify a rebellion. Clarendon has too much veneration for the English law to hold that any infraction or abuse of the law is a trifle, but he holds that common sense will dictate that no one gives to small matters the importance that truly belongs only to large. By simply refraining from making the necessary connection in the *History* between acts of misgovernment and Charles, he manages to create an impression that Charles was somehow, mysteriously, not involved in this part of the business of his own government. Clarendon's account of grievances justifies, intentionally or unintentionally, the reforms of 1641, though the justification is disguised by the fact that Clarendon so warmly emphasizes the goodness of Charles in granting so abundant a satisfaction for grievances.

Among his criticisms, he emphasizes the unwisdom and illegality of the ship-money exactions, which were planned, he says, "for a spring and magazine that should have no bottom, and for an everlasting supply of all occasions." [10] Those who had paid ship-money willingly before the judgment against Hampden, in the belief that by so doing they were performing a voluntary act of generosity for the King and that in case of necessity the law would protect them from such exactions, became refractory when they found the law perverted to serve the ends of state and ship-money confirmed by the judges "upon such grounds and reasons as every stander-by was able to swear was not law." [11] Such perversions of the function of the judges, which bent the decisions of the judges to the needs of state, contrary to the wise practise of former times, were an encouragement of and a useful excuse for the exorbitances of the two Houses in the Long Parliament. "If these men," Clarendon says of the judges, "had preserved the simplicity of their ancestors in severely and strictly defending the laws, other men had observed the modesty of theirs in humbly and dutifully obeying them." [12] In his idea of a connection between the misbehavior of the judges and the misbehavior of the Long Parliament, there is probably an element of hyperbole. Yet it arises naturally enough out of Clarendon's almost pedantic regard for the law and his sense that the state is an elaborately constructed, delicately balanced mechanism. If one part goes wrong, others will soon be affected, with the result that presently the whole structure feels the effect of the failure of one part. For us, the parallel is with a complex piece of machinery; for Clarendon's contemporaries, it was more likely to be with the human body.

To support such projects as ship-money and the exploitation of the forest laws, went an extension "to a vast extent" of the jurisdictions of the Council Table and the Court of Star Chamber. The Council Table took upon itself something similar to legislative functions, "by proclamations enjoining this to the people that was not enjoined by the law, and prohibiting that which was not prohibited." The Court of Star Chamber meanwhile undertook the enforcement of these injunctions, though the persons who presided at the Council Table and in the Court of Star Chamber were only "the same persons in several rooms." [13] Clarendon criticizes the public proceedings of the Council Table and Court of Star Chamber as wanting in tact and decorum: persons were needlessly affronted and even the respect shown by the public to these institutions was allowed to decline through ill management.

---

[10] *Ibid.*, I, 85.
[11] *Ibid.*, I, 86-88.
[12] *Ibid.*, I, 88-89. For his disapproval of the ship-money exactions, see also I, 92; Hyde to Secretary Nicholas, Feb. 12, 1646/7, *Clar. S.P.*, II, 336; Clarendon, *L*, II, 98.
[13] Clarendon, *HR*, I, 86; cf. I, 84, 92, 374.

Similarly, Clarendon objects to the mistreatment of Parliaments during the same period. "And here," he says in a passage of the *History* written in 1646, "I cannot but let myself loose to say, that no man can shew me a source from whence these waters of bitterness we now taste have more probably flowed, than from this unseasonable, unskilful, and precipitate dissolution of Parliaments; . . . ." [14] He briefly surveys the history of the first three Parliaments of Charles I. Though he concedes the rash behavior of some members of these three Parliaments, he states that "whoever considers the acts of power and injustice in the intervals of Parliaments, will not be much scandalized at the warmth and vivacity of those meetings." [15] These Parliaments would have been pliable to the good of the government if they had been intelligently handled, and their dissolutions served to alienate King and people. Finally, in 1629 the last of these was dissolved and a proclamation was issued forbidding men to speak of another Parliament. This proclamation had the double effect of encouraging suspicion among the people of the designs of the court to alter the form of government in church and state and of encouraging ill men, who now had no fear of Parliament, to exorbitant behavior in the service of the King. [16] The abrupt dismissal of the Short Parliament was also a mistake, as "It could never be hoped that more sober and dispassioned men would ever meet together in that place, or fewer who brought ill purposes with them." The enemies of the King, however, were well pleased with its dismissal. [17]

In his criticisms of the government of the church, Clarendon blames Laud gently yet more directly than he blames Charles anywhere for errors of the same period. He finds that Laud acted unwisely in the pursuit of morally good ends. Approving of Laud's desire to restore discipline to the church and seemliness to its services, he finds him defective in what would today be called public relations and points out the public resentment he provoked. Laud became Archbishop, he says, in "a time of great ease and tranquillity," when some grumbling existed about exactions made by the government upon the public but when the church "was not repined at." There was not at that time "the least inclination to alter the government and discipline thereof or to change the doctrine, nor . . . any considerable number of persons of any valuable condition throughout the kingdom who did wish either." Accordingly, Clarendon says in reproof of Laud, "the cause of so prodigious a change in so few years after was

---

[14] *Ibid.*, I, 5.
[15] *Ibid.*, I, 6.
[16] *Ibid.*, I, 84.
[17] *Ibid.*, I, 183, III, 181, 322.

too visible from the effects." [18] The unwisdom of Laud in affairs of the church was supplemented, he notes, by a certain roughness and sharpness in his treatment of other men. In accordance with the high value he put on friendship, Clarendon thought that the errors of Laud's political career could have been reduced if he had had a faithful friend to advise him of his errors, and he describes how he, a young lawyer, launched himself on the "bold enterprise" of giving good advice to the Archbishop.[19]

Friendship in the Clarendonian sense was hardly possible between persons as different in age and rank as Laud and his young acquaintance were, but their relations were cordial and Clarendon always remembered Laud with reverence and affection as "a man of the most exemplar virtue and piety of any of that age." [20] When he was mulling over his own fate in his second exile, he seems not to have compared his misfortunes to anything in the story of Charles I – to do so would probably have seemed to him little less than sacrilegious – but he did see something common to his life and Laud's. He "was guilty of that himself," he found, "which he had used to accuse the archbishop Laud of, that he was too proud of a good conscience." [21]

Clarendon's treatment of the clergy of the church of Charles I mingles approval and disapproval in a manner similar to that of his treatment of Laud, except that his treatment of the clergy is somewhat sharper in its criticism. Indeed, despite Clarendon's reverence for the Church of England and its loyal clergy, despite his patronage of the Laudian clergy and Laudian ecclesiastical ideas at the Restoration, he reveals occasional traces of something akin to anticlericalism. Almost but not perfectly suppressed, a Hobbesian critic of the clergy can be seen struggling for breath within him. His sharp remark in the *Life* about "clergymen" – it is not clear whether he is criticizing the clergy as a whole or only some of them – "who understand the least, and take the worst measure of human affairs of all mankind that can write and read," [22] might well have been uttered by Hobbes, and in fact in a passage of *Behemoth* already quoted in this study Hobbes does say something rather similar. Clarendon says that most sermons preached at court during the years of peace in Charles's

---

[18] *Ibid.*, I, 122-123, 126-128.
[19] Clarendon, *L*, I, 58, 61, 58-61.
[20] *Ibid.*, I, 57.
[21] *Ibid.*, II, 431; cf. Clarendon, "A Discourse, by Way of Vindication of my self from the Charge of High-Treason," p. 9, and "Reflections . . . By way of Essays," pp. 117-118, in *Miscellaneous Works*; and Clarendon, *HR*, I, 82.
[22] Clarendon, *L*, I, 61. For his adherence to Laudian ecclesiastical principles in his first exile and afterwards, see Robert S. Bosher, *The Making of the Restoration Settlement: The Influence of the Laudians 1649-1662* (Westminster, Dacre Press, 1957), pp. 55-56, 137-138, 218, and *passim*.

reign were of exemplary soundness but that a few were scandalous and presumptuous.[23] The molestation of the foreign Protestants in England occurred "when the power of churchmen grew most transcendent" and would not have occurred if the lay councillors had been sufficiently alert. The Bishops of Bath and Wells and of Ely "had with great pride and insolence provoked all the gentry, and in truth most of the inhabitants, within their dioceses." [24] When he comes to describe the act for the abolition of the Court of High Commission, he says:

But of late it cannot be denied that, by the great power of some bishops at Court, it [the Court of High Commission] had much overflowed the banks which should have contained it, not only in meddling with things that in truth were not properly within their conusance, but extending their sentences and judgments in matters triable before them beyond that degree that was justifiable; . . . .

Then, it was grown from an ecclesiastical court for the reformation of manners to a court of revenue, and imposed great fines upon those who were culpable before them, sometimes above the degree of the offence had the jurisdiction of fining been unquestionable, which it was not. Which course of fining was much more frequent and the fines heavier after the king had granted all that revenue, . . . to be employed for the reparation of St. Paul's church; . . . .[25]

Clarendon reflects on the animosity that developed between the common lawyers and the clergy, blames both, and concludes that their interests are so closely united that they should be defended as one.

In connection with Clarendon's historical treatment of the origins of the rebellion, two further problems need to be considered, first, his views on the role of Puritanism in the rebellion and, secondly, his views on the question of whether the rebellion was plotted in advance.

In treatments of the rebellion by seventeenth-century historians, some observations on the religious radicalism which can be comprehended roughly under the all-purpose name of Puritanism are common, though not universal. It will be remembered that Heylyn, Hobbes, Dugdale, and Nalson believed that religious dissidents promoted the rebellion, that Mrs. Hutchinson was aware that religion was an issue in dispute between the court and people before the rebellion, and that Baxter saw the importance of religion in drawing men to the Parliamentarian side in the fighting.

---

[23] Clarendon, *HR*, I, 96-97; see I, 95-97, for his general praise of the clergy. The quoted passage, p. 97, on "the best bulk of orthodox divinity" seems to come (indirectly?) from Bacon; see Francis Bacon, *The Advancement of Learning*, ed. G. W. Kitchin (London, Everyman's Library, 1958), pp. 218-219.

[24] Clarendon, *HR*, II, 417, I, 272.

[25] *Ibid.*, I, 372; cf. I, 125.

Clarendon, however, who is usually so detailed and comprehensive, dwells so little on the religious issues in the rebellion that Firth has been able to say that "his *History of the Rebellion* has the fundamental defect, that it is a history of a religious revolution in which the religious element is omitted" and that it is "an account of the Puritan Revolution which is unintelligible because the part played by Puritanism is misunderstood or omitted altogether." [26] More recent historians, holding other views on the importance of religion in the rebellion, have seen this lack of concern for religious issues as no defect and even as a virtue.[27]

Actually, these charges by Firth are most applicable to Clarendon's treatment of events before the meeting of the Long Parliament. For the subsequent period they need to be qualified slightly. But there can certainly be no doubt that Clarendon, who does not bother to discuss and barely even alludes to the origins of Puritanism in the *History,* thought it of little importance in the earlier of these periods. When Laud became Archbishop in 1633, he says, "the general temper and humour of" the kingdom was "little inclined to the Papists and less to the Puritan"; [28] for the subsequent discontent, as we have seen, he blames Laud. He does not, however, identify this discontent as specifically Puritan, nor does he describe any expansion of Puritanism. Though he describes the Arminian theological controversy and the accompanying controversy over the communion table which disturbed the peace of the kingdom, he gives no indication that he sees the Laudian policies as being confronted by a solid body of Puritans. He observes that very many of the opponents of Arminianism "were most affectionate to the peace and prosperity of the Church, and very pious and learned men." [29] Choosing to view the Laudian campaign for the improvement of church buildings and their services on a secular rather than a religious plane, he observes that it caused animosity towards the church because it was prosecuted "with too much affectation of expense, it may be, or with too much passion between the minister and the parishioners." [30] In speaking of the Parliament's declaration of April 8, 1642, for the reformation of the government and

---

[26] Firth, *Essays Historical & Literary,* pp. 119, 207. He adds to the latter observation, p. 208, that Burnet "succeeds in making the Revolution of 1688 intelligible while Clarendon leaves that of 1649 unexplained."

[27] Christopher Hill, *Puritanism and Revolution: Studies in Interpretation of the English Revolution of the 17th Century* (London, Secker & Warburg, 1958), pp. 199-200; H. R. Trevor-Roper, *Men and Events: Historical Essays* (New York, Harper & Brothers, 1957), p. 246.

[28] Clarendon, *HR,* I, 122-123.

[29] *Ibid.,* I, 124.

[30] *Ibid.,* I, 126-127.

liturgy of the church, he says that this declaration "would a year before have given great umbrage and scandal to the people, when generally there was a due submission to the government, and a singular reverence of the liturgy, of the Church of England." Even at this time, he suggests, the declaration was tolerated only because it seemed to hold out a compromise by which moderate reforms would prevent more radical injury to the church. He does, however, admit that the declaration was published "To confirm and encourage the factious and schismatical party of the kingdom." [31]

Clarendon, in fact, in dealing with this period before the meeting of the Long Parliament hardly seems to have anything in mind resembling the now familiar textbook images of a movement called "Puritanism" and a body of people called "Puritans." He tends to resolve the movement into its component parts or, more likely, refuses to synthesize these parts into a labelled whole. Thus he very largely though not quite exclusively sees a collection of hostile attitudes, or attitudes the government chose to regard as hostile to the dominant ecclesiastical order, rather than a definite "Puritan" movement of opposition. Some persons were anti-Arminian, some were Calvinists or Calvinistically inclined, some opposed the government of the church on various pretexts and to various degrees, some had a personal animus against individual bishops such as Laud, some may not have been enemies of the church at all, but simply persons who were accused of so being, and some, Clarendon says vaguely, were "those who were called Puritans in the worst sense." [32]

Religion of the Puritan variety looms slightly larger in Clarendon's narrative of events from the early months of the Long Parliament to the Restoration. There he refers to the incendiary Parliamentarian clergymen who preached up the rebellion, notes the proliferation of new sects and opinions in religion, and discusses the rivalry of the Presbyterians and Independents in England and the respective ways in which the Scottish Presbyterians and the English Independents translated their wickedness into political action. It is doubtful, however, whether he considered religion to be of major importance in causing the defeat of the King, and

---

[31] *Ibid.*, II, 70-72, 448-449, III, 221. In the midst of his account of Charles's visit to Scotland in 1633, he includes, I, 109-110, the observation that Charles feared the seditious possibilities of opponents of the ecclesiastical government and had, accordingly, "with the utmost vigilance caused that temper and disposition to be watched and provided against in England; and if it were then in truth there, it lurked with wonderful secrecy." This probably should be considered an extreme rather than representative statement of Clarendon's attitude. Cf. his remarks about London, I, 122, and about Laud and the "schismatics," Clarendon, *L*, I, 18.

[32] Clarendon, *HR*, *passim*; quotation from I, 241.

he is oblivious to the moral force of Puritanism. He is dealing, not with the convictions of saints, but with rascality and self-delusion.

Having examined Clarendon's views on the importance of Puritanism in the origins and progress of the rebellion, it is now possible to discuss his views on whether the fall of the monarchy was the result of a plot organized before the rebellion. Heylyn, it will be remembered, thought that it was. Dugdale's opinion seems to have been the same. Though it is hard to be sure that Hobbes saw the existence of a plot before the rebellion began, he certainly saw the existence of disloyal hopes of the sort that underlay the plot described by Heylyn, and it would be surprising to find that his views on the deliberateness with which the rebellion had been brought about were greatly different from Heylyn and Dugdale's. The notion that the destruction of the monarchy had been cold-bloodedly and clear-mindedly plotted and carried out was supported by belief in the wickedness of the Parliamentarian leaders and was not easily disproven or shaken given the information available to most seventeenth-century historians of the war. The appeal that it would have to such rigorously systematizing minds as those of Heylyn, Dugdale, and Hobbes is apparent. Clarendon, too, was convinced, at least by the time he came to write as a historian, of the wickedness of the Parliamentarian leaders; but he was more intimately informed of the events of the rebellion than either Heylyn, Dugdale, or Hobbes; and he distrusted such a severely intellectual approach to the problems of political life as they took. In his reply to *Leviathan* he says that

I should be very glad that Mr. *Hobbes* might have a place in Parliament, and sit in Counsel, and be present in Courts of Justice, and other Tribunals; whereby it is probable he would find, that his solitary cogitation, how deep soever, and his too peremtory adhering to some Philosophical Notions, and even Rules of Geometry, had misled him in the investigation of Policy, ...[33]

By minimizing the importance of Puritanism before the meeting of the Long Parliament, he undercuts the theory that the Puritan movement involved a plot to overthrow the monarchy.

What did Clarendon think about the original intentions of the Parliamentarian leaders, their intentions before the Long Parliament met? Though his statements do not permit a wholly satisfying answer to this question, it is sufficiently clear that he rejected the idea that there was any long organized pre-1640 plot to raise the rebellion and to overthrow

---

[33] Edward Hyde, Earl of Clarendon, *A Brief View and Survey of the Dangerous and pernicious Errors to Church and State, In Mr. Hobbes's Book, Entitled Leviathan,* 2nd impression (Oxford, 1676), p. 322.

the monarchy. It is also probable that he rejected the idea that there had been any plot at all, however recent its origin, before the Long Parliament met, but he does not absolutely exclude the possibility that a few [34] isolated or almost isolated individuals in this period may have hoped for and worked for a rebellion or the overthrow of the monarchy in a way which, had they worked in conscious conspiracy with each other rather than singly or almost singly, would have enabled one to speak of a "plot."

Clarendon's central statement on the problem of whether there was a plot behind the rebellion appears almost at the beginning of the *History*, when he writes that he will not

lead any man farther back in this journey, for the discovery of the entrance into these dark ways, than the beginning of this King's reign. For I am not so sharp-sighted as those who have discerned this rebellion contriving from, if not before, the death of Queen Elizabeth, and fomented by several Princes and great ministers of state in Christendom to the time that it brake out. Neither do I look so far back as believing the design to be so long since formed; (they who have observed the several accidents, not capable of being contrived, which have contributed to the several successes, and do know the persons who have been the grand instruments towards this change, of whom there have not been any four of familiarity and trust with each other, will easily absolve them from so much industry and foresight in their mischief;) ....[35]

The time from which he seems to see the rebellion taking its earliest rise is the period of Buckingham's dominance in the early years of the reign of Charles I. A "venom" of discontent which then took hold of the nation henceforth continued to increase in strength. This idea of a growing discontent he associates with his theory of a surfeit of peace and plenty. Thus men's minds in the remainder of the years of civil peace were filled with what Fuller, referring more narrowly to ecclesiastical matters, succinctly called "a mutinous tendency," which made them interpret events in the worst possible light. Unreasonably sensitive to injustice and misdeeds on the part of the government, people were unreasonably ungrateful for and indifferent to the benefits the government brought them.[36]

As Clarendon discusses the events which followed upon the meeting of the Long Parliament, he recurs from time to time to the problem of the intentions of the Parliamentarian leaders. He seems to see the worst designs as remaining long the property of only a few even among the body of Parliamentarian leaders. In 1641 the future regicide Henry

---

[34] See his remarks on the future Admiral Blake, Clarendon, *HR*, VI, 37.
[35] *Ibid.*, I, 3-4.
[36] *Ibid.*, I, 51, 96.

Marten, with whom Hyde at this time "lived very familiarly," confessed to him that he did "not think one man wise enough to govern us all." This, Clarendon says,

was the first word he had ever heard any man speak to that purpose; and would without doubt, if it had been then communicated or attempted, been the most abhorred by the whole nation, of any design that could be mentioned; and yet it appears it had even so early entered into the hearts of some desperate persons, that gentleman being at that time possessed of a very great fortune, and having great credit in his country.[37]

In speaking of events of March 1642, when the King was already at York, Clarendon is able to say:

And I am persuaded that even then, (and I was at that time no stranger to the persons of most that governed, and a diligent observer of their carriage,) they had rather a design of making themselves powerful with the King and great at Court, than of lessening the power of the one or reforming the discipline of the other: but no doubt there were some few in the number that looked farther, yet, by pretending that, kept up the mettle of writing, and inclined them for their honour to new declarations.[38]

Yet when he comes to describe the factions and attitudes which prevailed in Parliament immediately after the Battle of Edgehill, he speaks vaguely of those "who had contrived the mischieve, and already had digested a full change and alteration of government." As late as the Treaty of Oxford of 1643 there was a chance, he says, to frustrate "those violent and abominable counsels, which were but then in projection between very few men of any interest, and which were afterwards miserably put in practice." [39] On describing the death of Pym he is able to say, "No man had more to answer for the miseries of the kingdom, or had his hand or head deeper in their contrivance; and yet I believe they grew much higher even in his life than he designed." He similarly speaks of Lord Saye finding himself unable to restrain the forces of rebellion he had done so much to set in motion.[40] In a passage which is difficult to limit to a precise date, but which applies at least to the five months following the Battle of Marston Moor of July 1644, he says, without bothering to distinguish between the Independents inside Parliament and those out-

[37] Clarendon, *L*, I, 75-76. See also the conversation reported I, 75, in which Fiennes predicted war if the King resolved to defend the bishops. Gardiner, *HE*, IX, 389, mentions these conversations but does not attempt a precise dating of them.
[38] Clarendon, *HR*, II, 13-14.
[39] *Ibid.*, II, 378; Clarendon, *L*, I, 157, and the somewhat similar passage in Clarendon, *HR*, III, 212-213.
[40] *Ibid.*, III, 321, II, 547-548.

side Parliament, that the Scots discerned "that there was a purpose, if that party [the Independents] prevailed, to change the whole frame of the government, as well civil as ecclesiastical, and to reduce the monarchy to a republic." [41] In speaking of the Treaty of Uxbridge of 1645, he proposes to show "that they who governed the Parliament then had at that time the resolution to act those monstrous things which they brought afterwards to pass." Just possibly a distinction should be made here between resolution and intention. It was then that the Earl of Pembroke warned Hyde of the danger that the Parliamentarian extremists would establish a commonwealth.[42]

Evil leaders headed and managed the opposition to the King in the early Long Parliament and evil leaders continued to perform this function throughout the ensuing war. Clarendon never attempts to define at all closely what he means by this concept of a knot of evil leaders or to show what continuity of membership it maintained over the period of its existence, and he only occasionally mentions names of particular persons who belonged to it. Otherwise he refers to these leaders by names such as "They only who had contrived the mischieve," "a few men," "That violent party, which had first cozened the rest into the war, and afterwards obstructed all the approaches towards peace," "they who governed the Parliament then," "the party that steered," and "they who now governed in the Parliament." The ability of these men to dominate Parliament depended on their ability to hoodwink weaker but well meaning persons in both Houses who remained devoted to peace and well affected to the King even after the fighting was under way. Even loyalty to the church prevailed among the rank and file of both Houses after the outbreak of fighting.[43] He emphasizes that the dominance of the leaders depended on skillful management: often they were unable to exert their will as directly as they might have wished, but they knew how to guide the affairs of Parliament in such a way that in time events would take the course they desired. Clarendon's psychological awareness is revealed in his study of the methods of these leaders: he realizes how much their dominance depended on the intellectual and emotional weaknesses of other men and how ably they understood them. Yet his treatment of them is vague enough to be compatible with a good many theories about the nature of this continuing "knot" of leaders.

Although Clarendon does not believe that the Parliamentarian leaders,

[41] *Ibid.*, III, 453-454.
[42] *Ibid.*, III, 475, 494, For the intentions of the Parliamentarian leaders, see also II, 495-496, III, 81, 116, 136, 153, 205, 212-213, 216, 220, 322-323, 451.
[43] *Ibid.*, II, 378, 385, 438, III, 477.

at least as a body long united by one plan, deliberately plotted the war or the destruction of the monarchy, he does espouse the theory of what Wormald, in a useful phrase, has called their "original malignancy." [44] They early began to purge the House of Commons of persons not applicable to their "violent courses" by the expulsion of men involved in the abuses of the government of Charles I and by the settlement of disputed elections. Within six weeks "these terrible reformers" had caused the imprisonment of Strafford and Laud, frightened Finch and Windebank out of England, and intimidated many others. As a result of the use of such means, "they were like to find no very vigorous resistance or opposition in their farther designs." [45] Thus the crown was quickly "fallen so low that it could neither support itself and its own majesty nor them who would appear faithful to it." Their violent courses were consistent with their future rebellion but did not necessarily imply that rebellion, for they were willing to take office under the King.[46]

Though Clarendon realizes the isolation to which the King was reduced by the successful attack on some of his adherents and the temptation of others from their loyalty, he blames him for not managing his part in the contest more effectively. He should have advanced the popular leaders to office, he should not have made the disastrous attempt on the Five Members, and he should not have consented to the bill to exclude the bishops from the House of Lords. But his errors were political errors, not moral errors. When war came, moral issues were clear as the King at last made his stand against the constantly advancing aggressions of the Parliament and its leaders.

In the course of events we have been considering, which led from the disaffection of the thirties to the outbreak of fighting in 1642, Clarendon with his sense of the labyrinthine complexity of history seems to see a multitude of events as decisive. At every step in the march to disaster, a choice of possibilities stood before the nation. Among these decisive events, several stand out in his mind as being especially important: the Scottish war of 1639, when Charles could have crushed the Scots had he made up his mind to do so; the dissolution of the Short Parliament; the Irish rebellion (for without it "it is very probable all the miseries which afterwards befell the King and his dominions had been prevented"); [47]

---

[44] Wormald, *Clarendon,* p. 235.
[45] Clarendon, *HR,* I, 228, 236. Six weeks is a slight underestimate of the time.
[46] *Ibid.,* I, 241, 280-282, III, 322-323. Firth, "Clarendon's 'History of the Rebellion'," *EHR,* 36, describes more fully Clarendon's account of the devices used to dominate King and Parliament.
[47] Clarendon, *HR,* VI, 2-3; cf. Clarendon, *Religion and Policy,* II, 657-658.

and the decision of the Earl of Essex to be the Parliament's general, which alone made it possible for the Parliament to raise an army.

In the division of England into two parties, Clarendon, like Baxter and Corbet, sees a tendency to cleavage along class lines. He notes the tendency of corporations and great towns and, apparently, clothiers, to be on the side of the Parliament and of the gentry to be on the side of the King. In the battles men of note were lost on the Royalist side but on the other side the dead officers and soldiers were alike obscure. The national division sometimes had overtones of a simple struggle between the poor and the rich: in London, the poor were more devoted to the Parliament than were the rich, and at the beginning of hostilities there were outbursts of the rabble against their betters throughout the country. In an excellent analysis of Clarendon's remarks on class divisions and distinctions in the Civil War, an analysis which obviates the necessity of as full a study here of this subject as its importance would otherwise deserve, Christopher Hill observes that Clarendon "pointed out that men of new wealth were attacking the established ruling class." [48]

One of the results of the war was the rise of men hitherto of humble rank. On the publication of the declaration upholding the Vote of No Addresses, "persons of condition" withdrew from the Parliament's service and were replaced by "a more inferior sort of the common people" who henceforth lorded it over their erstwhile betters.[49] Defeated Royalists returning from the King's service "lived quietly and privately under the insolence of those neighbours who had formerly, by the inferiority of their conditions, submitted to them." The colonies submitted quietly to the yoke of the Parliament, "without any other damage or inconvenience than the having citizens and inferior persons put to govern them, instead of gentlemen who had been intrusted by the King in those places." Part of the degradation of Scotland under English rule was that the Scots were governed by plebeians. Richard's Parliament, he notes ironically, handled Oliver's peers "according to the quality they had been of, not that which they were in." [50] At the same time there was a levelling downward as lords, stripped of their former privileges, found themselves placed on the level of the common people.[51]

---

[48] Hill, *Puritanism and Revolution*, pp. 204-208, quotation from p. 207.
[49] Clarendon, *HR*, IV, 287-288, 315; Hill, *Puritanism and Revolution*, p. 208.
[50] Clarendon, *HR*, IV, 395, V, 262, VI, 2, 100.
[51] *Ibid.*, IV, 500, V, 184, VI, 4. Clarendon seems for a moment almost to touch on Harringtonian ideas of the connection between political power and property in his remark, IV, 495, about the "royal party" having suffered "loss of so much blood, and (which weakens almost as much) of so great estates." Cf. V, 287-288.

In contrast with his reflections as noted above, Clarendon largely ignores class conflicts and the economic relationships that lie behind them in his account of the rise of the war in the years before the outbreak of fighting in 1642. There he only implicitly and faintly touches on the strains of a class society, as in his idea of the surfeit of peace, which relates to the distribution of wealth in society, and in his remark that the burden of the forest laws exactions "lighted most upon persons of quality and honour, who thought themselves above ordinary oppressions, and [were] therefore like to remember it with more sharpness." [52]

Loyal though he was to the King's cause and person, Clarendon presents an unflattering portrait of part – perhaps a considerable part – of the Royalists. This is an aspect of his thought that is easily misunderstood. Clarendon's loyalty was first to the royal cause as he defined it, secondly and less strongly to the King as a person, and only thirdly and somewhat feebly to the Royalists, but he certainly considered them as a body morally superior to the Parliamentarians, and he wrote, as the opening lines of the *History* announce, to commemorate those defenders of the King who, though unsuccessful, had done their duty.[53] Nevertheless, his portrait of the Royalists, intentionally or unintentionally, conveys the impression that the defeat of Charles I was not very surprising. As he describes events, the King's court, army, and headquarters at Oxford began to be troubled by factions early in the conflict, the prosecution of Colonel Feilding in 1643 for his surrender of Reading being the event from which they took their origin. There was friction between the military men and the King's council, and the King failed to exact for his council as much respect as it deserved and the maintenance of his own dignity required. The Royalists proved troublesome to the sovereign they were defending by importuning him for rewards and favors. These troubles were paralleled by disorders in the field, which Clarendon, who seems to have been well equipped with the quintessential civilian's distrust of the military personality, censures severely. He complains that as the war progressed

those under the King's commanders grew insensibly into all the license, disorder, and impiety, with which they had reproached the rebels; and they, again, into great discipline, diligence, and sobriety, which begat courage

---

[52] *Ibid.,* I, 85.

[53] *Ibid.,* I, 1; "not" should be reinserted after "could" in line 4 of the first sentence of the *History* to make this sentence internally consistent and consistent with the similar remarks, IV, 2, 492, and with his letter of Aug. 14, 1646, quoted by Macray, *ibid.,* I, xiii-xiv. The "not" once existed in the manuscript (as the facsimile printed with the Macray edition and the original in the Bodleian show) but has been stroked out.

and resolution in them, and notable dexterity in achievements and enterprises. Insomuch as one side seemed to fight for monarchy with the weapons of confusion, and the other to destroy the King and government with all the principles and regularity of monarchy.[54]

The western army of which Hopton took command in January 1646 was "a dissolute, undisciplined, wicked, beaten army"; it contained "horse whom only their friends feared, and their enemies laughed at; being only terrible in plunder, and resolute in running away." [55] Extending his criticism to particular persons, he censures the wickedness of Lord Goring and Sir Richard Grenville – Grenville not Cromwell is the villain of the *History* – the roughness and rashness of Prince Rupert, and the flight of the Marquis of Newcastle from England after his defeat at Marston Moor.

In view of Clarendon's considerable acquaintance with Charles I, it is disappointing to find that Charles is such a dim figure in the *History* and *Life*. He shares no trace of the pulsating life that suffuses Clarendon's satanic figure of Oliver Cromwell. Clarendon is much less successful than the humble Warwick in portraying the King as a human being. Clarendon does succeed moderately well in the very different task of communicating a sense of the King's goodness: of the humility, kindness, patience, piety, and so forth of "the worthiest gentleman, the best master, the best friend, the best husband, the best father, and the best Christian, that the age in which he lived had produced." [56] Yet the picture of a good man which Clarendon has created is not the picture of any particular good man; it is the featureless picture of a type, not of an individual. No doubt the reason for this lies partly in Charles, whose personality seems to have made little impression on most people. The literary difficulty is also well known of painting a realistic portrait of a good man: Bunyan's Emmanuel in *The Holy War* is one of the few shining triumphs in this difficult field. It is interesting to speculate on the connection between Clarendon's failure to paint a more convincingly human portrait of the King and his strangely cursory treatment of the King's trial and execution.[57] Did Clarendon feel he lacked sufficient literary grasp of the King to paint the terrible last scenes of his life as they deserved?

Clarendon's treatment of his master contains criticisms fuller than

---

[54] Clarendon, *HR,* III, 222.
[55] *Ibid.,* IV, 130; cf. IV, 137.
[56] *Ibid.,* IV, 492.
[57] Clarendon's explanation of his briefness is given, *ibid.,* IV, 488. Cf. I, xlix, for the comments of the anonymous writer of the dedication to the third volume of the first edition.

those of any other Royalist historian of the century, but given the prevailing contemporary Royalist image of Charles as a good but unaggres-
sive man, unsuited by his temperament to grapple with the conditions of
harsh times, they were not of a kind likely to alter the average Royalist
or Tory reader's existing opinion of the King for the worse. The most
important criticism is the implicit one of the King's weakness. In his
account of the war, Clarendon represents him as a man who is almost as
unsuccessful in imposing his will on his followers as on his enemies, who
never quite rises to the level of the vigor and ruthlessness needed by the
situations in which he found himself, and who lacks the resolve to be
steady even to his own good judgment. Despite one or two unexpected
passages in which he favors great severity or even bloody-handedness,[58]
Clarendon gives the impression in his account of the war that his own
temperament was not sufficiently different from the King's to tempt him
to be a severe critic of or even to leave him deeply troubled by the King's
ineffectualness. In the King's place he would probably have been an
industrious administrator but would not have come much closer than
Charles did to the ruthless vigor of Oliver Cromwell. Along with this
implicit criticism Clarendon includes explicit criticisms, noting Charles's
impolitic dealings with the Long Parliament, his undue partiality for
Rupert, and his uxorious compliance with his wife.

Clarendon describes two incidents in Charles's career which may be
interpreted by a suspicious reader as evidence of Charles's duplicity. In
discussing Charles's attempt (which he deplored) on the Five Members,
he notes that Charles overlooked the promise he had made to him shortly
before not to act in matters relating to the House of Commons except
after consultation with Hyde, Falkland, and Colepeper.[59] In a passage
dealing with the Engagement of 1648 he says that

the three persons [Loudoun, Lauderdale, and Lanark] who were parties to
it were too wise to believe that it could be punctually observed; which they
used as the best argument, and that which only prevailed with the King,
that the treaty was only made to enable them to engage the kingdom of
Scotland to raise an army, and to unite it in his majesty's service, which less
than those concessions would never induce them to do; but when that army
should be entered into England, and so many other armies should be on
foot of his English subjects for the vindication of his interest, there would
be nobody to exact all those particulars, but every body would submit to
what his majesty should think fit to be done; which, though it had been

---

[58] *Ibid.*, V, 6, 376-377. See also the examples of his ill will toward Whitelocke,
Hyde to Secretary Nicholas, Dec. 12, 1653, and Hyde to Mr. Wright (Rumbold),
Jan. 16, 1659/60, *Clar. S. P.,* III, 202, 648.
[59] Clarendon, *HR,* I, 460-461, 463, 477, 487.

urged more than once before to induce the King to consent to other in-
conveniences, which they would never after release to him, did prevail with
him at this time.[60]

Sir James Fitzjames Stephen has pointed out the inconsistency between
this account of Charles's actions and Clarendon's verdict elsewhere in the
History that Charles "was, if ever any, the most worthy of the title of an
honest man; so great a lover of justice, that no temptation could dispose
him to a wrongful action, except it were so disguised to him that he believed it to be just." [61] The best that can be said in Charles's defense is
that if he is released from terms of his contract by the common submission
to his judgment of the other partners to it he will not be a violator of his
word in the fullest sense. Despite the inclusion of this passage, Clarendon
as a historian simply concealed Charles's intrigues with Glamorgan,
which he alludes to in his correspondence but does not mention in the
History or *Life*.[62]

In discussing the great opponent of Charles I, neither Clarendon nor,
presumably, any other Royalist historian felt any such temptation to
conceal wrongdoing, yet Clarendon produced one of the finest seventeenth-century historiographical tributes to Cromwell's greatness. In his
magnanimous mingling of praise and censure he was not, however, alone
among Royalists, for the author or authors (perhaps John Dauncey) of
The History of His Sacred Majesty (1660) and *An Exact History of the
several Changes of Government* (1660) and Manley and Warwick
provide, on a smaller scale and with a less skillful touch, portraits of
Cromwell similar in approach to Clarendon's.[63]

"Without doubt," Clarendon says in a passage which indicates his
divided judgment of Cromwell,

[60] *Ibid.,* IV, 302. Firth, *Essays Historical & Literary,* p. 178, says of the Engagement that "the details of the agreement were not revealed until the publication of
the second volume of Clarendon's *History of the Rebellion* in 1703." They are given
by Clarendon, *HR,* IV, 296-302.

[61] Sir James Fitzjames Stephen, "Clarendon's 'History of the Rebellion'," in his
Horae Sabbaticae, 1st ser. (London, 1892), pp. 320-321; Clarendon, *HR,* IV, 489.

[62] In a letter to Secretary Nicholas, Feb. 12, 1646/7, Hyde expresses pain at what
he has learned about Charles's intrigues with Glamorgan. *Clar. S. P.,* II, 337. Firth,
"Clarendon's 'History of the Rebellion'," *EHR,* 50n., discusses this passage. Clarendon
admits or almost admits, however, *HR,* V, 132-133, 107, that Charles II took the
Covenant. There are many indirect but severe criticisms of Charles II in the part of
the *Life* which deals with events after the Restoration; see, e.g., II, 466, 480, 501.

[63] H. R. Trevor-Roper, "Clarendon and the Practice of History," in F. R. Fogle
and H. R. Trevor-Roper, *Milton and Clarendon: Two Papers on 17th Century English Historiography presented at a seminar held at the Clark Library on December 12,
1964* (Los Angeles, William Andrews Clark Memorial Library, 1965), p. 34, over-
estimates the originality of Clarendon's portrait of Cromwell.

no man with more wickedness ever attempted any thing, or brought to pass what he desired more wickedly, more in the face and contempt of religion and moral honesty; yet wickedness as great as his could never have accomplished those trophies without the assistance of a great spirit, an admirable circumspection and sagacity, and a most magnanimous resolution.[64]

Though Clarendon recognizes him as being a master of hypocrisy and deception, all his interest in the art of managing men makes him reflect that Cromwell "must have had a wonderful understanding in the natures and humours of men, and as great a dexterity in the applying them." [65] He confesses that despite the roughness of his appearance in the early Long Parliament, which he suggests was affected in the interest of his ambitious designs, Cromwell later acted the part of a great man "without any indecency through the want of custom." [66] By his emphasis upon Cromwell as a farseeing schemer with a remarkable ability in arranging the course of events to favor him, he actually depicts Cromwell as a more masterful figure than he really seems to have been. Fixing his gaze too firmly on the dynamic soldier and administrator, he overlooks the dreamer of genius, continually surprised by events. He emphasizes his greatness at home, where he ruled "three nations, which perfectly hated him," by means of "an army that was indevoted to him and wished his ruin," but this greatness at home, Clarendon asserts, was nevertheless "but a shadow of the glory he had abroad," and he illustrates his greatness abroad by the deference which European powers paid to his wishes.[67] Unlike some contemporaries, he does not accuse Cromwell of betraying his country by making an easy peace with the Dutch in 1654 or raise the complaint (for which, in any case, he probably wrote too early) that Cromwell's alliance with France dangerously assisted the rise of that power. Yet for all his ungrudging acknowledgment of the stature of Cromwell, Clarendon was far from the temptations of mere hero worship. All human actions, he knew, were subject to the moral laws. Accordingly, just as he closed his treatise against Hobbes with hints that Hobbes would be damned, so he reminds the reader that Cromwell "had all the wickednesses against which damnation is denounced and for which hell-fire is prepared." [68]

With the death of Cromwell began a period of political instability which ended in the Restoration of Charles II. Clarendon denies Monck

[64] Clarendon, *HR*, VI, 91.
[65] *Ibid.*, VI, 91.
[66] *Ibid.*, VI, 91-92, IV, 305.
[67] *Ibid.*, VI, 94, 94-97; cf. V, 308-309.
[68] *Ibid.*, VI, 97; Clarendon, *Brief View and Survey*, p. 322.

the credit given him by many contemporaries for deliberately effecting the Restoration and instead emphasizes the importance of divine intervention in the Restoration. Even as late as February 1660, Monck had not "entertained any purpose or thought to serve" the King.[69] Clarendon says of Monck that

it was the King's great happiness that he never had it in his purpose to serve him till it fell to be in his power, and indeed till he had nothing else in his power to do. If he had resolved it sooner, he had been destroyed himself; the whole machine being so infinitely above his strength, that it could be only moved by a divine hand; and it is glory enough to his memory, that he was instrumental in bringing those mighty things to pass, which he had neither wisdom to foresee, nor courage to attempt, nor understanding to contrive.[70]

The Restoration was, Clarendon asserts in the same vein, "such a prodigious act of Providence as he hath scarce vouchsafed to any nation, since he led his own chosen people through the Red Sea," and was brought about "by such an extraordinary Influence of Divine Providence that there appears no Footsteps of Human Power in the Deliverance." [71] This idea that the Restoration was characterized by divine intervention was a commonplace in the historical thought of the time. Expressed with varying degrees of emphasis by persons as diverse as Baxter, and the famous Bishop Bossuet,[72] it could be combined, without much difficulty, with any view that the speaker wished to hold about the role of Monck in the Restoration. Sir Philip Warwick, for example, assigns the credit for the Restoration to God's interposition as fully as Clarendon does but also holds that although Monck

[69] Clarendon, *HR*, VI, 175.

[70] *Ibid.*, VI, 164.

[71] *Ibid.*, VI, 143; Clarendon, "Contemplations and Reflections upon the Psalms of David," *Miscellaneous Works*, p. 596. For Clarendon's expression of the idea that the Restoration was a miraculous event, see also *ibid.*, pp. 371, 552, 584-585, 640, 658-659, 679, 700, 726-727, 744-745; Clarendon, *HR*, V, 274, VI, 164, 234; the remarks on the revival of the Church of England at the Restoration in his *Animadversions Upon a Book, Intituled Fanaticism Fanatically Imputed to the Catholick Church, By Dr. Stillingfleet, And the Imputation Refuted and Retorted by S. C.*, 2nd ed. (London, 1674), pp. 96-97; and Wormald, *Clarendon*, pp. 238-239.

[72] Baxter, *RB*, Part I, 101, 105; J. B. Bossuet, *Oraisons funèbres panégyriques*, ed. Bernard Velat (Paris, Librairie Gallimard, 1951), pp. 69-96 *passim* and esp. pp. 94-95; for the idea of divine intervention in the Restoration, see also, W. G., *The Abridgement of the English History* (London, 1660), p. 353; William Younger, *A Brief View of The late troubles and confusions in England* (London, 1660), to the reader, sig. A3; pp. 147-148 correctly 147-149; Thomas Gumble, *The Life of General Monck* (London, 1671), ep. ded. to King; pp. 110-111, 215, 274, 280-281, 286, 426; Sir Winston Churchill, *Divi Britannici* (London, 1675), pp. 327, 351; Francis Sandford, *A Genealogical History* (In the Savoy, 1677), ep. ded., sig. [a2]-[a2]v; pp. 577-578. Clarendon, *L*, I, 268, says that events "made most men believe, both abroad and at home, that God had ... restored the king miraculously to his throne."

moved perchance, as a natural instrument at first, and discerned not, what would be the end; yet surely at last he was a voluntary and morall instrument in Gods hand; and by a loyall heart, prudent head, and stout hand designed and effected what was so happily brought about.[73]

Curiously enough, in the portion of Clarendon's work on the Psalms that he wrote during his first exile, we find him predicting and expecting the very thing that later (as he believed) came to pass: a divinely effected Restoration.[74]

In dealing with other matters, too, Clarendon follows the historical convention commonly found in his day of citing divine intervention as a cause of historical events – a convention which we should remember in examining the inconsistency which supposedly exists between the beginning and the end of the *History*. Firth held that Clarendon's

account of the close of the Great Revolution he had narrated contrasts curiously with his account of its beginning. In stating the causes of the Rebellion he had exaggerated the importance of personal influences, and attributed too much to the particular characteristics of individual men – to the pride of this man, the morosity of that, the ambition of a third, all like so many atoms contributing jointly to produce the great mass of confusion. In recounting the Restoration his point of view had altered. It is now the current of human affairs [sic] which guides men's acts, whither they know not, whether they will or not. The individual actor, even when he seems to direct the course of events, is in reality their creature.[75]

But in fact Firth in this passage misunderstands Clarendon. There is no inconsistency between the beginning and the end of the *History*. They reveal different applications of the divine intervention idea but this one idea unites and reconciles them. In the rise of the rebellion, divine intervention operated slowly and through what seemed, at the time at least, to be the normal workings of causation in society. In the Restoration, it acted more swiftly, and the "second causes," as contemporaries liked to call them, were much more evidently and dramatically subordinated to the divine hand than in the former case. Contemporaries knew that

[73] Warwick, *M,* p. 430. In speaking of the Restoration, he says, p. 429, that it seems "a sacriledge to rob Gods providence of any part of it; .... If he had not in this work made his own arme bare, and his interposition visible, mans wisdom or policy had never brought it about; ...."
[74] Clarendon, "Contemplations and Reflections upon the Psalms of David," *Miscellaneous Works,* p. 523. Cf. pp. 385, 546; Hyde to Secretary Nicholas, Nov. 4, 1651, *Clar. S. P.,* III, 36; Clarendon, *L,* I, 297, II, 407; Wormald, *Clarendon,* p. 177 and Part II, sec. 1, *passim.*
[75] Firth, "Clarendon's 'History of the Rebellion'," *EHR,* p. 483. Wormald, *Clarendon,* pp. 235-239, discusses Firth's charge; cf. p. 177. Perhaps I misread him, but it seems to me that the views I express on this charge are included in or supported by Wormald's remarks.

divine intervention operated in different ways. For one thing, they saw that it was much more direct, or at least much more evident, in some cases than in others. When Firth overlooks the divine element in Clarendon's account of the rise of the rebellion and speaks oddly of "the current of human affairs" in the Restoration, he needlessly secularizes Clarendon's thought and creates a conflict where none existed.

As we turn to Clarendon's discussion of foreign affairs, we find that he generally deals with this topic only insofar as the activities of foreign powers directly affected the Stuart kings or their dominions. He has no desire to paint the general background of continental events against which the English rebellion unfolded. He is aware that the English rebellion belongs to a group of rebellions troubling nations in recent years, but in any of his writings known to me he alludes to these "contemporaneous revolutions," these convulsions of the "general crisis of the seventeenth century," rather than discusses them.[76]

He finds that foreign powers had a baneful influence on the rebellions in Charles's kingdoms. He believes that Richelieu promoted the rebellion in Scotland once it was under way and is attracted to the belief that Richelieu helped to ignite it in the beginning. The Dutch fed the Scottish troubles by supplying the insurgents with credit for arms and ammunition. France, Spain, and the papacy aided and encouraged the Rebellion in Ireland once it had begun. He is even on record as suggesting that the papacy caused the Irish rebellion.[77] In England, at the time of the early Long Parliament, the French ambassador, the Marquis de La Ferté-Imbault, worked against Charles.

Clarendon is troubled by the practice of princes in encouraging rebellions in each others' territories and by their lack of a conviction that princes should unite to suppress rebellion in any particular prince's territory, to revenge a fellow prince's death, or to aid a fellow prince in affliction. Charles I was slighted by other monarchs during his troubles. If he had escaped from his imprisonment on the Isle of Wight in the autumn of 1648, there was "no court in Christendom so honourably or generously constituted, that it would have been glad to have seen him." [78] The news of his murder was placidly received by the continental princes

---

[76] Clarendon's meaning is not fully clear in one or two of the following passages, but some certainly and all perhaps allude to the "contemporaneous revolutions": Clarendon, *HR*, II, 420; Hyde to Secretary Nicholas, Jan. 1, 1646/7, April 13, 1652, July 11, 1653, *Clar. S.P.*, II, 318, III, 59, 178. See also Admiral Blake's remark as reported by Hyde to Nicholas, Feb. 9, 1651, III, 27.

[77] Clarendon, *Animadversions Upon a Book*, pp. 71, 246; cf. Clarendon, *Religion and Policy*, II, 657-658.

[78] Clarendon, *HR*, IV, 455.

("there was not a murmur amongst any of them at it"), who thereupon joined in the scramble for a share of his plundered possessions. Hyde and Cottington were hurried out of Madrid at the end of their futile embassy so that they would not be on the spot when "eighteen mules" loaded with the Spanish share of the loot arrived.[79] Charles II during his exile was slighted by his fellow princes, who neither contributed adequately to his support nor made practical efforts to effect his Restoration but who feared and courted the powerful tyrant Cromwell.

Clarendon's resentment at so much unkindness on the part of princes is understandable but somewhat naive. While he was under no obligation to accept the harsh, ungenerous principles of reason of state (of "that fathomless abyss," [80] as he calls it in another context), he had an obligation, as a statesman and historian, to understand them. Instead of doing so, he seems continually to be surprised that the continental powers should so steadfastly refuse to play the Good Samaritan to the advantage of Charles I or Charles II. Behind his surprise, there seems to be a feeling that the affairs of the continent were in some way less serious, less real, than the affairs of England, almost a notion that the continental princes should stop their play-acting long enough to take a hand in the "real" events in England. Yet if the *History* in many respects reveals an insular outlook, his essays and his vigorous and entertaining book on the papal power, *Religion and Policy*, do not; in other matters as well these works provide a good corrective to any temptation to think of Clarendon as a narrow man.

It now remains to fulfill a promise made at the beginning of this chapter and try to show the relationship of Clarendon to the other English language historians of the war who wrote their histories in whole or in early draft before the publication of the first volume of his *History* – historians who, if we wished to apply a convenient label to them, could be called the pre-Clarendonians. First, his debt to the existing printed histories of the war, so far as we know, was small or even non-existent. Secondly, he offers a more comprehensive indictment of the royal government and of the Royalists than any of the Royalists among the pre-Clarendonians. In part this indictment is owing to the superior length and thoroughness of his narrative, but it also arises from his emancipated willingness to be sharp in criticism where sharpness of criticism seemed to him to be justified and instructive. Thirdly, his historical method, though it is applied with all the formidable intellectual power and with the

[79] *Ibid.*, IV, 497-499, V, 151.
[80] *Ibid.*, I, 17.

assistance of the abundant historical data of its user, in itself marks no advance on the historical methods of the pre-Clarendonians. His emphasis on social conflicts and on psychology was important in his achievement, but there was nothing novel in historians being interested in these things or in dealing with them in their writings. Fourthly, Clarendon had resources of personal experience and personal communications equalled by no historian on his own side and by only Whitelocke on the other.

Fifthly and finally, there is the question of Clarendon's originality – a question which seems to me to be impossible to answer with any confidence, because our means of tracing the genealogy of ideas about the Civil War in his lifetime are imperfect to the point of being useless. Printed sources survive, but the great verbal source, that atmosphere of gossip, informed conversation, rumor, speculation, and common knowledge, which was probably, more than anything else, the storehouse from which the seventeenth-century historians drew their ideas about the war, has vanished but for a few traces. It does seem pretty certain to me, however, that a reader of Clarendon's newly published *History* in 1702-1704, if he had read industriously in the previously published histories of the war, would not find that Clarendon, in interpretation as apart from facts, had hit upon much that was both important and new, though he would find that he had used his materials with an effect that threw all the other writers in the shadow. This, however, proves very little – Clarendon may have independently reached the same conclusions as others. My own suspicion, for whatever it is worth, is that Clarendon picked up existing ideas with great avidity but was himself a conventional and even platitudinous thinker, that for all his very wide interests and matchless power of synthesis, he had not much more originality than we normally expect or find in a retired statesman who writes memoirs in his new-found leisure – but in this, I freely admit, I may be exceedingly wrong.

I do not mean by this suggestion to try to diminish Clarendon's towering stature; had he been more original, he would probably not have been so sound and therefore so great a historian. I shall be less open to criticism, for my spirit if not for the exact letter of my conclusions, when I claim that the *History* and *Life* together constitute what is still the most persuasive of all the histories of the Civil War, the one in which the machinery of the rebellion is most convincingly displayed. If we have since had to abandon aspects of its interpretation, it remains a work which is capable of capturing the imagination of the reader with immense force. Even the passages which incorporate those aspects of the interpretation with which we most disagree may usually (I except chiefly his weak account of the early and undivided Long Parliament) be compared with a poem that "convinces" the reader even though he knows that its particular events need not necessarily be supposed to have happened. The *History* and *Life* together may also be considered as constituting a great moral essay and a great essay on rebellion; time has eroded the relevance of many of the moral issues of this essay, but it is in many respects a faithful account of how rebellion works at this very day. The *History* and *Life* for this and other reasons repay their being read and re-read with an ever deepening understanding of our own time.

CHAPTER IX

CONCLUSION

Here it may be worthwhile to make some generalizations about how the historians examined in this study approached the historical problem of the Civil War.

From this study, it is apparent that there was no orthodox or prevailing set of interpretations of the war. Even within each of the two rival groups, the Parliamentarians and the Royalists, there were widely differing interpretations. That there should be differing interpretations within the Parliamentarian group is not surprising. This group contained such varied persons as Baxter, who followed the revolution as far as the beginning of the insubordination of the Roundhead army against the Parliament but no further; Ludlow and Mrs. Hutchinson, who followed it into republicanism but rejected the despotism of Oliver Cromwell; and Whitelocke, who accepted the despotism. One might expect that the interpretations of the Royalists would reflect the greater homogeneity of the Royalist group, which had the simplicity of defeat and of a singularly uncomplicated victory in 1660, yet their interpretations lacked uniformity as much as those of the Parliamentarians.

One of the most striking differences between the Royalist and Parliamentarian historians, as it has emerged in our study, is the greater confidence of the Royalists. The Royalists, unless they were mere chroniclers, based themselves in writing on a consciousness, which is often glaringly naked after the Restoration, of moral, legal, and logical superiority, but the Parliamentarians, with certain exceptions, were timid, bland, or ineffectual. The most notable of these exceptions were, of course, the republicans Ludlow and Mrs. Hutchinson. The historical value of the works of a few others who were exceptions, such as Lilly and Peyton, is so low as to make them of little weight. Since this generalization is true of Parliamentarian works published before the Restoration as well as after, the explanation of this contrast is not to be found in mere political

repression. The answer seems to be that the Parliamentarian historians
were simply demoralized by the unexpected turns their cause had taken.
From the early years of fighting onwards, it had sailed on an uninterrupted course of social, moral, and ideological disaster. The spread of
sectarianism, the insubordination of the New Model Army, the wreck of
the old constitution, the execution of the King, military rule, the despotism of the usurper, the turbulence of the military men after Cromwell's
death – these were so many obstacles in the way of any thoroughgoing
"Parliamentarian" defense of the "Parliamentarian" cause, a cause which
had for all practical purposes forfeited its claim to the "Parliamentarian"
title before these disillusioning events had half run their course. It is not
surprising that we find in Parliamentarian histories the coolness and
aloofness of May, the reticence of Rushworth, the total lack of zeal of
Whitelocke, and the irritated conservatism and imperfectly quieted conscience of Baxter. It can hardly be doubted that the Parliamentarian
historians and potential Parliamentarian historians came very largely to
accept the force of the arguments levelled against them. The republicans
alone had an ideological basis so firm that they could stand upon it with
a confidence equal to that of the Royalists. It is in this circumstance of
Parliamentarian demoralization that we must find part of the reason
why so few Parliamentarian histories were published or (so far as is
known) written between the Restoration and the end of our period.

Connected with the problem of the causes of the war, but more limited
and more strictly defined, is the structural question of how far back the
historian has to go to make his account of the war intelligible. If he begins his account with August, 1642, it will, admittedly, be truncated. The
year 1640 seems the latest date that is feasible, and the objections to
which it is open hardly need exposition. Apart from a preliminary survey
of earlier English and Scottish history, Gardiner began his great history
with the accession of James I in 1603; C. V. Wedgwood began her volumes on *The Great Rebellion* with the date 1637.[1] Of the twelve historians studied in detail in the above pages, three declared to the reader
their decision about a starting date for an intelligible account. Fuller
thought that the rise of the war could be traced from the Parliament of
1628-1629. Rushworth found that he could make his collection an adequate treatment of the war only by taking 1618 as his starting point.
Clarendon wrote that he would not "lead any man farther back in this
journey, for the discovery of the entrance into these dark ways, than the

---

[1] For criticism of her choice of this late date, see Trevor-Roper, *Men and Events*,
pp. 191, 193.

beginning of" the reign of Charles I.[2] Despite his inclusion of a discussion of the dominance of Buckingham in the reign of King James and of the Spanish journey, he is generally faithful to his date of 1625. This date, it is worth noting, would hardly have been tenable had he not thought Puritanism of little importance in causing the war. Other historians who set no precise dates often enabled the reader to deduce their opinions about a starting date for an intelligible account. By laying blame for the war on Protestant extremists of the sort who may be lumped under the all-purpose name of "Puritans," Heylyn, Dugdale, and Nalson pushed the history of the war back to the Reformation. Hobbes, who laid, however unfairly, part of the blame for the war on the English Roman Catholics and thought that the English reformed clergy, orthodox and unorthodox, retained too much of the old Popish insubordination to the civil authority, found roots of the war that extended back into the period before the Reformation. Mrs. Hutchinson, using Harringtonian ideas, traced its roots back into the middle ages.

While seventeenth-century thinkers who stressed the importance of Puritanism or, like Harrington, the redistribution of the monastic lands in causing the war did certainly link the Reformation and rebellion, it is surprising how little the English historians did to make the link explicit. Even Dugdale, Nalson, and, oddly enough, Heylyn, with his harsh realistic mind, his taste for astringent truths, and his drastic lack of favor for some aspects of Protestantism, do not give this link the importance it seems to deserve. One senses that there was a widespread awareness among the historians of this study of how harmful attention to this link could be to the Protestant cause and that in the interests of Protestantism they preferred not to expose it to the full light of day. Significantly, the future James II, in a conversation with Burnet, cited this link in defending his conversion to the Roman church.[3] We also find moralizing continental Roman Catholic writers calling upon standard contemporary notions about historical causation to represent the war as the outcome of the Reformation. The anonymous author of the *Abregé de l'histoire d'Angleterre, d'Escosse, et d'Irlande* (1652) suggests that Charles I died to expiate the crimes of Henry VIII, who drew down the divine wrath on England, "en y jettant les fondemens de l'Heresie, & prophenant le Sanctuaire sacré, pour assouvir sa lubricité demesurée." The Italian Bisaccioni thought the love of Henry VIII for Anne Boleyn an ulcer of such deep roots that they ruined Charles I's three kingdoms. Rather more

---

[2] Clarendon, *HR*, I, 3.
[3] Burnet, *OTA*, II, 29.

weightily, Bishop Bossuet in the valuable reflections on the English Civil War which he includes in his funeral sermon for Henrietta Maria applies to the war the words, "la séparation et la révolte contre l'autorité de l'Eglise a été la source d'où sont dérivés tous les maux," and says that Cromwell's triumphant career shows the "conseil de Dieu d'instruire les rois à ne point quitter son Eglise." [4]

Amidst all the discussion of religion and religious groups by the seventeenth-century English historians of the war, one fact that emerges is that among these historians there was no widely or generally accepted image of Puritanism. The Puritans seem strangely variable as one follows them from one history to another. Various terms, as we have seen, including "Puritans," "Presbyterians," and "the Dissenting Protestants," were used by historians to refer to Protestant dissidents; the list of terms cited earlier from Nalson shows the remarkable verbal ingenuity that one writer alone could reveal in discussing the Protestant threat to the monarchy. I have assumed throughout this study that whenever two writers use the same term for these dissidents it is not safe, except on the grounds of the strongest evidence, to assume that they mean the same thing by it. Perhaps it will be worthwhile here to repeat an observation I have included in a separately published piece of writing on *Behemoth*: that one senses that the historians had difficulty in finding an appropriate terminology for the multifarious religious groups, and that they often found a way out by adopting some convenient words that would roughly encompass their meaning while relying on the probability that their readers, who had also firsthand experience of the war, would simply "know" what the words meant.[5] Fuller, Hacket, Baxter, and Mrs. Hutchinson, in their interesting

---

[4] Mr M., *Abregé de l'histoire d'Angleterre, d'Escosse, et d'Irlande. Contenant les choses plus memorables qui se sont passées en ces trois Royaumes depuis leur origine iusques à present* (Paris, 1652), p. 524; Majolino Bisaccioni, *Gverras civiles de Inglaterra, tragica mverte de sv rey Carlos,* trans. Don Diego Felipe de Albornoz, 2nd impression (Barcelona, 1673), p. 4; Bossuet, *Oraisons,* pp. 84, 86, and 69-96 *passim*. See also Pierre Joseph d'Orléans, *The History of the Revolutions in England under the Family of the Stuarts, From the Year 1603, to 1690* (London, 1711), p. 128; cf. François Raguenet, *Histoire d'Olivier Cromwel* (Paris, 1691), ep. ded. and p. 6. In Samuel Dancer's *Metamorphosis Anglorum* (London, 1660), the passage on p. 106 suggests that the author is a Roman Catholic blaming the rebellion or some aspects of it on the Reformation, but these assumptions are inconsistent with the passage on pp. 110-111. Isaac de Larrey, *The History of the Reign of King Charles I,* 2 vols. (London, 1716), II, 289, cites a French writer as saying that Clarendon in exile attributed the first seeds of the Civil War to the lords' fear that Charles would take away their church lands. Perhaps Clarendon did say this, but about the Scottish, not English, lords.

[5] R. MacGillivray, "Thomas Hobbes's History of the English Civil War: a Study of *Behemoth*," *Journal of the History of Ideas,* 31 (1970), 189. My findings about the seventeenth-century meaning of "Puritanism" support C. H. George's article, "Puritanism as History and Historiography," *Past & Present,* No. 41 (Dec. 1968), 77-104.

remarks on the term "Puritan," must increase most modern readers' sense of its vagueness in the seventeenth-century through their emphasis on the manner in which it was used to libel people who were found objectionable because they were non-Arminians or more godly than their neighbours or for some other reason. It has been convenient for some later thinkers to treat Puritans as if they were a party almost clearly enough defined to have (if they wished) party membership cards and a centralized list of members, and to speak of the Puritan mind and the Puritan family, and the Puritan attitude to liberty, work, music, or sex, but this attempt to use "Puritan" as a term of precision conflicts obviously with Fuller, Hacket, Baxter, and Mrs. Hutchinson's statements. I do not think that the term "Puritan" should be abandoned by historians, but I do think that it is very dangerous.

Turning our attention from home to foreign affairs, as we continue our attempt to generalize about how the historians of this study approached the historical problem of the war, we find that they usually made little attempt to sketch the continental background of the war. In this respect, of course, there is something to be said for their insularity: continental affairs only occasionally impinged on events in the British Isles. One of the continental subjects on which they liked to speak was the complicity of Richelieu in the Scottish rebellion and – though they stressed this to a lesser degree – in the English troubles. The cunning of Richelieu seems to have deeply impressed the Englishmen of his time. Cromwell was censured for following his private rather than the public interest in making a disadvantageous peace with the Dutch and for aiding the rise of France. The Restoration should have been all the more welcome to friends of the monarchy because it curbed the disgrace they imagined England suffered in foreign countries for its tumults and its mistreatment of the royal family. One of them complained just before the Restoration that England's "distractions have (from the most glorious Nation of *Europe*) rendred her the most ridiculous Nation of the whole world, and made her Natives, once so highly respected in foreign parts, now ashamed to own her." [6] The realization that the English upheavals formed a family

---

[6] Dancer, *Metamorphosis Anglorum*, pp. 100-101. For Royalist sensitivity to the scorn of foreign nations, see also I[ohn?] D[auncey?], *The History of His Sacred Majesty Charles the II* (London, 1660), pp. 216, 233; William Younger, *A Brief View of The late troubles and confusions in England* (London, 1660), p. 146; J[ohn?] D[avies?], *The Civil Warres of Great Britain and Ireland* (London, 1661), preface, sig. [A3]. For similar feelings in a Parliamentarian, see Baxter, *RB*, Part II, 214. Filmer in his "Patriarca" in Sir Robert Filmer, *Patriarca and Other Political Works,* ed. Peter Laslett (Oxford, Basil Blackwell, 1949), p. 95, says that the Barons' War and the Wars of the Roses, our "two unnatural wars have dishonoured our nation among strangers."

with a set of European upheavals occuring about the same time as those
in England, that a ripple of rebellion passed within a relatively short time
through a number of countries, is well expressed in a work we have not
previously noticed, *A Political Essay: or, Summary Review of the Kings
and Government of England Since the Norman Conquest* (1698), by a
writer who is known only as W. P – y and who may have been William
Pudsey or Sir William Petty; and is also touched upon by Clarendon and
by Heath in *Flagellum*.[7]

The insularity with which the English historians regard the continent
finds an echo in the lack of understanding, sympathy, and even curiosity
so often evident in their treatment of Scotland and Ireland. For most of
the historians, these two closely neighbouring nations were very far away
indeed.

Though historians were able to trace the roots of the war into the
English past and to connect it, if somewhat diffidently, with the events of
neighbouring nations, they were unable, by reason of their nearness to it,
to trace its consequences very far into the future which it was to mark so
deeply. The question of what the war achieved, of its durable contribution to society, is legitimate in the broad perspective of the more than
three centuries that have elapsed since the Restoration, but it would have
seemed strange to many or most of the seventeenth-century historians of
the war. To the Royalists, it must have seemed that the war brought no
benefits worth the price, though it produced examples of loyalty, heroism,
and self-sacrifice, and many and salutary examples to prevent people
from provoking such a disaster again; to the Parliamentarians, while they
would agree as to the existence of edifying examples of loyalty, heroism,
and self-sacrifice, it must have seemed that whatever more substantial
benefits the war brought had been lost at the Restoration if not before.
Except in calling attention to such ambiguous benefits as these, no English historian of our period writing after the Restoration set himself to
show what good the war had brought. Historians who wrote before the
Restoration in praise of the Long Parliament or Oliver Cromwell said
or implied that their successes were good things and presumably wrote
under the assumption that their successes were likely to be perpetuated
in the form of lasting changes in the English government, but they never,
in any sort of historical book keeping, clearly balanced these successes
against what had been lost or damaged in the war.

[7] W. P – y, *A Political Essay: or, Summary Review of the Kings and Government
of England Since the Norman Conquest* (London, 1698), p. 142; references to Clarendon as in my chapter VIII, note 76; [James Heath], *Flagellum* (London, 1663),
to the reader, sig. A4-A4v.

While historians, unimpressed by its delusive achievements, often stressed the evils brought by the war, few if any of them seem to have doubted that it was a most exceptional historical event. We have already seen the claim of Lord North, the former Parliamentarian, that he had failed in his examination of histories to find any parallel to the English rebellion. Sir Roger Manley, stressing the singular nature of what had happened, wrote with a certain pride that "our Tragedies will scarce find Credit with Posterity, whilst the Ages to come, mistrusting the Reports of such enormous Villainies, will look upon our unheard-of Vicissitudes, but as the Fancies of Poetry, and the Decoration of Theatres." [8]

Of all the occurrences in the war that posterity might be expected to be aghast at, there was none, Royalists felt, that was likely to create a deeper sense of outrage than the mistreatment of the good King Charles I. There were of course attacks on Charles in the Parliamentarian histories and elsewhere, but Royalist historians seem generally to have regarded them as peevish libels which did not deserve a reply in detail.[9] Their apparent attitude is well expressed in words Thomas Fuller once wrote in another context: "in vain do staid heads make serious comments on light men's random expressions, where the knot is neither to be untied nor cut, but cast away." [10]

While the Royalist veneration of Charles often expressed itself in eulogy, it also often embodied a realistic sense of the King's weaknesses as a ruler. Royalist historians endlessly stressed the moral goodness of the King and the justness of his cause, but they rarely cared to distort history to make him seem more shrewd, energetic, and masterful than he actually was. At the same time, it was a good thing for Charles's reputation that his contemporaries and their successors later in the century had ideas less exacting than those prevalent today about the competence which a ruler of a country ought to show. Whether the historians in this period had a good opinion of Charles or a bad, their systems of values, which provided the channels in which their thoughts ran, were usually of a kind that led

[8] Sir Roger Manley, *The History of the Rebellions in England, Scotland and Ireland* (London, 1691), p. 2. The concept of "posterity," which Manley uses, is a valued, perhaps often emotive, concept of the historians covered in this study, who were often keenly alert to what posterity would think of their age and to their duty to inform posterity (cf. Clarendon, *HR*, I, 1). As these historians belonged to an important period in the development of the idea of progress, their preoccupation with posterity is intriguing. One wonders whether an analysis of what the concept of posterity meant to Tudor and Stuart writers would show any shift in emphasis that casts light on the development of the idea of progress.

[9] However, see the answer in Dugdale, *SV*, pp. 378-380, to an accusation of bad faith made against Charles.

[10] Thomas Fuller, *The Church History of Britain*, ed. J. S. Brewer, 6 vols. (Oxford, 1845), V, 155.

them to judge Charles much more in terms of political morality and such essentially non-political matters as dignity, gravity, genealogy, and private moral conduct than in terms of successful application to the tasks of government.

One opinion in particular about Charles is so frequently uttered by contemporaries as to deserve special attention. This is the opinion that Charles was a man of very good abilities but that through lack of confidence in them or excessive modesty he was inclined to submit to the judgment of persons who understood matters less well than he did. When one finds this opinion in the pages of Whitelocke and Clarendon,[11] they seem to be stating the results of their personal observation of the King, yet one finds it also in other writers who are most unlikely to have had firsthand experience of Charles. No doubt for Whitelocke, Clarendon, and some others who held and propagated this view of Charles, it really was verified by personal experience; still, it is hard to avoid wondering whether they would have thought to make this particular "firsthand" observation if the idea it expresses had not been part of the common coinage of ideas about the war.

In contrast to the Royalist eulogy of Charles stands the widespread detestation of Cromwell. Denounced by Royalists, republicans, and others, he stood for many or most of the seventeenth-century English as a monumental image of the bad man. This aspect of Cromwell's early reputation is so well known that there is no need to labor it further here. What must be emphasized is that, as the foregoing chapters have shown, there was also a tendency, even in Royalists, to see elements of greatness in Cromwell, while the Parliamentarian Baxter and the Whig Burnet saw good strangely mixed with the bad in him. Some few exceptions apart, the seventeenth-century English historical view of Cromwell was remarkable for its fairness. The mean and squalid attacks of Heath are untypical. In the eyes of Royalists and many others, the moral case against Cromwell was perfectly clear. During the seventeenth-century, practically no approach was made towards dissipating the evidence against him. Yet within the limits imposed by the prevailing belief in his guilt, historians were surprisingly willing to acknowledge whatever could be said in Cromwell's favor. At the same time, they showed virtually no tendency to cast aside moral considerations and admire Cromwell as a great man merely because he had been an astounding success in the world. This was – and the fact is worth remembering by anyone who wants to see

[11] References to Whitelocke as in my chapter V, notes 54, 55; Clarendon, *HR,* IV, 490; cf. Clarendon, *L,* II, 263-264.

Cromwell in the context of his own time – a century in which anything like mere power worship or blind devotion to an all-conquering politician was thoroughly alien to the minds of most educated Englishmen. Except in rare cases, perhaps these attitudes have only been possible when and where the Christian concept of man, man the weak and limited, man bound by the moral laws, has begun to fade.

We have turned over a good deal of evidence in the foregoing chapters about seventeenth-century ideas on historical causation. We have observed that the historians or some of them realized, though not always as fully as historians today, the importance of socio-economic and intellectual causes, and that they also recognized the importance of divine intervention as a form of historical causation. On the subject of these latter two forms of historical causation, a few remarks need still to be made.

None of the historians considered in this study placed more emphasis on the importance of intellectual causes than Hobbes, yet there was a widespread awareness among them that ideas influenced events in the war. Perhaps few if any historians went so far as to express this realization even to themselves in the form of the grandiose conception that ideas are among the moving forces of history, but even the most commonplace Parliamentarian or Royalist of the day was capable of the realization that right ideas about the laws and customs of the kingdom and about the teachings of Christianity were likely to express themselves in the form of aid for *his* party, while mistaken ideas on these subjects were likely to express themselves in the form of aid for the opposing party. Religious ideas were among those that were considered as influential in the war, yet recognition of their full force was undercut by the tendency to regard the differing religious ideas of others as a mere imposture, assumed in order to cover discreditable motives.

The most striking failure of the historians to give ideas the full weight they have today in studies of the war does not lie in any methodological reluctance on their part to study the war as a phenomenon in which events were influenced by ideas, but in their reluctance to turn their attention from the ideas that existed before it and study the war as a *generator* of ideas. Perhaps this latter unwillingness is part of the reason why so little attention is paid by nearly all of the historians to the Levellers and why the Diggers are even less noticed. One must suppose at the same time that even the more conservative historians did not notice or simply did not believe that these groups were any threat to the established order. If the Levellers and Diggers figure little in my pages above, it is because they made so slight an impression on the historians.

No idea about historical causation more sharply divides seventeenth-century historians from those of today than the seventeenth-century belief in divine intervention as a moving force in history. This belief still survives in the popular mind, as the observer of his fellow man will occasionally note, but even historians who are religious believers have dropped it from their written work and academically it is as dead as the phlogiston theory. As a result of this revolution of opinion, there even seems to be a tendency to regard this belief in divine intervention as a foible of past historians, which the most charitable observers of today will pass over in silence. In view of this attitude, I am uncomfortably aware that I have stressed the belief heavily in these pages. I have done the historians the honor of supposing that they were as serious in this part of their thought as in any other. Above all, I do not see how one can make sense of Clarendon's interpretation of the war if one overlooks a part of his thought which was so important to him. It is true, of course, that a historian who points out that divine intervention is at work in a certain event may also reveal his assumption that the event can be explained, at the same time, by the ordinary machinery of cause and effect in the world, by the "second causes." The divine intervention belief is thus to some degree superfluous in historical explanation. But then, this addition of the secular causes to the divine in historical explanation is not a contradiction in any way of the divine intervention belief but an integral part of it. My desire throughout this study has been to enter into the minds of the seventeenth-century historians and discover how *they* viewed the war. Obviously, there is a good deal in the furniture of their minds that is not to be found in ours, but I have merely described what I have observed. I suggest that their views on divine intervention should be taken as literally (barring certain obvious cases of metaphorical usage, exaggeration, and conventional pious talk) and as seriously as their views on the circulation of the blood, on the Copernican theory, and on the importance to England of the East India trade. We are all the more entitled to take the prevailing belief in divine intervention seriously because of the prevailing sobriety of the seventeenth-century English historiography of the war. Remarkably rich in variety though it was, it never produced any parallel to the fantastic history of the war published on the continent in the lives of Cromwell by François Raguenet or by Gregorio Leti who plagiarized Raguenet.[12]

[12] W. C. Abbott, ed., *The Writings and Speeches of Oliver Cromwell with an Introduction, Notes and a Sketch of His Life*, 4 vols. (Cambridge, Mass., Harvard University Press, 1937-1947), IV, 883-884, seems not to realize that Leti plagiarized Raguenet. An interesting attempt to improve the history of the war for literary pur-

Finally, it may perhaps be permitted me to remark on the confidence with which the historians, as they reveal themselves in their histories, looked upon their society even after the violent experience of the Civil War. They were impressed by the terrible and singular nature of this futile war and realized the continued existence within the nation of enemies they hated, and if they were Parliamentarians they had their own party reasons for demoralization and disillusionment. Yet neither the war nor the Plague and the Great Fire of London which some of them also describe provoked in the historians any deep social pessimism, any sense that society itself was fatally flawed or that in the face of such calamities human effort was of little avail. Instead, despite their disillusionment, unhappiness, and anger, they joined their contemporaries in facing the world with a rough and robust confidence very different from the pessimism which prevailed in some intellectual circles in the Jacobean and late Victorian periods and in the nineteen-twenties.

poses is Mrs. Aphra Behn's play, *The Roundheads or, The Good Old Cause* (London, 1682) in which Whitelocke appears. The seventeenth-century inclination to believe in portents and supernatural predictions makes occasional insignificant appearances in the historians of this study; I show its appearance there but, as I now feel, by implication greatly exaggerate its importance in my article "The Use of Predictions in Seventeenth-Century Historians," *Cithara,* 8 (Nov. 1968), 54-63.

THE SURFEIT OF PEACE AND PLENTY

We have already spoken in these pages of the idea that peace and prosperity tend to produce rebellion.[1] The epistolary essayist James Howell states this idea in a general sense, though perhaps the insubordination he has in mind stops short of outright rebellion:

The sword is the surest sway over all people who ought to be cudgelled rather than cajoled to obedience, if upon a glut of plenty and peace they should forget it. . . . Riches and long rest makes them [the common people] insolent and wanton.[2]

Clement Walker expresses a particularly full and elaborate form of the idea and applies it to the English Civil War in his *The Mysterie of the Two Ivnto's* (1647), later reprinted as part of his *The Compleat History of Independency* (1661):

Before I conclude, let me give you the pedigree of our Miseries, and of their Remedies. A long Peace begat Plenty, Plenty begat Pride, and her Sister Riot, Pride begat Ambition, Ambition begat Faction, Faction begat Civil War: And (if our evils be not incurable, if we be not fallen *in id temporis quo nec vitia nostra, nec eorum remedia ferre possumus*) our War will beget Poverty, Poverty Humility, Humility Peace again, *Sic rerum revertentibus vicibus annulus vertitur Politicus.* The declining spoak of the wheel will rise again. But we are not yet sufficiently humbled, . . .[3]

---

[1] See above pp. 19 (where an important passage from the *Britania Triumphalis* is quoted), 28, 54, 88, 200-201, 210, 215.

For the idea that peace and prosperity result in foreign or domestic war, see G. R. Waggoner, "An Elizabethan Attitude toward Peace and War," *Philological Quarterly,* 33 (1954), 20-33; Paul A. Jorgensen, *Shakespeare's Military World* (Berkeley and Los Angeles, University of California Press, 1956), pp. 192-200, and Sir George Clark, *War and Society in the Seventeenth Century* (Cambridge, Eng., Cambridge University Press, 1958), chapter 6.

[2] James Howell, *Familiar Letters or Epistolae Ho-Elianae,* 3 vols. (London, J. M. Dent and Co., 1903), III, 156 (letter XLVII).

[3] Clement Walker, "The Mysterie of the two Juntoes, *Presbyterian* and *Independent,* with some Additions," p. 17, in his *The Compleat History of Independency*

The idea is again applied to the English Civil War by the author of *The Civil Warres of Great Britain and Ireland* (1661), perhaps John Davies:

never were Nations (had they known and been sensible of it) so happy in two succeeding Kings (*James* and *Charles* of glorious memory) as these were, blessed under their Governments, with near Forty Years of a continued Peace; which in the end filled them with so great Plenty and Riches, that grown proud, they fell into such a Surfeit, that nothing but a violent Bleeding could effect a cure.[4]

Sir Winston Churchill, the author of *Divi Britannici* (1675), expresses the same idea except that he speaks in terms of peace alone rather than peace and plenty:

we may rather call him [Charles I] unfortunate then unhappy, since the infelicity of his, must be rather imputed to that of his Predecessors Government, who finding that the People had taken a surfeit of his long Peace, indeavoured, when it was too late, to divert the Distemper he foresaw coming on; but only moving, and not removing the peccant humour that was then predominant, he dispers'd the Malignity into all parts of the Body Politick, and so corrupted the whole Mass of Blood, that that which at first seem'd to be only an ordinary *Itch of Reformation,* turn'd at last to the *Leprosy of Rebellion,* the Contagion whereof spread it self in this Planet-strook Kings Reign thorow all his Dominions.[5]

As the last two quotations suggest, the idea of the corrupting effects of peace and plenty as it existed in the seventeenth century had medical overtones. In order not to place an over heavy emphasis on its medical associations, we should note that the historians of this period had a fondness for medical metaphors and showed it in dealing with other matters as well: thus (to take examples independent of the idea under consideration) Hacket speaks of "the Running Gout of Factions," and another writer, perhaps John Davies, complains that in the Civil War the English

---

(London, 1661). A passage describing a similar cycle based on peace, plenty, and pride appears in an anonymous play, *Andronicus: a Tragedy* (London, 1661), p. 38, and is quoted in James O. Wood, "Thomas Fuller's Oxford Interlude," *HLQ,* 17 (1953-1954), 207. Wood argues in this article that Thomas Fuller was the author of the play. In Fuller's *Church History* the idea of the surfeit of peace and plenty barely appears, but he does mention that England began in the reign of Henry III "to surfeit of more than thirty years' peace and plenty." Fuller, *Church History,* II, 183. Possibly Fuller was hinting at the outcome of a similar period of peace and plenty in his own century. The cycle of which Walker and the tragedy-writer speak is discussed in Jorgensen, *Shakespeare's Military World,* pp. 192-200, and in Clark, *War and Society,* chapter 6, though these writers are not cited there.

[4] Davies, *Civil Warres,* proem, sig. C. Manley, *History of the Rebellions,* p. 5, adopts or plagiarizes the last fifteen words of this quotation.

[5] Churchill, *Divi Britannici,* p. 342.

in fear of a disease (instead of remedy) had . . . taken so violent a Purge, as in the end proved their poison, and wrought so strongly upon them, that (not being sensible before they could not remedy it) they were brought over to the door of Death, to the jawes and brink of Destruction and Ruine; which they had assuredly fell into, had not God by his immediate hand helped them out.[6]

The idea under consideration sometimes takes the form of paralleling the sequence of corrupted satiety and upheaval in the people of a peaceful and prosperous state with the sequence of surfeit and the illness it introduces in the individual. This parallel, of course, is based on the standard comparison of the state to the human body, but probably is usually intended for illustration and vigor of expression rather than as a declaration that the writer is basing himself on a severely thought out comparison between the state and the human body and owes much more to reflections on society than to reflections on medicine. As the basic idea we have been considering remains the same in most cases, whether or not a specifically medical parallel is made and whether or not the word "surfeit" is actually used, we may, for the sake of convenience, constantly refer to the idea of the rebellious consequences of peace and plenty as the idea of the surfeit of peace and plenty. This term has already been used in the preceding chapters of this study.

Connected with the idea of the surfeit of peace and plenty or, perhaps, in some cases simply a form of it, was the idea that the war was a divine punishment for the abuse of peace and plenty. Clarendon perhaps touched on this latter idea when he saw the avenging hand of God working through the process of the surfeit of peace and plenty. Whitelocke reports himself as saying in a speech he made in the House of Commons in the summer of 1642:

> Butt S^r, I looke uppon another beginning of our Ciuill warre, God blessed us with a long and flourishing peace, & we turned his grace into wantonness, our peace would not satisfy us without Luxury, nor our plenty without debauchery, instead of sobriety & thankfullnes for our mercyes, we prouoked the giuer of them by our sinnes & wickednes to punish us (as we may feare) by a Ciuill warre to make us executioners of diuine Vengeance uppon our selues.[7]

Perrinchief says that when Charles I succeeded his father, "He seemed not so much to ascend a Throne, as enter upon a Theatre, to wrestle with all the difficulties of a corrupted State; whose long Peace had softned

---

[6] Hacket, *SR*, Part I, 78; Davies, *Civil Warres*, preface, sig. [A3].
[7] Whitelocke, "Annals," II (i.e., BM Add. MS 37343), f. 251^v, or Whitelocke, *Memorials* (London, 1732), p. 60.

almost all the Nobless into Court-pleasures, and made the Commons
insolent by a great Plenty." But retribution fell upon the English, who
were "wanton in Plenty." For God, "provoked by our sins, which had
profaned his Mercies, and abused the Peace and Plenty he gave us, would
chastise us by the scourge of Civil War, the corrective of too much felicity." [8] In the following quotation Gumble emphasizes that an event
leading up to the English rebellion was a punishment for the people's
ingratitude for the blessings of peace and plenty. Speaking of the Second
Bishops' War, he says that

> this ill managed War proceeded not only from the treachery of men, but
> certainly from the hand of God, to punish these Nations for their sins, who
> did not know how to prize their Peace and Plenty with Thankfulness to God,
> and Obedience to their King: for murmuring and discontent under Gods
> Mercies procures the greatest Judgments.[9]

The idea of the surfeit of peace and plenty has a number of other significant connections with the thought of the time. It is one aspect of the
suspicion with which contemporaries sometimes regarded peace. Peace
was, of course, recognised as being, in itself, a good thing, but there was
a feeling that if not properly tempered it could prove dangerous. Bacon
found that "a Forraine Warre, is like the Heat of *Exercise,* and serueth
to keepe the Body in Health." Perhaps the idea of the surfeit of peace
and plenty is itself being touched on when, with the same distrust of
peace, an early writer on Cromwell declares that "the best policy . . . is
to intermix" peace and war "so, as neither the State fall into a *plurisie*
by peace, nor *Hectique* Feaver or Consumption by war." [10] The idea of
the surfeit of peace and plenty also has, to modern ways of thinking,
obvious class implications, but these do not seem to have been prominent
if, indeed, they were present at all in the consciousness of most of the
seventeenth-century English users of the idea. No doubt if peace and
prosperity lead the people to rebellion, it should follow as a consequence
for conservatives that excessive prosperity for the people is a bad thing
and should be discouraged by governments. But in keeping with the

[8] Richard Perrinchief, "The Life of Charles I," *Works* of Charles I, 2nd ed.
(London, 1687), pp. 5, 28, 72, 11.
[9] Thomas Gumble, *The Life of General Monck* (London, 1671), p. 11; cf. [Henry
Fletcher?], *The Perfect Politician,* 3rd ed. (London, 1681), p. 3, for somewhat similar
remarks.
[10] Francis Bacon, "Of the true Greatnesse of Kingdomes and *Estates,*" *Essays*
(London, The World's Classics, 1966), p. 128; Richard Flecknoe, *The Idea of His
Highness Oliver, Late Lord Protector, &c. With certain brief Reflexions on His Life*
(London, 1659), p. 43. For other material on the dangers of peace belonging to the
age of Shakespeare, see Waggoner, "An Elizabethan Attitude," and Jorgensen,
Shakespeare's Military World, chapter 5.

usual moderation of the seventeenth-century English writers on the war, none of them, so far as I have discovered, unequivocally advanced this drastic argument, though some of them may have implied it. The idea of the surfeit of peace and plenty seems further to be connected with the idea that, as Heylyn said, "such is the vicissitude of humane affairs, that being carried to the height they begin to fall." [11] That is to say, it seems that peace and plenty are self-limiting, that they tend by some force in the mechanism of the universe to reach a certain critical level and then decline. Perrinchief does actually seem to link the two ideas when he writes that in the reign of Charles I

all things were so administred, that they seemed to conspire to the Publick good; except that they made our *Happiness too much the cause of all Civil Commotions*, and brought our Felicity to that height, that by the necessity of Humane Nature, which hath placed all things in motion, it must necessarily decline. And God provoked by our sins did no longer restrain and obstruct the arts and fury of some wicked men, who contemning their present certain enjoyments, hoped for more wicked acquisitions in publick Troubles; ...[12]

[11] Peter Heylyn, *Cyprianus Anglicus* (London, 1668), p. 449; see also Fuller, *Church History*, II, 296; cf. 208; Roger Ascham, "The Scholemaster," in Ascham, *English Works*, ed. W. A. Wright (Cambridge, Eng., Cambridge University Press, 1904), p. 286; Samuel Daniel, *The Complete Works in Verse and Prose of Samuel Daniel*, ed. A. B. Grosart, 5 vols. (New York, Russell & Russell, 1963), III, 52.

[12] Perrinchief, "Charles I," *Works*, p. 11. For further references to the idea of the surfeit of peace and plenty in connection with the Civil War see Peter Heylyn, *Cosmographie* (London, 1652), to the reader, sig. [A5]ᵛ; Mr. Brasy to Lord Chancellor Hyde, Dec. 2, 1659, *Clar. S. P.*, III, 619-620; [Thomas Frankland], *The Annals of King James and King Charles the First* (London, 1681), preface, sig. [b2]ᵛ; Sir Richard Bulstrode, *Memoirs and Reflections upon the Reign and Government of King Charles the 1st. and K. Charles the IId.* (London, 1721), p. 5; Robert Mentet de Salmonet, *The History of the Troubles of Great Britain*, trans. James Ogilvie (London, 1735), p. 204; Burnet in an omitted passage of his *Hamilton Memoires*, quoted in H. C. Foxcroft, "An Early Recension of Burnet's Memoirs of the Dukes of Hamilton," *EHR*, 24 (1909), 531; Edward Walsingham, "Life of Sir John Digby (1605-1645)," ed. Georges Bernard (London, Camden Miscellany XII, 1910), pp. 79-80; cf. Dugdale, *SV*, 63, 592. Many of these passages, being very brief or simple, may arise from the mere use of metaphor rather than from any conscious historical theory. I do not presume heavily upon them, but merely offer them for consideration. Thomas Wilson, in his "The State of England Anno Dom. 1600," ed. F. J. Fisher (London, Camden Miscellany XVI, 1936), p. 24, writing at about the beginning of the seventeenth century, remarks that "the longe continuance of peace hath bred an inward cankar and rest in menn's myndes." In 1621 James I, commenting on the desire of some of his subjects for a more bellicose foreign policy, complained that "we indeed find by experience, that a number of our Subjects are so pamper'd with Peace, as they are desirous of change, though they knew not what." Rushworth, *HC*, I, 48. H[amon] L['Estrange], *The Reign of King Charles*, 2nd ed. (London, 1656), p. 143, finds the root of the Laudian conflicts over ceremonies in "the spirit of *envy, emulation*, and *discord*, the inseperable companions of prosperity." Mr M., *Abregé de l'histoire d'Angleterre, d'Escosse, et d'Irlande* (Paris, 1652), p. 293, says "vne repletion de paix" and "vne démangeaison de broüiller," were among the causes to which persons attributed the war. According to J. N. de Parival, *Abregé de l'histoire*

The idea of the surfeit of peace and plenty was also a serviceable part of contemporary ideas of historical causation and helped to add logic and continuity to the history of the Civil War. Why did a monstrous rebellion arise out of the peaceful and prosperous times of James I and Charles I? The war seems to have swept over England with the sudden unexpected violence of a summer cloudburst. It is part of the duty of the historian, as these seventeenth-century historians knew, to discover causes, to beat back the element of the inexplicable, to discover continuity and order in the bewildering events of history. The belief in the incendiary capacities of peace and plenty was useful to historians who seem to have found the justification for the rebellion less evident than it has been to some of their successors in later centuries.

De ce Siecle de Fer, 3rd ed. (Brussels, 1658), p. 390, the prosperity which peace brought made the English almost forget God. Relying for part of his utterance on plagiarization of Bate, the anonymous author of *Les conspirations d'Angleterre, ou l'histoire Des troubles suscités dans ce Royaume, De puis L'an 1600. Jusques a L'an 1679, Inclusivement* (Cologne, 1680), pp. 156-157, says that the common cause of the English rebellion and the fall of the Roman Empire was too much prosperity. René de Lucinge, *The Beginning, Continuance and Decay of Estates,* trans. I. Finet (1606), reprinted in *The Frame of Order,* ed. James Winny (London, George Allen & Unwin Ltd, 1957), p. 141, notes the corrupting effects of "ease & plenty" on rulers; perhaps it is to the idea of the evil effects of peace and plenty on government that James Heath, *A Brief Chronicle Of the Late Intestine VVarr,* 2nd impression (London, 1663), p. 2, refers. In the ep. ded. to "All for Love" (1678) John Dryden says, "*And yet there are not wanting Malecontents amongst us, who surfeiting themselves on too much happiness, wou'd perswade the People that they might be happier by a change.*" *Dryden: Poetry, Prose and Plays,* ed. Douglas Grant (Cambridge, Mass., Harvard University Press, 1967), p. 590. The people of Israel seem to have been corruptible in something of the same way as the seventeenth-century English, for we are told that "Jeshurun waxed fat, and kicked." Deut. 32:15, Revised Standard Version.

BIBLIOGRAPHY

Studies, usually short, of the seventeenth-century historiography of the Civil War can be found in various sources, including *The Cambridge History of English Literature,* ed. A. W. Ward and A. R. Waller, 15 vols. (Cambridge, Cambridge University Press, 1908-1927), VII, chapters 8 and 9, both entitled "Historical and Political Writings," but the most useful guides I have found to this historiography are Abbott's *Bibliography* of Cromwell (for which see below in section C of my bibliography) and the various studies which C. H. Firth published of individual seventeenth-century English Civil War historians, often but not always in the *DNB*. I consider Firth my principal predecessor in this study.

Anyone who wishes to have a list of sources for the study of the life and achievement of any individual historian I have discussed at length in these pages may construct this list from the footnotes in the relevant section of my book.

A. *Histories of the Civil War to 1702*

The following list contains the histories which form the basis of this study as defined in my preface. It is, therefore, a list of histories of the Civil War or some aspects of it written in England or by Englishmen or Englishwomen or published in England up to 1702, the year in which the first volume of Clarendon's *History* was published. As this body of works merges imperceptibly into works which are not in any sense histories, I have sometimes been forced to decide arbitrarily whether a certain work should be included or not. Without much doubt as to the rightness of doing so, I have omitted very minor works, works which are merely reports of current events and thus are "histories" only in the special sense in which similar reports in newspapers and magazines today are "histories," and works in which the historical element is slight or incidental. I have been forced to be especially arbitrary in deciding when to include biographies and autobiographies. Here I have often followed the rule of thumb of including those biographies and autobiographies which make as much contribution to the general history of the war as do the poorer general histories. Histories of the reign of James I belonging to the same period as these Civil War histories and chosen on the same principles so far as these are applicable to them have been given their own special list in the following section B, but I realize that many or most of them could with equal logic have been put in the present list. As chance has it, only one of these histories of James's reign was *not* first published in the 1650's and that one (by Goodman) was written in the 1650's. I am well aware of the subjective element at work in the compilation of these lists, but I trust that they would not differ gravely from lists of an equal number of titles compiled by other researchers who accepted the principles of selection I have indicated in my preface and in the present chapter.

A[lexander], W[illiam]. *Medulla Historiae Scoticae: Being a Comprehensive History of the Lives and Reigns of the Kings of Scotland, from Fergus the First, to our Gracious Sovereign Charles the Second.* London, For Randal Taylor, 1685.

Ashburnham, John. *A Narrative by John Ashburnham of His Attendance on King Charles the First from Oxford to the Scotch Army, and from Hampton-Court to the Isle of Wight.* Ed. George, third Earl of Ashburnham. 2 vols. London, Payne and Foss, Baldwin and Cradock, 1830.

Aubrey, John. *'Brief Lives,' chiefly of Contemporaries, set down by John Aubrey, between the Years 1669 & 1696.* Ed. Andrew Clark. 2 vols. Oxford, Clarendon Press, 1898.

Augustus Anglicus. See under Cook.

B., W. H. *The Royall Martyr. Or, King Charles The First no Man of Blood but a Martyr for His People. . . . To which is Added, a Short History of . . . Charles the Second.* London, For Henry Bell, 1660.

Baker, Sir Richard. *An Abridgment of Sr Richard Bakers Chronicle of the Kings of England. In a Succinct History of the Successions of the English Monarchy.* London, For John Kidgell to be sold by Richard Janeway, 1684. This work also appeared as Edward Cook or Cooke, *The History of the Successions of the Kings of England. From Canutus the First Monarch* (London, For Thomas Simmons and John Kidgel, 1682), and as the first part of L. S., *A short Historical Account of the Kings of England. From Canutus the First Monarch, and from William the Conquerour* (London, For Tho. Simmons, 1684). These volumes have Wing numbers B499, C6000, and S3594. The connection with Baker is probably imaginary.

—. *A Chronicle of the Kings of England. From the Time of the Romans Government, unto the Death of King James. . . . Whereunto Is Added, The Reign of King Charles the First, and The First Thirteen Years of His Sacred Majesty, King Charles the Second,* 7th impression. London, For George Sawbridge and the assigns of Thomas Williams, 1679.

Bate, George. *Elenchus Motuum Nuperorum in Anglia: or, a short Historical Account of The Rise and Progress of the Late Troubles in England. . . .* [to which is added Thomas Skinner,] *Motus Compositi: or, the History of the Composing the Affairs of England By the Restauration of K. Charles the Second, And the Punishment of the Regicides: And other Principal Occurrents to the Year 1669.* London, For Abel Swalle, 1685. Translated by A. Lovel from the Latin works whose names are still retained in this title; the name of the translator is given by Wood, *AO,* III, 828.

Baxter, Richard. *The Autobiography of Richard Baxter Being the Reliquiae Baxterianae Abridged from the Folio (1696)*. Ed. J. M. Lloyd Thomas. London, J. M. Dent & Sons Ltd., 1925.

—. *Reliquiae Baxterianae: or, Mr. Richard Baxter's Narrative of The most Memorable Passages of His Life and Times*. Ed. Matthew Sylvester. London, For T. Parkhurst, J. Robinson, J. Lawrence, and J. Dunton, 1696.

Berkeley, Sir John. *Memoirs of Sir John Berkley, Containing an Account Of his Negotiation with Lieutenant General Cromwel, Commissary General Ireton, And other Officers of the Army, For Restoring King Charles the First to the Exercise of the Government of England*. London, By J. Darby for A. Baldwin, 1699.

B[orlase], E[dmund]. *Brief Reflections on the Earl of Castlehaven's Memoirs Of his Engagements and Carriage In the Wars of Ireland. By which, the Government at that time, and the Justice of the Crown since, are Vindicated from Aspersions cast on Both*. London, For George West, 1682.

[—]. *The History Of the Execrable Irish Rebellion Trac'd from many preceding Acts, to the Grand Eruption The 23. of October, 1641. And thence pursued to the Act of Settlement, MDCLXII*. London, For Robert Clavel, 1680.

[—?]. *A Letter in Answer to a Friend, Upon Notice of a Book Entituled, A Short View of the Late Troubles in England, Wherein in the VIII*th *Chapter the Occasion of the Execrable Irish Rebellion XLI. is egregiously mistaken*. London, For Randall Taylor, 1681. 4 pp. Written by Borlase? Some remarks of the Earl of Anglesey suggest so. Anglesey to Borlase, May 31 (no year stated), BM Sloane MS 1008 f. 264.

—. *The Reduction of Ireland To the Crown of England. With the Governours since the Conquest by King Henry II. Anno MCLXXII. With some Passages in their Government. A Brief Account of the Rebellion Anno Dom. MDCXLI*. London, By Andr. Clarke for Robert Clavel, 1675.

Bos, Lambert van den. *Florus Anglicus or an Exact History of England, from the Reign of William the Conquerour to the Death of Charles the I. By Lambert Wood Gent.*, 3rd ed. London, For Simon Miller, 1658. See also under Dauncey.

—. *The Life and Raigne of King Charles, From his Birth to his Death. Faithfully and Impartially performed By Lambert Wood Gent*. London, For Simon Miller, 1659.

Bramston, Sir John. *The Autobiography of Sir John Bramston, K. B., of Skreens, in the Hundred of Chelmsford*. Ed. P. Braybrooke. London, Camden Society, 1845.

Britania Triumphalis: a Brief History of the Warres and Other State-Affairs of Great Britain. From the Death of the late King, to the Dissolution of the last Parliament. London, For Samuel Howes, 1654. Reissued with an additional section as *Britains Triumphs* (London, For Edward Farnham, 1656).

[Buchanan, David]. *L'histoire véritable de ces derniers troubles, qui ont commencé en Escosse, et continuent à present, en touts les trois royaumes d'Escosse, d'Angleterre et d'Irelande*. Thomason describes the origin of this fragmentary history in a note on his copy in the Thomason Tracts in the British Museum. The *Catalogue* of the Thomason Tracts, ed. G. K. Fortescue, 2 vols. (London, British Museum, 1908), I, 734, fails to supply the full name of the author, identified by Thomason only as "D.B.," but it may be obtained by comparing this passage with Fortescue's preface, I, p. iv, or by consulting Lois Spencer, "The Professional and Literary Connexions of George Thomason," *The Library*, 5th ser., 13 (June 1958), 107-108.

Burnet, Gilbert. *Bishop Burnet's History of His Own Time: with Notes by the Earls of Dartmouth and Hardwicke, Speaker Onslow, and Dean Swift. To Which Are Added Other Annotations.* Ed. M. J. R[outh]. 2nd ed. 6 vols. Oxford, At the University Press, 1833.

—. *Burnet's History of My Own Time: a New Edition Based on That of M. J. Routh, D. D.: Part I: the Reign of Charles the Second.* Ed. Osmund Airy. 2 vols. Oxford, Clarendon Press, 1897-1900.

—. *The Life and Death of Sir Matthew Hale, Kt· Sometime Lord Chief Justice of His Majesties Court of Kings Bench.* London, For William Shrowsbery, 1682. 8vo.

[—]. *The Life of William Bedell, D. D. Bishop of Kilmore in Ireland.* London, For John Southby, 1685.

—. *The Memoires of the Lives and Actions of James and William Dukes of Hamilton and Castleherald, &c. In which an Account is given of the Rise and Progress of the Civil Wars of Scotland: with other great Transactions both in England and Germany, from the Year 1625, to the Year 1652. Together with many Letters, Instructions, and other Papers, Written by King Charles the I. Never before Published. All drawn out of, or Copied from the Originals.* London, By J. Grover for R. Royston, 1677.

—. *A Supplement to Burnet's History of My Own Time Derived from His Original Memoirs His Autobiography His Letters to Admiral Herbert and His Private Meditations.* Ed. H. C. Foxcroft. Oxford, Clarendon Press, 1902.

Burton, Richard or Robert. See under Crouch.

C., H. *The Plain Englishman's Historian: or, a Compendious Chronicle of England, From its first being Inhabited to this present Year 1679.* London, For Langley Curtis, 1679.

C., W. *The History of the Commons Warre of England. Throughout These three Nations: Begun From 1640. and continued till this present Year 1662.* London, For Joshua Coniers, 1662.

Cabala: sive Scrinia Sacra. Mysteries of State & Government: in Letters Of illustrious Persons, and great Agents: in the Reigns of Henry the Eighth, Queen Elizabeth, K: James, and the late King Charls. London, For G. Bedel, and T. Collins, 1654.

Carrington, S. *The History of the Life and Death Of His most Serene Highness, Oliver, Late Lord Protector. Wherein, from his Cradle to his Tomb, are impartially transmitted to Posterity, the most weighty Transactions, Foreign or Domestique, that have happened in his Time, either in Matters of Law, Proceedings in Parliaments, or other Affairs in Church or State.* London, For Nath. Brook, 1659.

C[arter], M[atthew]. *A Most Trve And exact Relation of That as Honour-*

able as unfortunate Expedition of Kent, Essex, and Colchester. N.p., 1650.

Castlehaven, James Touchet, third Earl of. *The Earl of Castlehaven's Review: or His Memoirs of His Engagement and Carriage in the Irish Wars. Enlarged and Corrected.* London, For Charles Brome, 1684.

Cholmley, Sir Hugh. *The Memoirs of Sir Hugh Cholmley, Knt. and Bart. Addressed to His Two Sons. In Which He gives some Account of his Family, and the Distresses they underwent in the Civil Wars; and how far he himself was engaged in them.* N.p., 1787.

Churchill, Sir Winston. *Divi Britannici: Being a Remark Upon the Lives of all the Kings Of this Isle, from the Year of the World 2855. Unto the Year of Grace 1660.* London, By Tho. Roycroft to be sold by Francis Eglesfield, 1675.

Clarendon, Edward Hyde, first Earl of. *The History of the Rebellion and Civil Wars in England Begun in the Year 1641.* Ed. W. Dunn Macray. 6 vols. Oxford, Clarendon Press, 1888.

—. *The History of the Rebellion and Civil Wars in Ireland, with The true State and Condition of that Kingdom before the Year 1640; and the most material Passages and Actions which since that Time have contributed to the Calamities it hath undergone.* London, For J. Wilford, 1721.

—. *The Life of Edward Earl of Clarendon, Lord High Chancellor of England, and Chancellor of the University of Oxford: in Which Is Included, a Continuation of His History of the Grand Rebellion. Written by Himself.* 2 vols. Oxford, At the University Press, 1857.

Coke, Roger. *A Detection of the Court and State of England during The Four Last Reigns And the Inter-Regnum,* 3rd ed. 2 vols. London, For Andr. Bell, 1697.

Collins, John. "Mysteria Revelata," HMC, *Report on the Manuscripts of F. W. Leyborne-Popham, Esq. of Littlecote, Co. Wilts.,* ed. Mrs. S. C. Lomas (Norwich, HMSO, 1899), 198-239.

[Cook, Aurelian]. *Augustus Anglicus: A Compendious View of the Life and Reign of That Immortal and Glorious Monarch, Charles II.* London, For Samuel Holford, 1686. A shortened version of Cook's *Titus Britannicus.*

—. *Titus Britannicus: an Essay of History Royal: in the Life & Reign of His Late Sacred Majesty, Charles II.* London, For James Partridg, 1685.

Cook or Cooke, Edward. See under Baker.

Corbet, John. *A true and impartiall History Of the Military Government Of the Citie of Gloucester: From the beginning of the civil War between the King and Parliament, to the removall of ... Col. Edward Massey: ... to the Command of the Western Forces,* 2nd ed. London, For Robert Bostock, 1647.

Courthop, Sir George. "The Memoirs of Sir George Courthop 1616-1685." Ed. Mrs. S. C. Lomas. London, Camden Miscellany XI, 1907, pp. 91-157.

Cox, Richard. *Hibernia Anglicana: or, the History of Ireland From the Conquest thereof by the English. To this Present Time.* 2 Parts. London, By H. Clark for Joseph Watts, 1689-1690.

[Crouch, Nathaniel]. *The History of Oliver Cromwel: Being an Impartial Account Of all the Battles, Sieges, and other Military Achievements, wherein he was Ingaged, in England, Scotland and Ireland. And likewise,*

Of his Civil Administrations. . . . Relating only Matters of Fact, without Reflection or Observation. London, For Nath. Crouch, 1692. Attributed on title page to "*R.B.*"

[—]. *The Wars in England, Scotland and Ireland. Or An Impartial Account of all the Battels, Sieges, and other Remarkable Transactions, Revolutions and Accidents, which have happened from the beginning of the Reign of King Charles I. in 1625, to His Majesties happy Restauration, 1660.* London, For Nath. Crouch, 1681. To the reader is signed "*Richard Burton.*"

[Dancer, Samuel]. *Metamorphosis Anglorum, or, Reflections Historical and Political, upon the late Changes of Government in England, From the Death of Oliver Lord Protector, to the last Dissolution of the Parliament. As it was represented by a Person of Quality, to the most Excellent Don Lewis de Haro, Chief Minister of State to his Majesty of Spain.* London, For William Palmer, 1660. The name of the author is supplied in *A Transcript of the Registers of the Worshipful Company of Stationers; from 1640-1708 A.D.,* 3 vols. (London, Privately Printed, 1913-1914), II, 256.

D[auncey?], I[ohn?]. *The History of His Sacred Majesty Charles the II. King of England, Scotland, France, and Ireland, Defender of the Faith, &c. Begun from the Murder of his Royall Father of Happy Memory, and continued to this present year, 1660.* London, For James Davies, 1660.

D[auncey?], J[ohn?]. *An Exact History of the several Changes of Government in England. From the horrid Murther of King Charles I. to the happy Restauration of King Charles II. With The Renowned Actions of General Monck. Being the second Part of Florus Anglicus.* London, For Simon Miller, 1660. See also under Bos.

Dauncey, John. *The History of the Thrice Illustrious Princess Henrietta Maria de Bourbon, Queen of England.* London, By E. C. for Philip Chetwind, 1660.

D[avies?], J[ohn?]. *The Civil Warres of Great Britain and Ireland. Containing an Exact History of Their Occasion, Originall, Progress, and Happy End.* London, By R. W. for Philip Chetwind, 1661.

[Dawbeny, Henry?]. *The Pourtraiture of His Royal Highness, Oliver Late Lord Protector &c. In His Life and Death; With a short View of His Government.* London, By T. N. for Edward Thomas, 1659.

[Dugdale, Sir William]. *A Short View of the Late Troubles in England; Briefly setting forth, Their Rise, Growth, and Tragical Conclusion. As also, some Parallel thereof with the Barons-Wars in the time of King Henry III. But chiefly with that in France, called the Holy League, ... To which is added a Perfect Narrative of the Treaty at Uxbridge in an. 1644.* Oxford, At the Theater for Moses Pitt, 1681. For a reply to this work, see above under Borlase.

Eglesfield, Francis. *Monarchy Revived, in the Most Illustrious Charles the Second. Whose Life and Reign Is Exactly described in the ensuing Discourse.* London, By R. Daniel for Francis Eglesfield, 1661. First published as *The Life and Reigne of Our Sovereign Lord King Charles the II* (London, By R. Daniel for Francis Eglesfield, 1660).

Fairfax, Thomas, third lord. "Short Memorials of some things to be cleared during my Command in the Army" and "A Short Memorial of the Northern Actions; during the War there, from the year 1642 till the year 1644," *Stuart Tracts 1603-1693*, ed. C. H. Firth (Westminster, Archibald Constable and Co., Ltd., 1903), 351-398.

[Fletcher, Henry?]. *The Perfect Politician: Or, a Full View of the Life and Actions (Military and Civil) of O. Cromwel. Containing also a History of the late Civil War, so far as he was concerned therein*, 3rd ed. London, For J. Crumpe, 1681.

[Frankland, Thomas]. *The Annals of King James and King Charles the First. Both of Happy Memory. Containing a Faithful History, and Impartial Account of the Great Affairs of State, and Transactions of Parliaments in England, from The Tenth of King James, M.DC.XII. To The Eighteenth of King Charles, M.DC.XL.II.* London, By Tho. Braddyll for Robert Clavel, 1681.

Fuller, Thomas. *The Appeal of Iniured Innocence: unto The Religious Learned and Ingenuous Reader. In a Controversie betwixt the Animadvertor Dr. Peter Heylyn and The Author Thomas Fuller.* London, By W. Godbid to be sold by John Williams, 1659.

—. *The Church History of Britain; from the Birth of Jesus Christ until the Year M.DC.XLVIII.* Ed. J. S. Brewer. 6 vols. Oxford, At the University Press, 1845.

F[uller], T[homas], [*et al?*,] ed. *Ephemeris Parliamentaria; or a Faithfull Register Of the Transactions in Parliament, in the third and fourth years of the reign of our late Sovereign Lord King Charles.* London, For John Williams and Francis Eglesfield, 1654.

G., G. *The History of the Church of Great Britain, from the Birth of our Saviour, untill the Year of our Lord, 1667.* London, For Philip Chetwin, 1674.

G., W. *The Abridgement of the English History: Giving a true and an exact account of all the memorable Battels fought, all the magnificent Structures, all prodigies and Comets in the Air, and whatsoever by Sea or Land hath been wonderful. From the coming of William the Conqueror. . . . unto the restoring of . . . Charles the Second, . . . in the year. 1660.* London, For W. Gilbertson, 1660. Perhaps by Gilbertson?

Gumble, Thomas. *The Life of General Monck, Duke of Albemarle, &c. With Remarks upon his Actions.* London, By J. S. for Thomas Basset, 1671.

Hacket, John. *Scrinia Reserata: a Memorial Offer'd to the Great Deservings of John Williams, D.D. . . . Containing a Series of the Most Remarkable Occurrences and Transactions of his Life, in Relation both to Church and State.* [London], In the Savoy, by Edw. Jones for Samuel Lowndes, 1693.

Heath, J. *Englands Chronicle: or, the Lives & Reigns of the Kings and Queens From the time of Julius Caesar To the present Reign of K. William and Q. Mary.* London, For Benj. Crayle, N. Bodington, and G. Conyers, 1689. This author (good authorities to the contrary) is probably *not* the following James Heath.

[Heath, James]. *A Brief Chronicle of All the chief Actions so fatally falling out in these three Kingdoms; viz. England, Scotland & Ireland, From the year, 1640. to this present twentieth of November, 1661.* London, For William Lee, 1662. Also published as a section of *Royall and Loyall Blood* (q.v.). For evidence of Heath's authorship of this *Brief Chronicle,* see (a) the reappearance of some of its material in Heath's much larger *Brief Chronicle,* 2nd impression, of 1663 (b) "The Book-Seller to the Reader" of the same (c) Wood, *AO,* III, 664.

—. *A Brief Chronicle Of the Late Intestine VVarr in the Three Kingdoms of England, Scotland & Ireland . . . From the Year of our Lord 1637. to this present Year 1663,* 2nd impression greatly enlarged. London, By J. Best for William Lee, 1663.

[—]. *Flagellum: or The Life and Death, Birth and Burial of Oliver Cromwel The late Usurper. Faithfully described in an Exact Account of His Policies and Successes. Not heretofore Published or Discovered. By S. T. Gent.* London, For L. R., 1663.

—. *A New Book of Loyal English Martyrs and Confessors, Who have endured the Pains and Terrours of Death, Arraignment, Banishment, and Imprisonment, for the Maintenance of the Just and Legal Government of these Kingdoms, Both in Church and State.* London, For R. H. to be sold by Simon Miller, n.d. [1665?].

Herbert, Sir Thomas. "Sir Thomas Herbert's Memoirs, &c.," in Sir Thomas Herbert and others, *Memoirs of the Two last Years of the Reign of that unparallell'd Prince, of ever Blessed Memory, King Charles I* (London, For Robert Clavell, 1702), 1-144. See under Mackenzie in Section C below.

Heylyn, Peter. *Aerius Redivivus: or, the History of the Presbyterians. Containing The Beginnings, Progress and Successes of that active Sect. Their Oppositions to Monarchical and Episcopal Government. Their Innovations in the Church: and, Their Imbroylments of the Kingdoms and Estates of Christendom in the pursuit of their Designes. From the Year 1536, to the Year 1647.* Oxford, For J. Crosley, to be sold in London by Tho. Basset and Chr. Wilkinson, 1670.

[—]. *A Briefe Relation of the Death and Sufferings of the Most Reverend and Renowned Prelate the L. Archbishop of Canterbury: VVith, a more perfect Copy of his Speech, and other passages on the Scaffold, than hath beene hitherto imprinted.* Oxford, 1644.

—. *Certamen Epistolare, or, the Letter-Combate. . . . With. 5. An Appendix to the same, in Answer to some passages in Mr. Fullers late Appeal.* London, By J. M. for H. Twyford, T. Dring, and J. Place, 1659.

—. *Cyprianus Anglicus: or, the History of the Life and Death, of The most Reverend and Renowned Prelate William . . . Lord Archbishop of Canterbury, ... Containing also The Ecclesiastical History of the Three Kingdoms of England, Scotland, and Ireland from His first rising till His Death.* London, For A. Seile, 1668.

—. *Examen Historicum: or a Discovery and Examination of the Mistakes, Falsities, and Defects In some Modern Histories. Occasioned By the Partiality and Inadvertencies of their Severall Authours.* London, For Henry Seile and Richard Royston, 1659.

—. *Extraneus Vapulans: or the Observator Rescued from The violent but vaine Assaults of Hamon L'Estrange, Esq. and The Back-blows of Dr. Bernard, an Irish-Deane.* London, By J. G. for Richard Lowndes, 1656.

[—]. *Observations on the Historie Of the Reign of King Charles: Published by H. L. Esq. For Illustration of the Story, and Rectifying some Mistakes and Errors in the Course thereof.* London, For John Clarke, 1656.

[—]. *A Short View of the Life and Reign of King Charles, (The second Monarch of Great Britain) from his Birth to his Burial.* London, For Richard Royston, 1658. Also published in *Reliquiae Sacrae Carolinae: the Workes of . . . Charles the 1st.* (Hague, By Sam: Browne, n.d. [1658?]).

The Historians Guide. In Two Parts. First, The Recovery of lost Time; Being a Compendious Chronology of the World, from the Creation, to this present Age. Translated out of Italian. Second, Englands Remembrancer; Being a Summary Account of all the Actions, Exploits, Battles, Sieges, Conflicts, &c. And all Remarkable Passages in His Majesties Dominions. London, For W. Crook, 1676.

The History of England. Faithfully Extracted from Authentick Records, Approved Manuscripts, And the most Celebrated Histories of this Kingdom, 2nd ed. 2 vols. London, For Isaac Cleave, Abel Roper, A. Bosvile, and Richard Basset, 1702.

Hobbes, Thomas. *Behemoth or the Long Parliament.* Ed. Ferdinand Tönnies. London, Simpkin, Marshall, and Co., 1889.

Hodgson, John. *Autobiography of Captain John Hodgson, of Coley Hall, near Halifax; His conduct in the Civil Wars, and his troubles after the Restoration.* Ed. J. Horsfall Turner. Brighouse, A. B. Brayes, 1882.

Holles, Denzil Holles, Baron. *Memoirs of Denzil Lord Holles, Baron of Ifield in Sussex, From the Year 1641, to 1648.* London, For Tim. Goodwin, 1699.

[Howell, William]. *Medulla Historiae Anglicanae. Being a Comprehensive History of the Lives and Reigns of the Monarchs of England. From the Time of the Invasion thereof by Julius Caesar, to the Death of King Charles II,* 3rd ed. London, For Abel Swalle, 1687.

Husbands, Edward, ed. *A Collection Of all the publicke Orders Ordinances and Declarations Of both Houses of Parliament, from the Ninth of March 1642. Untill December 1646.* London, By T. W. for Ed: Husband, 1646.

—, ed. *An Exact Collection Of all Remonstrances, Declarations, Votes, Orders, Ordinances, Proclamations, Petitions, Messages, Answers, and other Remarkable Passages . . . December 1641, . . . untill March the 21, 1643.* London, For Edward Husbands, T. Warren, R. Best, 1642.

Hutchinson, Lucy. *Memoirs of the Life of Colonel Hutchinson Governor of Nottingham.* Ed. C. H. Firth, new ed. London, George Routledge & Sons, Ltd, 1906.

Iter Carolinum, Being a Succinct Relation of The Necessitated Marches, Retreats, and Sufferings Of His Majesty Charls the I. From January 10, 1641. till the time of His Death 1648. London, By W. Godbid, 1660. Has been attributed to Sir Edward Walker and to Thomas Manley.

Jones, D. *A Continuation of the Secret History of White-Hall; From the Abdication of the late K. James, ... Together with the Tragical History of the Stuarts, from the first Rise of that Family, . . . to the Death of Her late Majesty.* London, By R. Baldwin, 1697.

L['Estrange], H[amon]. *The Reign of King Charles. An History, Disposed into Annals. The second Edition revised, and somewhat enlarged. With a Reply to Some Late Observations upon that History; By The Same Author. And at the End of All, The Observators Rejoynder.* London, By F. L. and J. G. for Hen: Seile, Senior and Junior, and Edw. Dod, 1656.

Leycester, John. See under Ricraft.

The Life and Death of Charles the First, King of Great Britain, France and Ireland: Containing an Account of his Sufferings; His Tryal, Sentence, and Dying Words on the Scaffold. London, By J. Bradford, n.d. [1690?].

Lilly, William. *Monarchy or No Monarchy in England . . . .* [including] *Passages upon the Life and Death of the late King Charles.* London, For Humfrey Blunden, 1651.

Lloyd, David. *Memoires of the Lives, Actions, Sufferings & Deaths of . . .* [Royalists] *with the Life and Martyrdom of King Charles I.* London, For Samuel Speed to be sold by Samuel Speed, John Wright, John Symmes, and James Collins, 1668.

Ludlow, Edmund. *The Memoirs of Edmund Ludlow Lieutenant-General of the Horse in the Army of the Commonwealth of England 1625-1672.* Ed. C. H. Firth. 2 vols. Oxford, Clarendon Press, 1894.

Manley, Sir Roger. *The History of the Rebellions in England, Scotland and Ireland: . . . from The Year 1640. To the Beheading of the Duke of Monmouth.* London, For L. Meredith and T. Newborough, 1691. Part I of this previously appeared in Latin as his *Commentariorum De Rebellione Anglicana Ab Anno 1640. Usque ad Annum 1685. Pars Prima* (London, For L. Meredith and T. Newborough, 1686).

May, Thomas. *A Breviary of the History Of the Parliament Of England,* 2nd ed. London, By J. Cottrel for Thomas Brewster, 1655. First published in Latin as his *Historiae Parliamenti Angliae Breviarium Tribus partibus explicitum* (1650).

—. *The History of the Parliament Of England: Which began November the third, M.DC.XL. With a short and necessary view of some precedent yeares.* London, By Moses Bell for George Thomason, 1647.

[May, Thomas, M. P.]. *Arbitrary Government Displayed to the Life, in The Tyrannic Usurpation of a Junto of Men called the Rump Parliament. And More especially in that of the Tyrant and Usurper, Oliver Cromwell.* London, For Charles Leigh, 1682. Also issued as his *An Epitomy of English History,* 3rd ed. (London, For W. C., 1690).

Meriton, George. *Anglorum Gesta; Or, a Brief History of England. . . . since the first Attempt by Julius Caesar . . . to . . . 1677,* 2nd ed. London, By T. Dawks for Tho. Basset, 1678.

Metamorphosis Anglorum. See under Dancer.

A Modest Vindication of Oliver Cromwell From the Unjust Accusations of Lieutenant-General Ludlow in His Memoirs. Together with some Observations on the Memoirs in general. London, 1698.

Nalson, John. *An Impartial Collection of the Great Affairs of State, From the Beginning of the Scotch Rebellion In the Year MDCXXXIX. To the*

Murther of King Charles I. Wherein The first Occasions, and the whole Series of the late Troubles in England, Scotland, & Ireland, Are faithfully Represented. Taken from Authentick Records, and Methodically Digested. 2 vols. London: vol. I for S. Mearne, T. Dring, B. Tooke, T. Sawbridge, and C. Mearne, 1682; vol. II for A. Mearne, T. Dring, B. Tooke, T. Sawbridge, and C. Mearne, 1683.

—, ed. *A True Copy of the Journal of The High Court of Justice, for the Tryal of K. Charles I. As it was Read in the House of Commons, and Attested under the hand of Phelps, Clerk to that Infamous Court.* London, By H. C. for Thomas Dring, 1684.

Nani, Battista. *The History Of the Affairs of Europe In this present Age, But more particularly of the Republick of Venice.* Trans. Sir Robert Honywood. London, By J. M. for John Starkey, 1673.

Newcastle, Margaret Cavendish, Duchess of. *The Life of William Cavendish Duke of Newcastle to Which Is Added the True Relation of My Birth Breeding and Life.* Ed. C. H. Firth, 2nd ed. London, George Routledge & Sons Limited, n.d.

[North, Dudley, fourth Baron North]. *A Narrative of Some Passages in or Relating to the Long Parliament.* London, For Robert Pawlet, 1670.

P – y, W. *A Political Essay: or, Summary Review of the Kings and Government of England Since the Norman Conquest.* London, 1698. Perhaps by William Pudsey or Sir William Petty?

Parival, Jean Nicolas de. *The Historie of This Iron Age:* . . . [European History, 1500-1659] *rendred into English, by B. Harris, Gent.,* 2nd ed. London, For J. Crook, Simon Miller, and Thomas Davies, 1659.

Perrinchief, Richard. "The Life of Charles I," Βασιλικα. *The Works of King Charles the Martyr,* 2nd ed. (London, For Ric. Chiswell, 1687), 1-74.

Peyton, Sir Edward. *The Divine Catastrophe of The Kingly Family Of the House of Stuarts: or, a Short History of the Rise, Reign, and Ruine Thereof. Wherein the most secret and Chamber-abominations of the two last Kings are discovered, Divine Justice in King Charles his overthrow vindicated, and the Parliaments proceedings against him clearly justified.* London, For Giles Calvert, 1652.

Price, John. *The Mystery and Method Of His Majesty's Happy Restauration, Laid Open to Publick View.* London, For James Vade, 1680.

[Reily, Hugh]. *Ireland's Case Briefly Stated; or, a Summary Account of the most Remarkable Transactions in that Kingdom since the Reformation.* N.p. [London?], 1695.

Ricraft, Josiah. *A Survey of Englands Champions, and Truths faithfull Patriots. Or, a Chronologicall Recitement of the principall proceedings of the most worthy Commanders of the* [Parliamentarian Army]. London, By R. Austin to be sold by J. H., 1647. Reissued with an additional section as John Leycester, *The Civill VVarres of England Briefly Related* (London, For John Hancock, 1649).

Ross, Alexander. *The History of the World: The Second Part, in Six Books: Being a Continuation of the famous History of Sir Walter Raleigh, Knight.* London, For John Clark, 1652.

Royall and Loyall Blood Shed by Cromwel and his Party, &c. . . . To which is annexed a brief Chronicle of the Wars & Affairs of the 3. Kingdoms, from 1640 to 1661. London, By H. B. for W. L., 1662. For authorship of the chronicle, see under Heath. According to "An Advertisement to the Reader" in John Reynolds, *The Triumphs of Gods Revenge Against the crying Sin of Murther* (London, For Will: Lee, 1662), *Royall and Loyall Blood* was also published as a section of that edition of Reynolds' book, but it is absent from the one copy I have seen.

Rushworth, John. *Historical Collections.* 7 vols. London, 1659-1701. Title (after the above two words) and printers vary through the set.

—, ed. *The Tryal of Thomas Earl of Strafford.* London, For John Wright and Richard Chiswell, 1680.

S., L. See under Baker.

Sanderson, William. *A Compleat History of the Life and Raigne of King Charles from His Cradle to his Grave.* London, For Humphrey Moseley, Richard Tomlins, and George Sawbridge, 1658.

—. *Peter pursued; or Dr. Heylin Overtaken, Arrested, and Arraigned upon his three Appendixes, ... For which the Doctor is brought to Censure.* London, By Tho. Leach, 1658.

Sandford, Francis. *A Genealogical History of the Kings of England, and Monarchs of Great Britain, &c. From the Conquest, Anno 1066. to the Year, 1677.* [London], In the Savoy, By Tho. Newcomb for the author, 1677.

Scobell, Henry, ed. *A Collection of Acts and Ordinances . . .* [made in Parliaments held Nov.] *1640 . . .* [to 1657]. London, By Henry Hills and John Field, 1658.

—, ed. *A Collection Of several Acts of Parliament, Published in the Years 1648, 1649, 1650, and 1651. . . . VVhereunto are added some Ordinances of Parliament.* London, By John Field to be sold by W. Lee, D. Pakeman, and G. Bedell, 1651.

The Secret History, of the Four last Monarchs of Great Britain: Viz. James I. Charles I. Charles II. James II. To which is added, An Appendix, Containing the Later Reign of James the Second, from the Time of his Abdication of England, to this present January, 1691. With Particular Remarks on his Private Actions in Ireland. London, 1691.

The Secret History of the Reigns of K. Charles II. and K. James II. N.p., 1690.

Seller, John. *The History of England. Giving a True and Impartial Account of the most Considerable Transactions in Church and State, in Peace and War, during the Reigns of all the Kings and Queens, from the coming of Julius Caesar into Britain.* London, By Job and John How for William Gwillim, 1696.

Shirley, John. *Ecclesiastical History Epitomiz'd. Containing* [lives of Christ and prominent Christians] *to this present Age.* 2 Parts. London, For Tho. Passinger and Will. Thackery, 1682-1683.

Skinner, Thomas. *The Life of General Monk: Duke of Albemarle.* Ed. William Webster, 2nd ed. London, For J. Graves, J. Isted, and J. Hooke, 1724. For Skinner, see also under Bate.

Sprigge, Joshua. *Anglia Rediviva; Englands Recovery: Being the History Of the Motions, Actions, and Successes of the Army under the Immediate Conduct of His Excellency Sr. Thomas Fairfax, Kt. Captain-General Of all the Parliaments Forces in England.* London, By R. W. for Iohn Partridge, 1647.

Temple, Sir John. *The Irish Rebellion: or, an History Of the Beginnings and first Progress of the General Rebellion raised within the Kingdom of Ireland, ... With the Barbarous Cruelties and Bloody Massacres which ensued thereupon.* London, By R. White for Samuel Gellibrand, 1646.

[Vicars, John]. *England's Worthies. Under Whom, All the Civill and Bloudy Warres since Anno 1642, to Anno 1647 are related. Wherein Are Described the severall Battails, Encounters, and Assaults of Cities, Townes, and Castles at severall times and Places; .... As Also, Severall Victories by Sea, by the Noble Admirall, Robert Earle of Warwick.* London, For J. Rothwell, 1647.

——. *Magnalia Dei Anglicana. Or, Englands Parliamentary-Chronicle. Containing a full and faithfull Series, and Exact Narration of all the most memorable Parliamentary-Mercies, and mighty (if not miraculous) Deliverances, great and glorious Victories, and admirable Successes, of the Counsels and Armies of this present Parliament, both by Sea and by Land, over the whole Kingdom of England, in the most just defence and Vindication of her Religion, Laws, and Liberties, from the yeer, 1640, to this present yeer, 1646.* London, For J. Rothwell and Tho. Underhill, 1646.

[——]. *True Information of the Beginning and Cause of all our troubles: how they have been hatched, and how prevented. Wherein VVe may see the manifold contrivances and attempts of forraigne and home-bred Enemies, against the Parliament, Kingdome, and purity of Religion. And How all their Endeavours whether by Force or fraud, never prospered. A Work Worthy to be kept in Record, and to bee communicated to Posterity.* London, 1648.

Walker, Clement. *The Compleat History of Independency. Upon the Parliament Begun 1640. By Clem. Walker, Esq; Continued till this present year 1660. which fourth Part was never before published.* London, For Ric. Royston and Ric. Lownds, 1661. The Fourth Part is by "T.M. Esquire."

Walker, Sir Edward. *Historical Discourses, upon Several Occasions.* London, By W. B. for Sam. Keble, 1705.

Walsingham, Edward. "Life of Sir John Digby (1605-1645)." Ed. Georges Bernard. London, Camden Miscellany XII, 1910, pp. 59-149.

Warwick, Sir Philip. *Memoires Of the reigne of King Charles I. With a Continuation to the Happy Restauration of King Charles II.* London, For Ri. Chiswell, 1701.

Wellwood, James. *Memoirs Of the Most Material Transactions in England, for The Last Hundred Years, Preceding the Revolution in 1688,* 3rd ed. London, For Tim. Goodwin, 1700.

Whitelocke, Bulstrode. *Memorials of the English Affairs: or, An Historical Account of what passed from the Beginning of the Reign of King Charles the First, to King Charles the Second His Happy Restauration,* new ed. London, For J. Tonson to be sold by J. and J. Knapton and others, 1732.

[Winstanley, William?]. *Englands Triumph. A More Exact History of His Majesties Escape After the Battle of Worcester, with a Chronologicall Discourse of His Straits and dangerous Adventures into France, and His Removes from place to place till His return into England, with the most Remarkable Memorials since, to this present September, 1660*. London, By J. G. for Nathaniel Brook, 1660. Listed with a query under Winstanley's name in the British Museum catalog.

—. *England's Worthies. Select Lives Of the most Eminent Persons of the English Nation, from Constantine the Great, Down to these Times*. London, By J. C. and F. C. for Obadiah Blagrave, 1684. Essex, Lilburne, and Cromwell are included in the first edition (1660; dated by Thomason February 1659/60), but in the 1684 edition Lilburne and Cromwell are missing, Essex survives only with an apology, and more Royalists are included.

—. *The Loyall Martyrology; or Brief Catalogues and Characters of the most Eminent Persons who Suffered for their Conscience during the late times of Rebellion.... Together with those who were Slain in the Kings Service. As Also, Dregs of Treachery: With the Catalogue and Characters of those Regicides who Sat as Judges on our late Dread Soveraign of ever Blessed Memory: with others of that Gang, most Eminent for Villany*. London, By Thomas Mabb for Edward Thomas, 1665.

Wood, Anthony à. *Athenae Oxonienses. An Exact History of All the Writers and Bishops Who Have Had Their Education in the University of Oxford. To Which Are Added the Fasti, or Annals of the Said University*. Ed. Philip Bliss. 4 vols. London, For F. C. and J. Rivington and others, 1813-1820.

Wood, Lambert. See under Bos.

Wren, M. "Of the Origin and Progress of the Revolutions in England," *Collectanea Curiosa; or Miscellaneous Tracts*, ed. John Gutch, 2 vols. (Oxford, Clarendon Press, 1781), I, 228-253.

Yonge, William. *Englands Shame: or the Unmasking of a Politick Atheist: Being a Full and Faithful Relation of the Life and Death of that Grand Impostor Hugh Peters*. London, By Da. Maxwel for Theodore Sadler, 1663.

Younger, William. *A Brief View of The late troubles and confusions in England, begun and occasioned by a prevailing Faction in the Long Parliament: Deduced to the auspicious coming in of General Monck, And the most glorious and happy Restitution of King Charles the Second*. London, For Robert Gibbs, 1660.

B. Histories of the Reign of James I to 1702

Goodman, Godfrey. *The Court of King James the First; ... to Which Are Added, Letters Illustrative of the Personal History of the Most Distinguished Characters in the Court of That Monarch and His Predecessors*. Ed. J. S. Brewer. 2 vols. London, Richard Bentley, 1839.

[Osborne, Francis]. *Historical Memoires on the Reigns of Queen Elizabeth and King James.* London, By J. Grismond to be sold by T. Robinson, 1658.

[Sanderson, William]. *Aulicus Coquinariae: or a Vindication in Answer to a Pamphlet, Entitvled The Court and Character of King James. Pretended to be penned by Sir A:W: and published since his death, 1650.* London, For Henry Seile, 1650. See under Weldon.

—. *A Compleat History of The Lives and Reigns of Mary Queen of Scotland, And of Her Son and Successor, James The Sixth, King of Scotland; And (After Queen Elizabeth) King of Great Britain, France, and Ireland, The First (Of ever Blessed Memory.).* London, For Humphrey Moseley, Richard Tomlins, and George Sawbridge, 1656.

[Sparke, Michael?]. *The Narrative History of King James, for the first fourteen Years. In four Parts.* London, For Michael Sparke, 1651.

Spottiswoode, John. *History of the Church of Scotland, Beginning the Year of Our Lord 203, and Continued to the End of the Reign of King James VI.* Ed. M. Russell. 3 vols. Edinburgh, Oliver & Boyd, 1851.

[Weldon, Sir Anthony?]. *A Cat May look upon a King.* London, For William Roybould, 1652.

W[eldon], Sir A[nthony]. *The Court and Character of King James. Whereunto is now added the Court of King Charles: Continued Unto the beginning of these Unhappy Times. With some Observations upon Him in stead of a Character.* London, By R. I. to be sold by J. Collins, 1651.

Wilson, Arthur. *The History of Great Britain, Being the Life and Reign of King Iames the First, Relating To what passed from his first Accesse to the Crown, till his Death.* London, For Richard Lownds, 1653.

C. The Context of the Histories

The following remarks and list of suggested readings are offered as a further guide to any reader of this book who wishes to read some of the histories covered in it. Special attention is given to (1) the ideas about historical writing current when these histories were written, (2) the place of these histories in the history of English historical writing.

Because someone who studies the historical writing of a period finds himself studying a complete or almost complete cross section of the thought of the period, works on the intellectual history of the period are often useful to him. For this reason I have included the works by Bury and Snow in the list, though these are not directly concerned with historical writing, and I could have included many others of little less utility.

There is as yet no comprehensive study of seventeenth-century English ideas about the method and purpose of historical writing, though they are touched upon in several works listed below. I suggest that a good way to get an understanding of these ideas is to read the statements of them which appear in the prefaces and other prefatorial matter of seventeenth-century histories and to compare the theorizing of this prefatorial matter with the actual practice of the historians in the body of the books.

I have devoted considerable attention to these ideas, but as my findings provide part of the general intellectual background for my book rather than the principal material for any section of it I have not documented them anywhere in detail. I should mention, however, that I base my understanding of these ideas on extensive reading in contemporary statements of them wherever they appear – not only in the prefaces and other prefatorial matter mentioned above, but also in seventeenth-century essays, courtesy books, treatises on education and on historical study, biographies and autobiographies, and other works including histories written on various topics.

The lives of seventeenth-century historians in the *DNB* and by Wood are of the highest importance for the understanding of seventeenth-century English historical writing.

Abbott, W. C. *A Bibliography of Oliver Cromwell: a List of Printed Materials relating to Oliver Cromwell, together with a List of Portraits and Caricatures.* Cambridge, Mass., Harvard University Press, 1929. Because the entries in this work are arranged chronologically, it gives an excellent idea of the course of historical writing on the war over the centuries. See also Abbott's introduction to this work and his essay "The Fame of Cromwell" printed in *The Writings and Speeches of Oliver Cromwell,* ed. W. C. Abbott, 4 vols. (Cambridge, Mass., Harvard University Press, 1937-1947), IV, chapter XVI, for views of Cromwell by successive historians.

Baker, Herschel. *The Race of Time: Three Lectures on Renaissance Historiography.* Toronto, University of Toronto Press, 1967.

Barnard, John. *Theologo-Historicvs, Or the True Life of the Most Reverend Divine, and Excellent Historian Peter Heylyn.* London, For J. S. to be sold by Ed. Eckelston, 1683. Fascinating life of a seventeenth-century historian.

Bolingbroke, Henry St. John, Viscount. *Letters on the Study and Use of History,* 2 vols. New York, Garland Publishing, Inc., 1970.

Bolton, Edmund. "Hypercritica, or a Rule of Judgment for Writing or Reading Our History's," *Critical Essays of the Seventeenth Century,* ed. J. E. Spingarn, 3 vols. (London, Oxford University Press, 1957), I, 82-115.

Bury, J. B. *The Idea of Progress: an Inquiry into Its Origin and Growth.* New York, Dover Publications, Inc., 1955.

Carr, Edward Hallett. *What Is History?* London, Macmillan & Co Ltd, 1961.

Delany, Paul. *British Autobiography in the Seventeenth Century.* London, Routledge & Kegan Paul, 1969.

Douglas, David C. *English Scholars 1660-1730,* 2nd ed. London, Eyre & Spottiswoode, 1951.

Ewald, Ursula. *Studien zur Entwicklung der britischen Gegenwartschronistik im 17. und 18. Jahrhundert: Inaugural-Dissertation zur Erlangung der Doktorwürde der Philosophischen Fakultät der Ruprecht-Karl-Universität in Heidelberg.* 1964.

Fahey, David Michael. "Historical Interpretations of the English Civil War, Particularly since the Middle of the Eighteenth Century," unpub. diss., University of Notre Dame, 1964.

Firth, C. H. "The Development of the Study of Seventeenth-Century History," *Transactions of the Royal Historical Society,* 3rd ser., 7 (1913), 25-48.

—. "Modern History in Oxford, 1724-1841," *The English Historical Review*, 32 (January 1917), 1-21. For the same topic see also his *Modern History in Oxford, 1841-1918* (Oxford, Basil Blackwell, 1920) and his *Modern Languages at Oxford 1724-1929* (London, Oxford University Press, 1929), chap. I.

Fussner, F. Smith. *The Historical Revolution: English Historical Writing and Thought 1580-1640*. New York, Columbia University Press, 1962.

Lenglet du Fresnoy, Pierre Nicolas. *A New Method of Studying History: Recommending more Easy and Complete Instructions for Improvements in that Science Than any hitherto Extant: With the whole Apparatus necessary to Form a Perfect Historian*. Trans. and improved by Richard Rawlinson. 2 vols. London, For W. Burton to be sold by J. Batley and others, 1728.

Levy, F. J. *Tudor Historical Thought*. San Marino, The Huntington Library, 1967.

Love, Walter D. "Civil War in Ireland: Appearances in Three Centuries of Historical Writing," *The Emory University Quarterly*, 22 (1966-1967), 57-72.

Mackenzie, Norman H. "Sir Thomas Herbert of Tintern: a Parliamentary 'Royalist'," *Bulletin of the Institute of Historical Research*, 29 (1956), 32-86. Interesting piece of historical detective work concerning Herbert's memoirs.

Snow, Vernon F. "The Concept of Revolution in Seventeenth-Century England," *The Historical Journal*, 5 (1962), 167-174.

Thompson, James Westfall, and Bernard J. Holm. *A History of Historical Writing*. 2 vols. New York, The Macmillan Company, 1958.

Usher, Roland G. *A Critical Study of the Historical Method of Samuel Rawson Gardiner with an Excursus on the Historical Conception of the Puritan Revolution from Clarendon to Gardiner*. St. Louis, Publications of Washington University, 1915.

Wheare, Degory. *The Method and Order Of Reading both Civil and Ecclesiastical Histories in Which The most Excellent Historians are Reduced into the Order in which they are Successively to be Read; and the Judgments of Learned Men, concerning each of them, Subjoin'd*. Trans. Edmund Bohun. London, For Charles Brome, 1698. Contains material added by Bohun, Nicolas Horsman, and Henry Dodwell.

Wright, Louis B. *Middle-Class Culture in Elizabethan England*. Ithaca, N.Y., By Cornell University Press for the Folger Shakespeare Library, 1958. Chap. IX, "The Utility of History," has useful material on the motives for writing and publishing histories.

INDEX